The New Naturalist Library
A Survey of British Natural History

Ferns
Their Habitats in the British and Irish Landscape

Editors

Max Walters, ScD, VMH
Professor Richard West, ScD, FRS
David Streeter, FIBiol

Photographic Editor

Eric Hosking, OBE, Hon FRPS, FBIPP

The New Naturalist

FERNS

Their Habitats in the British and Irish Landscape

Christopher N. Page

With 21 colour photographs, and over
160 photographs and diagrams in black and white

COLLINS
Grafton Street, London

William Collins Sons & Co. Ltd

London · Glasgow · Sydney · Auckland
Toronto · Johannesburg

First published 1988
© C. N. Page 1988

Designer: Glynis Edwards

ISBN 0 00 219383 3 (hardback edition)
ISBN 0 00 219382 5 (limpback edition)

Typeset by Phoenix Photosetting, Chatham
Printed and bound in Great Britain by
Mackays of Chatham PLC, Chatham, Kent

Contents

Editor's Preface

Some New Naturalist volumes have a very long gestation period, and this welcome new book on Ferns brings to fruition a project that was seriously discussed more than forty years ago when the New Naturalist library was in its infancy. Dr Page, in his Author's Preface, indeed, tells us of a charming coincidence in a Devon lane that reminded him of this fact. We are extremely fortunate to have found, in the new generation of pteridologists, an author as competent and enthusiastic as Chris Page to write this book for us. Not only is the author a professional scientist interested in the Pteridophyta of the world, but he is also an amateur naturalist with a love for the ferns of the British Isles. This combination of talent is ideal for the New Naturalist series, which has always aimed to combine a high standard of accuracy with a stimulation of the natural pride of the British public in their wild animals and plants.

The relationship between the contents of this volume and Dr Page's earlier book on *The Ferns of Britain and Ireland* (Cambridge University Press, 1982) perhaps needs a little clarification. The two books are designedly complementary: the 1982 volume is a modern, detailed Pteridophyte Flora of the British Isles, in which full taxonomic treatment is given to every native species, whilst our present volume deals essentially with the ecology of British pteridophytes, grouping them mainly under contrasting habitats and discussing their adaptations to the conditions of those habitats. Ideally, the reader might possess both books, but of course the New Naturalist volume is totally self-explanatory and provided with an appended checklist of species.

There is a further reason for pleasure in adding this volume to our series. It is in fact 25 years since the last purely botanical New Naturalist book was published (Sir Edward Salisbury's classic on *Weeds and Aliens*, a revision of which is currently being undertaken by Dr Akeroyd), and the Editors greatly welcome this move to redress the balance somewhat between the different branches of natural history. Let us hope that in the near future we can fill other long-standing gaps in our botanical coverage as satisfactorily as the fern gap has been filled.

Author's Preface

Shortly after completing an earlier taxonomic book for the indentification of the ferns of Britain and Ireland (Cambridge University Press, 1982), I was teaching one of my field courses at Slapton Field Studies Council centre in south Devon. One evening, I left my group working in the laboratory, while I wandered out into the nearby lanes to photograph ferns that I had seen there earlier in the day. It was a beautifully still, warm, Devonshire evening. The light remained good, and only at this time of day did the lane seem free enough of traffic to set-up my camera and tripod with any great safety.

Whilst giving an attractive spleenwort due photographic attention, I was surprised by an elderly, Devonian voice from behind me. Its owner had clearly been watching my antics, and had arrived unseen. 'I'm photographing ferns growing amongst the lanebank stones', I explained to him, with all the speed of purpose that the infectious pace of rural Devonshire, and my own west-country upbringing, usually muster.

'I once photographed ferns' was the surprising reply, and, of course, we fell into one of those mutually curious conversations on the chance meeting of two fellow interests that seems to happen on but few occasions in most lifetimes.

He went on to explain that he had been a professional photographer, and that one of his jobs before he retired had been to photograph British ferns. Fascinated I probed further, and was amazed as he recounted that this had been as a commission to illustrate a book on ferns.

I asked, in great curiosity, what book this was. 'It was for Collins, for their New Naturalist series' he detailed, and added: 'That was about 1947, but the book was never written'.

There have been few times in my life, as a scientist, that I have ever felt quite so amazed at the statistical improbability of such an event. For it was now my turn to explain to this benevolent and aged gentleman that the person he had just told that tale to was the one who, just a few months before, had been approached by Collins to write just the book he is talking about. We eventually retired, each still continuing to recount the story to the other again, just in case the whole conversation had been merely the misheard echo of a quiet Devon lane.

This book is thus the result of those labours (or at least of mine), and of this strange co-incidence of events. For there is regretfully no longer any trace of these former photographs. But this meeting eased me into the knowledge of the gestation period of this particular book which, as I calculate it, was conceived (by others), as part of the *New Naturalist* series, when I was about five years old.

About that time, however, and unknowing of more worldly things, I was busy adopting two impressions of plants of my own. One took the form of many piles of rocks, gleaned like a jackdaw and examined with ever-increasing delight and curiosity. These came from the numerous spoil heaps of small coal workings, from which I could collect ample specimens, in the Forest of Dean. The many fossils in these were distinctly of plants, of recognisable fragments of wood, many curiously jointed stems, and distinctive and beautiful foliage, not unlike that of the ferns that grew around me. All of these I treasured. The other occurred in annual holidays to the Cambrian coast of Wales, where the beach sand fascinated me less than did the thick masses of succulent, white-stemmed, jointed shoots of plants through which I had to push to get there. They seemed to tower around me like something out of a fairy tale. I came to regard them as something special, about which I wanted to know more, the more so because I could also see a likeness between them and some of my fossils. Thus both horsetails and ferns each came to have a special and enduring fascination. Nature knew how to capture the attention of a small boy; rather more than did many school lessons of the day.

Nearly forty years on, and a university thesis on horsetails somewhere in between, it is perhaps due time therefore that this book appeared. I can therefore only apologise to those readers who have duely passed-on while waiting.

The resulting account is, whatever else, a personal narrative of the field experience gained during this time. I have written about the habitats and natural history of the native ferns and fern-allies of Britain and Ireland, as I have found them. It is thus essentially a biogeographical study of an insular pteridophyte flora, encompassing all of what I have come to view as the more important habitats for ferns and fern-allies within these islands. In most of these, ferns still form a significant, and sometimes unexpected, component. It is especially about wild and, indeed, sometimes nearly inaccessible places, because most pteridophytes are most abundant in places which are free from despoilation, air-pollution and especially such hazards as artificially-high animal grazing pressures. It is therefore especially about our islands' more distant and rural corners, which, as a west-countryman who has spent his life as a professional botanist mostly in Scotland, I have had the good fortune to live near enough to visit very frequently, at all times of year.

Throughout this account I have, to avoid confusion, followed closely the nomenclature for species given in Page (1982), to which the reader is also referred for any further details of fern and fern-ally identification. Each habitat is thus viewed from the standpoint of a taxonomist, but with an awareness of its landscape and environmental setting and of the ecology, biology and evolution of the plants within it. The ecology of pteridophytes is itself a highly unusual one. It is unusual partly because of the pteridophyte life-cycle, with a free-living prothallial generation, about which we are just beginning to know something in the field; and partly because of the extreme range of habitats which pteridophyte species tolerate, the latter resulting from their own innate abilities which have ensured their survival against competition from the vegetatively more aggressive flowering plants. In general, the ecology of ferns and fern-allies is to me one dominated by the often unusual ecological tactics of ecological escapists and fugitives from an angiosperm-dominated world. Ferns thus often succeed where flowering-plants most fear-to-tread.

Further, within Britain and Ireland, much of the landscape itself has, since ancient times, been the subject of extensive modification by man, and is still ever-changing. I have thus tried, wherever appropriate, to set the ecology of the modern pteridophyte communities against a broader perspective of deductions about the history of their habitats, inferred from the wealth of literature dealing with many otherwise apparently disparate aspects of the British and Irish environment and known landscape history. Lastly, from this basis, I have drawn any relevant conclusions about the conservational status of pteridophyte species and plant communities concerned.

In preparing this account, although the ultimate responsibility for the views and ideas expressed is entirely my own, I am nevertheless conscious of an immense debt of gratitude to very many colleagues, friends, botanists and naturalists in many spheres, both amateur and professional, with whom I have had the opportunity to discuss points over very many years, very often in the field in very many separate parts of Britain and Ireland. It would be impossible to list them all here. Nevertheless special debts of gratitude must go to those who fostered and helped to mould my bourgeoning interests in this plant group, especially to Drs T. G. Walker, M. G. Shivas and Professor (now Sir John) Burnett, at the University of Durham (latterly University of Newcastle upon Tyne), to A. C. Jermy and J. A. Crabbe of the British Museum (Natural History),

London, to J. W. Dyce of the British Pteridological Society, to Dr A. F. Dyer of the University of Edinburgh and to B. L. Burtt, Professor D. M. Henderson, Professor J. McNeill and Dr J. Cullen at the Royal Botanic Garden, Edinburgh. Amongst the many others to whom I also owe a debt of gratitude for help in many ways are Mrs F. Bennell, P. M. Benoit, Dr J. Birks, Mrs D. M. Bolitho, R. P. Bowman, the late J. C. Brownlie, A. R. Busby, Mrs J. Castle-Smith, the late Dr W. A. Clark, Dr R. Dickson, A. Douglas, P. J. Edwards, R. Eudall, Dr R. E. C. Ferreira, Mrs M. A. Fyfe, J. C. Gardiner, Dr R. Gemmel, Dr M. Gibby, K. Grant, Mrs S. Grierson, J. Grant Roger, Dr G. Halliday, Miss R. Hollands, A. Kenneth, Major E. W. M. Magor, J. Margetts, Dr A. G. Long, the late Miss M. McCallum-Webster, Miss H. McHaffie, Dr B. Moffat, Miss R. Murphy, Mrs C. Murray, A. C. Page, Mrs A. Prain, Dr F. H. Perring, Dr J. Proctor, M. H. Rickard, R. H. Roberts, Miss A. Rutherford, Miss M. J. P. Scannel, M. Scott, Dr A. Sleep, Dr R. A. H. Smith, R. Smith, the late Professor D. H. Spence, Mrs O. M. Stewart, A. McG. Stirling, Professor G. A. Swan, Professor J. A. Taylor, Professor J. Tivy, Dr J. Turner, the late Professor D. H. Valentine and P. J. Wormell. Miss H. McHaffie and Mrs M. A. Fyfe kindly commented on much of the text, and Mrs D. Brunton and Miss Z. C. Page provided assistance with preparation of the artwork. All photographs, are by the author except the aerial views, for which I am particularly grateful to Cambridge University for permission to reproduce material from their collections. There is also a considerable debt of gratitude to my various students, both undergraduate and postgraduate and on Field Study Council and Scottish Field Study Council courses, and to my children, who have accompanied me on many excursions.

Finally, I would like to thank Dr S. M. Walters (recently of Cambridge University Botanic Garden) for reviving the idea of a fern book for the *New Naturalist* series, and to Myles Archibald of Collins for seeing the resulting text through to publication.

C.N.P.
Churchdown, Gloucestershire.
March, 1988.

Dedication

This book celebrates the two hundredth anniversary of the publication of the first book on ferns in these islands (and the first book on ferns in the world), that of James Bolton's *Filices Britannicae*, published in Leeds and Huddersfield, Yorkshire in 1785–1789. It also commemorates the enormous stimulus to pteridology of the work of Professor Irene Manton, FRS (1904–1988), from her first second-generation student.

Our Fern-rich Heritage

CHAPTER I

'We have the receipt of fern seed – we walk invisible'
William Shakespeare, Henry IV Part I, Act II, Scene I (1598).

Mention of the word 'fern' probably immediately conjures up
certain images in most readers' minds. Exact pictures will vary
according to individual experience, but common ingredients
may well include finely sculptured, delicate, softly-waving
foliage, a myriad of hues of different greens, of frond-
festooned banks along trickling brooks, or of quiet ferny
coombs on misty mornings. At the same time the plants themselves may also present an aura of some mystery, prevalent as
many are in moist dark places, lacking in flowers or large seeds,
and representing survivors of an extremely ancient group,
whose ancestors dominated the distant silent forests of some
prehistoric world. Indeed their retiring ecology, their fine deli-
cacy of architectural form, the curiosity of their life-cycles and
their ancient allegiances, convey much of the essence of the
modern scientific interest in the structure, ecology, biology and
evolution of the worldwide multitude of species we call ferns.

But probably none of these interests are really new. For
within Britain and Ireland, the distinctive, curious, flowerless
ferns, as well as the equally obscure horsetails, quillworts and
clubmosses botanically allied to them, and which are therefore
included with them in this account, have long played their own
particular and often curious roles in culture, folklore, literature, agriculture, science and medicine throughout rural life
within these islands.

Ferns in Myth, Magic and Mystery

Within these islands, the magical and mysterious uses to which
ferns and fern-allies have been put have been many and varied.
For, since probably very ancient times the generally curious
and often delicate form of ferns has been held to endow them
with mysterious and magical properties. Such repute was held
widely in country lore in both Britain and Ireland, as well as
probably in Europe more generally. Indeed, in France, the

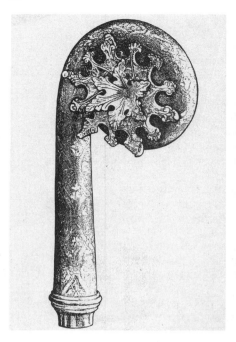

Left. A 12th-century, British, gilt and enamel crozier of ecclesiastical use, with exacting pteridological detail, including stylised laterally expanding pinnae with circinnate vernation, clearly derived from observation of the morphological structure of an expanding fern frond (Royal Museum of Scotland). See p. 43.

Right. The somewhat mystical unrolling of each fern frond, in this case Polystichum setiferum. *Cardiganshire, late May*

apparent diversity of powers with which ferns were believed to be endowed earned them the old French name 'herb aux cent miracles'.

Amongst ferns, the unusual-looking Moonwort (*Botrychium lunaria*), was especially held to be so-endowed. This plant was clearly well-known to country folk to a degree which it is not today, and must have been much more common among the grassy swards of lowland meadows and pastures in former times than at present. It had the repute of being able to undo shackles and locks and to remove horses' shoes should they step upon it. Alchemists believed it to have the power of turning quicksilver (mercury) into real silver, whilst witches and sorcerers held its reputed magical powers in high regard. Fairy-like connotations also surrounded this plant, the separate leaflets of which were held to be used as saddles on appropriate occasions by fairy-sized people and their appropriately diminutive horses. Such a myth is aptly recalled in James Hogg's poem the *Witch of Fife* (1813):

'The first leet night, quhan the new moon set,
Quhan all was douffe and mirk,
We saddled our naigis wi' the moon-fern leif,
And rode fra Kilmerrin kirk.'

It's lock-opening powers perhaps relate to the key-like appearance of the leafy segments of Moonwort, whilst the fact that each, sometimes semi-closed leaflet is shaped like the crescent moon and were believed to wax and wane with the moon's phases, doubtless helped confirm its magical properties.

More directly, in the field, Moonwort also gained the repute of being injurious to the sward of grass amongst which it grew. Nowadays it is seldom abundant, although its appearance and apparent non-appearance at the same spot in different years still remains something of a mystery to science. It is known to be dependent for survival on an intimate mycorrhizal association with soil fungi, which are themselves saprophytic on decaying vegetable matter in the surface layers of the soil around them. Whether this association could in any way be responsible for its Medieval repute of decay of the grass sward itself remains unknown.

Some of the supposed applications of Moonwort derive from the 'Doctrine of Signatures,' in which drug dispensers, herbalists and astrologers studied the characteristics ('signatures') of different plants, in the hope that the fern of the plant itself would suggest its medicinal uses.

Fig. 1
Ophioglossum
vulgatum *(left) and*
Botrychium lunaria
*(right), both the subject
of extensive legend and
repute*

Related to Moonwort is another fern of curious appearance, Adder's-tongue (*Ophioglossum vulgatum*). The ecology of this plant is similar to that of Moonwort, and Adder's-tongue too was probably much more common in moist lowland pastures over clay soils in the past than it is today. Its unusual common name seems to derive from the ensheathing leaf-like portion of its fertile shoot, held to be reminiscent of the mouth of an adder, with the fertile protruding shaft likened to a serpent's tongue. With such an appearance the plant was consequently accepted as the standard antidote to adder-bite, which was perhaps also more frequent in former times than today. As with Moonwort, Adder's Tongue was widely employed by witches and sourcerers, and used in spells and incantations:

'And I ha' been plucking plants among, Hemlock, Henbane, Adder's Tongue; Nightshade, Moonwort, Libbard's Bane, And twice by the dogs, was like to be ta'en.'   Ben Jonson, 1573–1637

Some ferns were believed to endow protective properties. Washing one's hair in a decoction of the fronds of Maidenhair fern (*Adiantum capillus-veneris*) was supposedly good for a maiden's tresses, whilst, if worn, this fern, as well as Wall Rue (*Asplenium ruta-muraria*), were regarded as good antidotes to witchcraft. Hart's Tongue (*Phyllitis scolopendrium*) is sometimes mentioned specifically in this respect, due to the cut stem (stipe) having a pattern of vascular tissue in the form of an X, and this was believed symbolic of Christ. Other genera have stipe vasculature of different shape, and this did not fail to be noted in Medieval times. Some, with mushroom-shaped strands, were likened to an oak tree and, on finding such a plant, the more closely it resembled an oak tree the luckier the finder would be. Oak Fern (*Gymnocarpium dryopteris*) was accredited with being beneficial for curing 'fearful and troublesome sleeps or dreams', and if ferns were grown on the roof of a house, they were believed to protect it and its occupants from thunder and lightning.

Other ferns had more romantic connotations. The rhizome of Male Fern (*Dryopteris filix-mas*) applied gently to the sleeping eyelids was supposed to be a love-philtre, that the wearer might fall in love with the first person who he or she thereafter sees. A similar property seems to have been associated with the juice of Maidenhair Spleenwort (*Asplenium trichomanes*), for, according to Turner's Herbal of 1598 'the juice stayeth the heart that falleth off, and if they be falleth off, it restoreth them agayne'. The anonymous ditty 'T'was the maiden's matchless beauty, That drew my heart a nigh; Not the fern-root potion, but the glance of her blue eye' seems to suggest that such attachments could form spontaneously anyway!

Hart's Tongue (*Phyllitis scolopendrium*) had even more extensive properties in this connection. In many a rural setting the plant must have been much better known than it is today, for it was probably an abundant colonist of the interior surfaces of most village wells. Here its apparently spontaneous appearance, as well as its unusual and evergreen form, were doubtless the main attributes responsible for endowing it with magical properties. Beside the medicinal uses of a decoction of its fronds similar to those attributed to other ferns, its long tongues of evergreen foliage arising from heart-like bases gave it romantic connotations. The distilled water of Hart's Tongue was held to be 'very good against the passions of the heart', whilst if the plant was 'uprooted on a dark moonless night and hung like an amulet around the neck' it had the repute that it would be effective in preventing conception. Just how effective seems not to have been recorded.

Fern-allies in the form of the clubmosses were not without mystical connotations either. Members of the clubmoss genus *Lycopodium* were widely held to possess potent aphrodisiacal properties. Perhaps it was for this reason that garlands made from the tough stems of the whole plant (especially of Fir Clubmoss *Lycopodium clavatum*) were woven into mats, wreaths or armlets, and worn on festive occasions as items of rustic personal adornment. On such occasions they doubtless endowed the wearer with all sorts of magical properties. An old legend which seems to relate to this plant has it that if properly gathered with due ceremony, clubmoss conferred the power of

The hoary leaves of Lycopodium clavatum, *particularly characteristic of this species. Mid-Perthshire, June*

Dryopteris filix-mas
*showing how the spores,
produced in sporangia,
cluster into
characteristic shapes
(sori) on the backs of
fern fronds, to be
released by the million
when mature from
mid-summer on. West
Cornwall, mid-August*

Phyllitis
scolopendrium
*showing the large and
distinctive linear soral
rows of the numerous
fertile fronds. South
Devon, early August*

being able to understand the language of beast or bird. 'Properly gathered' appears to have included the collector walking barefoot, with feet washed, clothed in white and having offered a sacrifice of bread and wine.

A further belief of Medieval times relating especially to ferns lies in the magical properties with which their spores were endowed. These, if falling under certain conditions on one's shoes, would confer on the bearer the somewhat enviable power of temporary invisibility. The argument in favour of this unique attribute in the plant world seems a tortuous but logical one, bearing in mind the total ignorance about the life-cycle of

ferns until comparatively recent times. The brown spores that
fell from the back of the fronds of ferns from summer onwards
were clearly widely known to be their 'seed', and are usually
referred to in literature as such. If ferns produced seed then, by
analogy with all other large plants, they must, of course, first
flower. But try as people might, even the most ardent observer
of ferns could never seem to be able to actually catch them in
flower, nor find the remains of any withered flower, even once
the seeds had started to appear. From the Medieval standpoint,
failure to see the flowers could not be taken as failure on the
part of the plant to produce them, for seed was certainly set.
The logical conclusion was that the flowers, when they came,
must be invisible ones. Equally clearly, as the fronds were, one
day in summer, shedding seed by the million, when the previous day they were not shedding at all, these invisible flowers
must have appeared in some quantity during the previous
night. Bearing in mind the time of year when ferns mature, and
the existing repute of midsummer's night (then 12 days later in
the calendar than now) when all sorts of magical things were
held to generally happen anyway (a belief dating back to the
time of the Druids), the repute became that all ferns everywhere produced these minute, invisible, short-lived flowers
only on that night of the year. If the flowers were invisible, then
probably so too were the seeds at a very early stage, and only by
the light of morning did they become visible to the eye. If the
seeds possessed this power of invisibility conferred on them
from the flower, then so too could they transfer this property to
anything else that they touched, at least until dawn. So if you
chanced to walk amongst the ferns early on the midsummer
morning following the special features of this magic night,
should any of these newly formed seeds chance to fall upon
you, you too could be influenced by this property of invisibility.

This belief was held widely not only in English folklore, but
also in that of Wales, Scotland and Ireland too. Indeed, such
tradition dictated the necessity of ceremonies designed to
catch the fern seed, in which various elaborate precautions and
observances were needed, varying from barefootedness,
silence and adopting a kneeling position to catch the quiet fall
of seed, to the use of a silver or pewter plate on which to collect
it and the operator being wrapped in a white cloth previously
boiled in spring water from near the fern's place of growth on
the third day of the moon! Indeed so mystical were these
properties of the fern, that witches were said to find it expedi-
ent to make escape during their various occupations by assum-
ing invisibility with the aid of this much-sought-for substance.
Shakespeare, Henry IV Part 1 of 1598, clearly considered that
he needed little introduction when referring to this property

(see the quote at the head of this chapter), whilst in Ben Jonson's *New Inn* (i, 1), written in the early 1600s, it is similarly mentioned; 'I had no medicine Sir, to go invisible; no fern-seed in my pocket.'

Many of these varied mystical beliefs about ferns were probably far from new even by the Middle Ages, and may well have their origins dating back to a mixture of Christian ceremony and the pagan festivals of the Druids.

Practical Uses of Pteridophytes

From at least the Middle Ages, if not earlier, many ferns and fern-allies appear to have been put to more directly applied uses. Some of these, especially in folk medicine, probably grew out of original mystical beliefs. Others had, perhaps, a firmer scientific foundation.

Practical Uses of Ferns

Traditional rural uses of native ferns appear to have been especially varied, and include many of our common native species.

Infusions of Male Fern *(Dryopteris felix-mas)*, Lady Fern *(Athyrium filix-femina)*, Hard Fern *(Blechnum spicant)*, Rustyback Fern *(Ceterach officinarum)* and various other unspecified ferns, were held to bring relief from a wide manner of ills, including inflammatory, asthmatic, rheumatic, urinary, pulmonary, bronchial and other disorders, whilst the spleenworts (members of the genus *Asplenium*) in particular, were held (and are, by some, still held) in high esteem to be of particular value for any complaint in which the spleen could be supposed to have had any share. Adder's-tongue, if plucked during the wane of the moon, was regarded as a cure for tumours, whilst to bite on young croziers of ferns in spring was once a rural remedy for toothache. Polypody *(Polypodium* spp.) was formerly employed as a purgative and also 'in cases of coughs and pectoral affections'. It was especially used against whooping-cough. Royal Fern *(Osmunda regalis)* was valued in parts of Ireland in which it is plentiful, as a cure for rickets. Hart's Tongue *(Phyllitis scolopendrium)* was used as a popular healing remedy for burns whilst a green-coloured healing preparation, Adder's-spear ointment, based on an extract from Adder's-tongue fern *(Ophioglossum vulgatum)* has a particularly long history of popular rural use as an application to speed-up the healing of wounds.

The thick, green, fleshy-textured shoots of Ophioglossum vulgatum *have a particularly long history of use in popular medicine. Midlothian, June*

Of especially popular use appears to have been the ability of Common Male Fern (*Dryopteris filix-mas*) and Bracken (*Pteridium aquilinum*) to yield rhizome extracts which were held to be effective as vermifuges in the treatment of tapeworm. Such a use of these ferns is probably extremely ancient, for the use of an oil extract of fern to expel worms appears to go back to at least 300 BC, when it was recommended by the Greek botanist and physician Theophrastus.

The successful application of some of these treatments were probably acts of faith, and their efficacy must, of course, be treated with some scepticism today. However, this does not imply that they should necessarily all be dismissed out-of-hand. Many were accepted by long and popular usage over centuries. Although many ferns wait to be more fully analysed and investigated by modern science, we already know that ferns contain mucilages and an enormous range of secondary plant chemical compounds, many of which are unique to pteridophytes. The strong antihelminthic properties of the rhizomes of nearly all species of *Dryopteris* for example, although their medicinal use is regarded as obsolete and dangerous today, are attributable to the presence of acylphloroglucinol components, of which as many as fifty variants have been analysed from a range of species of this genus, with several occurring simultaneously in some plants.

An, as yet, unknown pteridophyte function, however, appears to have been in the use of the spores of Royal Fern

Osmunda regalis once occurred widely in western districts. West Argyll, early August

(*Osmunda regalis*), along with Meadowsweet and Heather, in the preparation of mead, known from an ancient Celtic culture on the Isle of Rhum, Inner Hebrides (Dr Brian Moffat, personal communication).

Turning to more modern uses of ferns, or at least those which have persisted, it is Bracken (*Pteridium aquilinum*), the commonest and most familiar of all native ferns, that has probably attracted the most widespread rural usage and exploitation from at least Roman times, or probably very much earlier, until the present day. Its role, however, seems to have reached its zenith from about the Middle Ages to the beginnings of the Industrial Revolution. As a growing plant, it provided cover and shelter for game. Old fronds cut and dried were widely used as a plentiful source of bedding for stock. They were also used, perhaps equally widely, as a bedding for humans either in a raw state or as a stuffing for mattresses. In both these uses they had the repute of keeping down pests and parasites. Recent analyses of Bracken fronds have shown them to contain a great number of chemical substances which are toxic or particularly repellent to insects, and its reputed value as a bedding medium thus seems to be founded on a good scientific basis. Perhaps relating to this property, recent investigations have shown that Bracken fronds were strewn on the floor in the forts of Hadrian's Wall in northern England, whilst in Medieval times it appears also to have been used as a sort of under-floor insulation, where doubtless its repellent properties were also of incidental benefit. Fronds cut when in a green state could also be used as a mulch or compost. If dried fronds were burned, the ash which was yielded was used (especially in Scotland) as an important top-dressing for peatlands, particularly valued in the cultivation of potatoes. The beneficial results of application of its ash are known to result from its exceptionally high potash content, which the extensive and deep-seated rhizomes enable to be brought to the surface.

Indeed, so important a source of potash was Bracken that a whole Medieval 'chemical industry' seems to have been founded upon it. Locally, in many districts, soap was manufactured by 'boiling tallow with the ashes of the Brake.' More directly, when rolled into balls, the ash was used as a primitive soda by washerwomen, whilst it also seems to have gained a wide later use in Ireland and in northern Britain as a bleach in the preparation of linen and wool respectively. Alkali obtained from the ash of Bracken was also used in tanning leather and in glass manufacture. Its use in both glass and soap making seems to have been recognised at least as early as the 10th century AD, and not to have become finally displaced as an important source of alkali until probably the early 1800s. In the English

Lake District, specially constructed pits dating from before the 17th century and used for Bracken burning, still survive.

In the absence of other media in upland areas, Bracken too found widespread Medieval usage as thatch. The stalks alone were sometimes used for this purpose in the Highlands. It was generally considered less durable than straw, although the latter medium was seldom equally available. In England its use for this purpose is known from at least the 1300s, although such a role for Bracken may well go back to pre-Roman and even Iron-Age times. Another use of Bracken, as standing crop, was as a rural thermometer of the season, the late summer and autumn colour changes indicating the state of the onset of winter temperatures, by which other agricultural activities could be closely timed.

Other rural purposes for which Bracken was valued included the use of its rhizome in the Scottish Highlands to dye wool yellow, and it was regularly used for this purpose, along with other vegetable dyes, to obtain some of the soft ochreous hues of older Scottish tartans. In the Forest of Dean in Gloucestershire, and probably elsewhere, the rhizomes were sometimes cooked and fed to pigs. Perhaps the widespread repute of the rhizome of Bracken, along with that of Common Male Fern, as an antihelminthic against tapeworm, may also have been significant in this particular application.

Cutting of Bracken for control, it has been found in recent years, has to be carried out during mid-summer, but the former importance of Bracken as a recurring annual crop and vital raw material for so many purposes is underlined by the decrees and rules which governed its cutting and harvesting. These prevented, on penance, its cutting before certain dates, usually in September. To have the right to cut Bracken over certain areas or 'fern bounds' was a privilege which could be forfeited by cutting earlier than the prescribed dates, and by these means the continuance of a regular and undiminished annual crop of fronds was assured. Sometimes, where agricultural rents were paid partly in kind, this might include a specified annual number of cartloads of cut Bracken fronds to the landlord. Nevertheless, during this period it seems likely that the annual onslaught on the Bracken fronds probably did serve to keep its populations generally within bounds, and it is the cessation of such cutting this century which is probably one of the causes of Bracken's modern uninhibited spread.

An important everyday use to which fern fronds in general were put, during the 19th century but probably also much earlier, was as a packaging medium in which produce of various kinds could be safely transported. In both Ireland and the Isle of Man, fronds of ferns were widely used for packaging fish. In

England, fresh fruit (especially strawberries) were also frequently packed in fern fronds for transport to London markets, a custom also long followed on the Continent, where an old French name for Bracken 'Fougère a cerises' alludes to its widespread use in similarly packing cherries for travel. In Scotland in particular, but perhaps elsewhere too, Bracken fronds were traditionally used as a packing material for potatoes, and once the crop was laid down for the winter, a covering of the fronds also helped to protect it from frost. Fern fronds, and especially those of Bracken were valued for this work, not just because of their ready availability, but because they had the repute of helping the fresh crop to resist mould and decay during lengthy periods of transit.

We now know that ferns of many species contain complex biochemical substances which help prevent them being eaten and render them remarkably resistant to most diseases. Some of these, such as cyanide in Bracken fronds, are volatile and released into the air around them whenever frond tissue becomes broken or crushed. Others are insect repellent. It is probably these properties which so regularly helped to reduce decay in fresh fish, fruits or vegetables packed in amongst them. In these days of refrigeration, it is doubtful if most modern fishmongers, dutifully displaying their wares on city slabs in neatly arranged rows separated by plastic fern fronds, are really aware that there is a significance to this tradition which is much deeper than purely aesthetic.

Another packaging use of fern fronds, for which Bracken in particular was usually gathered, relates to their physical properties. This was in the transport of Welsh slates. Cushioned by sandwiches of Bracken fronds, slates were transported by cart and canal barge from Welsh slate quarries to all parts of Britain. Spores of Welsh strains of Bracken would doubtless have been particularly regularly conveyed in quantity to towns in the developing areas of industrialisation in the north of England and elsewhere by this means, doubtless helping along the route to add good Welsh strains of Bracken to the populations already existing elsewhere. In dockland areas of Britain too, with the development of the wool trade and the importation of wool as a raw material from distant parts of the globe (especially from Australia and New Zealand), there is evidence of importation of pieces of dried spore-yielding Bracken fronds tangled in the raw wool. It is perhaps for this reason that at least one specimen of Bracken collected last century from a colony in the docklands of east London and preserved in the herbarium of Edinburgh Royal Botanic Garden looks much more like the Bracken of New Zealand than it does like that of south-east England.

Practical Uses of Horsetails

Certainly by the Middle Ages and probably from Roman times onward, if not earlier, the practical everyday uses to which horsetails have been put were also many and varied.

A minor use, certainly from at least Roman times, has been that the shoots of some horsetails have been eaten as vegetables. Presumably what was eaten were the early spring cone shoots of the two species that produce these: that is Common Horsetail (*Equisetum arvense*) and Great Horsetail

(*E. telmateia*). The former is widespread in these islands, the latter is more especially a southern species. Both would certainly have been widely available in early spring, long before most other edible plants would have been in evidence.

Most of the uses of horsetails, however, concern the undoubted asperous properties of their vegetative shoots, which have been put to good use throughout the ages.

The green summer shoots of Common Horsetail (*Equisetum arvense*) have a very long tradition of use like extremely fine sandpaper, for finishing and polishing wood in cabinet making and marquetry, and also for scouring wooden, pewter and brass cooking vessels and for wooden pails—hence one of the former English names for horsetail, Pewterwort. In a similar fashion, certainly in the Middle Ages, and doubtless long before, horsetails were particularly favoured for polishing armour and in the smoothing of the shafts of arrows. Another English name for horsetail, Shavegrass, reflects its finishing properties on metals to set a fine edge, and in a similar manner it was also used by watchmakers for the most delicate finishing work after coarser filing.

Doubtless all horsetails were used for such purposes, but especially valued most have been the so-called Dutch Rush (*Equisetum hyemale*). Although a native species the name probably derives from the fact that demand clearly exceeded native supplies, for bundles of its rush-like shoots were imported in great quantity from Holland through the Middle Ages, to be sold in London markets for all manner of scouring. Other reports show it to have been used as a file for enlarging and rounding holes made in flutes and other musical instruments or by fletchers and comb-makers to polish their work.

There are good scientific reasons why horsetails were appreciated for their asperous properties. The microscopic structure of the surface of all species of horsetail, when viewed with the aid of a hand-lens, or better still, with the aid of the modern scanning electron microscope (Page, 1972a), can be seen to be armed with very many silica points, knobs and beads, somewhat resembling the grains used to make modern fine-grade sandpaper. It is these that give the rough 'feel' to the plants, and especially to *E. hyemale*, and give all the members of this group their particularly fine burnishing properties.

A quite separate Medieval use of horsetail also derives from their minutely rough surface property. This was in staunching the flow of blood from wounds (presumably a well-tried and necessary handy household necessity in times when the sword ruled so widely). 'Horsetail', probably most often the green summer shoots of *Equisetum arvense*, was 'held in the highest regard in rendering incomparable service' in this application.

Indeed, we know today that clotting of blood is stimulated by minute roughness of the surface, adding weight to the probable effectiveness of the minute surface structure of *Equisetum* in probably speeding this. Perhaps relating to this property too was the use of a decoction of horsetail applied externally as a compress to heal troublesome sores and skin disorders, whilst taken internally, it was regarded as a powerful remineralising agent of value in anaemia, skin complaints and in causing white spots on the fingernails to disappear. In this respect, the mineral content of *Equisetum* which, in addition to silica is known to be high in base elements and iron, may well have played a relevant role.

Two final uses of horsetails derive further from their ability to accumulate silica and also from their ability to take up various heavy metals from a very dispersed state in the soil, and to accumulate these within their tissues. Gold is one such metal which horsetails can accumulate. The quantities involved are, in fact, fairly small, but they are nevertheless sufficiently high compared with the quantities in which they occur in the soil, for it to be practical to prospect for such metals by chemically analysing the horsetails present instead of the soil. This little-known aspect of *Equisetum* has been particularly exploited in prospecting for gold in North America, but it seems likely that wherever horsetails occur over soils in which heavy metals are present, then these plants are likely to accumulate them into detectable quantities.

Finally, the strongly siliceous structure of the vegetative shoots of *Equisetum* is particularly apparent when the shoots are burned. A quite separate, and spectacular, native use of *Equisetum*, derives from this property. The exceptionally high silica content of some species, such as Dutch Rush (*Equisetum hyemale*) endows it with the ability to maintain its cylindrical form after combustion. With the advent of the age of gas, bundles of lengths of shoots of this species were sold for use as early gas mantles, for they have the ability to glow incandescently when burnt in this way.

Practical Uses of Clubmosses

Besides their use as garlands for personal adornment, some of the species of native clubmoss also have an interesting history of other traditional use. This is in the yielding of 'Lycopodium powder': the spores collected *en masse*, especially from *Lycopodium clavatum* and perhaps other species too.

L. clavatum at least was formerly a frequent member of heath and moorland communities throughout lowland Britain, and

'Lycopodium powder' derived from its cones was widely primitively used as a sort of talcum-powder, said to be soothing and cooling in application. Later, it was also used in the manufacture of pills.

This bright yellow powder also gained an unusual theatrical use, for it could be ignited with spectacular effect, producing an explosive flash of light. Behind such a flash presumably appeared many a theatrical demon or magician's rabbit, whilst the powder also found a similar use in the manufacture of fireworks.

This unusual property of the spores seems to derive from an exceptionally high oil content, and was doubtless responsible for bringing something of an awe of magic to the curious native plants that produced them.

The probably well-established principal uses of clubmosses, however, appear to have been in the preparation of coloured textile fabrics.

Pteridophytes in Textiles

Certain pteridophytes are known to have had a former and perhaps widespread use in Britain and Ireland in the preparation of woollen yarn, destined for incorporation into woven textile fabrics.

The involvement of various pteridophytes in such craft industries is certainly of long standing, stretching back at least to the 8th century AD, and very probably much earlier.

Pteridophytes were especially used in the initial preparation of the yarn, and as a mordant or colour fixative subsequent to dyeing with other plant dyes, although some also yielded a colour themselves. As a dressing, along with other agents, in the initial preparation of the yarn during spinning or prior to weaving, they helped to give the threads strength. As dyes and mordants, they helped to create some of the softer, more ochrous hues of the finished materials, long associated with traditional rural textiles, such as those of Scottish clan tartans.

Literature records of the effects of native pteridophyte dye-plant use, attribute yellow-green and green colours to horsetails (*Equisetum* spp.), and other greens to Common Male-fern (*Dryopteris filix-mas*). In addition, modern dye tests show that *Blechnum spicant* produces a pinkish brown and dark brown pigment with alum and iron mordants respectively and that vegetative shoots of Common Horsetail (*Equisetum arvense*) produce Naples yellow with alum mordant (Susan Grierson, personal communication), and it seems likely that use would have been made of these species too.

Bracken has also been widely used as a dye-plant. The Statistical Survey of Co. Tyrone of 1802 notes that Bracken root was cut into short pieces, bruised in a mortar, and the 'oil' pressed through a cloth bag. This was then used as a dressing in spinning. Additionally, many modern craft books also still refer to the use of Bracken 'fiddleheads' (ie young, expanding croziers) as the source of a yellow dye, whilst use of the rhizome for this purpose was still recommended in Scotland at the end of the 19th century (Ross, 1895). Further, fern ashes (probably usually of Bracken) are widely noted to have been used in dyeing and bleaching of cloth. Lack of older written or direct archaeological evidence for most species precludes more exact information on the antiquity of dye use, but it seems most likely that such applications are far from entirely modern.

There is, however, emerging evidence of especially wide and ancient use of clubmosses in rural textile industries in these islands. Literature accounts of the use of clubmosses in Scotland as dye mordants are known as early as 1777, in the *Flora Scotica* published by Lightfoot. The native clubmosses particularly associated with such use are Alpine Clubmoss (*Diphasiastrum alpinum*), Stag's-horn Clubmoss (*Lycopodium clavatum*) and Fir Clubmoss (*Huperzia selago*). These clubmosses appear to have been used as a substitute for the more common mordant alum (potassium aluminium sulphate), perhaps because of a natural possession by these plants of the element aluminium, possibly in combination with potash and iron, and it seems likely that at least in Scotland, and probably elsewhere, these species may well have had a long tradition of rural use in this way.

It is interesting to note that two of these traditional dye-plants exist still as the clan badge plants of at least two ancient Scottish clans: Stag's-horn Clubmoss (*Lycopodium clavatum*) of Clan Munro and Fir Clubmoss (*Huperzia selago*) of Clan Macrae (Cameron, 1883).

As all of these species are almost impossible to cultivate in the normally accepted sense, long periods of very extensive wild gathering from upland moorland areas must have been involved. By comparison, modern wild populations of these species could never support such a trade, and their very considerably greater abundance in the past seems to be indicated: before modern air pollution levels were achieved, and before the annual use of rotational moorland burning ('muirburn' in Scotland) was so widely practised, for these two factors are almost certainly the most potent modern events limiting the general abundance of these species today.

Modern experiments carried out in Scotland (by Susan Grierson of Perth, to whom I am indebted for much of this information) confirm the ability of such clubmosses in making fast the colours achieved from other traditional plant dyes, such as Madder root, Woad, Weld and Willowherb. A comparison with the effects of alum mordant on the same original dyes has shown that the colours produced by clubmoss mordants are softer, less bright, ones than are produced by the same dyes when alum mordants are used. A comparison of ultimate durability however, shows that whilst the colours produced by traditional plant dyes and alum mordants slowly fade under exposure to daylight, those created with plant dyes plus clubmoss mordants retain a permanency of shade not achieved with alum. Clubmosses used without other dye-plants also impart a colour to wool, generally that of a soft, pale straw shade.

Some evidence of the ancientness of the use of clubmosses in such industries in Britain, as well as of direct involvement of yet another very surprising clubmoss species, comes from archaeological sources. Detailed accounts of archaeologically proven ancient plant dye-stuff assemblages are, in practice, very rare—for satisfactory taxonomic verification of ancient residues suspected of being those of former plant dyes can be notoriously difficult. This is partly because of the generally poor state of preservation of the used material itself, and partly because so many plant species formerly incorporated in dyeing may also have had numerous other uses. Nevertheless, in two ancient dye-stuff assemblages which have been recently studied by archaeologists, there is convincing evidence of pteridophyte, and especially clubmoss, involvement, in textile dyeing.

These assemblages come from excavations in Medieval (12th century) Perth and from Viking (10th century) York.

In Perth, waterlogged organic material sampled from occupation floor levels and from middens beneath sites of ancient silver-smithing furnaces, associated workshops and living quarters in a Medieval urban site, contained substantial shoot fragments of both *Diphasiastrum alpinum* and *Lycopodium clavatum*. These were accompanied also by remains of several other possible dye-plants, including Heather (*Calluna vulgaris*, as shoot tips and flowers), Dyer's Rocket or Weld (*Reseda luteola*, formerly much cultivated for a flavone dye), Birch (*Betula* sp., as bark slivers), Tormentil (*Potentilla erecta*, as seeds), and Bracken (*Pteridium aquilinum*, as frond fragments). In some samples, clubmoss remains made up a significant proportion of the material, and the quantity involved and the other associated materials suggest that residues from the dyeing process are almost certainly represented here (M. A. Robinson, personal communication).

In York, richly organic, waterlogged deposits of deep red peaty materials and associated textile fragments have provided similar evidence. In back-yards of 10th century houses and workshops at Coppergate, artifacts indicative of a variety of trades are known, including woodworking, metalworking, and cloth production. Evidence of cloth fragments and the presence of spindle whorls, loom-weights and other items associated with cloth production, suggests such activity to have been a ubiquitous family industry. Absorption spectrum analysis of the red-stained deposits has revealed a predominance of the dye alizarin, derived from Madder (*Rubia tinctoria*), whilst analysis of textile fragments has shown also Woad (*Isatis tinctoria*), a lichen purple, and other dyes to have been in use. Two other plants present as leaf and stem fragment remains within the deposits are Dyer's Greenweed (*Genista tinctoria*) and the clubmoss *Diphasiastrum complanatum*. The latter is present as distinctive portions of dichotomously branching shoots to about 3 cm in length, mostly preserving their characteristic, ranked, scale-like leaves, and, in one sample, an 8 cm length of the creeping axis was found.

The occurrence of the remains of Bracken at the 12th century Perth site may indicate its use as a dye-plant too at the time, or for other purposes associated with yarn production.

As for the clubmoss residues, to judge from the quantities probably consumed, some considerable trade in such materials, involving their transportation over distances, must have been involved. Whilst it is possible that in Perth much of the clubmoss might have been of local origin, this appears not to have been the case in York, where the clubmoss used, *Diphasiastrum complanatum*, is a species not native to Britain today, but widespread in continental northern Europe (including Norway, Sweden and Denmark).

The sites of each of these archaeological dye-plant assemblages are in towns which were inland North Sea ports, and ones which were particularly closely influenced by Viking North Sea trade. The dye-plant assemblages of 10th century York occur in association with other artifacts known to be Scandinavian in origin, at a time when the importation of a great variety of materials from Scandinavia is known to have been active. Indeed, so strong were the Scandinavian ties, that the language of the day then spoken in York ('Jorvik') was not Old English, but Old Norse. There is also evidence of ancient use of this clubmosses as a dye-plant in both Norway and Sweden, and such use was probably widespread in areas under Scandinavian influence, at least as far as the Faeroes.

It would thus seem likely that Scandinavia was the main source of the clubmoss of the York dye-plant industry of the time, and that ten centuries and more ago, such clubmosses were perhaps once an important item of buoyant North Sea trade, across which they were doubtless diligently conveyed, perhaps ultimately to many parts of these islands, in proud wooden longboats.

Old and More Local Names of Ferns and Fern-allies

Various former (sometimes archaic) English names of ferns or fern-allies provide interesting associations with either their appearance, habitat or supposed properties or usage. These include Cypress-moss or Heath Cypress (*Diphasiastrum alpinum*), Fox-feet, Wolf's-claw and Knife-and-Fork (*Lycopodium clavatum*), Merlin's Grass (*Isoetes lacustris*), Puddock Pipes and Trowie Spindles (*Equisetum fluviatile*), Snake Pipes and Joint-weed (*Equisetum arvense*), Pewterwort and Shave-grass (*Equisetum hyemale*), Fairy-tree (*Equisetum sylvaticum*), Adder's-tongue, Serpent's-tongue or Dragons (*Ophioglossum vulgatum*), Pepper-grass (*Pilularia globulifera*), Bog Onion, Heart of Osmund and Herb Christopher (*Osmunda regalis*), Goldylocks (*Hymenophyllum tunbrigense*), Golden Locks, Ever-fern, Brake-of-the-Wall (*Polypodium vulgare*), Venus'-hair, Dudder-grass (*Adiantum capillus-veneris* but perhaps also *Asplenium trichomanes*), Petty-fern (*Asplenium adiantum-nigrum*), Waterwort (*Asplenium trichomanes*), Tentwort (*Asplenium ruta-muraria*), Brownwort, Finger-fern, Miltwaste (*Ceterach officinarum*), Bearsey-fern (*Dryopteris cristata*), and Mekkin (*Dryopteris filix-mas*). Many of these names, often local, are probably of considerable antiquity, whilst even such modern names as Polypody (*Polypodium vulgare*), Pillwort (*Pilularia globulifera*) and Osmunda (*Osmunda regalis*) are known to date back at least to the 14th–16th centuries. Many may be much older, the latter being suggested to be derived from Osmund, a Saxon waterman, who was said to have hidden his children within clumps of this plant (which, when aged, often have hollow centres) to protect them during an incursion by the Danes.

In English usage, the words 'fern' and 'bracken' derive from Anglo-Saxon *fearne* or *fearnig* and Old English *braecen* or *braku* respectively, the latter itself probably originating from an Old Norse name for this plant. However, Bracken was sometimes specifically referred to in Anglo-Saxon as *wylde brake* or *eagle brake* (of at least 12th century or earlier derivation); the latter probably referring to the general appearance of the expanding frond of the plant in May, when a pair of almost fully-expanded and arching wing-like pinnae are topped by a coiled-down, tawny crozier-head, resembling somewhat dramatically the stance of an alighting eagle. The pattern of vascular strands in the cut-across stem of the plant has also been held to resemble the double-headed eagle of fable.

In all the ancient Celtic languages surviving in the corners of our islands, closely similar words for fern (sometimes also meaning Bracken) also exist. Thus *roineach/raineach/rathain* of Scots Gaelic is paralleled by *raithreach* in Irish and *rhedyn* in Welsh and perhaps Cornish. All of these terms have been suggested to be derived from *reath*, a revolution or turning about or *rat* or *rath*, motion, circle or wheel, from the circinnate uncoiling of the young croziers of ferns.

Although many of the applications of these terms are probably fairly general to either ferns or Bracken, species of ferns are sometimes much more specifically recognised in these Celtic languages, as in English. These, often rather delightful, alternative names include *Faile raineach* (which translates as 'Scented Fern') for Sweet Mountain Fern (*Oreopteris limbosperma*) in Scots Gaelic, whilst *Marc raineach* ('Horse Fern') is Common Male-fern (*Dryopteris filix-mas*) in Scots and Irish Gaelic, and just *March* or *March rhedyn* in Welsh. *Raineach Mhuire* ('Mary's Fern', alluding to Christian connotations) is Lady-fern (*Athyrium filix-femina*) in both Scots and Irish Gaelic and *Rhedyn nair* in Welsh. *Creamh mac fiadh* (Scots) or *Creamh nam muc fiadh* (Irish Gaelic) ('Wild Boar's Wort') are used for Hart's Tongue Fern (*Phyllitis scolopendrium*), whilst *An raineach mhor* ('large fern') was sometimes used in Scots Gaelic as a particular word for Bracken (*Pteridium aquilinum*). *Lus na teanga* (Irish) or *Lus na nathraith* (Scots) ('Serpent's weed') is, appropriately, used for Adder's-tongue (*Ophioglossum vulgatum*) in Gaelic. *Tafad y neidr* in Welsh, *Lus na miosa* in Irish or *Luan lus* in Scots are Moonwort (*Botrychium lunaria*). *Raithneach riuil* (Irish) or *Raineach rioghail* (Scots) are Royal Fern (*Osmunda regalis*). *Rhownyn y march* ('Stallion tail') is horsetail (*Equisetum*) in Welsh, and *Gwair Merllyn* ('Hay of the stagnant pool') is Quillwort (*Isoetes*). Fir Clubmoss (*Huperzia selago*) is *Garbhag an sleibhe* in Scots Gaelic ('the rough one of the hill'), whilst *Raineach Meall Ghaordie* ('Meall Ghaordie Fern') is an ancient name for Mountain Bladder-fern (*Cystopteris montana*) in Scots Gaelic, making reference to a famous Highland locality for this species, where it still occurs today. *Cloh-reathneach* ('Stone fern') refers to Polypody (*Polypodium*) in Scots Gaelic, whilst its Irish equivalent *Ceis chrainn*, seems literally to mean 'tree tax', presumably because it was thought to draw forth substance from the trees on which this commonly epiphytic fern grows.

Pteridophytes in Place Name and Surname Origins

It is in the origin of many rural place names within these islands, as well as in many British surnames, that pteridophytes and especially ferns, have left one of their most lasting marks.

In the case of place-names, many examples of the use of *fearne* or *brackni* exist, although ferns and Bracken might not necessarily always have been very specifically distinguished in a taxonomic sense. Many of these names date from the period between the 11th and 15th centuries or earlier.

Examples include names of towns, districts, villages, hamlets, roads, fields and sometimes other topographic features. In Britain, examples of old settlement names deriving from *fearne* or *brackni* include: Farnham (Dorset, Essex, E Suffolk, Surrey, W Yorks, Bucks), Farningham (Kent), Farnley (W Yorks), Farnefield (Notts), Farnworth (Lancs), Farndon (Notts, Northants, Cheshire), Farndale (N Yorks), Farncombe (Surrey), Farnborough (Warwicks, Hants, Berks, Kent), Farmcote (Glos, Somerset), Farmborough (Somerset), Farlow (Shrops), Farlington (N Yorks), Farley/Farleigh (Berks, Glos, Hants, Surrey, Wilts, Staff, Shrops), Farlam (Cumbs), Farington/Faringdon/Farringdon (Berks, Lancs, Oxon, Hants, Dorset, Devon, Somerset), Farthinghoe (Northants), Farthingdale (Surrey), Ferndale (Glam), Ferndown (Dorset), Fernham (Devon, Berks), Fernhurst (W Sussex), Fernedge (London), Fernilee (Derbys), Ferneyhough/Fernyhalgh (Lancs), Ferniegair (Lanark), Fernley (Lancs/Glos), Ferniehill (Midlothian), Fern (Forfar), Fearnhead, Fernhead (Lincs, London), Vernhams (Hampshire), Brackenfield (Derbys), Brackenthwaite (Cumbs, N Yorks), Brackenborough (Lincs, N Yorks), Brackenbottom (N Yorks), Brackenhall (W Yorks), Brackenber (Westmorland & Cumberland), Brackenholme (W & E Yorks), Brackley, (Northants), Brackenhurst (Notts), Brackenwood (Cheshire), Brackleymore (Argyll), Brecknock (Powys) and Brecon (Powys). Similarly old, more minor names, especially of old fields and topographic names which derive from a similar basees include: Farne Fields (Middlx), Farne Breek (Lancs), Farnham Field (Herts), Farndune Hill (Herts), Fern Close (Berks, Argyll), Fern Cote (Berks), Fernel (Nthumb), Fern Field (Derbys), Fern Furlong (Oxon), Fernhill (Cheshire, Dorset, Leics, Worcs, Oxon, Shrops, Som, Staff), Fernhill Furlong (Oxon), Ferney Bank (Cheshire), Ferny Field (Hants, Surrey), Ferny Hay (Derbys), Fern Acre (Lancs), Fernacre (Devon), Ferncliffe (W Yorks), Ferne Park (Wilts), Ferneybeds (Nthumb), Ferney Cross (Gwent), Fern Gone (Lancs), Fern Grove (Lancs), Fernhill Heath (Worcs),

Ferny Common (Worcs), Bracken Hill/Brackenhill (E Yorks, N Yorks, W Yorks, Cumb, Notts), Brackenrigg (Westmorl), Brackendale (E Yorks), Brackenlands (Cumbria), Brackenside (Nthumb), Bracklestone (W Sussex), Brackley Fields (Northants), Brackley Hatch (Northants), Bracken Bed Wood (W Yorks), Finbracken Hill (Argyll), Breck Ness (Orkney), and Breckland (Norfolk/Suffolk). If Bracken (rather than other ferns) is commemorated in the appropriately-based names, then their predominant location in heathy or upland areas of Britain is notable, while Breckland is still an area in which particularly large stands of Bracken still occur throughout the region, as they have for many years.

The non-English-speaking parts of these islands were not forgotten in place-name origins either. I have found a few of these, though it is probable that many others exist. North of the Scottish Border, these include: Blawrainy (Kirkcudbright— 'ferny plain'), Culrain (Sutherland—'Wood' or 'nook of the ferns'), Rathen (Inverness—'ferny place'), Creag Rainich (Inverness—'Bracken rock'), Frenich (Argyll—'place of ferns'), Ruidh Reinnich (Perthshire—'ferny shieling'), Sron Raineach (Inverness—'Bracken point'), Camus Rainneach (W Argyll—'Bracken bay') and Loch Rannoch (Perthshire— 'Bracken loch'), all of which derived from the Scots Gaelic *roineach* or *raineach* for Bracken or *rathain* for fern. Thus Kinloch Rannoch is 'head of the Bracken loch' and Blackwood of Rannoch its pinewood. In Wales, Cilrhedyn (Dyfed) is 'nook of the ferns.' Similarly in Ireland are: Rahan ('ferny spot'), Ardrahan ('height of the ferns'), Coleraine ('nook of the ferns'), Drumraney/Drumraine ('ridge of ferns'), Kilrane ('church of the ferns') and Mallaranny /Mulrany ('hill-brow of the ferns'). Even in Cornwall, in far south-west Britain, Redannick ('place of the ferns') on the Lizard peninsula derives from a similar base in ancient Cornish.

Equally pteridophytic seems to be Auchlunachan ('field of the jointed grass') in the Highland region, presumably deriving from a healthy stand of nearby horsetail when the village was founded.

In the West Highlands in particular there are also several replicated references to different mountains called *Beinn Bhuidhe* ('Yellow Mountain') or *Fair Bhuidhe* ('Yellow Height'), which all derive from a conspicuous yellow colour of the hillsides, which is very probably that produced by extensive stands of Golden-scaled Male-fern (*Dryopteris affinis* subsp. *affinis*) around their lower flanks, the western mountain distribution of which these names seem to closely follow.

There are probably many examples of surnames which appear to have pteridophyte associations. Some of the more

widespread of these in English are: Crozier, Fern/Ferne/ Ferns, Fernie/Ferney, Fernley, Fernall/Fernell, Fernback, Fernbank, Ferncombe, Ferneyhough/Fernyhough, Redfern/ Radfern, Blackfern, Brack/Bracks/Breck, Bracken, Brackenridge/Breckenridge, Brackenbridge/Breckenbridge, Brackenbury, Brackenberg, Brackenborough, and Brackenburg. Many of these surnames probably derive from personal associations with place names of the same spelling, while others may have more direct pteridophyte associations, perhaps deriving from ancient trades associated with ferns or bracken.

The distinctive golden-green, freshly emerged fronds of Dryopteris affinis *subsp.* affinis. *West Argyll, July*

Fern Influence in Art, Architecture and Artefact

Two structural aspects of ferns are especially readily-observed and characteristic features of the group. One is the finely-divided form of the fully-expanded fern frond, with, in many species, a repeated pinnate division giving a fine degree of dissection to form a delicately-textured frond. The other is the fern crozier. This is the circinnately-coiled, watchspring-like spiral bud, from which the fern frond ultimately develops.

Phyllitis
scolopendrium
showing the form of the
fern crozier often
immitated in many
aspects of art,
architecture and
artifact. West
Cornwall, May

Whilst the expanded frond is characteristic of the summer growing season, the fern croziers are most noticeable in spring, when they somewhat dramatically expand by a steady process of unrolling, intimately coupled with a sideways-extension of the pinnate divisions of the frond ('the pinnae') which are, at first, also curled tightly within the main spiral and only appear after the initial unrolling.

Both features occur in only a few other groups of plants. Fine leaf-dissection is also seen in many Umbelliferae, but is usually less regularly pinnate in form than in most ferns. The coiled crozier occurs in the Sundew genus *Drosera* of bog-plants, but its leaves are very small at this stage, and not easily seen. But only in the ferns are these features common both taxonomically and geographically throughout the group, in temperate and especially in tropical parts of the world, and they are large and characteristic, and hence easily noted, features of this section of the plant world.

Against this background it is of interest to find that frond-like form and spiral motifs occur very widely in art, architecture and in many ornate artefacts throughout much of human history.

Certainly, these shapes in artwork may have been independently derived on many separate occasions and for many purposes, without reference to a fern plant. However, bearing closely in-mind the significance of ferns in folklore through history, both in these islands and elsewhere, in many cases the occurrence of such shapes may have been consciously or unconsciously influenced by these shapes occuring in nature. In other cases, the influence may have been more indirect, on designs which perhaps had abstract beginnings, but which nevertheless came to look more closely like the form of the fern frond or crozier as the designs themselves have been adapted and evolved through time.

The significance of the spiral symbol in art usually appears to have been in indicating renewed life (Dr J. Perani, personal communication). One explanation for this may lie in the repetitiveness of the spiral form itself. Could another, however, also be that it derives from a widespread phenomenon in nature: the recurring annual appearance of fern croziers in the spring, a visible and assured herald of new life to be?

Certainly, in Victorian times in Britain, the fern-frond, either as a crozier or in a more fully unfurled form, was prevalent in the ornate cast-iron architecture of glasshouse and conservatory construction, and reflected too in the patterns of cast-iron garden furniture designs of the day. Elsewhere, ferns of all sorts have appeared as the unashamed ornamentation of many items of chinaware of English Victorian and later origin.

More widely, in primitive art, the spiral form has been independently used in different cultures from ancient times. Such spiral forms are extensively present, for example, in the Viking art of Scandinavia, in the Maori art of New Zealand, in New Guinea art and in pre-Columbian art of South America, though not, so far as is known, in that of the African continent. It is perhaps no mere coincidence, that the art-cultures in which these spiral-forms have been widely (and presumably independently) adopted are each in parts of the world in which ferns abound in the natural vegetation of the regions, and absent in Africa, where they do not. In New Zealand, such spiral forms can be seen not only in Maori art and carvings and on the cheeks of Maori warriors, but with a derived form today adorning the more modern location of the tail-fins of aircraft of New Zealand's national airline, while the fern-frond itself has

Fig. 2
*Corinthian capital of
classical architectural
design, showing
multiple, fern-crozier
like volutes ensheathed
at the base by stylised
Acanthus leaves*

become New Zealand's national emblem. Nearer to home, and from an independent source, fern-crozier-like shapes also once adorned the prows of raiding Viking longboats.

In architecture, a similar type of crozier-like structure, usually referred to as a 'volute', has frequently also adorned architectural stonework within these islands, derived from those of classical architecture elsewhere. These seem especially to be found as stonework ornamentation on the capitals forming the crowning members of columns, piers and pilasters, widely used in monastic, cathedral and other architecture of the Middle Ages. One of these is the 'Corinthian capital', formed of several separate crozier-like volutes ensheathed at the base by rows of stylised Acanthus leaves, and here these volutes may bear an especially close affinity with the form of expanding fern croziers.

Elsewhere, and presumably of totally independent origin, the scroll at the head of violins and the whole string-family of musical instruments, as well as on some Welsh and Irish harps, is also a crozier-like and very traditional design. Indeed, in America, the link has somewhat turned the other way, for fern-croziers are referred to as 'fiddle-heads' in general parlance!

But perhaps of the most spectacular affinity with a fern crozier is in the Bishops crozier of Christian religion (see p. 16). For not only do some old croziers bear a special resemblance to a fern-frond in bud, but some even appear to be complete with ornate pinnules. Perhaps such use also relates to the fern crozier as a primitive symbolisation of renewed life?

Ferns — the Modern Commercial Image

Today, in the latter part of the 20th century, there is every sign that fern-influences even in everyday life are far from extinct. Ferns appear on the coinage and banknotes of at least one British Commonwealth country, and have made their appearance on postage stamps, including on one issue in these islands. But perhaps more than ever before, the fern has become seen as a marketable, commercial commodity. One significant aspect of this is in their widespread availability for amateur cultivation through both the general and specialist horticultural trade, and in the commercial reappearance of

The distinctive, white-scaled croziers with early-expanding pinnae of Oreopteris limbosperma. Midlothian, May

associated literature and even of excellent modern pseudo-Victorian Wardian cases (see Chapter 2).

Especially, however, the fern has become quite naturally adopted as a symbol of an implicit forest fragrance yet purity as well as pleasantness and perhaps softness of use, of many a modern commercial cosmetic product, to be found on the shelves of almost every high street chemist's shop and store through these islands.

Perhaps it in some way still underlines an inherent belief in the mystery and magic of these plants, that living potted ferns and commercial products depicting them are now perhaps, most often to be found side-by-side in many a modern home, on the half-secret places of the modern bathroom windowsill, from the tins and jars of which we still hope to receive some magical and perhaps rejuvenating effects, through daily ceremonial application of their hidden and obscure contents.

The History of Pteridology CHAPTER **2**

In the last two centuries or more, two major aspects of the interest in pteridophytes have developed. One, at the popular level, was the great interest in cultivation of ferns of the late 19th century, which we reflect upon, from the perspective of a hundred years on, as the Victorian fern craze. The other, which began over two hundred years ago, but which has had more lasting effects, has been the process, gradual at first but strengthening greatly with time, of the coming of science to pteridology.

The Victorian Fern Craze

It was undoubtedly in the drawing-rooms of Victorian Britain, that interest in native ferns reached an all-time historic zenith. To have an interest in ferns became fashionable, and the fashion reached epidemic proportions before it declined, with unfortunate repercussions for the conservation of the plants themselves. The aspect of pteridophytes which so suddenly and wholly caught the Victorian imagination was an avidly horticultural one—the growing of ferns and the quest for the ever more rare and obscure of them—a craze which has subsequently been aptly dubbed 'pteridomania' (Allen, 1969).

Origins of the Craze

Pteridomania seems to have first begun to take a grip on the Victorian imagination in about the 1830s. Prior to this, living ferns had trickled into Britain from more tropical climes since about 1795, when Bligh (of 'Bounty' fame) first successfully brought back living tropical ferns from the West Indies. Knowledge of how to propagate ferns from their spores had been gradually emerging since the very late 1700s, and this knowledge, allowing ferns to be raised by the hundred, was the first main advance which made their cultivation widely possible. The second was the advance which enabled ferns once propagated to be maintained indefinitely within the environs of

The large and beautiful, thin-textured, pellucid fronds of Trichomanes speciosum, *a rare fern now legally protected*

the Victorian drawing-room. This was the invention of the closely-glazed 'Wardian Case'—a sort of ornate miniature greenhouse on legs. Such cases enabled ferns to be grown in the midst of the smoke of Victorian London, where the numbers of chimneys had led all previous efforts to cultivate ferns to be unsuccessful. From such small cases, measuring a few feet in length, it was but a short step to the fully fledged, glazed, Victorian conservatory abutting on to the house and abounding with ferns deriving from all corners of the British Empire.

One of the original purposes of the Wardian case was to permit exotic species to be imported and once here, to be grown. However, imported ferns tended to be expensive to buy and required heat to survive through the British winter.

The desire to cultivate ferns, however, transcended the social barriers of Victorian Britain, and for those who could not or did not want to acquire tropical ferns and go to the expense of permanently heating them, then the cultivation of hardy British ferns which were available free and needed no artificial heat, provided an attractive alternative. The number of native species was, however, more limited than the ever-different range of tropical specimens arriving with almost every ship. The quest amongst the hardy ferns for variety, and as a result, the ever more unusual, brought value to those plants or varieties of them which were not so readily obtained.

Urged on by a new-found freedom to travel to more distant parts of Britain and Ireland, which the coming of the railways and their numerous rural branch lines brought, more and more fern-rich habitats fell within the grasp of the mid-Victorian

Left. Equisetum sylvaticum *is unusual among the horsetails in having whorled branches which are themselves branched, to form an intricate and distinctive branch architecture. Mid-Perthshire, early August*

Right. The distinctive architecture and soft texture of a typically downhill-pointing frond of Phegopteris connectilis. *Mid-Perthshire, late June*

collector. For those not able to travel themselves, the commercial collector of ferns for the blossoming nursery trade followed hard on the heels of the amateur, bringing ferns for commercial sale in Victorian cities from ever more remote parts of these islands, sometimes by the cartload. Such wholesale collection of naturally rare species very soon rapidly exceeded what the wild populations of these plants could possibly stand, and such slow-growing plants as the alpine Woodsias from northern Britain or the Killarney fern (*Trichomanes speciosum*) from south-west Ireland rapidly suffered sad and wanton devastation of their well-known wild populations, from which they have never recovered.

By the standards of the day, we can understand, although not condone, this highly unfortunate episode. The beauty and intricacy of architecture of the fronds of ferns fitted in well with the intricacies of Victorian furnishings and elegance of living. Such plants were brought back for observation and study in the comfort of the Victorian drawing-room or conservatory, where either live or pressed they were objects of curiosity. They seemed to have come into much the same category of desiderata as the stuffed-moose head looking benignly down at its captor from the wall, or the tiger-skin rug lying passively

The spectacular croziers of Dryopteris dilatata. *West Cornwall, May*

underfoot. Under such conditions, nature was tamed and, removed from the more sordid trappings of its natural environment, became socially acceptable.

The vogue for fern-filled conservatories (as well as many including palms, oranges, camellias and other exotica) which were green all the year round, led to the more grandiose of these being termed 'Winter Gardens'. From such structures of glass and iron, considerable architectural advances were made, of which the climax was Sir Joseph Paxton's Crystal Palace, first opened in 1851. Many ambitious, though typically Victorian, glasshouse structures still survive to be seen today, often with impressive curvilinear or clerestory domed roofs, supported by stonework or cast-iron columns and intricate networks of ornamented girders. Surviving examples include Bicton, Devon (1838); Chatsworth, Derbyshire (1840); Syon Park, Middlesex (1847); Sefton Park, Liverpool (1896); Sheffield Botanical Gardens (1836); Grimston Park, Yorkshire (1840); Belfast Botanical Garden (1839, 1853); Glasnevin, Dublin (1850 and 1884); Kibble Palace and Peoples Palace, Glasgow (1872 and 1880); and the great Palm Houses at Royal Botanic Gardens, Kew, London (1847) and Edinburgh (1858) Royal Botanic Gardens.

The interior of a classic Victorian fernery, Kibble Palace in Glasgow. Most of the ferns present date from specimens originally-planted in the 19th-century

The Hardy Fern Varieties

From about 1850 onwards, however, one aspect of the search for the unusual amongst native ferns took an altogether different direction. This was the more constructive approach of finding wild varieties and raising these from spores in cultivation. Those specimens which differed from the normal, often no matter how grotesquely, were particularly prized, and by selecting their progeny, increasingly extreme forms of some of the more common species were obtained. Thus the native species of *Dryopteris*, *Athyrium* and *Polystichum* gave rise remarkably rapidly to literally hundreds of named 'varieties' often variously forked, frilled, crisped, congested or finely cut. Many were sheer monstrosities. A few were quite beautiful. Many were listed in nurserymen's catalogues of the time.

Fig. 3
*Examples of two
Victorian hardy British
fern varieties,* Phyllitis
scolopendrium *(left)
and* Adiantum
capillus-veneris
*(right). (After Lowe,
1865)*

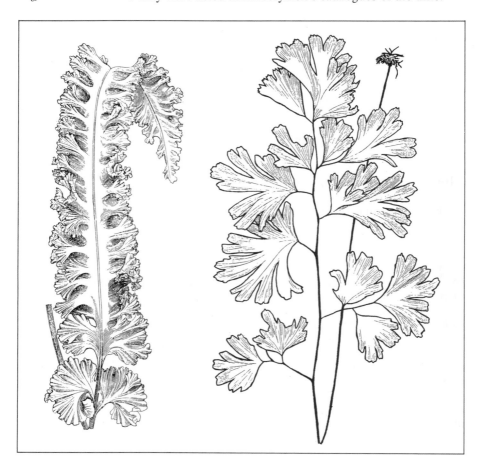

Curiously enough, it remains somewhat of an enigma today, just how the Victorian pteridologists succeeded in finding and acquiring such an extraordinary range of variation over so short a period of time and how, contemporary accounts tell us on so many trips into the wild, the starting-materials for this cultivation sub-cult could so readily be found. No similar situation seems to have ever arisen anywhere else in the world but in Britain, and even here, no similar range of wild finds or sports in cultivation have ever appeared since.

Perhaps it was the sheer volume of plants which the Victorian growers raised which was responsible for this. Nevertheless, the range of these Victorian 'finds' were truly enormous, although only a small fraction of those which were once cultivated have survived in the hands of a few keen propagators to the present day. A small dedicated body of fern-growers was thus born, who by far outlasted and survived the eventual decline of the popular Victorian fern-craze towards the close of the 19th century. It was these amateur growers and enthusiasts, with very considerable expertise in fern propagation, as well as in the finer points of their taxonomy and nomenclature, who founded the British Pteridological Society in 1892, with the objectives of growing and serious study of ferns of all kinds. The Society still survives, and indeed flourishes, and just short of a century in age, is now the oldest and most respected such organisation in the world.

The Coming of Science to Pteridology

It was, however, more than a century before the founding of the British Pteridological Society that the more scientific study of ferns and fern allies in all their aspects had first begun in Britain.

By the latter part of the 1700s mere superstition about fern spores and their function in the life-cycle began to give way to more exact knowledge based on serious observation and experiment. As early as 1699, there is a recorded experiment in which the 'powder' from mature leaves of Hart's Tongue Fern scattered on moist soil were found to produce, the following year, 'many plants with delicate leaves'. From these beginnings, the subsequent discovery of the life-cycle of ferns was, in no small way, due to the close involvement that the disciplines of medicine and botany then had (and often still do) with one another. Discovery of the essence of the complex life-cycle of the fern fell to John Lindsay, a former student of Dr John Hope, the then Professor of Medicine and Botany and Superintendent of the Royal Garden (now Royal Botanic Garden) at

Edinburgh. John Hope was himself the son of an Edinburgh
surgeon, and had trained as a student in medicine, but was an
enthusiastic Botanical experimenter, pioneer investigator of
the Scottish flora, and teacher. Hope's teaching and his
enthusiasm was clearly a lasting influence on Lindsay, who,
although himself becoming a surgeon, maintained a strong
botanical interest when he eventually travelled to Jamaica.
Here Lindsay noted how young ferns appeared in quantity:

'after the rains in marle and gravel pits, and on the shaded banks of
rivers which had been broken down by the floods; and indeed in every
place where the earth had been dug into, and left shaded and
untouched for a few months . . .'

Lindsay considered this an opportunity to investigate how
these young ferns arose. Combining his field observation with
experiment, and with the aid of a microscope, he watched
spores germinate and subsequently form 'bilobate, liverwort-
like scales'. From each of these, he observed, eventually arose a
small membranous leaf (the first true leaf of the young fern)
followed rapidly by a sequence of successively larger leaves.
Lindsay recorded and sent these observations back to Dr John
Hope in Edinburgh, who was sufficiently impressed by them to
propose 'to lay the observations before the Royal Society of
Edinburgh'. Hope's death unfortunately intervened before he
had been able to do this. The work of a busy surgeon in Jamaica
then occupied much of Lindsay's time until a request arrived
from Sir Joseph Banks at Kew in a letter dated 29 March 1789
for live specimens of Jamaican ferns. Doubting the ability of
whole ferns to make the journey to Kew successfully, Lindsay
records that he offered instead to send Banks 'some of their
seeds, which being properly sown, I had reason to believe
would grow'. Banks replied to Lindsay that if Lindsay could
show him how successful growth of ferns could be achieved in
England from such seed, Lindsay would have 'the credit of
making a very valuable discovery'.

Lindsay sent to Banks a copy of his notes and observations,
and these subsequently formed the basis of a paper by Lindsay,
communicated by Banks, which was published in the Trans-
actions of the Linnean Society for 1792.

Within Britain and Ireland, although it is the more popular
aspects of the Victorian fern craze which tend to dominate our
memory of this period, it should not be overlooked that the
century before and Victorian times were a period of an important developing interest in our native ferns, from a botanical
rather than a horticultural standpoint, and that the foundations
of a great deal of our modern knowledge about the British
species were made by several very competent observers during

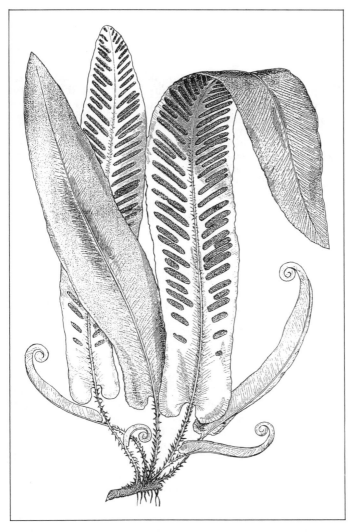

Fig. 4
Phyllitis
scolopendrium *from a*
19th-century
illustration

this period. The first book on British Ferns (and, indeed, the first book on the ferns of any country in the world) was published in Britain between 1785 and 1789. This was *Filices Britannicae* by James Bolton, an ardent Yorkshire naturalist and explorer of native plants. Bolton influenced, in Victorian times, several very competent observers, amongst whom James Sowerby, E. J. Lowe, Edward Newman, James Britten and J. G. Baker stand out in the author's esteem as having laid the foundations of much of the modern field studies of these plants in Britain and Ireland.

Polystichum
lonchitis, *a rare and
spectacular Arctic-
Alpine species. East
Perthshire, September*

*Cascading
herringbone-like fronds
of an old clump of*
Blechnum *spicant in a
steep, ungrazed site, are
attractive in all
seasons. Wester Ross,
August*

One great emphasis of Victorian botany was on collecting. Specimens were gathered and pressed, and in this way, permanently-preserved collections of plants (herbaria) could be accumulated. In several cases, whole plants were collected, and the number of amateur botanists forming such collections must, in these cases, have put further pressure on the already depleted populations of rarer plants in the wild. In most cases, however, single fronds were gathered, and often immaculately and beautifully preserved. Once preserved, the collections had the benefit of being permanent, and usually outlasted their original owners. Gifted or bequeathed to local county museums, or to the major national collections at the Natural History Museum, London, or the herbaria of the two Royal Botanic Gardens at Edinburgh and Kew, they have been carefully maintained and preserved, where they act as valuable records of the plants of the day, whilst forming the basis of the taxonomy of these plants.

It is in these essential scientific aspects, and in fern natural history in general, that the main interest in ferns and their allies has gradually focussed in Britain and Ireland during the 20th century. Early milestones here were marked particularly by the publication of D. H. Campbell's *Mosses and Ferns* (1895) and by F. O. Bower of his now-classic works *The Ferns* (1923–28) and *Primitive Land Plants* (1935), whilst in a field-orientated sphere, the many observations and publications of Irish botanists, amongst whom R. L. Praeger stands pre-eminent, did much to establish the rightful place of our native ferns in ecological studies.

During the period when ferns had been coming from all corners of the Empire, so too had ferns and fern-allies from another source—as fossils, and these too required description. Britain itself has a remarkably complete geological record, and fossils of land plants from as young as the relatively recent Tertiary fossils of south-east England, to very much older ones from the Carboniferous and Devonian were found within these islands. Amongst prominent palaeobotanical investigators have been J. Lindley, W. Hutton, Robert Kidston, W. H. Lang, D. H. Scott, M. E. J. Chandler, E. M. Reid, A. C. Seward, John Walton and T. M. Harris, whilst many researchers continue these excellent traditions today. Amongst the especially notable contributions of native fossils, Kidston and Lang's description of *Rhynia* from the chert beds of Rhynie in Aberdeenshire—the then earliest known vascular plant and first pteridophyte—still mark a milestone in evolutionary thinking.

But by the middle of this century, if the mould had not been altogether broken, at least a new one had become very properly launched – a new one which was to have, and is still having, far-reaching effects upon our ideas about evolutionary processes and interrelationships in pteridophytes. This was their study through the interpretation of their chromosomes (promptly ever after known as their 'cytology') expounded with a degree of accuracy hitherto unknown, by the work of Professor Irene Manton at Leeds, published in 1950. Her work was to both revolutionise and revitalise pteridology worldwide. She also brought scientific pteridology back to the study of the living-plants, both in the field and in the greenhouse, where plants could be reared, and their hybrids successfully synthesised.

From this point onwards, the amateur grower of ferns and the professional botanical researcher again began to have an inkling that each other existed and of what each other were generally about.

The existing British Pteridological Society became the forum for renewed interest in ferns and fern-allies both by amateurs and professionals, and it is to their eternal credit that those amateurs, who were nevertheless the unsurpassed authorities on our native species, and who had long maintained the Society, were able to adapt to the new methods, new purposes and new findings of a taxonomically now rapidly-advancing field. A particularly significant milestone was reached with the publication of distribution maps of all the native Pteridophyta (Jermy et al., 1976) based on the collated recording work of very many amateur members.

Thus, by the beginning of the last quarter of the 20th century, we have come to know much about the taxonomy and detailed geographic distribution of the species of ferns and fern-allies native in Britain and Ireland, to a probably greater degree of accuracy than in any other part of the world.

But although we may now know much about their taxonomy and geography, we seem still scarcely to be beginning to probe the boundaries of further significant questions about the biology and ecology of these fascinating plants, as well as their natural history and conservation, and it is in these important areas that the rest of this book is concentrated.

The Influences of Climate and Soil on Pteridophyte Range

The inter-related effects of climatic and edaphic (rock and soil) influences form a vital background to the understanding of the evolution, ecology, phytogeography and natural history of our native pteridophyte flora. The geographic ranges of most of the climatic factors discussed here are mapped in detail for the whole of Britain and Ireland in Page (1982). For convenience of discussion, predominantly Latin names of pteridophytes are used throughout this chapter. English names will be found in Appendix 1 and in the habitat sections of this text.

Climatic Influence

The accumulated effect of the daily weather conditions—the climate—is a powerful factor governing the geographic range of plant species. The effects of climate on plant ranges operate both directly and indirectly. Directly, the climate determines the ability of a species to survive, and how well it can do this. Indirectly, the climate influences the edaphic conditions, and also determines the ability of all other competing species to survive. The climatic-edaphic-biotic effects resulting thus together play the major role in determining the geographic range which any native pteridophyte is able to achieve and maintain.

When split into some of its many component factors, correlations between the distribution of certain of these and the distribution of individual pteridophyte species can be seen. Amongst other lower plant groups, similar relationships have been found amongst Atlantic bryophytes (Ratcliffe, 1968) and epiphytic lichens (Coppins, 1976). Such comparisons can provide valuable pointers to the factors probably involved in helping determine species ranges, although some caution in their interpretation must be exercised. Clearly, more than one climatic component may show a similar distribution, whilst the

ranges of the plants themselves are probably governed by a
constant interplay of many such factors. Further, boundaries of
plant ranges are formed where one or other factor becomes
limiting, and this may well not be the same factor in all parts of
the range, even of a single species. Throughout its range,
species are likely also to be genetically variable, differing subtly
in the degree of conditions which they are able to tolerate,
whilst even in one area, the occurrence of one set of conditions
at one time of the year (eg. good summer growing conditions)
may enable a plant to withstand greater extremes of other conditions (eg. prolonged or severe winter cold), than it can
elsewhere.

Responses of plants are often further modified by the local
microclimatic conditions in which they occur, whilst even an
individual plant may respond differently to the same climatic
factor at different stages in its life-cycle. This is particularly
relevant to pteridophytes, where both generations in the life-
cycle are free-living and structurally different. Even a single
individual sporophyte may become more demanding of specific conditions, and less tolerant of extremes of them, as it ages,
compared with its tolerances when young. Perhaps it is such an
increasing demand for specificity of conditions which finally
limits the eventual age of most individuals.

Such comparisons of distribution of plant ranges and climatic factors thus do not give exact measures of the precise degree
of any one factor which limits a species. But they can be valuable in comparing the general trends of the distribution of
species and those of climatic factors, and allow hypotheses
about relationships to be suggested. These form pointers
towards likely factors, which should be investigated experi-
mentally for their effects on both the sporophyte and gametophyte generation of the species concerned.

Temperature

Temperature is one of the principal aspects of climate
influencing pteridophyte distributions, and can be split into a
number of independent factors.

Summer temperature maxima In summer, the heat
received from the sun is the dominant factor controlling temperatures, and there is an effect caused by latitude producing
progressively cooler temperature maxima northwards. Interior
regions also show great contrasts with coastal ones, with the
interiors, especially in periods of clear, settled weather,
warming up rapidly to a high daily temperature, which may,

however, drop off quickly again at night, so there is a large diurnal temperature range. By contrast, this behaviour is moderated in all coastal parts of Britain and Ireland by the effect of the sea, which limits the temperature rise by day and its fall by night. Because the prevailing winds blow from a WSW direction, this oceanic effect is greatest on western coasts, from which its influence is felt some distance inland.

Summer temperature maxima probably more or less directly limit the southward extent of the ranges of many, more northern pteridophytes. This is most conspicuously seen, for example, in the ranges of most of the 'Arctic–Alpine' pteridophytes and especially, perhaps, of *Cryptogramma crispa*, both species of *Woodsia* and both alpine *Athyrium* species.

Winter temperature minima   In winter, temperatures in Britain and Ireland are beneficially influenced to a very large extent by those of the surrounding seas. The overall minimum temperatures are higher by far than is generally characteristic of continental areas at equivalent latitudes, to the extent of about 20°F (ca. 11°C) higher in London (lat. 51°30′N), 30°F (ca. 17°C) higher in Edinburgh (lat. 55°58′N), and 40°F (ca. 22°C) higher in Shetland (lat. 62°20′N). Edinburgh, for example, is further north than Moscow, whilst winter minimum temperatures on the Scottish west coast are more nearly equivalent to those of the south of France. Regional differences of minimum temperature are, however, profound. Regions nearest the coast remain warmer than inland districts. Off western coasts the winter temperatures are most directly and continuously influenced by the effect of the impinging warm Gulf Stream current (North Atlantic Drift), and are always a degree or so warmer than the waters off the eastern coasts, so that western coastal areas tend to be warmer than eastern ones.

Although the winter temperature minimum is likely to be far from the only factor involved, it probably has a profound influence in limiting the northernmost range of many of the more tender southern 'Mediterranean' and 'Atlantic' pteridophytes in Britain and Ireland, especially in habitats very close to western coasts. Amongst others, the northward extension of the ranges of *Osmunda regalis*, *Trichomanes speciosum*, *Asplenium billotii*, *Dryopteris aemula* and *Ophioglossum azoricum*, as well as the occurrence at all in these islands of more Mediterranean pteridophytes such as *Isoetes histrix*, *Ophioglossum lusitanicum*, *Adiantum capillus-veneris* and *Asplenium onopteris*, can almost certainly be attributed, at least in large part, to the mildness of the winter temperatures.

Distribution of frosts   Frosts occur in nearly all parts of

Britain and Ireland, although their frequency, severity, and the times of the year over which they are prevalent vary widely. The most frost-free areas occur around the extreme Atlantic periphery, especially in south-west Ireland, extreme west Cornwall and the Channel Islands. In such areas, temperatures descending below 0°C are likely on no more than 10 occasions per year (5 in the Scilly Islands), and severe frosts are extremely rare. The frost-free period of the year is also long, extending from the end of February (mid-February in the Channel Islands) until almost the end of the year (about 11 months). Away from the west coast, however, as well as with increasing latitude northward and increasing altitude, likelihood of frosts increases rapidly. The most severely frosted areas are probably those of the eastern Scottish Highlands, where the temperature is likely to drop below 0°C on well over 100 days during the year, and where severe and prolonged frosts are frequent. Here, the season of the year when frosts are likely is also long, and lasts from mid-August to the beginning of the following June (a frost-free season of only 2½ months). In such areas, the severity of frosts is further influenced by local topographical details, with the mean minimum temperature on a frosty night becoming at least 2°C lower in well-sheltered 'frost-hollows' than on nearby, more windy slopes.

Prolonged exposure to frost causes damage to the plant not only through cold, but also through desiccation, especially if accompanied by wind. At altitude, cold as well as desiccation are largely ameliorated in areas where snow accumulates deeply. The varying altitudinal limits reached by most pteriodophytes probably, at least to some extent, reflect differing frost-sensitivities. Bracken (*Pteridium aquilinum*), for example, although so abundant on the lower parts of hillsides, ceases fairly abruptly at an altitude of about 2,000 ft. (ca. 610 m) in Scotland, where the damaging effect on the young growth of late spring frosts probably becomes the limiting factor. Amongst other species which seem frost-sensitive are our various southern Atlantic and Mediterranean species which reach northerly stations in southern and western districts, such as *Adiantum capillus-veneris* and *Trichomanes speciosum*, whilst surprisingly frost-sensitive is *Asplenium marinum*. Its sites— close to the sea and only where wave action creates winter spray—are ones where the severity of cold nights is greatly tempered locally by the presence of warm winter sea. Its range around much of Britain and Ireland thus reflects not so much the range of a salt-demanding plant, but the range of a very frost-sensitive one, which has evolved a considerable tolerance of salt (Page, 1982) thus enabling it to benefit from the relative warmth of the sea in winter.

Length of thermic growing season If other factors are not limiting, most vascular plants cease active growth when the temperature drops below a certain critical minimum, and resume once this threshold is crossed again. A generally accepted figure for this temperature for the majority of plants is about 5–6°C. Exact limits probably vary with individual species, although for pteridophytes, these are in need of study. Some measure of the length of the growing season for plants can be derived from 'temperature sums', in which the number of accumulating day degrees of temperature above the determined threshold value can be assessed, either annually or for certain portions of the year. In practice, it seems unlikely that metabolic activities of pteridophytes differ very substantially in their temperature responses from those of the bulk of vascular plants, and such summed or accumulated temperatures have been used extensively by climatologists and agrometeorologists for the establishment of agroclimatic zones.

Particularly high annual accumulated temperatures with over 3000 day–degrees F (ca. 1,650 day–degrees C) occur over much of southern England, and in coastal regions of southern Ireland extend northwards somewhat on west coasts. By contrast, the eastern Scottish Highlands have under 500 day–degrees F (ca. 275 day–degrees C)—less than one-sixth of the English south coast.

Fronds of the highly frost-tolerant, deciduous-fronded Athyrium filix-femina, *etched by winter's rime. Midlothian, early February*

The length of the thermic growing season gives a good impression of the distribution of annual or seasonal thermic conditions, and also shows interesting comparisons with several pteridophyte distributions, corresponding, in large part, to regions where there is a high annual accumulated temperature. These appear to be those pteridophytes occurring most extensively through southern and eastern England with northward extensions along the west coasts. Amongst these appear to be especially *Osmunda regalis*, *Thelypteris palustris*, *Pilularia globulifera* and *Equisetum telmateia*, whilst *Ophioglossum vulgatum* shows a similar, but somewhat more extensive, trend, as does the introduced *Azolla filiculoides*. It seems noteworthy that all these are species associated in some degree with rather wet, often pond, or lake-marginal habitats, which presumably require a considerable amount of heat-input to warm sufficiently to stimulate growth in spring.

The geographic distributions of significant amounts of accumulated temperature in the winter months also shows some interesting pteridophyte range comparisons. The mean *winter* accumulated temperature shows that there is a significant accumulated temperature of over 300 day–degrees during the period December–March only in the Channel and Scilly Islands and in the coastal fringes of south-west England and south-west Ireland (Page, 1982). When interpreted in terms of length of growing season this is the only area of Britain and Ireland where the growing season exceeds nine months, and in places (probably west Cornwall, the Scilly and Channel Islands) approaches twelve. Four species of native pteridophytes occur only in these areas: *Adiantum capillus-veneris*, *Ophioglossum lusitanicum*, *Isoetes histrix* and *Anogramma leptophylla*. In each case, these are species which achieve most or all of their annual growth in the winter half of the year.

Precipitation

Precipitation is also a principal aspect of climate in influencing pteridophyte ranges, and like temperature, can be split into a number of independent factors.

Amount of precipitation The amount of rain falling in Britain and Ireland varies widely, from under 800 mm (less than 31 inches) over a large part of lowland England, to well over 3,200 mm (over 126 inches) in upland parts of south-west Ireland, North Wales and western Scotland. The patterns of rainfall show both an increase westwards and an increase with ascending altitude. High precipitation usually results in frequently high groundwater tables, high surface run-off, creation of streamside erosion habitats, and a high frequency of standing water in the form of small pools and lakes. Over much of lowland England and Wales, standing waters in the form of surface lakes and ponds are correspondingly sparse, and occupy less than 0.5% of the land area (Smith & Lyle, 1979). Much higher percentages occur in North Wales, the English Lake District and almost throughout Highland Scotland and the Islands, where many regions have up to 5% of their area occupied by lakes and ponds, or over 5% for parts of the north-west Scottish coast and the Outer Hebrides.

Many aquatic or semi-aquatic pteridophytes in both Britain and Ireland correspond in their greatest frequencies to areas of particularly high amounts of precipitation and extensive standing and running waters, as well as with often hard, mostly mineral-poor rocks, set usually in rather bleak and barren landscapes. Resulting lakes and pools are thus of mostly acidic waters which are relatively mineral and base-poor (oligotrophic). Within such lakes and pools, throughflow scouring stony bottoms in some places and the deposition of peaty silts in others, helps maintain relatively open habitats, whilst vegetative competition in such sites is also often low. Particularly thriving under such conditions are the lake-bottom-dwelling *Isoetes lacustris* and *I. echinospora* and lake-margin *Equisetum fluviatile, E. palustre* and *Osmunda regalis*. Species more prevalent in the gravel-fans and erosion slopes of running-waters of

Oreopteris limbosperma at the edge of a bog of Myrica gale, *a community characteristic of high-rainfall northern climates.*
Kirkudbrightshire, July

such regions include *Equisetum variegatum* and *Selaginella selaginoides*, whilst the abundance of *Oreopteris limbosperma* and *Athyrium filix-femina* seems linked in such areas to the large numbers of available sites of moving acidic water along the margins of small rills and streams.

Snow-lie   During winter months, much of the precipitation may fall as snow. The amount of snow falling varies widely from month to month and from year to year, as does the time for which the resulting snow-cover lies on the ground. Falls of snow tend to be greater and more frequent over higher ground, whilst long-term averages show strong regional contrasts in the time for which the snow cover can be expected to remain. Over most of the lowland parts of Britain and Ireland, snow lies over extensive stretches of ground on an average of only about 5–10 days or less per winter, and in southern and western districts, this is usually much less. Duration of snow-lie increases rapidly with rise in altitude, latitude and distance from the west coast, so that in upland Wales, the Pennines and over much of upland Scotland, it is common for snow to lie on over 30 days per year, and often on over 100 days in the Cairngorms area of Scotland. In upland areas, snow often accumulates most deeply where it drifts into slight hollows in the landscape, especially those on slopes of north-easterly aspect, to become finally dispersed only by the arrival of warm spring rain.

The most important effect of snow-lie on vegetation occurs in upland areas, where frosts are most severe. The snow-cover forms an effective thermal blanket to the vegetation below it, for at depths of only 10–20 cm within the snow, the temperature seldom falls as low as it does on the surface, fluctuating through only a few degrees, whilst the diurnal temperature above may range through 20°C or more (Geiger, 1959). The blanket also provides a period of continuing, fairly uniform cold, holding back flushing of fronds until final snow-melt, providing a single, safe end to winter, and thus discouraging premature frond flushing on early mild days. A regular, deep snow covering can thus be thermally beneficial to plants, and snow-lie hollows usually develop a characteristic vegetation often rich in ferns. *Cystopteris montana, Athyrium distentifolium* and *A. flexile* are largely exclusive to these, whilst *Blechnum spicant, Oreopteris limbosperma, Dryopteris expansa* and *Cryptogramma crispa*, in the upper parts of their altitudinal ranges, also become largely confined to such long snow-lie (chionophilous) 'fern-beds'.

Frequency of precipitation   The *frequency* with which rain (or snow) falls in Britain and Ireland emphasises the considerable differences between the climates of western and eastern districts. There is a very pronounced westward increase in the frequency of days with rain, reaching a maximum of rain on well over 250 days in the year (ie. on over 68% of days) in south-west and north-west Ireland, and most of the Inner and Outer Hebrides and western Highlands of Scotland. This contrasts with under 175 days in the year (ca. 48% of days) in the drier parts of eastern Scotland and eastern and southern England. The frequency of rainfall probably gives a better biological index of the effective wetness of climate than does the total amount of rain falling, and its results are more direct, closely affecting the temperature and humidity on which evaporation rates depend. High frequency of rainfall is also associated with high frequency of cloud cover and thus reduced insolation.

High frequency of light rainfall causes enhanced soil mineral loss by leaching, and hence except where this is neutralised by appropriately lime-yielding rock, acidic soils and peat-covered landscapes are widespread. The greatest densities of several acid-loving pteridophytes correspond with such environments, especially *Huperzia selago, Diphasiastrum alpinum, Equisetum sylvaticum, Osmunda regalis, Oreopteris limbosperma, Cryptogramma crispa, Phegopteris connectilis, Gymnocarpium dryopteris, Dryopteris aemula, D. expansa* and *D. affinis.*

Reminiscent of a Carboniferous swamp in miniature, finely-branched Equisetum sylvaticum *grows densely in a sheltered, ungrazed site under frequent cloud cover and soft light rain. Inverness-shire, mid-August*

Frequent, light rainfall, is probably also a pertinent factor in bringing down airborne pteridophyte spores from their highly dispersed state in the atmosphere (Page, 1978). The ground surface conditions resulting, with frequent high humidity and presence of extensive surface water films, also seems to provide ideal conditions for prothallial growth and fertilisation, almost wherever existing ground vegetation becomes disturbed. Increased opportunity for spore establishment plus resulting increased opportunity for outbreeding between different neighbouring prothalli are likely consequences. Such effects are probably in-part responsible for the greatly increased number of individuals and increased vigour of growth of many pteridophytes in such areas, reflected too in the significantly increased numbers of pteridophyte hybrids in areas of most frequent precipitation (Page & Barker, 1985).

Oceanity and Continentality

The degree of oceanity or continentality of our climate is also a very important factor in governing pteridophyte ranges, especially in these islands on the western fringe of Europe.

In Britain and Ireland, the climate is everywhere an oceanic (maritime) one, but important consequences for vegetation derive from the regional distribution of the degree of oceanity. The enormous volume and extent of the adjacent Atlantic Ocean, with the warming effect of its water in winter and its cooling effect in summer, tends to minimise the differences between winter and summer temperature in the land areas closest to the ocean. Thus over much of the extreme western coastal strip of south-west England, western Ireland, western Scotland and the Orkneys and Shetlands, an annual range of temperature of below 16°C is common, and in exceptional years this has been as little as 8.6°C in the Scilly Islands, 8.0°C in Kerry, 7.7°C in the Outer Hebrides, and 7.5°C in Shetland.

The prevailing WSW wind direction helps ensure that this oceanic effect penetrates much further inland on west coasts than on east coasts, so that the areas least oceanically influenced, and hence of more continental climates, are displaced eastwards, to occur in SE Ireland (with an annual temperature range of over 18°C), the eastern Scottish Highlands (over 20°C) and the East Anglian area of lowland England (where the annual temperature range exceeds 23°C). An important reason for the concentration of particularly continental conditions in the south-east of Britain is the lack of a large volume of ocean water in this direction and the nearness of the adjacent land-mass of continental Europe.

The oceanic, western climates are also those with the most frequent cloud-cover, highest humidity, least frost occurrence, greatest length of thermic growing season, and least potential summer water deficits.

Cloud cover is frequent over the whole of Britain and Ireland, but increases steadily both westwards and northwards. The portion of daytime for which the cloud density is sufficient for bright sun to be obscured varies from around 55% of possible annual daylight time in the Channel Islands, through about 60% in southern England, to 65–70% over much of the rest of England, Wales and almost the whole of Ireland, and reaches 80% or more almost throughout the Scottish Highlands. Such cloud cover influences the general temperature, by preventing penetration of sunshine by day and acting as a thermal blanket against heat loss by night. Frequent clouds thus further temper diurnal extremes of temperature, whilst also important from a pteridological point of view, they reduce overall levels of daytime illumination.

Coupled with oceanity and frequent cloud cover and precipitation, are the effects of high humidity. Relative humidity (RH) increases enormously with lowered temperatures, and decreases with higher ones. Distance from the sea as well as frequency of precipitation plays a large part, not only by providing much of the available moisture, but also by influencing temperature. Thus, although the climate of the whole of Britain and Ireland is a rather humid one, humidities become least in south-east England in mid-summer, but remain high along the western Atlantic fringe of both Britain and Ireland, where average values of relative humidity for the year exceed 80%.

Most ferns seem particularly sensitive to exposure to direct, strong sunlight, and have photosynthetic mechanisms which probably reach their greatest efficiency in semi-screened daylight conditions. High relative humidity is also of great significance to most ferns. It helps reduce desiccation at both prothallial and sporophytic stages, and is perhaps particularly important for the growth of epiphytic and lithophytic (rock-growing) species, whose water-balances are closely tied to prevention of excessive moisture loss by evapotranspiration. In association with high cloud cover, conditions of high relative humidity seem thus of significance in enabling ferns to spread outside woodland environments, especially into sheltered, low vascular-competition habitats, such as those of epiphytic and lithophytic sites.

All three native species of *Polypodium* (*P. vulgare*, *P. australe* and *P. interjectum*, as well as their three hybrids, thus become most abundant as well as most frequently epiphytic in western areas of frequent precipitation, high frequency of cloud-cover, and high humidity (especially where average RH means exceed 75%). The range of the filmy ferns (*Hymenophyllum wilsonii, H. tunbrigense* and *Trichomanes speciosum*), which loose water rapidly if exposed to dry air, also closely follows this pattern. Other terrestrial as well as mural species which become more abundant and extend more freely into open sites under these conditions include *Athyrium filix-femina, Blechnum spicant, Dryopteris affinis, D. dilatata, Phyllitis scolopendrium, Polystichum setiferum, Equisetum telmateia, E. sylvaticum, Cystopteris fragilis, Asplenium trichomanes, A. adiantum-nigrum, A. ruta-muraria* and *Ceterach officinarum*.

Potential summer water deficit   Average rates of evaporation of moisture from plant surfaces vary widely from place to place throughout Britain and Ireland, as well as with the seasons, and are influenced by the distribution of relative humidity. Potential water deficit (or potential water surplus if rainfall is in excess) is a measure of the difference between rainfall and the potential water evapotranspiration from the surface of vegetation, and is thus a measure of by how much one exceeds the other. Over almost the whole of Britain and Ireland, precipitation exceeds evapotranspiration during the winter six months of the year, leaving a potential water surplus. The patterns of the potential summer water deficit (calculated as April–September) however, vary greatly, and strong regional differences occur with the smallest deficit (of under 0.5 inches, ca. 1.27 cm) in upland western Ireland, upland Wales, the English Lake District and the western Scottish Highlands. By contrast, a high potential water deficit of about 3–6 inches (ca. 7.6–15.2 cm) may build up in summer in central eastern Ireland and throughout much of lowland England, with the highest deficits in Essex. Potential water deficits are not always the same as actual water deficits, as the latter depends also upon the amount of stored water in the ground to which the roots of the plant have access, and maps showing 'soil moisture deficit' (not currently available) could prove of further pteridological interest.

Potential water deficits seem likely to influence distribution of species through possible limitations on gametophyte development as well as growth of the sporophyte, especially in habitats in which stored water around the roots is not great, or can be easily seasonally influenced. Native pteridophytes which become generally scarce or are absent from areas where the potential water deficit is annually greater than about 7.6 cm, and hence which are always most abundant where this factor is less than this, include several rather delicate species: the largely mural *Cystopteris fragilis*, and species associated with more or less permanent shallow flushes such as *Equisetum variegatum* and *Selaginella selaginoides*, or damp earth slopes such as *Phegopteris connectilis, Gymnocarpium dryopteris* and *Equisetum sylvaticum*.

Under the amalgam of environmental conditions of high oceanity and low potential summer water deficits, a number of pteridophytes whose overall ranges are otherwise far-south of Britain and Ireland have been able to spread either widely in our oceanic islands, or far northward along our western coasts. Essentially southern or Mediterranean ones include *Isoetes histrix, Equisetum telmateia, Ophioglossum lusitanicum, Anogramma leptophylla, Adiantum capillus-veneris, Polypodium australe, Phyllitis scolopendrium, Asplenium billotii, A. onopteris* and *Ceterach officinarum*. Additionally, a number of ferns which elsewhere occur on more southerly, North Atlantic archipelagos, especially the Azores, Madeira and the Canary Islands, reach some of the most northerly parts of their ranges along the oceanic, western fringe of Britain and Ireland, but do not penetrate far into more inland regions. Such species include *Asplenium*

Hymenophyllum tunbrigense is confined to western climates of high oceanity and low potential summer water deficits. Merionethshire, September

marinum, Polystichum setiferum, Ophioglossum azoricum, Osmunda regalis, Trichomanes speciosum, Hymenophyllum tunbrigense, H. wilsonii and *Dryopteris aemula.*

Ironically, the low maximum temperatures found in the oceanic climates of our western fringe often do not exceed those of higher mountains in the more interior regions, enabling many more typically montane pteridophytes to descend to particularly low altitudes near west coasts, especially in the extreme west of Scotland and in the west of Ireland. Mountain species descending into such habitats in either Britain or Ireland include especially *Equisetum variegatum, Oreopteris limbosperma, Asplenium viride, Polystichum lonchitis, Dryopteris oreades* and *D. expansa.* Consequently, in our most oceanic climates, such species may meet, and grow alongside, northerly extensions of southern species, opening interesting possibilities for unusual hybridisation (see Chapter 13 and Appendix 2).

Rock and Soil Influences

Exposed to the effects of weathering at the surface of the earth, all rocks slowly soften and disintegrate. Through a series of stages, the decomposed rock fragments eventually form the basis of soils, in which micro-organisms, plants and animals gradually become established.

The whole process of rock breakdown and soil formation is the result of a complex interplay of both physical and chemical processes, as well as of climatic and ultimately also of biotic ones. In considering the ways in which different original rock types influence the distribution of species and vegetation in general, it is common to concentrate especially on the significances of different soil types, their structural differences and those of the soil horizons which they form. Such a concentration of edaphic interest on the end-products of soil genesis, would, in my view, be an entirely incorrect focus with which to try to understand edaphic influences on pteridophyte distributions. For in most mesic soils ultimately formed, unless some other factor is limiting, such as shade, pteridophyte vegetation is almost always mainly displaced by more vigorous flowering plant competition, and the distributions of detailed classification of soil types often seem not greatly relevant to comparison of pteridophyte ranges.

Vastly more important, however, in determining sites where pteridophyte vegetation, as a whole, can come into dominance, seems to be the distribution of the early stages of the rock breakdown process which are least suitable for great flowering plant success. Further, it is the physical components of this process which seem of the greatest importance in determining general site suitability for pteridophytes at all, whilst the chemical ones come only more secondarily into play in determining which species then best succeed.

Significant Physical Edaphic Aspects

Principal amongst the contributions of the physical aspects of the underlying geology is, of course, the relief of the landforms created. For, in general, the higher and more rugged the relief, the more diverse are likely to be the range of resulting habitats. Many of these will involve direct rock exposures and rapid rates of erosional processes, especially suited in appropriate climates to pteridophyte colonisation.

At a more detailed topographic level, within such landscapes, especially at altitude, the freeze–thaw cycle of clear winter weather is a particularly potent factor in initially opening small cracks in rock, and removing surface flakes through stresses induced by thermal contraction and expansion. Such cycles cause relatively rapid break-up of even the hardest rocks, especially where they are exposed to warm daytime sunshine alternating with cold winter nights. Almost all rock-inhabiting ferns probably continually re-pioneer such sites, to which the airborne spores of pteridophytes give considerable advantages of rapid accessibility.

In cliffs, once cracks, joints and bedding planes in rock are exposed, infiltration by water, micro-organisms and fern roots can take place. Fern roots have no secondary thickening process, and although they may penetrate considerable distances through fissures, they thus seem to seldom break up the rock as may flowering plants, thus not destroying their firm 'foothold' for the duration of the life of the plant.

Once soils start to form, these become further modified by the effects of climate as well as plant and animal life upon them. The structure of soils ultimately formed has its greatest significance to pteridophytes in sites where other aspects of the environment limit flowering plant competition, such as in the shade of woodlands. Amongst the general physical aspects of the structure of such mature soils of particular importance to pteridophytes, seem to be the soil's ability to both retain moisture and contain air. Indeed, the constancy of the maintenance of the balance between these two conditions seems paramount for many woodlands species. Such conditions are perhaps met most closely in sandy loam soils, of widely assorted particle size, into which there has long been a steady incorporation of organic matter.

Significant Chemical Edaphic Aspects

The chemical content of the rock particularly influences distribution of pteridophytes, through the presence or absence of available minerals, especially bases. Such differences operate very widely to create habitats appropriate for varyingly base-loving or acid-loving species. Other mineral aspects of the substrate may also be additionally important. Many small ferns (especially *Asplenium*), for example, are able to flourish on rocks with high heavy-metal yielding abilities, including ultrabasic ones (see Chapter 9) largely because of their tolerance to these minerals and relative freedom of such habitats from competition by the many plants to which such minerals are poisonous. Another example is seen in most species of *Equisetum*, where there is almost certainly a strong edaphic requirement for a combination of good base content plus adequate silica availability for successful growth. In this case, combinations of lime-rich seepage-water irrigating the aluminium-silicates of clays can provide particularly successful habitats.

From the geological point of view, the mineralogical content of particular types of rock is well known, and rocks can be readily classified accordingly. The geologist classifies rocks according to the minerals which they contain, and uses, as a measure of acidity the amount of silica, SiO_2. Geologists recognise four categories:

Acidic	more than 66% SiO_2
Intermediate	66–52% SiO_2
Basic	52–45% SiO_2
Ultrabasic	less than 45% SiO_2

The presence or absence of other characteristic mineral elements are often also associated with these groupings. Acidic rocks, for example, are characteristically low in iron, magnesium and phosphorous. Basic rocks are usually high in iron, magnesium, calcium, and sodium, and ultrabasic rocks high in magnesium, iron, nickel and chromium, but low in calcium.

By contrast, the botanist tends to classify rocks into a less exact grouping, but one which reflects more closely the effects which they have on plant life as the rock weathers. This grouping is less easy to define, but separates rocks according to their base-yielding properties when exposed at the earth's surface. There are wide contrasts too between the presence of particular minerals within a rock, and their availability to plants as rocks decompose, the availability being influenced not only by the chemical combination of the elements present, but also by such factors as the acidity of the habitat.

There is, nevertheless, a broad band of overlap between

geological and botanical rock classification, for all rocks which are geologically acid, give rise also to botanically acidic conditions, although the exact type of soil formed may be strongly influenced by other minerals present in the parent rock, as well as by climate. But not all rocks which are geologically basic are botanically so, although many are base-yielding (and of these, most are lime-yielding). Much botanical attention therefore centres on the release of carbonates from weathering rock. Basic carbonates have a high solubility, and strongly influence the type of vegetation present through their ability to neutralise acidic soils. The effects of carbonates can be most readily seen by the effect on soil pH (a measure of concentration of hydrogen ions, which can be relatively easily recorded). The pH ranges of most normal soils are conventionally regarded as acidic or basic as follows:

less than pH 4.0	strongly acidic
pH 4.0–5.0	acidic
pH 5.0–6.0	mildly acidic
pH 6.0–7.0	circum-neutral
more than pH 7.0	alkaline or basic

Other factors can, however, influence this essentially simple picture. If base-yielding rocks occur in areas of high rainfall, then the rate of base supply may be insufficient to offset the continual losses of bases from the soil by the leaching action of the rain, resulting in a soil which is less basic than it would have been under lower rainfall conditions. Subsequent movement of flushing water containing dissolved bases may serve to neutralise other soils through which it passes, with resulting effects on the vegetation. This can result in base-rich springs and flushes, especially in mountain areas, and the flushing of lowland peats by base-rich water to give lowland fens.

Further, local differences in base-status can occur even in the same rock, and these are usually closely reflected in the pteridophyte species present. In mountain areas, even in predominantly acidic rocks, there may be local secondary deposits of more base-rich minerals, such as veins of calcite. In such sites, a niche of more calcareous soil may be produced, whilst elsewhere nearby, bases may have leached away. Conversely too, in predominantly base-rich rock areas, although cliffs may be exposed with flushes of base-rich seepage water at their feet, the predominantly downward movement of rainwater may prevent the bases from greatly affecting the soils accumulating on their tops. Here, caps of acidic, peaty soil may thus develop directly over the tops of such base-rich rock outcrops, bringing calcicole and calcifuge pteridophytes into sometimes close and bewildering proximity (see especially Chapter 13).

CHAPTER 4

Other Influences on Pteridophyte Range

In this chapter, I have tried to include the remaining factors which have together had an influence on the distribution and composition of our native pteridophyte flora. Included are therefore the known palaeo-historic influences and the geographic elements which they have helped to form. Some phytogeographic comparisons between our pteridophyte flora and that especially of continental Europe are made, and the significance of hybrid pteridophytes in our flora discussed.

Palaeo-historic Influences

Present distributions are the result not only of the interplay of environmental factors acting today, but also of those which have been operative in the past. Such historic factors have played a role in not only influencing overall ranges, but also in determining which species are present at all.

Glacial Floristic Effects

In the past, in Britain and Ireland, the widespread glaciation of the late Pleistocene period—the last 'Ice Age'—very greatly influenced the flora. The number of species which were present was probably many times greater before the ice advance than after it. The pteridophytic component seems to have been extensively reduced in much the same way as were other vascular plants. A comparison with Japan, similar latitudinally and in size, but unglaciated, suggests that, in Europe, only about 1/10th of the former Tertiary pteridophytes may have eventually survived into Post-glacial times.

The last Ice Age had four major phases of glacial advance, with long periods of relative warmth ('interglacials') between. The last phase—the Weichselian glaciation—ended about 12,000 years BC. During this phase, the extent of the ice sheets was less than it had been in the previous two phases, leaving much of southern England and some of south-western Ireland unglaciated. It may well be that some of the existing species still present here survived through this last (and even through previous) glaciations, especially in niches in mild coastal areas influenced by the Atlantic. Indeed for a few pteridophyte species (eg. *Selaginella selaginoides*) there seems positive fossil evidence of this (Godwin, 1975), and it is at least a possibility that a substantial number of other pteridophyte species still present are glacial survivors too.

The Role of Palynological Evidence

Much direct evidence of Late-glacial and Post-glacial progress of vegetation in Britain and Ireland has been accumulated in recent years through the botanical science of palynology—the identification of sub-fossil plant remains, especially pollen grains and spores, preserved in peat. Palynology provides valuable fragments of jigsaw-like evidence, which is continually improving in quality, and amassing in quantity, to help more exactly place the occurrence of species in the past both geographically and at certain identifiable points in time (divided by palynologists into various periods or 'pollen zones').

As a result of the widespread occurrence of peaty deposits in Britain and Ireland, much of this data has been collected on a regional basis, especially in Ireland, northern and eastern England, and Scotland. A synthesis of this data has been presented by Godwin (1965, 1975), from which much of the pteridophyte data summarised here has been derived.

Palynological evidence of Late-glacial pteridophyte spread Early pteridophyte influence was doubtless felt by widespread expansion of glacial-margin, rather Arctic species, including many pioneers, which doubtless skirted the border of the slowly receding ice sheet. With rapid spread by airborne spores into newly exposed habitats, spores from both local and more distant sources may well have both played a role, even for the same species.

Species of Pteridophyta for which there is direct palynological evidence of presence in the early post-glacial (Late Weichselian—pollen zones I–III) and which have probably survived more or less continuously to the present day, include *Lycopodium annotinum*, *L. clavatum*, *Lycopodiella inundata*, *Huperzia selago*, *Diphasiastrum alpinum*, *Selaginella selaginoides*, *Isoetes lacustris*, *I. echinospora*, *Equisetum fluviatile*, *Botrychium lunaria*, *Ophioglossum vulgatum*, *Cryptogramma crispa*,

Polypodium vulgare, Phegopteris connectilis, Gymnocarpium dryopteris, Cystopteris fragilis and *Blechnum spicant.*

Lakes and glacial streams were undoubtedly widespread in these Late-glacial times, and genera such as *Lycopodium, Lycopodiella, Huperzia, Diphasiastrum, Selaginella, Isoetes* and *Equisetum*, may well have played a widespread and vegetationally especially significant role during this period. The number of these recorded species which are today members of generally upland habitats, mainly in open (rather than wooded) situations, is impressive. The list is, of course, of those species whose sub-fossil fragments have been recognised, and seems perhaps notably short in some genera such as *Equisetum, Asplenium* and *Dryopteris.* Poor representation of the former is probably largely due to lack of preservation of its thin-walled spores, *Asplenium* due to its real absence or to its small spore output in rocky places least likely to become fossilised, and *Dryopteris* perhaps through difficulty of specific separation of palynological material. Bearing these difficulties in mind, and comparing their modern ecology, other native species which might have shared a native history for a similar amount of time might well also include *Equisetum hyemale, E. variegatum, E. pratense, E.*

Equisetum pratense
*was probably
widespread in the
Late-glacial, and still
survives in northern
districts.
Clackmannanshire,
June*

sylvaticum, E. palustre, Asplenium septentrionale, A. viride, A. trichomanes subsp. trichomanes, A. trichomanes subsp. *quadrivalens, Athyrium filix-femina, Dryopteris oreades, D. affinis, D. montana* and *D. carthusiana.*

The distinctive ecotypic variation seen in *Equisetum variegatum* and *Isoetes lacustris* in both Britain and Ireland today, as well as their differences across the Irish Sea, may well result from extensive Late-glacial and early Post-glacial spread and diversity, before subsequent range-restriction through lowland forest development. A similar history may also lie behind the variation of *Dryopteris expansa, Polystichum lonchitis* and the upland *Athyrium* species, confined to northern Britain today.

As pointed out by Ratcliffe (1968) in connection with the Atlantic bryophytes of Britain and Ireland, there is so little evidence about the effects of past climatic events on such species, especially concerning their possible survival during, or re-immigration after, the Pleistocene glaciations, that much of the historic story must rest upon inference gained from knowledge of the ecology of the surviving species today. The Atlantic ferns provide an exactly parallel problem. The proven Late-glacial and early Post-glacial spread of glacial-margin species, does not rule out the possibility of the successful contemporaneous existence of more 'Atlantic' species in local, sub-maritime niches, closely influenced by cool, but highly oceanic, climates, although there is no direct evidence for this. But in a similar manner today, luxuriant growths of highly oceanic ferns, including many epiphytes and filmy-ferns, as well as tree-ferns, occur in sites such as New Zealand's South Island, where apparently tender plants thrive within distances of a few kilometres from the ends of impressive glaciers and permanent mountain snowfields (Page, 1979a). Such apparently incongruous mixtures of tender plants and harsh environments under highly oceanic conditions clearly impressed Seward (1941) (see his frontispiece) as much as they have the present author. There seems a strong possibility that some of the British and Irish fern species with highly Atlantic distributions today, could well have survived nearby glaciations in similar niches within these islands, lapped by west-coast oceanic winter warmth under conditions of frequent light precipitation.

Palynological evidence of subsequent Post-glacial range changes Habitats for the widespread occurrence of essentially woodland and forest ferns would initially have been limited to the cloudiest regions, before the widespread arrival of much forest-forming angiosperm vegetation. But such vegetation undoubtedly began to become established as the Post-glacial climate continued to warm.

With final glacial retreat from Britain and Ireland, rises in sea-level cut off first Ireland from Britain, then Britain from Europe. The dates of closing of these migration routes are probably primarily of significance to the pteridophytes through the effect they may have had on restricting the numbers of angiosperm competitors, for such water distances seem well within the normal biological capability of pteridophytes to continue to invade by airborne spores.

With increasing warmth towards the 'climatic optimum,' of 2,500–7,000 years ago, many more warmth-loving pteridophytes would undoubtedly have entered these islands and spread, whilst those of the original, more open, glacial-margin habitats, must have become simultaneously more geographically restricted. In addition to more widespread occurrence of forest-dwelling ferns, species of pteridophytes now regarded as tender, and today confined to regions of milder winter temperatures, may also have had wider British and Irish ranges than they do today, contracting again with the general climatic deterioration of the Sub-Atlantic (pollen zone VIII). Subsequent to the Late-glacial, the palynological record valuably illustrates how the ranges of some pteridophytes have changed.

Species for which there is clear palynological evidence of considerable general contraction in range are especially those which were vegetational pioneers in the open habitats of the Late-glacial periods, which were later largely displaced northwards by warming climates and spread of forest vegetation. These include particularly *Lycopodium clavatum* and *Huperzia selago*, which have shown a progressive diminution in area since the early Post-glacial, and *Lycopodium annotinum*, which was more widespread in Scottish sites in the early Post-glacial, but which has become progressively more restricted to the Cairngorms area since (although surviving until recent time also in Snowdonia and Yorkshire—Godwin, 1975). *Selaginella selaginoides* appears to have been particularly widespread across Britain in the late Weichselian time, with restriction to its present, mostly northern, area during the Flandrian (from pollen zone IV onwards). There is, however, a rise in site frequency of *Selaginella* again in pollen-zone VIII (Sub-Atlantic period) which seems to reflect a response to woodland clearance and spread of grassland vegetation. *Botrychium lunaria* also declined rapidly in abundance after the close of the Pre-boreal, along with the extensive displacement of open *Juniperus-empetrum* heath by spreading *Corylus–Betula* woodland (Godwin, 1975).

For *Equisetum*, total palynological site records also appear to have declined suddenly to a much lower, more constant level, by the end of pollen zone IV, from the increasingly high frequencies they established during the Late-glacial. Although individual species of *Equisetum* have not been generally distinguished by palynologists, an ecological interpretation of this change might very well be a large decline in horsetail species of open, sub-Arctic habitats, especially *Equisetum variegatum* and *E. pratense*, with extensive persistence through Boreal and Atlantic time of those of lowland river banks, lake margins and woodlands, such as *E. fluviatile, E. sylvaticum, E. palustre, E. telmateia* and *E. hyemale*.

Evidence from palynological studies suggests other species to have had essentially similar ranges during much of the Holocene, to those they have at present in Britain and Ireland. The preference of *Cryptogramma crispa* for scree habitats may have more or less always confined it to essentially mountain areas (although its possible former more widespread occurrence on Dartmoor, is not ruled out). *Gymnocarpium dryopteris* seems to have had a range from Late Weichselian or early Flandrian time, mostly concentrated in the north of Britain, and especially in the English Lake District and West of Scotland in much the same way as it is today. *Lycopodiella inundata* may have had as local and sporadic occurrence in the past as it does today, as judged by its scattered palynological records from Lancashire and Yorkshire. It is, however, a rare species today, and can be particularly difficult to find. Despite its occurrence in readily-fossilisable habitats, its discovery as sub-fossil material possibly indicates that it has not always been as rare.

Unusual, however, amongst plants for which palynological data discloses no evidence for altered range (Godwin, 1975), is *Diphasiastrum alpinum*. At least on grounds of its modern ecology, this species would have seemed likely to have been a more widespread pioneer, along with *Lycopodium clavatum* and *Huperzia selago*, in Late-glacial Britain, and evidence of the continued persistence of *Diphasiastrum* × *issleri* in southern England points also to the likely former more extensive occurrence of parental *D. alpinum* too (see Chapter 10) .

For a few pteridophyte species, there is evidence that there has been a generally increasing trend in abundance through Post-glacial time. It could be surmised that, with expansion in forest cover, there may indeed have been a great increase in very many of the larger woodland fern species, although there is very little direct evidence for this as the palynological record for herbaceous woodland plants is always sparse.

Of species for which there is a good fossil record, however, several of generally contrasting ecology show similar periods of rise, perhaps pointing towards a general pteridophyte expansion in many habitats during Atlantic time-onwards.

Fig. 5a
Time sequence of Post-Glacial vegetation change in Britain and Ireland, and the known occurrence of pteridophytes within each time zone. (After Godwin, 1949, 1975; West, 1963, 1968; Birks and Birks, 1980)

In aquatic situations, the submerged species of *Isoetes* increased steadily up to pollen zone VIIa (Atlantic period), whilst *Thelypteris palustris* and *Osmunda* show rather similar patterns, *Osmunda* also reaching a maximum in Atlantic time. In the case of *Isoetes*, based on megaspore identitification in North Wales (Nant Ffrancon), Seddon (1962) suggests that *Isoetes echinospora* was present in the early Post-glacial, and was joined by *I. lacustris* only later, particularly in the warmer Boreal and Atlantic periods (Godwin, 1975). In lowland England, *Thelypteris palustris* has clearly been present right

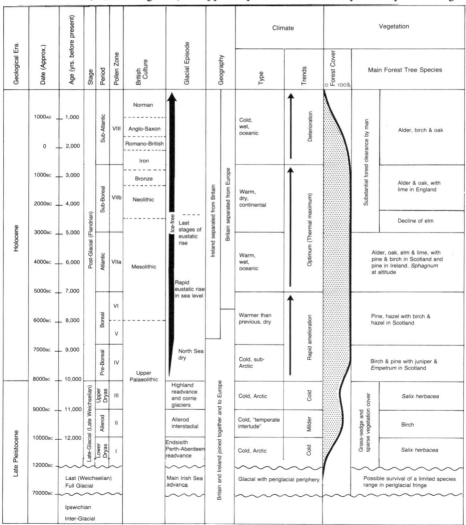

Geological Era	Date (Approx.)	Age (yrs. before present)	Stage	Period	Pollen Zone	British Culture	Glacial Episode	Geography	Climate Type	Climate Trends	Forest Cover 0–100%	Main Forest Tree Species
Holocene	1000 AD	1,000	Post-Glacial (Flandrian)	Sub-Atlantic	VIII	Norman	Ice-free	Ireland separated from Britain / Britain separated from Europe	Cold, wet, oceanic	Deterioration	Substantial forest clearance by man	Alder, birch & oak
						Anglo-Saxon						
	0	2,000				Romano-British						
						Iron						
	1000 BC	3,000		Sub-Boreal	VIIb	Bronze			Warm, dry, continental	Optimum (Thermal maximum)		Alder & oak, with lime in England
	2000 BC	4,000				Neolithic						
	3000 BC	5,000					Last stages of eustatic rise					Decline of elm
	4000 BC	6,000		Atlantic	VIIa	Mesolithic			Warm, wet, oceanic			Alder, oak, elm & lime, with pine & birch in Scotland and pine in Ireland. *Sphagnum* at altitude
	5000 BC	7,000					Rapid eustatic rise in sea level					
	6000 BC	8,000		Boreal	VI				Warmer than previous, dry	Rapid amelioration		Pine, hazel with birch & hazel in Scotland
	7000 BC	9,000			V		North Sea dry					
	8000 BC	10,000		Pre-Boreal	IV	Upper Palaeolithic			Cold, sub-Arctic			Birch & pine with juniper & *Empetrum* in Scotland
Late Pleistocene	9000 BC	11,000	Late-Glacial (Late Weichselian) — Upper Dryas		III		Highland readvance and corrie glaciers	Britain and Ireland joined together and to Europe	Cold, Arctic	Cold	Grass-sedge and sparse vegetation cover	*Salix herbacea*
	10000 BC	12,000	Allerod		II		Allerod interstadial		Cold, "temperate interlude"	Milder		Birch
			Lower Dryas		I		Endsisith Perth-Aberdeen readvance		Cold, Arctic	Cold		*Salix herbacea*
	12000 BC		Last (Weichselian) Full Glacial				Main Irish Sea advance		Glacial with periglacial periphery			Possible survival of a limited species range in periglacial fringe
	70000 BC		Ipswichian Inter-Glacial									

from zone V (Early Boreal) through to zone VIII (Atlantic), and thick mats of its roots and rhizomes occur in sub-forest layers representing a transition from fen to raised bog (Godwin, 1975). In *Osmunda regalis* too, preserved spores become increasingly frequent throughout the Post-glacial, from zone V (Early Boreal) to VIIb (Sub-boreal), often in sites where the fern still flourishes.

In more terrestrial situations, expansion is also indicated for *Pteridium* which is present, in small quantities, through pollen zones I–V, presumably as a rather minor component of the

Fig. 5b
Presence of pteridophytes within each time zone. Data from various palynological and macrofossil studies

Pteridium aquilinum	*Cryptogramma crispa*	*Blechnum spicant*	*Athyrium filix-femina*	*Thelypteris palustris*	*Dryopteris filix-mas*	*Polypodium spp.*	*Osmunda regalis*	*Ophioglossum spp.*	*Botrychium spp.*	*Equisetum telmateia*	*Equisetum fluviatile*	*Equisetum palustre*	*Huperzia selago*	*Lycopodium clavatum*	*Selaginella selaginoides*	*Isoetes lacustris*	*Isoetes echinospara*	*Diphsoastrim spp.*	*Lycopodium annotinum*	*Lycopodiella inundata*	*Isoetes sp.*	*Cystopteris spp.*	*Gymnocarpium dryopteris*	*Phegopteris connectilis*	*Pilularia globulifera*	*Adiantum cupillus-veneris*
●		●	●	●		●	●	●	?	?	●		●	●	●	●	●	●	●	?					●	
●		●		●	●	●	●				●		●	●	●	●	●		●	?						?
●			●	●	●	●					●		●	●	●	●	●									
●			●	●	●	●	●				●		●	●	●	●	●	●								●
●			●	●	●	●					●	?	●	●	●	●	●	●		●						●
●	●	?			●	●	●	●			●		●	●	●	●	●	●	●			?	●	●	●	
●	●	●	?		●		●	●			●		●	●	●	●	●	●	●	●		?	●	●	●	●
●	●	●	?		●		●	●			●		●	●	●	●	●	●	●				●	●	●	
●	●	●			●		●	●					●	●	●	●	●	●	●		?		●	●	●	
										?		?														

vegetation. From pollen zone VI (Late Boreal) onwards, there begins a great increase through Mesolithic and Neolithic times, where it clearly responded rapidly to fire and early forest opening by man.

Also showing considerable evidence of expansion in Flandrian time is the *Polypodium vulgare* aggregate, which seems of particular significance because of the frequent association of these plants with lithophytic and epiphytic habitats in environments of generally high humidity. The spores of *Polypodium* show a fairly high frequency through the Late-glacial and early post-glacial, declining somewhat in early Boreal times. Thereafter there is a big increase, from pollen zone VI (Late Boreal) into zones VIIa–VIIb, declining slightly again in VIII (Sub–Atlantic). Site records occur over the whole of the British Isles, although the largest number are in Scotland and the English Lake District (Godwin, 1975). The species of *Polypodium* are not separated by palynologists because of the close similarity of their spore type and size. It seems likely however, that many of the Late-glacial stations, as well as those at higher-altitude in the Post-glacial, probably refer to *P. vulgare sensu stricto* (the tetraploid species), whilst the spore increase from pollen zone VI onwards, associated with a time of extensive forest development and Post-glacial optimum of climate, may result from the widespread additional establishment of both *P. australe* and *P. interjectum* at this time.

Finally, during the climatic optimum, it seems possible that species of ferns and fern-allies which are totally absent from the native flora today, may have invaded Britain and Ireland through their ability to spread over water barriers by their aerial spores. It seems very probable that such a past native range may have been true for the horsetail *Equisetum ramosissimum*, to account for the existence of its hybrid, *E. × moorei*, in Ireland in modern times, and the clubmoss *Diphasiastrum complanatum*, to account for the current persistence of its hybrid, *D × issleri*, in widely scattered localities in Britain.

Geographic Influences

With the exception of two species which are possibly endemic—*Athyrium flexile* and *Dryopteris submontana*—all the native Pteridophyta occurring in Britain and Ireland have ranges which extend elsewhere in the European mainland. Some extend far further afield across Eurasia or elsewhere.

Within Europe, the geographic ranges of pteridophyte species have been mapped in detail by Jalas & Suominen (1972). Certain similarities of ranges outside Britain and Ireland allow species to be grouped according to their general range-types, or geographic elements. An extensive analysis of such elements in Britain and Ireland and their percentage contribution to the flora was carried out by Mathews (1937), in which eleven separate elements were recognised. This survey did not include the Pteridophyta.

More recently, Birks (1976) has carried out a computer-based comparison of the ranges of European pteridophytes, in which twenty-one different floristic elements have been recognised in Europe as a whole. This survey is of particular significance to the British and Irish pteridophyte flora in that it shows objectively that Britain plus Ireland plus adjacent north-west France form a distinctive pteridological floristic region of Europe, characterised by a high representation of Atlantic and Mediterranean elements, together with northern, montane and Arctic–Alpine ones. Such a mixture occurs nowhere else in Europe, and results largely from the climatic characteristics of Britain and Ireland, especially the high degree of oceanity which enables separate elements to co-exist remarkably close to one another (see also chapters 3 & 13).

Birks' computer-based survey is an objective and complex one, but, by the nature of the method, forms what seem to me to be sometimes uncomfortable species groupings. I have thus devised a slightly different classification here, formed entirely around the British and Irish species which, although more subjective in construction, is also rather simpler.

Mediterranean–Atlantic Species

These are species which have their main headquarters in the Mediterranean area or jointly in the Mediterranean and North Atlantic Islands (especially the Canary Islands, Madeira or the Azores), but reach either the extreme south of Ireland, extreme south-west of England or the Channel Islands. These species include: *Isoetes histrix, Equisetum telmateia, Ophioglossum lusitanicum, Anogramma leptophylla, Adiantum capillus-veneris, Polypodium australe, Phyllitis scolopendrium, Asplenium adiantum-nigrum, A. onopteris, Ceterach officinarum,* and *Polystichum setiferum*. Of these, *Anogramma leptophylla, Asplenium adiantum-nigrum,* and *Adiantum capillus-veneris,* are wide-ranging on a global scale, and *Phyllitis scolopendrium* perhaps approaches closely the range of the Atlantic species.

In Britain and Ireland, members of this element occur mostly at low altitude, in stations near warmer coasts, often on south-facing slopes or banks which warm rapidly in spring sunshine. Many are evergreen, and several make all or part of

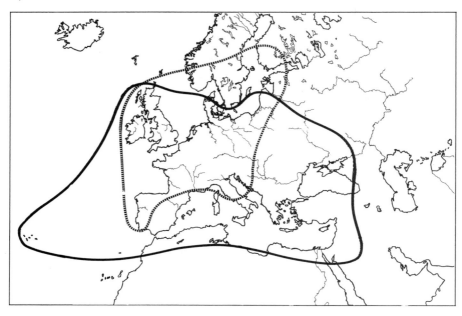

Fig. 6
Mediterranean–
Atlantic distribution of
Equisetum telmateia
(solid line) and sub-
Atlantic Pilularia
globulifera (dotted
line)

their growth in the winter months. Cytologically they include a range of both diploid and polyploid species.

Atlantic Species

These are species whose ranges extend chiefly along only the Atlantic seaboard of Europe, mainly from Britain and Ireland southwards (or which sometimes just reach south-west Norway), and most of which also occur in the North Atlantic Islands (especially the Azores, Madeira and the Canaries). They include: *Ophioglossum azoricum, Osmunda regalis, Hymenophyllum tunbrigense, H. wilsonii, Trichomanes speciosum, Asplenium billotii, A. marinum, Dryopteris affinis*, and *D. aemula*. Of these, *H. wilsonii* extends further northward than most, and approaches the range of a sub-Atlantic species. All native subspecies of *Dryopteris affinis* are tentatively grouped here, although ssp. *borreri* approaches a more sub-Atlantic range.

This element includes mostly cold-sensitive species of markedly west-coast distribution in Britain and Ireland, most of which occur in habitats which are sheltered and permanently moist. Most probably form part of an original European–Macaronesian element of Tertiary age (Page, 1973a), and the large number of cytologically diploid species amongst this element is particularly noteworthy.

Fig. 6 Mediterranean–Atlantic distribution of Equisetum telmateia (solid line) and sub-Atlantic Pilularia globulifera (dotted line)

Sub-Atlantic Species

These are essentially oceanic, west European species, with a predominance along the Atlantic coast, often reaching north-wards to Iceland and Scandinavia, and spreading some distance into the continent north of the Mediterranean. They include: *Lycopodiella inundata, Huperzia selago, Isoetes lacustris, I. echinospora, Polypodium interjectum, Oreopteris limbosperma, Asplenium trichomanes* subsp. *quadrivalens, Polystichum aculeatum, Dryopteris oreades, D. dilatata, Blechnum spicant,* and *Pilularia globulifera.* Amongst these, *Polypodium interjectum* approaches an Atlantic distribution, *Dryopteris oreades* an

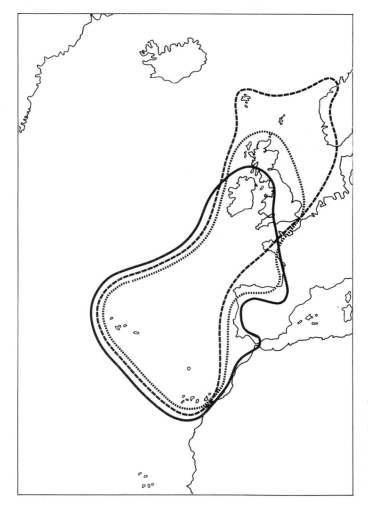

Fig. 7
Atlantic distribution of three native pteridophytes: Trichomanes speciosum *(solid line),* Hymenophyllum wilsonii *(dashed line) and* Dryopteris aemula *(dotted line)*

Arctic–Alpine (especially alpine) range, and *Pilularia globu-lifera* is somewhat continental. *Asplenium trichomanes* subsp. *quadrivalens* is grouped here provisionally, although at sub-species level its range has been imperfectly mapped. *Asplenium trichomanes* subsp. *trichomanes*, by contrast, can probably be included under the Continental element.

The Sub-Atlantic element contains plants of a wide range of native habitats, most of which are moist and some aquatic, and includes a wide assortment of cytological ploidy levels.

Continental Species

These are species which have their main headquarters in more central areas of Europe, spreading westwards to reach Britain and sometimes Ireland. They include: *Ophioglossum vulgatum, Thelypteris palustris, Asplenium septentrionale, A. ruta-muraria, A. trichomanes* subsp. *trichomanes, Gymnocarpium robertianum,* and *Dryopteris cristata.*

Of these *Asplenium ruta-muraria* has a particularly extensive range near to the Atlantic coast of Europe, and this closely approaches a Sub-Atlantic species in range, while *A. septentrio-nale* occurs also particularly extensively through southern Nor-way and Sweden, where it approaches a Northern Montane species.

In Britain and Ireland, members of this element seem largely either marsh/fen or other lowland wetland species, or are plants of relatively dry, mural, inland habitats. Many are scarce or absent around the Atlantic fringe of Britain and Ireland, and this element contains a notably high proportion of cytologically polyploid species.

Arctic–Alpine Species

This element includes British and Irish Pteridophyta which have their main European centres of distribution split between the mountains of Scandinavia and the Alps of central-southern Europe. They include: *Diphasiastrum alpinum, Selaginella sela-ginoides, Cryptogramma crispa, Athyrium distentifolium, Cystop-teris montana, Woodsia ilvensis, W. alpina, Polystichum lonchitis,* and *Dryopteris expansa.* Of these, *Cryptogamma crispa* approaches the range of a Sub-Atlantic species, and is prob-ably amongst the most frost-sensitive members of this element. *Woodsia ilvensis* has a more extensive northern-European range than has *W. alpina,* and approaches that of a Northern Montane species, to which the whole of this element is, indeed,

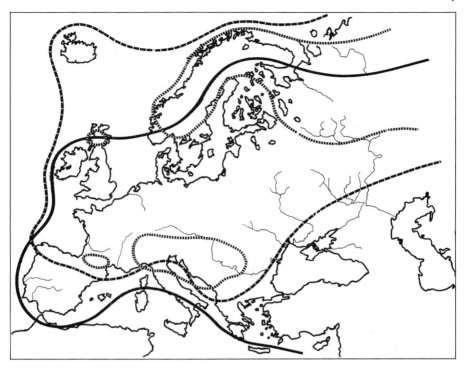

probably closely related. The same seems true of *Dryopteris expansa*, which also has taxonomic links with North America.

In Britain and Ireland, this element includes species which are typical of high mountain cliff or turf-ledge habitats, but many of which also descend to reach low altitudes near extreme west coasts. It is another element that contains a particularly substantial proportion of cytologically diploid species.

Fig. 8
Continental distribution of Thelypteris palustris *(solid line), Northern Continental* Equisetum sylvaticum *(dashed line) and Arctic–Alpine* Cystopteris montana *(dotted line)*

Widespread Northern–Continental Species

These are essentially species which have the main parts of their range in the mountains of Scandinavia, often spreading through large parts of northern Europe or the greater part of Europe as a whole, but with special concentrations in the north. Many spread widely across Eurasia to Siberia and Japan, and to the New World. Several belong to species or species-groups which are very wide-ranging on a world scale. They include: *Equisetum hyemale, E. fluviatile, E. arvense, E. sylvaticum, E. palustre, Botrychium lunaria, Polypodium vulgare, Pteridium aquilinum, Phegopteris connectilis, Athyrium filix-femina, Gymno-*

carpium dryopteris, Cystopteris fragilis, Dryopteris filix-mas, and
D. carthusiana. Equisetum sylvaticum approaches the range of a
Northern Montane species, like *E. pratense,* as do *Phegopteris
connectilis, Gymnocarpium dryopteris* and *Cystopteris fragilis.
Dryopteris filix-mas* and *D. carthusiana* perhaps have affinities in
their ranges with ones of continental type, whilst *Athyrium
filix-femina* probably has with those of sub-Atlantic type.

In Britain and Ireland, the members of this element are all
rather hardy species, most of which are winter-deciduous, and
grow in habitats with the high levels of moisture they require,
through a wide range of altitude. This is another element
which contains a particularly high proportion of cytologically
polyploid species.

Northern-Montane Species

These are species whose ranges have their main headquarters
in the mountains of northern Europe, especially Scandinavia,
with only a smaller representation in alpine areas. They
include: *Lycopodium annotinum, L. clavatum, Equisetum variegatum, E. pratense, Asplenium viride,* and *Cystopteris dickieana.*
All the members of this element are clearly related to the
Arctic–Alpine ones, *Asplenium viride* perhaps especially so.

In Britain and Ireland, they are mostly species of high
altitude sites, often growing alongside more truly Arctic–
Alpines, but not all of which necessarily descend to lower
altitudes along the west coast, as do many of the Arctic–Alpine
ones. They also differ from the Arctic–Alpines in embracing a
wide assortment of cytological ploidy levels.

Endemic Species

Only two pteridophytes in Britain and Ireland are endemic as
far as is known (although there are several endemic hybrids).
These species are: *Athyrium flexile* and *Dryopteris submontana.*
Both are probably local segregates of more widespread
European complexes, in which *Athyrium flexile* probably has
Arctic-Alpine affinities, and *Dryopteris submontana,* more con-
tinental ones. Both are cytologically polyploid.

Some Phytogeographic Comparisons

A few thousand years is a very short time in terms of phytogeography and evolution for an archipelago of islands, such as

Britain and Ireland, to acquire a largely new flora and fauna.

Not only has the poorness of the number of species been influenced by a relatively decimated source stock in Europe following the glacial advances, but also by the isolation of Ireland from Britain and the British Isles from Europe some 7–8,000 years ago, as sea levels rose and as a result of post-glacial melting of glacial and polar ice.

One consequence of our insular position is that several plants and animals which today occur widely across the northern European mainland are absent from the British Isles, although the climate here seems suitable for them. Such absentees indeed include animals, such as hamsters, lemmings, bears, chamois, elk and reindeer amongst the mammals, and plants, such as Silver Firs (*Abies*), Larches (*Larix*) and Spruces (*Picea*) amongst the coniferous trees. Despite the very small size and airborne dispersal capability of the spores of pteridophytes, very similar absences are also reflected in this group of plants. Thus absent in Britain and Ireland but present in continental Europe are *Matteucia struthiopteris*, *Dryopteris fragrans*, *Cystopteris sudetica*, *Woodsia glabella*, *Polystichum braunii*, *Asplenium cuneifolium*, *A. adulterinum*, several northern European species of *Botrychium* (*B. simplex*, *B. boreale*, *B. matricariifolium*, *B. lanceolatum*, *B. multifidum*, *B. virginianum*), *Diphasiastrum complanatum*, *D. tristachium*, *Equisetum scirpoides*, and numerous subspecies of *Dryopteris affinis*.

In the case of these northern European species, their absence from the British Isles must be presumed to be either because they require more Arctic climates, or that they have been unable to get here. Yet two of the more northerly species *Dryopteris fragrans* and *Equisetum scirpoides* appear to grow here successfully when cultivated, although it may be that there are aspects of their life-cycles and establishment which cannot be successful in our climate. Less surprising, perhaps, are the absence in the British Isles of several fern genera present in more southern areas of Mediterranean or Atlantic Europe. These genera include *Cheilanthes*, *Notholaena*, *Pteris*, *Marsilea* and *Salvinia*, all of mainly Mediterranean affinity, and *Culcita*, *Davallia*, *Cyclosorus*, *Pleurosorus*, *Elaphoglossum*, *Woodwardia* and *Psilotum*, all of Atlantic, European and North Atlantic Island (Azores, Madeira, Canaries) distribution. These, it must be assumed for climatic reasons, have probably never been able to reach this far north in Post-glacial time, although like the northern species, some of these, such as *Woodwardia*, are able to maintain themselves vegetatively when introduced in some of the milder western parts of these islands.

Ireland shows some similar contrasts when its pteridophyte flora is compared with that of Britain. Despite the general wetness and humidity of the Irish climate and its mild winter temperatures, only about 59 of the 70 or so species of pteridophytes present in Britain also occur in Ireland (subspecies, varieties and hybrids excluded). Notable absentees in this case include mostly Northern–Montane species plus a few more characteristic of particularly continental, eastern climates: *Athyrium distentifolium, A. flexile, Woodsia ilvensis, W. alpina, Cystopteris montana, C. dickieana, Dryopteris submontana, D. expansa, D. cristata*, and *Lycopodium annotinum*. Additionally at least ten further species are present but particularly rare or very local in Ireland: *Pilularia globulifera, Asplenium septentrionale, A. viride, Phegopteris connectilis, Gymnocarpium dryopteris, G. robertianum, Dryopteris oreades, Polystichum lonchitis, Cryptogramma crispa* and *Equisetum pratense*.

On the other side of the coin, however, Ireland has at least one Mediterranean species, not known to be present in Britain: *Asplenium onopteris*, although two others of similar geographic affinity, *Ophioglossum lusitanicum* and *Isoetes hysterix* are present in Britain in the Channel Islands and extreme south-west England but have not, to date, been found in Ireland. *Asplenium onopteris* might reasonably be sought in south-west England. A further species, *Asplenium billotii*, present in the Channel Islands and south-west England is very rare in its occurrence in Ireland. However, Ireland more than makes up for these pteridological deficiencies by several bonuses. The Irish flora is remarkable for its development and exuberance of several species of Atlantic affinity: *Osmunda regalis, Dryopteris aemula, Hymenophyllum tunbrigense, H. wilsonii* and *Trichomanes speciosum*, whilst the southern *Ceterach officinarum* and *Adiantum capillus-veneris* are also better developed in Ireland than in any other part of the British Isles.

There is also a particularly large number of pteridophyte hybrids in Ireland, mainly in the genera *Asplenium, Asplenophyllitis, Dryopteris* and *Equisetum* (especially *E. × litorale, E. × rothmaleri, E. × dycei, E. × trachyodon* and *E. × moorei*). The latter hybrid is of particular phytogeographic interest as one of its parents, *E. ramosissimum*, is apparently absent as a native plant from both the floras of Britain and Ireland at the present time, although the presence of this hybrid locally on the Wexford–Wicklow coast seems to indicate the former presence of this parent in the near historic past. Ireland also boasts, more perhaps than the rest of Britain, of several pteridophytes which have evolved their own morphological or ecological peculiarities. These notably include *Ceterach officinarum, Asplenium onopteris, Isoetes lacustris* and *Equisetum variegatum*. All of these species have forms which appear to be unique to Ireland and have either evolved as such in post-glacial times or are survivors in Ireland of isolated pre-glacial forms which have become extinct elsewhere. In the case of these plants and the hybrids, the combinations of the peculiar climatic oceanic conditions of Ireland and the relative paucity of species in its flora, have presumably combined to promote the ecological success and persistence of these isolated forms in this area of the British Isles (Page & Barker, 1985).

Hybrid Pteridophytes

Hybrid pteridophytes are of enormous evolutionary significance, and consequently their study in the native flora has occupied considerable pteridological time and expertise.

In addition to 74 known specific or subspecific/varietal taxa of native ferns and fern-allies, a current count (to 31 December 1987) shows the occurrence of at least 35 wild hybrid pteridophytes to be known within Britain and Ireland (a ratio of nearly 0.5 hybrids to each potential parent taxon). It is difficult to know for sure whether this apparently extremely large percentage reflects some biologically unusual facet of our native pteridophyte flora, or merely the concentration of study by pteridologists. My belief is that it reflects both, and that while the degree with which our native pteridophyte flora has been studied is certainly a more exacting one than for any other part of the world, this high proportion of hybrids is also in itself particularly notable.

Further details of most of the hybrids are included in Stace (1975), Jermy et al. (1978) and Page (1982), to which the reader is referred for further details (see Appendix 3). From this accumulated information it is clear that almost all known pteridophyte hybrids in our flora are closely structurally (morphologically) intermediate between their parents, and where the parents are themselves of very different form, the appearance of the hybrids can be striking. Such hybrids often occupy habitats which are either also approximately intermediate between those of the parents, or the hybrids are sometimes of very flexible ecology and occupy virtually the whole range of habitats of both. Hybrids also often gain a certain amount of hybrid vigour ('heterosis') and this may often be of significance in enabling those which do to succeed in the face of established plant competition.

The potential availability of habitats probably plays an important part in determining whether hybrids are able to survive, and on this aspect, it seems likely that the species-poorness of the existing British and Irish floras, resulting from their glacial history, perhaps contributes substantially towards creating circumstances in which newly-formed hybrids are able to hold niches in which they are able to survive due to the number of niches available.

Once produced, most pteridophyte hybrids are sterile, and remain as single (though often long-lived) generations in the localities in which they are formed. In a few hybrids, a limited degree of fertility and mobility occasionally occurs. Relatively good spores have occasionally been observed in *Equisetum* × *font-queri* (Page, 1973) and *Diphasiastrum* × *issleri* (Jermy *et al.*, 1978), and may also occur in certain fern populations of hybrid origin. This is particularly so in hybrids involving an apogamous species in their parentage (eg. hybrids with *D. affinis*, q.v.), and a limited amount of reproduction and local dispersal may occur by this means. Occasionally, too, pteridophyte hybrids are able to spread locally about their site of origin by vegetative growth, especially if they have long-lived creeping rhizomes, as in *Equisetum* and *Pteridium*, and extensive local colonies may build up. In *Equisetum* too, there is evidence of dispersal along rivers and coasts by water-borne shoot fragments in *E.* × *trachyodon* (Page & Barker, 1985), and this may also occur in *E.* × *litorale*.

Polypodium × mantoniae (P. interjectum × P. vulgare). *South Devon, August*

Although there are a few exceptions, allowing for the relatively small number of sites of some hybrids, the trend seems to be for a generally increasing number of hybrid sites westwards or south-westwards in Britain and Ireland. And this pattern seems particularly often repeated in hybrids in *Asplenium* and × *Asplenophyllitis* (mostly south-westwards), *Dryopteris*, *Polypodium*, *Polystichum* and *Equisetum* (either south-westwards or westwards; see Appendix 3).

Some evidence of contrasting field success is provided by *Equisetum*, where the number of inter-specific hybrid combinations and the frequency of their stations in Britain and Ireland, is probably the highest known in the world. Two native hybrids in subgenus *Equisetum*, *E.* × *rothmaleri* (*E. arvense* × *palustre*) and *E.* × *dycei* (*E. fluviatile* × *palustre*) are rare, despite the widespread occurrence of both parents. Furthermore, at their known stations, both are also small and weak plants, apparently lacking hybrid vigour, and both are mostly confined to man-made, open, roadside ditches. By contrast, in the same subgenus and same geographic areas, two other hybrids, *E.* × *litorale* (*E. arvense* × *E. fluviatile*) and *E.* × *font-queri* (*E. palustre* × *E. telmateia*), are large and vigorous plants. Once formed they spread by vegetative means to form extensive, often vegetationally dominant, stands, sometimes ecologically displacing their parents, and spreading into surrounding vegetation. Their intermediacy in structure between their greatly different-looking parents is particularly striking.

Evidence of the inter-specific relationships in this group established independently on sporophytic micro-morphological grounds (Page, 1972a) suggests that the weak hybrids are those between ecologically similar, yet not very closely related, pairs of species, whilst the vigorous ones are those between species pairs which are ecologically more different, yet closely interrelated (Page 1973). In this genus, it seems that it is hybrids between the latter types of parents which are the most vigorous ecologically and the most successful in the field (Page & Barker, 1985). Further details of the taxonomic occurrence of hybrids within the native pteridophytes and their British geographic range are given in Appendix 2.

The significance of such hybrids is that, evolutionarily, they provide one of the more or less immediate sources of new variation upon which natural selection can act. Evolution is a generally slow process, but one important method by which Pteridophyta can make rather rapid evolutionary progress is by genetic stabilisation and isolation of such hybrids, especially by the doubling of their chromosome numbers, thereby restoring their fertility. Investigation of hybrids in the field thus enables information to be gathered about this one particularly important method by which evolution is progressing in this order of plants.

Taxonomic trends

Taxonomically there are quite strong contrasts in the frequency of occurrence in the field between different hybrid combinations. Several, including *Dryopteris* × *brathaica, D.* × *pseudoabbreviata, Polystichum* × *illyricum, P.* × *lonchitiforme, Asplenium* × *murbeckii, A.* × *clermontiae, A.* × *contrei,* × *Asplenophyllitis confluens, Equisetum* × *dycei* and *E.* × *rothmaleri* are very rare. By contrast, others, including *Dryopteris* × *deweveri, D.* × *tavelii, Polystichum* × *bicknellii, Asplenium* × *sarniense,* × *Asplenophyllitis microdon, Polypodium* × *mantoniae, Equisetum* × *font-queri* and *E.* × *litorale* are locally quite common.

In part, these differences in abundance are probably due to the different relative frequencies of their respective parents species, and the opportunity for ecological associations to develop in which parents can come into sufficiently close field association for chances of crossing to be high. In part too, genetic factors are probably also operative, which prevent hybrids forming with ease between some species, even when growing in close proximity. *Asplenium* × *clermontiae* may provide such an example, for it is known only once (in Ireland), although its two parents, *Asplenium ruta-muraria* and *A. trichomanes* subsp. *quadrivalens*, frequently occur together on walls in large quantities in many parts of both Britain and Ireland. Clearly, however, such barriers do not always exist, and may vary anyway between populations and between the direction of hybridisation. Higher polyploids, for example, can sometimes act as the female but not the male parent in such crosses.

Such factors concern chiefly the ability, or otherwise, of hybrids to form. Equally important, but much less investigated, seems to be the ability of hybrids, once formed, to survive.

Coastal Pteridophytes CHAPTER 5

As relatively small islands, Britain and Ireland enjoy particularly extensive coastlines—6,000 miles (over 9,600 km) of coast, for example, around Britain alone. Because of the wide range of rock types present, as well as differing exposures and aspects, the coastal landscapes and their habitats are also extraordinarily varied. Widely differing glacial histories, depending on latitude and location, and consequent sea-level changes and land movements, have additionally added to this diversity. Further, the coastline as a whole is in a more or less continuous and dynamic state of change, and new habitats are constantly formed, either through the action of despositional or erosional processes.

Coastlines thus provide habitats for a very great range of different types of wildlife, each adapted in an almost equally varying number of ways to the unusual, and often quite exacting, habitats in which they succeed. The coastal communities so-formed include associations of animals and plants which are rarely found very extensively inland, although some of their component species may range more widely. The numerous pteridophytes of these coastal regions also show adaptations to their unusual environments which are of special ecological interest.

Pteridophytes succeed in the many coastal habitats because they are often able to more or less continuously re-pioneer the areas of low-competition often mineral-rich surfaces created by the dynamic state of the erosional/depositional processes, while the enhanced humidity of coastal sites is particularly well tolerated. Further, the buffering of temperature amplitudes brought about by such close proximity to the sea, and the immediate effects of the impinging warm Gulf Stream water on western shores, enables a number of relatively tender and especially southern pteridophyte elements to reach particularly northerly outposts in our coastal habitats.

For our purposes, the differing environments of our coasts can be best discussed according to the differing hardness of the underlying substrates. For these result in coastal landscapes of very different type, each containing appropriately different habitats and species.

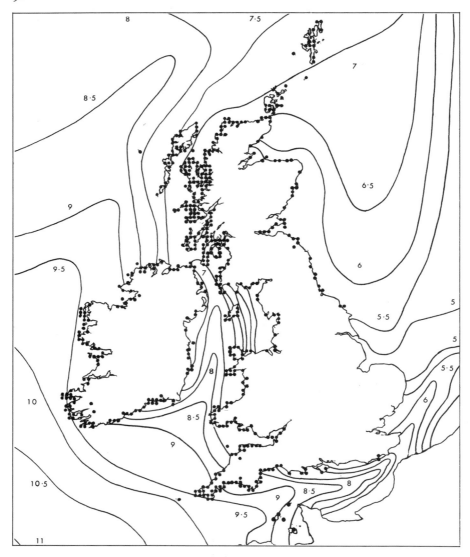

Fig. 9
The distribution of
Asplenium marinum
on hard rock coasts in
relation to mean winter
minimum sea surface
temperatures (°C).
(After Hohn, 1973 and
Jermy et al., 1978)

Hard Rock Cliffs

Sea cliffs are very widely scattered around the British and Irish coastline, and they account for a particularly high proportion of the coasts which form the main bulwark directly against the Atlantic, especially in counties such as Cornwall, Devon, Pembrokeshire, and many parts of western Ireland. They also form a very large component of the coasts of many of the smaller outlying islands, from the Channel Islands in the south to the many Inner and Outer Hebridean Islands of Scotland, the Orkneys and Shetlands in the north, and of the more remote rock outcrops such as St Kilda and Rockall in the Atlantic.

Habitats on hard rock cliffs clearly vary widely, and in particular the exposure of the site and the location of each niche on the cliff profile appear to be powerful factors in the determination of the local distribution of any plants present. Amongst these, the small and ecologically unusual group of ferns present show a characteristic zonation of their cliff-face distribution.

Sea Spleenwort Communities

The most extremely maritime pteridophyte community is that of Sea Spleenwort (*Asplenium marinum*). *Asplenium marinum* is essentially a western North Atlantic fern in its distribution, occurring outside the British Isles along the west and south-west coasts of Europe and in the islands of Madeira, the Canaries and the Azores. Around Britain's coasts, Sea Spleenwort is most abundant on Atlantic coasts, but spreads around northern Scotland with the flow of Gulf Stream water reaching southward down the north-east coast of England to Yorkshire. It is present all around the Irish coast, but is most abundant in the west, whilst along the south coast of England it does not spread further east than Kent, and seems to be excluded from those coasts where the ocean surface temperatures are coldest.

Within this range, Sea Spleenwort seldom occurs far beyond the immediate spray zone of the sea, where it is confined to rock faces which receive appreciable wave break and where spray drift is strongest. It occurs higher on cliffs only where their topography and the prevailing wind directions combine to regularly funnel ocean spray to higher elevations. It is absent from coasts most sheltered from the Gulf Stream, and even on Atlantic coasts it is absent from deep inlets where there is insufficient fetch of water and wave-break to produce adequate spray drift. It is thus on the lower parts of the most exposed cliffs that the most luxuriant plants of Sea Spleenwort usually occur. It is here that the environments produced by the proximity of the sea can also be most forcibly felt. On cliffs of any aspect, but particularly on aspects facing away from the sun, a high atmospheric summer coolness coupled with permanent high humidity, darkness, and often locally a surprising stillness of the atmosphere can be all pervading. On northerly aspects too, levels of light may also be considerably reduced. Around partly undercut cliffs, and especially into arches and caves, the darkness and stillness generally increase, and in such habitats,

dripping freshwater seeping from cave roofs and beneath overhangs often provide particularly suitable habitats in which Sea
Spleenwort can form especially large plants. In such sites they
succeed in their somewhat ponderous existence because of the
remarkable constancy of their environment and the very low
levels of competition from any other vascular plants. Despite
their highly maritime sites, plants seem to require little, if any,
salt. The importance of the fine saltwater spray is that it carries
the winter warmth of the ocean on to nearby rock faces,
minimising the occurrence of frost, to which this species is
extremely sensitive.

Many of the morphological features of the plant seem to
adapt it particularly closely to these curious, and pteridologically, unusual sites. Its shining, fleshy, lobed fronds are green
throughout the year, usually a pale apple-green when young,
maturing to a deep, glossy green with age. The bluntly rounded
pinnae are usually held stiffly inclined towards the light whilst
the whole frond often adopts a sinuous and winding habit. In
specimens from the most exposed areas, the fronds are usually
held firmly pressed along natural crevices in the rock faces, but

in more sheltered spots are usually better developed and spread more widely over the rock faces. Its fronds arise in a slow succession, sometimes beginning as early as mid-April, and continue to unfurl, till most are fully expanded by late July. Fronds on most plants are usually abundantly fertile and, even on small specimens, the linear sori bulge heavily at maturity with numerous brown sporangia from August onwards. These highly fertile fronds persist from summer through the following winter until the early summer of the following year, not finally withering to creamish-white skeletons until well after the succeeding year's flush of new green fronds has fully expanded. Its fleshy fronds seem to act as considerable stores of freshwater in its highly saline environments, and in this feature they parallel the leaves of many salt-tolerant flowering plants of maritime habitats. The shining waxy cuticle presumably helps to further minimise water loss, and the evergreen habit of the fronds probably helps secure hard-won reserves within the plant until fully transferred to the subsequent year's growth. At all times the stiffness of the stipe and rachis helps hold each frond firmly against undue spray-battering, whilst in such frequently wetted habitats the unusually winged stipe and rachis may help to draw excess moisture droplets away from the sensitive crown.

Unusually too, *Asplenium marinum* is not known to hybridise with any other species of *Asplenium* or other related genera.

The glossy textured and long-persistent fronds of Asplenium marinum tuck into a natural rock crevice where they benefit from winter warmth brought by wave-splash from the Atlantic. West Cornwall, September

Partly this results from the unusualness of its habitat. But it may also be because it is not particularly closely related to other native spleenworts. There is another species of maritime spleenwort, *Asplenium obtusatum*, in the southern hemisphere, which looks similar to *A. marinum*, whilst most of the other species of this large, worldwide genus, which appear to have morpholigical affinities with it, are essentially Old World lithophytes or even epiphytes of rainforests of the tropics. It is perhaps with these that *A. marinum* has its closest taxonomic affinities today.

Where sea caves penetrate higher and deeper, away from the most regularly sea-secured levels of the cliffs, other ferns may occasionally appear. In dark recesses of caves, there may be Lady Fern (*Athyrium filix-femina*), Broad Buckler Fern (*Dryopteris dilatata*) and Common Male Fern (*Dryopteris filix-mas*). In such sites, these species usually occur in lank and etiolated forms in deep cave recesses where they are only slightly splashed by the sea, and where seeping fresh water from the cave roofs above creates a more or less constant high humidity. These species, all more typically plants of woodland, succeed in small numbers in these unusual habitats chiefly through their tolerance of the exceptionally low-light conditions prevailing, whilst benefiting from the summer coolness, shelter, humidity and absence of substantial flowering plant competition.

Dickie's Bladder-fern Communities

On a small area of the Kincardineshire coast of eastern Scotland, an unusual fern present in certain sea caves is Dickie's Fern (*Cystopteris dickieana*). This fern had its first, known locality anywhere discovered on this coast by an amateur naturalist in 1842, who drew it to the attention of the then Professor of Botany at Aberdeen University, George Dickie.

Today, more than a century later, the fern still exists in, and continuously recolonises the walls and roof of, the Kincardineshire sea cave in which it was first found and described, and which hence represents the type locality for the species. It is, on the whole, a smaller fern than the widespread and much more familiar Brittle Bladder-fern (*Cystopteris fragilis*), although I have measured individual fronds in its native cave reaching more than 9 inches (ca. 23 cm) in length. The pinnae are altogether broader, less divided and more closely-spaced along the rachis than are those of *C. fragilis*, giving the frond a more congested appearance, whilst the ultimate divisions are also much blunter. Technically, however, the main character by which *C. dickieana* differs from *C. fragilis* (which itself is a complicated group of interrelated distinct genetic entities of differing ploidy) is that its spores have an outer coat (the 'perispore') which is typically wrinkled into irregular folds, ridges and low projections (described as 'rugose-verrucose') in contrast to the very spiny ('echinate') spores which characterise all plants of *C. fragilis*. It is this spore character which unites these curious Kincardineshire sea cave plants with other plants which are now known to be widely and discontinuously scattered in other corners of Europe today—either in the mountains of the south (mainly in the Alps and Pyrenees) or in high Arctic areas to the north (chiefly in Iceland, Lapland and on into northern Asia), although nowhere is it very abundant.

In its Kincardineshire sea-cave locality, this fern grows on the sides and roof of deep, broad-mouthed, tide-washed caves. The caves are always very damp, with freshwater dripping

Cystopteris dickieana, *an extremely localised native plant, in its sea-cave type-locality in Kincardineshire.* September

freely from their roofs, much of the moisture persisting even through the driest of summers. The exposed rock of the cave interiors—a highly stratified, low-grade metamorphic schist, traversed by numerous, lime-rich veins and further influenced in its base-status by constantly dripping water seeping from andesitic lavas above—is, in places, quite loose and extremely unstable. Massive roof falls seem frequent, and most of the floor is made up of smashed, fallen boulders deriving directly from the roof. Dickie's Fern grows scattered in amongst the loose rock floor debris where this has built up above the level of regular tidal inundation. It also hangs somewhat precariously from the steep rock walls and from remaining, more stable pieces of persistent cave ceiling, from where it rapidly reco-lonises the bared areas revealed by each new rock fall. The cave mouths are east-facing, and their interiors are dark, damp and constantly cool. The only other plants to grow with Dickie's Fern are several species of moss, although large plants of Sea Spleenwort fringe the mouths of the cave recesses, and scat-tered, sterile plants of Lady Fern (*Athyrium filix-femina*) and Broad Buckler-fern (*Dryopteris dilatata*) survive near to drip-ping water in the dank cave interiors.

Lanceolate Spleenwort Communities

Moving above the sea-cave zone of hard cliff faces, and to else-where in Britain, higher up on the cliff faces themselves, Lanceolate Spleenwort (*Asplenium billotii*) may be present. This plant has a scattered and distinctly southern and western distribution around our coasts, but is usually only found with any frequency on coastal cliffs of the Channel Islands, Devon, Cornwall and West Wales. Like *A. marinum, A. billotii* has rather stiff short-stiped fronds, and in its more exposed situations, the fronds often spread stiffly over the rock surfaces. Its fronds are, however, much more finely divided than those of *A. marinum* and are of a less thick and altogether less fleshy texture. Plants of *A. billotii* seem more tolerant of stronger light than *A. marinum*, but frequently plants initially arise in deep narrow fissures, and it is not uncommon to find only the outer parts of their fronds emerging into more fully lit conditions.

Both *Asplenium marinum* and *A. billotii* occur on cliffs of a very wide range of differing rock types, including volcanic, metamorphic and harder sedimentary ones such as basalts, granites, mica and hornblend schists, slaty shales, schistose grits, conglomerates, well-bedded sandstones and harder limestones, the former also occasionally spreading to more unusual rock types such as dolerite, serpentine and picrite.

Asplenium billotii *amongst sunny, coastal rocks. Caernarvonshire, March*

Indeed both plants seem less influenced by the type of rock than its physical characteristics, amongst which a combination of sufficient hardness to resist too rapid a rate of erosion, with a physical structure of well formed narrow cracks, crevices or bedding planes, into which plants can establish, seem to be the most important.

In rocks with small fissure size, each of these ferns may dominate locally. Where, however, rock fissures become larger and pockets of rudimentary soil develop, especially where these are a little above the immediate splash zone of the sea, then the competition of flowering plants tends to increase. Near to Sea Spleenwort may occur Rock Samphire (*Crithmum maritimum*), Cliff Sand-spurrey (*Spergularia rupicola*), Buck's-horn Plantain (*Plantago coronopus*) and Sea Scurvy-grass (*Cochlearia danica*), whilst in the slightly higher cliff zone which

Lanceolate Spleenwort usually typifies, additional species frequently include Sea Plantain (*Plantago maritima*), Sea Thrift (*Armeria maritima*), Sea Campion (*Silene maritima*) and Wall Pennywort (*Umbilicus rupestris*).

Cliff-face Royal Fern Communities

The steep faces of sea cliffs from place to place intersect the seaward drainage from the land, and here water discharging from surface streams may form small cascading waterfalls, whilst that arising from natural fissures, geological fractures, or from the water tables within the rock faces themselves, forms moist and sometimes dripping seepage lines. In both cases the water is moving and often well-oxygenated, and may be relatively permanent through all seasons. Where the water originates directly from surface run-off, especially if it has come from peaty upland areas, the water may be quite acidic and mineral poor. Where it originates as seepage lines or small

Dense colonies of Osmunda regalis fringe a sheltered sea cove. West Cornwall, July

In sea-cliff sites numerous small Osmunda *plants may cling to near-vertical rock faces. West Cornwall, July*

springs, the water may have passed through substantial amounts of intervening rock since it originally sank into the surface, and it may have had abundant opportunity to dissolve minerals from the rocks through which it has flowed. Lime is particularly soluble, and if present in the rocks through which the water has passed (especially limestone), then the water that emerges may be highly charged with lime which can precipitate on the rocks of the cliff faces or amongst cushions of mosses growing upon them, to form creamy-white spongy deposits of tufa. Patches of such emerging water, either by their erosive properties or their depositionery ones, seem to continue to create new surfaces which mosses and ferns are often particularly well able to pioneer. Especially where such sites are on shaded cliff aspects, the locally enhanced moisture can form suitable habitats for two other local cliff-face ferns. These are *Osmunda regalis*, if the water is peaty and acidic, and *Adiantum capillus-veneris*, if the water is particularly lime-rich.

When *Osmunda* is present in cliffside habitats it usually occurs mainly as very numerous but mostly juvenile plants with fronds varying from under 10–50 cm in height, each plant with a small number of broad triangular-outlined blades borne on long pale upright stipes. Only occasional plants have fertile fronds, and these merely have one or more pairs at the tip of the frond highly reduced into narrow, non-leafy, soriferous pinnae, forming a small fertile 'tassel' to the top of the blade. Sometimes plants of *Osmunda* occur singly in these sites, but where the spread of run-off water creates fairly large areas of permanently damp rock, quite dense colonies with numerous plants may occur, giving patches of a vivid green hue to the early summer vegetation of the cliffs. Limitations on the ultimate size of individual plants imposed by the general precariousness of the habitat itself seem to help ensure the maintenance of these colonies in a state of almost permanent juvenility, and in the absence of a creeping rhizome, the new plants filling vacant areas arise through repeated spore colonisation, including from spores most probably arriving from more mature plants in other more inland sites nearby.

Adiantum capillus-veneris, *a lime-loving species, confined to only the mildest fringes of these islands. West Cornwall, May*

Cliff-face Maidenhair Fern Communities

In contrast to the potentially large size of Royal Fern, plants of Maidenhair Fern, *Adiantum capillus-veneris* always remain very

much smaller, but can be highly fertile locally. Maidenhair Fern is an attractive plant, with delicate, finely-divided fronds which, in this habitat, seldom exceed more than 30 cm in length and are very often under 8 cm. Larger sized specimens usually occur only as more solitary individuals, often in the local shelter of deep, moist cliffside fissures, whilst on more exposed cliff faces where tufa is accumulating, small plants may occur in profusion and in a highly-crowded condition, forming dense, bright-green cushion-like mats. The fronds are more or less winter-deciduous, but each spring they make a new and particularly early start. In North Cornwall, expansion of the new season's growth may begin as early as mid-March, bringing them into full leaf by mid-April, when most of the other surrounding vegetation still has a distinctly wintry look. *Adiantum* begins shedding its spores as early as mid-May, after which the fronds generally persist to late summer, or, if the season has been a particularly dry one, they become dilapidated, if not entirely shrivelled, by late August.

Like *Asplenium bilottii*, *Adiantum capillus-veneris* is an essentially Mediterranean–Old World sub-tropical species of fern, which just succeeds in reaching our shores to thrive only in occasional, scattered far southern and western localities, where it occurs mainly around the coasts of Cornwall, Cardigan Bay and Co. Clare, with a few isolated western localities elsewhere north to the Isle of Man and the northern shore of Donegal Bay. Its strongly calcicolous habits restrict Maidenhair Fern totally to often inaccessible patches of high cliff-faces, where there is particularly active accumulation of tufa rock. Plants spread locally over such wet, tufaceous surfaces by horizontal growth of their thin creeping rhizomes as well as, presumably, by spore re-establishment from the usually numerous fertile fronds. The tufaceous substrates can be particularly soft, and seem to eventually naturally fall away in whole chunks during winter storms. These expose new patches of underlying rock upon which new tufa deposits immediately begin building, and into which the Maidenhair Fern soon starts to recolonise.

Almost all of the ferns in these cliff-face habitats seem well adapted to make particularly good use of the potentially long growing season available: both *Asplenium* species by their evergreen habits, *Cystopteris dickieana* by long remaining green in autumn, and *Osmunda* and *Adiantum* by their completion of much of their frond expansion and maturity before summer drought and possible crowding by upgrowth of surrounding, more rank vegetation. The winter and early spring growth habits of the southern species point to plants which, in most cases, are beginning to reach the northern limits of their overall geographic ranges around the British coasts. Here they seem to be clearly benefiting from the proximity of the effects of our warm winter Gulf Stream water.

Soft Rock Cliffs

The extensive outcrop in sea-cliffs of softer geological strata which tend to crumble substantially on erosion, is usually marked by the formation of long, semi-mobile screes. This is especially true of the outcrops of such readily-cleaved rocks as shales or slates. Rocky valleys also often mark areas of change in the geological strata, where streams flowing to the sea have followed lines of natural rock weakness, the streams (or glacial action before them) cutting down through the rocks and often themselves becoming flanked by tumbled boulder slopes. The most exposed coastal screes can appear to be fairly devoid of vegetation from a distance, although their chinks may contain several low-growing species, and especially ferns. Rocky valleys, by contrast, may be better vegetated, and if not too extensively grazed, some woody overgrowth may be present, and more luxuriant growths of pteridophytes may occur.

Black Spleenwort–Western Polypody Communities

The habitats of tumbled rocky screes differ from those of coastal valleys in being generally drier and more exposed. One fern in particular is characteristic of these sites. This is Black Spleenwort (*Asplenium adiantum-nigrum*).

Black Spleenwort is a fern which ranges very widely outside Britain and Ireland across mainly southern Europe, and on into Africa and the sunnier warm-temperate parts of the Old World. Its distribution in coastal screes in Britain and Ireland closely reflects this, being particularly characteristic of warm, well-lit, dark-coloured, coastal shale or slate screes with a general westerly or southerly aspect—rock types often poor in such elements as calcium and magnesium, but high in others such as aluminium and silica. In such sites, it can sometimes be numerous, either as scattered plants or, more usually, as many scattered clumps of plants, often up to a foot or so (ca. 30 cm) in diameter. Its shining-surfaced, evergreen, fronds seem tolerant of direct exposure to full sun. The plant itself seems tolerant of considerable summer desiccation and baking. Its habitats are usually ones where the scree itself is already lying at a steep and delicately-balanced angle of repose, with accumulations of small islands of marginally more stable small rock-fragments dammed behind occasional boulders usually extensively colonised by this fern.

In some shale screes, generally, although not necessarily always, those with a little more shelter, Black Spleenwort sometimes co-dominates with a second, numerous, fern. This fern is Western Polypody (*Polypodium interjectum*). Western Polypody too seems very tolerant of the relatively desiccating summer conditions, and during particularly dry summers, its annual frond-replacement is often delayed in these sites until the beginning of a wetter period. The plant nevertheless generally succeeds in forming extensive patches, with its scaly rhizome creeping far over, or amongst, loose surface fragments of rock. The numerous, but often small, stiff, fleshy and rather yellow-green fronds born in abundance in these sites, seem to well adapt Western Polypody to this type of habitat, which is much less well, if at all, exploited to any significant degree by the other two lower-ploidy, thinner-fronded species of this genus in our flora.

Associates of Black Spleenwort, or of this species plus Western Polypody, in these coastal scree habitats, are not always numerous, but form a fairly characteristic assemblage. They include very frequent patches of Wild Thyme (*Thymus drucei*) and English Stonecrop (*Sedum anglicum*), with occasional ground-trailing Ivy (*Hedera helix*) and Stone Bramble (*Rubus saxatilis*), small plants of Gorse (*Ulex europaeus*), and scattered plants of Wood Sage (*Teucrium scorodonia*), Birdsfoot-trefoil (*Lotus corniculatus*), Lady's Bedstraw (*Galium verum*), Rock Sea-spurrey (*Spergularia rupicola*), Sea Campion (*Silene maritima*), Hawkweeds (*Hieracium* spp.), Red Fescue (*Festuca rubra*), Early Hair-grass (*Aira praecox*), cushions of mosses such as *Hypnum cupressiforme* and *Dicranum scoparium*, and often abundant *Xanthoria parietina* and *Ramalina siliquosa* lichens. Sea Thrift (*Armeria maritina*) and Rock Samphire (*Crithmum maritimum*) are often present on more stable slopes nearby.

At the feet of such screes, where they may merge on to well-vegetated, sandy foreshores or on to the plateaux of former raised-beach levels, large scattered clumps of *Polypodium interjectum* can sometimes be found amongst densely grass-covered swards. In one such site investigated in some detail by the author, at the foot of a sunny, south-facing coastal slope in Kirkudbrightshire, the clumps of *P. interjectum* were found to either mark the sites of shallow soils resulting from the presence of a hidden boulder just beneath the ground, or, much more often, the almost equally-hidden, dome-shaped, hard tops of the nests of the small yellow-brown ant *Lasius flavus*, which were often still in active occupation beneath.

Sheltered, undisturbed, and often fairly inaccessible sites are also often the habitats of particularly rich insect and reptile faunas including the Common Adder (*Vipera berus*), which can be extremely well camouflaged amongst these ferns and often unappreciative of sudden disturbance.

Although it is screes of slates and shales on which Black Spleenwort most frequently reaches its characteristically extensive development, it is by no means confined to such rock types, and can also occur on coastal scree slopes formed by a number of other rocks, including thinly-bedded sandstones, mudstones, cementstones, conglomerates and breccias, schists, basalts and dolerites. It seldom seems to occur very extensively on limestones, and usually avoids also the very hardest and most acidic rock types such as granites and gneiss. It is however, present, sometimes in unusual abundance, on ultrabasic rocks such as serpentines and peridotites, including in the rare localities where these outcrop to form loose cliff screes. Some particularly notable examples of this unusual type of habitat occur in the Lizard peninsula of Cornwall, as well as more locally on the Shetland islands and on Rhum. In each of these localities, *Asplenium adiantum-nigrum* can reach a considerable abundance and occurs in an unusual form in which the tips of the segements of the fronds are unusually blunt and the whole frond of quite distinctive and atypical form. This odd plant has a strong superficial resemblance to the European spleenwort of ultrabasic rock, *A. cuneifolium* (which, when discovered, it was first thought to be, until it was found to differ from it in ploidy), and seems to be a uniquely insular and characteristic fern of such ultrabasic rock screes in Britain and Ireland, no matter how isolated and wherever they may occur.

Rocky Coastal Valley Communities

Along the flanks of coastal valleys, scattered plants of Black Spleenwort may mix in tumbled boulder slopes with Common Male Fern (*Dryopteris filix-mas*), Soft Shield-fern (*Polystichum setiferum*) and Hart's Tongue Fern (*Phyllitis scolopendrium*), especially on less acidic rocks on western coasts, whilst on rocks of different types, all three species of *Polypodium* (and sometimes patches of their hybrids) may occur over boulders. Lanceolate Spleenwort (*Asplenium billotii*) can be present more locally and usually amongst softer and well-fissured rock outcrops on the coasts of Wales, Devon, Cornwall and the Channel Islands, and in the latter region, Guernsey Spleenwort (*A. × sarniense*) may also grow. In shaded, more acidic and sheltered spots, especially where there is some tree overgrowth,

Lady Fern (*Athyrium filix-femina*) and Broad Buckler-fern replace several of the above, whilst in local, usually shaded, moist and cool, highly Atlantic situations, drought-sensitive, acid-loving species, including Hay-scented Buckler-fern (*Dryopteris aemula*), Northern Buckler-fern (*D. expansa*), Tunbridge and Wilson's Filmy-fern (*Hymenophyllum tunbrigense* and *H. wilsonii*), and occasional clumps of Hard Fern (*Blechmum spicant*), add considerably to the diversity (see also chapter 13).

Where small stream-carrying valleys intersect the cliffs and splashing water is present, Royal Fern (*Osmunda regalis*) can sometimes occur on western coasts, especially if the water is peaty and acidic, and in a few, rare, well-sheltered sites, Killarney Fern (*Trichomanes speciosum*) is known.

Where such water is less acidic, Great Horsetail (*Equisetum telmateia*) and Dutch Rush (*E. hyemale*) can occur locally, whilst in sites where streams tumble on to and eventually cross the upper parts of pebbly foreshores, Shore Horsetail (*E.* × *litorale*) can occur in communities with Yellow Flag (*Iris pseudacorus*), Meadowsweet (*Filipendula ulmaria*), Hemp Agrimony (*Eupatorium cannabinum*), Hemlock Water Dropwort (*Oenanthe crocata*) and Purple Loostrife (*Lythrum salicaria*). Quite frequently, the parents of this hybrid are also to be found nearby, Common Horsetail (*E. arvense*) in neighbouring rough grass slopes or cliff-top ledges, and Water Horsetail (*E. fluviatile*) in standing water, where this ponds from flowing streams behind pebble-banked foreshores. Here, such a diversity of species can be brought into close proximity with cool, moist, sea-sprayed rocks, bearing colonies of Sea Spleenwort (*Asplenium marinum*).

Clay Coasts

Where clays outcrop in coastal areas, rates of erosion are typically high and the landforms resulting are of an altogether lower and more gently sloping profile than are those of more rocky coasts. Such coats are thus often ones of long, sweeping bays, interrupted by occasional, low headlands where scattered harder strata intervene. Rates of clay coast erosion are often at their greatest during winter, when the slippery and plastic water-saturated clays readily slump, opening new bare surfaces and numerous small chasms and moist crevices within their seaward slopes. A small number of ferns and several horsetails succeed in these eroding habitats, largely because such sites possess a continual openness and temporary freedom from dense plant competition after each new erosional phase which the ferns and horsetails are able to colonise and utilise before further slippage or enchroachment by other plants occurs.

Clay Coast Fern Communities

The base-retaining capacity of clays often enables base-loving species to be present on the most recently-exposed mineral slopes, whilst more acid-loving ones can occur nearby where small pockets of raw plant humus have accumulated. Thus, most characteristic basic clay sites, especially on milder, Atlantic, coasts, are Soft Shield-Fern (*Polystichum setiferum*) and Hart's-Tongue (*Phyllitis scolopendrium*), whilst in more acidic spots there may be nearby Male Fern (*Dryopteris filix-mas*), Common Golden-scaled Male Fern (*D. affinis* subsp. *borreri*), and in moist patches, Broad Bucker-fern (*D. dilatata*) and Lady Fern (*Athyrium filix-femina*). In many cases, the densest stands of these ferns are in moist, recessed niches, especially near to small streams, where they are often accompanied by low shrub overgrowth. The most common associates noted in sites in which Hart's Tongue and Soft Shield-fern are particularly characteristic, include mainly trailing stems of Ivy (*Hedera helix*) with Slender False-brome (*Brachypodium sylvaticum*) and sometimes Red Campion (*Silene dioica*). In such sites, many of the ferns can be seen to freely recolonise newly bared erosional surfaces as these arise, where their successs to maturity is in part also promoted by the absence of larger grazing animals.

Clay Coast Horsetail Communities

More extensive on clay coasts than are ferns, however, are sometimes horsetails, which usually occur in local stands on more rapidly eroding and more exposed slopes, which they regularly and continuously reinvade.

The most widely spread horsetail in these sites is the Common Horsetail (*Equisetum arvense*), which is particularly characteristic of the shoulders of the banks. Although its sites appear to be ones in which the surface of the ground dries out most in summer, its very deep-seated and extensive creeping rhizome system provides a network which continuously feeds from deeper, moister layers below. On the surface, its shoots adopt a very wide range of habits according to the degree of exposure of the site, from tall and erect to low-growing and decumbent or totally prostrate. Its associates vary from a dense, grassy sward marking its more stable habitats, to a small number of scattered herbs in its more mobile ones. These commonly include a range of sub-maritime plants and ones of grassland or disturbed ground, such as Coltsfoot (*Tussilago farfara*), Buck's-horn Plantain (*Plantago coronopus*), Birdsfoot-trefoil (*Lotus corniculatus*), Silverweed (*Potentilla anserina*), Yarrow (*Achillea millefolium*), Tufted Vetch (*Vicia cracca*),Ragwort (*Senecio jacobaea*), Scarlet Pimpernel (*Anagallis arvensis*), Common Mouse-ear Chickweed (*Cerastium holosteoides*) and Oat-grass (*Arrhenatherum elatius*).

More impressive, however, are the large stands of Great Horsetail (*Equisetum telmateia*) which sometimes occur in these sites, occasionally in spectacular colonies of considerable extent. Its colonies typically mark spring lines along which outcropping rock aquifers discharge a steady seepage of base-rich moisture through slumping clay banks, and where the clays are sufficiently deep and kept moist enough on a year-round cycle for the horsetail to achieve both extensive subterranean rhizome growth and to maintain its appreciable annual crop of massive aerial shoots.

Wherever successful, Great Horsetail tends to form dense stands, with its fertile cone-shoots in April each year often numerous around the drier upper margins of each colony, and

Bottlebrush-like shoots of Equisetum telmateia *on a slumping clay coast, marking an area of subterranean freshwater seepage. Berwickshire, June*

its sterile, white-stemmed, green-branched bottlebrush-like vegetative shoots following in large numbers in early summer like a miniature forest of Carboniferous Calamites. By mid-summer, its vegetative shoots are regularly 4–6 feet in height, and in some sheltered localities, I have measured shoots over eight feet (nearly 2.5 m) high. Some of its more classic coastal localities include the exposures of late Pleistocene boulder clays overlying Silurian rocks of the Cambrian coast of

Complex slumping of coastal soft rock cliffs. Isle of Wight, rich in Great Horsetail. (Cambridge University Collection: copyright reserved)

Cardigan Bay as well as those facing from the other side of the Irish sea on the Wicklow coast and over a very similar geological sequence on the Galloway Peninsula of south-west Scotland, the Jurassic lias clays of both the Yorkshire and Dorset coasts, and the Oligocene gault clay exposures on the coasts of the Isle of Wight. In each of these sites, Great Horsetail itself is typically the vegetationally dominant plant within much of the areas in which it occurs, but a range of other species which characteristically occur with or around it in many of its coastal sites often includes scattered plants of Meadowsweet (*Filipendula ulmaria*), Wild Angelica (*Angelica sylvestris*), Cow Parsnip (*Heracleum sphondylium*), Marsh Thistle (*Cirsium palustre*), Marsh Bedstraw (*Galium palustre*), Marsh Marigold (*Caltha palustris*), Water-pepper (*Polygonum hydropiper*), Great Hairy Willow-herb (*Epilobium hirstutum*), Hemp Agrimony (*Eupatorum cannabinum*), Fleabane (*Pulicaria dysenterica*), Hard Rush (*Juncus inflexus*), Remote and Great Pond Sedges (*Carex remota* and *C. riparia*). Along their upper margins, such colonies of Great Horsetail usually mingle with tall herb and meadow-grassland communities including abundant Ribwort Plantain (*Plantago lanceolata*), Restharrow (*Ononis repens*) and tall grasses such as Oat-grass (*Arrhenatherum elatius*), Yorkshire Fog (*Holcus lanatus*) Cock's-foot (*Dactylis glomerata*) and Tall Brome (*Festuca gigantea*); these usually marking the beginnings of more stable slopes.

In its typical, wet, slumping, sites of well-irrigated, soft clay substrates, Great Horsetail probably gains an essential combination of both adequate bases and adequate soluble silicates (presumably deriving from the alumino-silicate composition of the clay matrix itself) to satisfy the massive annual mineral demand of this species. Its clay sites are thus ones which are often surface-wet and soft and slippery even in summer, and in high ot steep terrain, should be explored only with appropriate caution.

Near to some of the clay coast sites in which Great Horsetail grows in south-eastern Ireland, another horsetail, Moore's Horsetail (*Equisetum × moorei*) is of localised occurrence (see Chapter 13).

Coastal Sand-dunes

Sand-dune systems of greater or lesser extent occur fairly widely around the coasts of Britain and Ireland, especially in regions where both the immediate hinterland and the submerged marine platform are of long and shallowly-shelving profile.

Wind is the transporting agent in sand-dune building.

The successional mosaic of sand dune ridges and slacks. Morfa Harlech, Merioneth. (Cambridge University Collection: copyright reserved)

Coastal sand dunes are formed gradually inland from marine sites where there is an abundant sand supply from offshore sand flats, and where these are regularly exposed at a sufficiently high level at each low tide for their surface grains to dry and be picked up and transported landward by the prevailing wind. The sand removed from the foreshore is continually replenished there from more permanently submerged tidal zones during each period of regular tidal submergence. Meanwhile, the sand grains carried landward by the wind over the regular surface of the beach become re-deposited wherever the smooth wind-flow is broken into turbulence and made diffuse by striking its first main barriers of emergent terrestrial vegetation.

The vegetation itself hence induces new sand deposition to take place mainly in a narrow zone immediately adjacent to the coast. Growth of the sand-dunes thus occurs in a predominantly seaward direction, and there may be an appreciable hinterland of older dune ridges increasing in age and in vegetational stabilisation with increasing distance from the sea. Coastal sand-dunes so-formed thus often occur as a series of ridges parallel to the coast and separated by a system of valleys—the sand-dune 'slacks'. Furthest from the sea, the oldest parts of the sand-dune system usually develop into a more stable, level or undulating, well-grassed, fixed dune-pasture—widely referred to as sand-dune 'links'.

Significant differences in the species present in different dune systems result, in part, from their formation by sands of different geological and biological origins. The sand may be derived from marine erosion of nearby coastal rocks or from fluvial deposits arriving by longshore drift, with or without the addition of a component from local organic sources in the form of broken fragments from a myriad of marine molluscan shells. Such 'shell sand' is by no means uncommon around the shores of Britain and Ireland, and can result in a calcium carbonate component amounting to up to 5% of the sand (but reducing from such an initial amount in the surface layers by gradual leaching in the older parts of calcareous sand-dune systems). Such basic dune systems are almost always the richest in pteridophytes as well as of most other plants.

The sand-dune environment is characteristically a very windswept one, with the general windspeeds lessened only slightly in the slacks and links. All of the pteridophytes of sand-dunes are species which can adopt aerial growth with relatively low wind-profiles, and at the same time are tolerant of exposure of salt-laden air and full sun. Despite these limitations, the general success of pteridophytes in these habitats seems due largely to the greatly reduced competition from both aggressive and tall vegetation which characterises many dune pteridophyte sites.

Dune Ridges and Gulleys

The dryness of most dune ridges usually limits the representation of pteridophytes to occasional horsetails (*Equisetum*), and even these, in most sites, are either absent or are limited to a few scattered shoots arising from extremely deeply-running rhizomes. Such shoots may become locally more frequent, however, where traversing streams carve broad gulleys through the dunes, and dune water-tables occur near to the surface. In some sites, especially in high rainfall, calcareous dune systems, shoots of several horsetails may be present in such sites. The most frequent of these are Common Horsetail (*Equisetum arvense*) and Marsh Horsetail (*E. palustre*), the former sometimes extending short distances into the drier parts of adjacent dunes. Very locally other horsetails, and especially horsetail hybrids, may be present in the vicinity of streams and small rivers crossing sand-dune ridges, including especially Shore

Horsetail (*Equisetum × litorale*), and very locally Mackay's
Horsetail (*E. × trachyodon*) and Moore's Horsetail (*E. × moorei*), the latter confined to the dunes of the Wicklow–
Wexford coast (see chapter 13). Also very locally in Scotland
(East Lothian), I have found Ditch Horsetail (*E. × rothmaleri*)
in this habitat, and in one Pembrokeshire site found what is
probably a hybrid between *E. arvense* and *E. telmateia*, both
parents of which were nearby.

An unusual local abundance of a horsetail in one rather dry
area of a calcareous dune site, however, is that of Dutch Rush
(*Equisetum hyemale*) in one locality in east Sutherland, where it
locally co-dominates with Marram Grass (*Ammophila arenaria*). Other associates here include Red Fescue (*Festuca*

Equisetum palustre
*growing luxuriantly
where flushed
marshland fringes
calcareous dunes.
Morfa Harlech,
Merionethshire, late
June*

rubra), Cat's-foot (*Antennaria dioica*), Lady's Bedstraw (*Galium verum*), Bridsfoot-trefoil (*Lotus corniculatus*), Lesser Meadow Rue (*Thalictrum minus*), Hairbell (*Campanula rotundifolia*), Yellow-Rattle (*Rhinanthus minor*), Red Fescue (*Festuca rubra*), Meadow-grass (*Poa pratensis*), and the mosses *Campalothecium lutescens* and *Tortula ruraliformis* (R. Ferreira, personal communication). It is of interest that the shoots of *E. hyemale* in this habitat are of a particularly slender and slightly anomalous form, ressembling forms which I know elsewhere only in Denmark, where they also occur in such dunes.

Dune Slacks

Adjacent to the dune ridges, the slacks are usually broad and flat bottomed, their base levels marking where their sand surface remains more or less permanently damp through close contact with the regular water-table within the whole sand-dune system. These slacks frequently become flooded to depths of several inches in winter. The irrigation of the slacks is derived mostly from rainfall, but the water table itself frequently floats on a deeper layer of infiltrated seawater, and the resulting water of the slacks may thus be partly brackish. Such dune slacks, in base-rich dune systems, may contain a number of scattered pteridophytes.

In sand dune systems in which any of the above horsetails are present, they also usually spread to occupy parts of the margins of adjacent dune slacks. However, by far the most typical horsetail of dune slack habitats, but mostly confined to highly calcareous ones, is Variegated Horsetail (*Equisetum variegatum*). In slacks of appropriately basic character this species occurs in widely scattered sites in both the north and south of these islands, its abundance varying from scattered and fairly isolated shoots to occasional dense local colonies. It typically thrives around the edges of moist slacks, avoiding those areas which are most permanently flooded in winter as well as those which dry out too excessively in summer. When abundant, it thus frequently forms a fringe towards the outer edges of slacks, marking the edge of winter pools, where sheets of ice meet the surface of the sand.

Variegated Horsetail is, however, a remarkably variable plant between different sites, and sometimes even at different levels around the same site its shoots appear to adopt a differing vegetative appearance. Experimental cultivation of cuttings shows that dune slack races of this species are genetically distinct ecotypes, mostly of moderate potential size (larger, for example, than those of mountain streamside habitats, but smaller than many inland forms in Ireland), which usually also adopt a more decumbent habit. Differing local environmental conditions frequently, however, further modify their appearance, and may induce them, for example, to be nearly prostrate. Their strong-growing leading shoots, which do not arise from surfacing rhizome apices until late spring or early summer, typically form single, semi-decumbent shoots which may later also develop sparse basal branches. In some sites, these evergreen main axes are almost invariably damaged (or are positively suppressed) either by grazing by rabbits or by both summer sand-blasting and by winter pool-margin ice movements, and such environmental effects then often stimulating more vigorous development of the basal branches into a flush of secondary shoots. These side branches are often more prostrate and flexuous in their growth than the original main shoot, and in some whole colonies they may arise abundantly, leaving little trace of the original main shoot, which they sometimes come to approach in size. Brought into experimental cultivation from cuttings, specimens established from such laterals ultimately grow into exactly the same form of the plant as do those from strong-growing shoots from the same dune locality, but all remain distinct from those of mountain and inland Irish, indeed, even from some inland British habitats.

In many of its more northern sand dune slack sites, *Equisetum variegatum* is associated also with small, diffuse patches of Lesser Clubmoss (*Selaginella selaginoides*), although the presence of this plant, usually growing as widely scattered individuals, is easily overlooked. It is, however, probably not infrequent in the most calcareous dune-slack sites, especially in moist hollows where tall vegetation is not dense. In one northern British site where these two pteridophytes occur together, flowering plants noted included mainly Silverweed (*Potentilla anserina*), Birdsfoot-trefoil (*Lotus corniculatus*), Mouse-ear Chickweed (*Cerastium* spp.) and locally frequent Coral-root (*Corallorhiza trifida*), with mosses forming at least a partial component of the cover.

Also widespread in calcareous dune slacks, although of somewhat local and rather sporadic occurrence is Common Adder's-tongue (*Ophioglossum vulgatum*). This species may occur as quite gregarious colonies within fairly sparsely-vegetated slacks, or as much sparser individuals in denser slack vegetation, especially in hollows which regularly become flooded to depths of several centimetres during the winter months. Plants typically occur mostly as low growing but upright individuals, sometimes as small as 2–3 cm in height, but becoming larger than this in damp and progressively more sheltered hollows, where it can sometimes reach as much as

10 cm or so in height, and many tens of individuals may occur in an area of a few square metres. Despite such numbers, the plant is sometimes difficult to spot, especially if not fertile, for the colour and texture of the leaf alone is very similar to that of a number of other calcareous dune slack plants with which it sometimes grows, including the leaves of the Marsh Pennywort (*Hydrocotyle vulgaris*), Common Spotted Orchid (*Dactylorhiza fuchsii*), Northern Fen Orchid (*D. purpurella*), Meadow Orchid (*D. incarnata*), Fen Orchid (*D. praetermissa*), Coral-root (*Corallorhiza trifida*), Autumn Lady's Tresses (*Spiranthes spiralis*), and Marsh and Dune Helleborine (*Epipactis palustris* and *E. dunensis*). It is perhaps of significance that many of these species also share with *Ophioglossum* the possession of roots which are fleshy and highly mycotrophic.

In some calcareous dune slacks, a second species of *Ophioglossum* may be present; Small Adder's-tongue (*Ophioglossum azoricum*). This tiny plant, of somewhat diminutive and plantain-like appearance, is a highly Atlantic species in its discontinuous native distribution around the coasts of Britain and Ireland, from where it spreads south to the Azores and Canary Islands and north to Iceland. Only some of its stations are in sand-dune slacks, the majority being on exposed, grassy headlands. In sand-dune slacks it sometimes reaches its greatest abundance, however, occurring in generally well-vegetated patches of either fixed dune pasture or of low-lying, damp, calcareous slacks, although in some of the latter there is also plenty of bare ground. In sand-dune slacks, associates commonly include a particular abundance of Marsh Pennywort (*Hydrocotyle vulgaris*) and Lesser Spearwort (*Rannunculus flammula*), which typically occur as the main vegetational dominants. Where the Common Adder's-tongue (*Ophioglossum vulgatum*) also occurs in nearby dune-slack sites, *O. azoricum* is typically confined to those which are somewhat less extensively flooded in winter and are ones which perhaps warm up more readily and earlier in spring presumably extending the growing season for this plant, although the reasons for its preference for these sites and its competition with *O. vulgatum* remains unclear. This small species is clearly susceptible to grazing pressure, particularly that of rabbits, which may take its aerial part in considerable numbers by early summer, while on the Cumbrian coast I have also seen the large, roaming caterpillars of the White Ermine Moth (*Spilosoma menthastri*) consume both the sporangia and the leafy parts with great facility. In their most extensive sand-dune sites, plants of both Common Adder's-tongue *Ophioglossum vulgatum* and Small Adder's-tongue *O. azoricum* typically occur in relatively large, diffuse colonies, presumably marking dune-slack sites which have remained stable over particularly long periods of time, thus allowing these small plants time to proliferate. When they occure in these numbers they can be quite easy to spot.

Fixed Dunes and Sand Dune Pasture

Progressing inwards from the sea, the older parts of the dunes become more stable. Upon these is eventually established a denser, more continuous vegetation forming fixed dune 'links' or sand-dune pasture, and beneath its vegetation mantle, the sand surface is sufficiently stabilised for a shallow humus layer to begin to build up. All of the species of pteridophytes already seen in the sand-dune slacks are often able to persist in this vegetation for shorter or longer periods, whilst some others may make their first appearance at this point.

Of those which persist from the dune slack stage, some, such as Lesser Clubmoss, Variegated Horsetail and Common Horsetail generally do so only in a very much reduced and scattered form. This is also true for the rare sites where Mackay's Horsetail and Moore's Horsetail occur, although the latter two, and to some extent also Variegated Horsetail and Common Horsetail, are able to return to fuller vigour in the temporarily reduced competition of erosional blow-outs (where the presence of these horsetails can do much to help stabilise and re-vegetate the damaged surface). Marsh Horsetail persists only infrequently, except where natural streams or man-made drainage ditches cross the links, where it too can return to form a densely-colonising fringe, and Shore Horsetail also persists from stream gullies nearer to the dune

Ophioglossum vulgatum *in calcareous fixed-dune links. East Lothian, June*

front, to occur most typically in the semi-stable, sandy erosion-margin communities of such sites.

Within the fixed dune pasture, Common Adder's-tongue, and more rarely Small Adder's-tongue, can persist rather more permanently, if rather more diffusely, in the rich turfy sward, where their mycotrophic roots presumably gain enhanced sustenance from the increased rate of supply of decaying surrounding matter.

Of the species which enter the natural succession here usually for the first time, an especially characteristic additional member of the community of the grassy links is Moonwort (*Botrychium lunaria*)—although it is also sometimes present in old, sand-dune slacks which have almost reached the vegetational stability of links. This diminutive fern, sometimes as tall as about 8 cm in sand-dune links, but more often having a full stature of under 2 cm in such sites, can be extremely difficult to see amongst a rich, grassy, dune links sward, but may occur locally in considerable numbers. Plants generally thrive under less damp and generally better-drained ground conditions than are typical for Common Adder's-tongue, and on the not-infrequent occasions in calcareous dune links where the two grow close to one another, Moonwort usually occupies only the better-drained hummocks and knolls, whilst Adder's-tongue (often in nearly equally diminutive form) only occupies the nearby damper hollows. These two highly mycotrophic plants thus form fairly discreet aspects of the same vegetation communities, without generally coming into direct vegetational competition.

Associates of Moonwort in sand-dune slack vegetation can be many, but frequently include patches of low-growing Wild Thyme (*Thymus drucei*), Clovers (*Trifolium* spp), Lady's Bedstraw (*Galium verum*), and Birdsfoot-trefoil (*Lotus corniculatus*), in a dense and species-rich turf. Scattered thin and diminutive shoots of *Equisetum variegatum* are sometimes present near to or even intergrown through the Moonwort patches, representing something of a last seral stage of success of this horsetail, gradually succumbing to the competitive pressures of closure of the vegetation in which the Moonwort thrives.

One unusual fern occurring occasionally in patches where the dune sand surface starts to become fixed, is Polypody. Colonies of this fern are known especially from some East Anglian coastal dune sites and from ones in Anglesey. Perhaps both Common Polypody (*Polypodium vulgare*) and Western Polypody (*P. interjectum*) may occur occasionally in such sites, and more research on these is needed. At one of its Norfolk sites, observations have shown that the plant began to increase through the years following the disappearance of the rabbit populations from 1954 (White, 1961). As with many ferns, this genus seems highly sensitive to grazing, and presumably rabbit populations everywhere play a significant role in restricting this normally-epiphytic fern from such unusual terrestrial sites.

A not uncommon invader of the inland edge of the fixed dune pasture, and often also forming islands within it, are low-canopied, harsh-fronded forms of Bracken (*Pteridium aquilinum*), with their rhizomes penetrating sometimes deeply through the sandy substrate. Such communities occur widely, their spread perhaps, in this case, aided by herbivore pressure on the surrounding vegetation.

Of very much more rare occurrence, however, was a community which I have found only once (in Pembrokeshire) in a moist hollow within low fixed dunes, where there occurred on the sand an apparently natural, small, highly-sheltered, thin, miniature woodland of low-canopied Hornbeam trees (*Carpinus betulus*). This unusual woodland had as its understorey an equally unusual, nearly continuous stand of Hart's Tongue Fern (*Phyllitis scolopendrium*), growing luxuriantly on the white, calcareous sand in the dappled Hornbeam shade. At the time when I stumbled upon this memorable site, it was a warm and sunny day, and I could not help re-imagining this place to be akin to the vegetation of one I had once previously seen, where, amongst a thin canopy of palm trees, I was once equally surprised to come across a dense terrestrial vegetation of rather similar-looking Bird's-nest Fern (*Asplenium nidus*), growing equally luxuriantly on the smashed white coral rock of a remote Pacific atoll.

The Pteridophytes of
Man-made Landscapes

Throughout Britain and Ireland, since man first entered the scene, he has continually wrought change to the vegetation and the landscapes around him. Most of this change has progressively diminished the habitats available for pteridophytes, especially those of the original, natural, forest. Some of the many new landscapes created, however, have eventually themselves become suitable for at least a limited recolonisation by appropriate native pteridophyte species, which in several cases have come to form communities which although different from the original native ones, are now nevertheless closely and characteristically associated with some of these habitats. The most distinctive of these are in sites of abandoned industrial activity or with habitats resulting from the construction of various massive communication systems. Pteridophytes have succeeded in these sites because they often combine several important features for pteridophyte success, especially variously reduced plant competition, availability of unusual (and especially mineral-rich) subtrates, and relative freedom from grazing. The history of many of the sites can be traced both in general and sometimes quite specific terms, usually with considerable accuracy, and hence the history of the pteridophyte communities concerned may be able to be fairly closely inferred. Today, such sites often also owe their importance to their having additionally become biological refuges for a number of different pteridophytes originating in different ways in different historic periods, but each from subsequent change, often becoming eliminated in the habitats around them.

South-western Hedgebanks

Steep 'hedgebanks' or 'lanebanks' along a myriad of minor roads and trackways, and similar structures forming field divisions, are a particularly characteristic feature of the rural landscape of much of the south-west of England. They also occur extensively in the Channel Islands and in many parts of

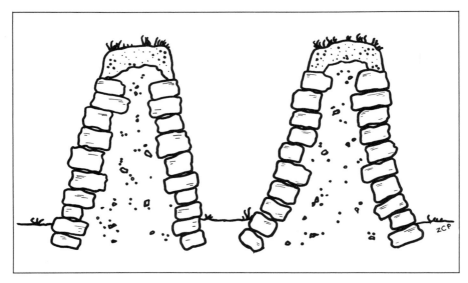

Fig. 10

Cross-sections of typical western hedgebanks, approximately 4 feet (ca. 120 cm) high and 4¹/₂ feet (ca. 140 cm) wide at the base, with a rough facing of local stones, earth filling and turf capping. (After Cornwall County Council, unpublished records)

southern Ireland. Often 2–3 metres or so in height, such hedgebanks are usually massive, and often ancient, winding structures built of earth and stone, and capped by a hedge. Although manifestly man-made, their exposed surfaces support a particularly characteristic vegetation, of which the fern component is an integral and frequently abundant one.

In the areas in which they most abound, hedgebanks and lanebanks of this type have long formed substitutes for more traditional types of hedge. They occur in regions which typically enjoy a mild though damp and windy climate, often with appreciable summer sun and sometimes winter snow, but in which there is a considerable maritime influence. The latter helps buffer the greatest extremes of temperature and, indeed, it is the frequently windswept nature of the more exposed parts of the terrain that is generally responsible for the success in such regions of this type of 'hedge'.

Even in their origins, these hedgebanks differ fundamentally from the majority of hedgerows of other regions. They occur mostly in areas in which, through historic time, Anglo-Saxon influence has been least and where Celtic traditions have remained strong. Their location and frequency often reflected progressive consolidation of ancient holdings of land with boundaries along even more ancient bridle-ways and cart-tracks. Many also marked parish or estate boundaries. Much of the present landscape in which they occur had been already enclosed by the beginning of the 16th century, and in south-west England in particular, in many cases its enclosure into small squared fields was carried out over a period of at least three centuries before this date, and many may be very much older. Much of their original construction would have been carried out on a piecemeal basis, gradually and directly from the original woodlands, always by hand, and usually with only small medieval implements. It frequently included the digging of a trench, with the soil removed incorporated into the 'hedge', whilst stones already lying at or near the surface of the surrounding fields were used to 'face' the superstructure. The bank was then traditionally capped by turves and left as grass, or, more usually, planted with a quickset hedge of Oak, Ash or Hazel. So constructed, such hedgebanks and lanebanks have a mark of permanence against the elements, and have usually changed little since their original construction.

In bleak, windswept upland parts of south-west England, only a few species of pteridophyte are usually present on the hedgebanks, and those which succeed are generally of low stature or grow deeply recessed within fissures of the banks. *Polypodium* is a particularly distinctive genus of usually the tops of the banks in exposed sites, and either Common Polypody (*Polypodium vulgare*) or low-growing plants of Western Polypody (*P. interjectum*), but especially the latter, may occur in

Polypodium interjectum has its rhizomes deeply recessed between massive stone blocks, and is a frequent member of the flora of both the sides and tops of western hedgebanks. West Cornwall, October

extensive windswept patches, with fronds of a markedly yellow-green colour and fleshy texture. *Polypodium* here is often · accompanied by low-growing flowering plants of Stonecrop (*Sedum*) and Thyme (*Thymus praecox*). On the sides of these same banks, small plants of Black Spleenwort (*Asplenium adiantum-nigrum*) occupy only dark narrow recesses, and sometimes stunted plants of Maidenhair Spleenwort (*Asplenium trichomanes* subsp. *quadrivalens*) are also present. There may also be scattered and usually stunted specimens of Common Male Fern (*Dryopteris filix-mas*), Soft Shield-fern (*Polystichum setiferum*), Hart's Tongue (*Phyllitis scolopendrium*), and, where pockets of more acidic humus accumulate, occasional Golden-scaled Male-fern (*Dryopteris affinis* subsp. *borreri*), Lady Fern (*Athyrium filix-femina*) or Broad Buckler-fern (*Dryopteris dilatata*) in their sheltered lees. On the tops of windswept moors such as Bodmin Moor, the low, stony banks typically also have many plants of Hard Fern (*Blechnum spicant*) along their bases, and observations suggest that in such sites this fern has become much less frequent through the last half-century (E. W. M. Magor, personal communication).

In the more sheltered situations, however, which characterise the very great majority of low-altitude hedgebanks along tracks, paths, lanes, bridle-ways and roads descending along

Polystichum setiferum *is a very widespread and sometimes frequent member of ancient hedgebank communities, especially of deep water-lanes. West Cornwall, August*

narrow coombes to the sea, the luxuriance, abundance and diversity of ferns present increases greatly. Indeed, in the sheltered lanebanks of South Devon and the water-lanes of the Channel Islands, ferns may dominate the banks. Here, many of the species seen in more exposed sites come much more into vegetative prominence, with the most abundant usually being Hart's-tongue (*Phyllitis scolopendrium*) and Soft Shield-fern (*Polystichum setiferum*). Indeed, the luxuriance of these two species, and especially *Phyllitis*, may very largely replace *Polypodium* in some coastal sites. Mostly in south Devon, Hard Shield-fern (*Polystichum aculeatum*) and Lowland Hybrid Shield-fern (*P.* × *bicknellii*) are sometimes also present, mainly on soil slopes at the bases of banks. On very many sheltered hedgebanks, Black Spleenwort (*Asplenium adiantum-nigrum*) remains an often abundant species, especially in sites where there is not dense tree overgrowth, and occurs both in the deep interstices of the rock wall matrices and on accumulations of earth at the foot of the banks, especially on their sunnier aspects. Here this species, like *Phyllitis scolopendrium* and *Polystichum setiferum*, is particularly variable in size and in many details of the form and cutting of the frond, even in single localities. Specimens with unusually finely divided fronds (notably in parts of South Devon) are sometimes strongly

Asplenium adiantum-nigrum, *in widely varying forms, are particularly abundant colonists of ancient hedgebank communities, almost wherever such structures exist in our western landscapes. West Cornwall, September*

reminiscent of the related *Asplenium onopteris*, which is, so far as is known, confined to lanebank sites only in southern Ireland, where it has an unusually finely dissected frond form compared with its continental European equivalents. In other lanebanks at low altitude, especially in south-west England and the Channel Islands, *A.adiantum-nigrum* may be joined by Lanceolate Spleenwort (*A. billotii*). This species has a size and blade dissection not greatly different from that of *A. adiantum-nigrum*, and when it grows deeply recessed between boulders, with only the tips of its fronds emerging, may be easily over-looked. Old field records suggest that *Asplenium billotii* is also much scarcer today in south-west England in this habitat than it was a century or more ago, but still occurs very widely in the hedgebanks of the Channel Islands. It occurs mainly on hedgebanks which are sheltered but sunny and which enjoy considerable winter warmth through close proximity to the sea. Occasional plants in these habitats in South Devon and in the Channel Islands also look near, in their frond form, to the European Obovate Spleenwort (*Asplenium obovatum*), which grows in adjacent Brittany, and which some of these British plants may be.

The several species of *Asplenium* in these lanebank sites are occasionally also involved in hybridisation both with each other and also with the related Hart's Tongue (*Phyllitis scolopendrium*), which is in the same family (Aspleniaceae). Taking first the purely *Asplenium* hybrids, the one with the most numerous lanebank stations is Guernsey Spleenwort (*Asplenium ×
sarniense*), recorded as scattered individuals in various parts of the south and west of Guernsey, in one locality with over 20

A sheltered, Guernsey bridle-track flanked by ancient hedgebanks where over 20 plants of Asplenium × sarniense *grow. South-west Guernsey, early April*

plants along about quarter of a mile of a single sheltered bridle-track. A second *Asplenium* hybrid, Hybrid Black Spleenwort (*A.* × *ticinense*), the hybrid between *A. adiantum-nigrum* and *A. onopteris*, is known only from the area of occurrence of the *A. onopteris* parent in southern Ireland. But as *A. onopteris* could yet be found elsewhere, especially in south-west England or the Channel Islands, so could this hybrid; whilst *A.* × *sarniense* might also yet be found in lanebank habitats of the mainland parts of south-west England where both parents occur. The three remaining hybrids of various species of *Asplenium* all have *Phyllitis scolopendrium* as their other parent. Confluent Maidenhair Spleenwort (× *Asplenophyllitis confluens*), the hybrid of *Asplenium trichomanes* subsp. *quadrivalens* × *Phyllitis scolopendrium*, is known in lanebank habitats in south-western Ireland as well as in damp, shaded wall habitats further north in England (north-east Yorkshire and Westmorland). Jackson's

× Asplenophyllitis microdon, *here with both parents, is apparently restricted to such hedgebank communities. South-west Guernsey, late March*

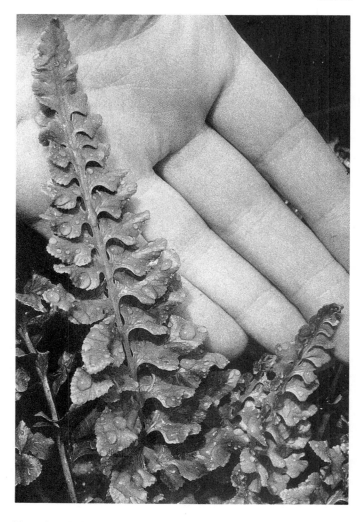

× Asplenophyllitis microdon, *which inherits its unusual appearance from parents which have very different structures. South-west Guernsey, April*

Fern (× *Asplenophyllitis jacksonii*), whose parents are *Asplenium adiantum-nigrum* × *Phyllitis scolopendrium*, was known in the mid-19th century from widely scattered stations in the Channel Islands, Devon and Cornwall, growing in similar lanebank habitats to Black Spleenwort. Guernsey Fern (× *Asplenophyllitis microdon*), which is *Asplenium billotii* × *Phyllitis scolopendrium*, is known wild still today in the Channel Islands (Guernsey) and as unconfirmed 19th century records also from Cornwall, Devon and Wales. In hedgebank habitats of south-west England or southern Ireland almost any of these hybrids too could yet be refound.

Plants of *Polypodium* are also often extremely abundant in sheltered lanebank habitats in south-west England and southern Ireland. Western Polypody (*Polypodium interjectum*) is perhaps the most frequently encountered, being aptly described by the Cornish botanist L. J. Margetts as the 'most abundant Polypody in the Lizard where it often makes a continuous fringe at shoulder height on the Cornish hedges'. Common Polypody (*P. vulgare*) is more typical of inland acidic sites in Devon and Cornwall. Southern Polypody (*P. australe*) may also be present on hedgebanks where base-yielding rocks have been incorporated, such as in the vicinity of the Devonshire limestones and in many places in southern Ireland. All of these species of *Polypodium* show considerable environmentally-induced variation in these habitats, mostly related to exposure, but *P. interjectum* and *P. australe* also show considerable genetic variation in frond form, even sometimes between different plants in the same locality, some plants of each having variously cut, lobed or serrated pinnae. Diagnosis of species of these hedgebank polypodies is further complicated by the occurrence of at least one hybrid between them, that of *P. interjectum* × *vulgare* (= *P.* × *mantoniae*) in this habitat. This plant is probably not rare in hedgebanks, and other hybrids may occur near to sites for *P. australe*.

On permanently moist, mainly south-facing lanebanks, where there is slight regular erosion of soft clay surfaces, the Annual Fern (*Anogramma leptophylla*) occurs very locally in the Channel Islands of Guernsey and Jersey. The annual habit of this small fern, with erect fronds seldom more than about 10 cm in height, is particularly unusual among pteridophytes. Plants regenerate anew each spring, presumably from spores shed from one or more previous years' generations, which have overwintered as young prothalli. Sporophytes begin to appear by late March, after which they rapidly produce fronds of successively increasing size. In its Guernsey site at least, *Anogramma* is known to have persisted along the same length of a single south-facing lanebank for more than a century, although constant annual recolonisations seem involved.

Man's regular cutting of the verge sides (formerly by scythe, nowadays more often by tractor) probably helps to maintain the fern communities by reducing the heights and seed-bearing properties of any surrounding flowering plant vegetation. Nevertheless, numerous flowering plants do usually occur, varying in density from sparsely scattered individuals to a fairly toughly interwoven mass. Species particularly frequently associated with ferns include Ivy (*Hedera helix*), Wall Pennywort (*Umbelicus rupestris*), Red Campion (*Silene dioica*), Lesser Celandine (*Ranunculus ficaria*), Herb Robert (*Geranium robertianum*), Wood Sage (*Teucrium scorodonia*), Slender False-Brome (*Brachypodium sylvaticum*) and Cock's-foot (*Dactylis glomerata*). Cuckoo-pint (*Arum maculatum*) sometimes occurs along the bottoms of fern-rich hedgebanks whilst hawthorn (*Crataegus monogyna*) in sheltered sites and Gorse (*Ulex europaeus*) in more exposed ones are now amongst the most frequent shrubs capping their tops.

Two evolutionarily interesting aspects of the many ferns of these hedgebanks are the great variation shown between individuals in very many of the fern species present and, secondly, the large number of hybrids which occur from time to time. These two aspects are, I suspect, not unrelated. For very much of the variation in the several species of ferns in which it occurs (especially *Polystichum, Phyllitis, Asplenium, Polypodium*) appears to be genetic in origin, and the frequent appearance of structural differences even between neighbouring individuals in single sites suggests a degree of genetic diversity not usually encountered in the populations of ferns of other man-made habitats. The frequency of inter-specific hybridisation may itself also be in part a reflection of this genetic diversity. This variation is of special interest in relation to the age and method of origin of the hedgebank habitats themselves.

The stones originally incorporated into the banks were usually ones which had already long lain exposed to the elements and hence existed in a considerably weathered condition even before their ancient incorporation into these sites. The habitats we see within the hedgebanks today thus differ from place to place according to the local stone used. The stones used were seldom moved far by man, and in the largely unglaciated regions of Britain in which these lanebanks exist, such stones are usually relatively typical of the particular locus of the bank. Over Devon, Cornwall and the Channel Islands they include, for example, granites, diorites, syenites, felsites, gneiss, quartzites, sandstones, shales, mudstones, limestones, conglomerates, dolerites, gabbros, serpentines and schists set within locally dug soils which themselves include alluvium, clays, marls, and silts, thus producing complex matrices of mineral and base availability, but each distinctive to the area in which it occurs. Their construction at a time when the surrounding vegetation probably existed in relatively undamaged condition, almost certainly made these lanebanks available for colonisation by an initial immigration of fern populations incorporating a wide cross-section of local and ancient genetic variation. It is thus my belief that, for the pteridophytes, the hedgebank habitat has acted subsequently as a uniquely important refuge for this variation, through an especially long period of historic time.

Hedgerows and Ditches

Hedgerows, often with ditches beside them, form a conspicuous feature of the landscapes of much of rural, and especially lowland, Britain and Ireland. Indeed, they are a feature of most parts of western Europe, wherever the climate is particularly suitable for the growth of pasture grasses and there has been a need to include or exclude browsing stock.

In these islands, the history of hedgerows is one of progressive enclosure of land over a very long period of human history. In Britain, some hedgerows result from enclosures which probably date back to Roman times. Others are perhaps Norman. Very many date from the time of growth of the wool trade under the Tudors between about 1485 and 1600, and later, with increased arable production and the Enclosure Acts between about 1760 and 1830. In many cases, fields were enclosed directly from former common grazing land (rather than usually from the original forest, as were the southwestern hedgebanks). The lines of the hedgerows created were often irregular and formed irregularly-shaped fields in earlier plantings or more regular ones with later plantings. Although the initial fauna was limited, hedgerows have, over the intervening period of time, gradually evolved a greater diversity of species. Slowly, the species present have come to form fairly characteristic communities within a uniquely linear habitat.

The general effects of a hedge are to cause windspeed to decrease and become more diffuse in its lee, whilst also providing an aspect of greater shade, ground moisture and longer snow-lie. Although the woodier parts of the hedgerow may well have been subject to periodic disturbance over a very long period of time, especially where intermittently coppiced or cut-and-laid, the ground beneath and immediately around will have probably remained relatively undisturbed since the date when the hedge was originally founded.

Although hedgerows are seldom the sites of very luxuriant pteridophyte growth, old hedgerows blend together certain features of both ancient woodland, ancient pasture and woodland margin habitats, whilst also occasionally including areas of banking and stone retaining work. Where ditches run parallel to hedges, new habitats which have more affinity in their species with marshes and seepage lines may be brought into close array with the miniature shrubbery of the hedge. Hedges and ditches thus allow unusual mixtures of species to grow in particularly close proximity, and have acted as refuges, albethey less ancient ones than south-western hedgebanks, for a small range of ferns and fern-allies. Amongst these, those of several different elements can be recognised.

The woodland element is represented in the hedgerow pteridophytes mainly by a number of larger statured ferns, particularly of the genus *Dryopteris*. The most frequent is Common Male Fern (*Dryopteris filix-mas*), which is very widely spread in hedgerow communities throughout lowland Britain, especially those of not excessive acidity. It is also accompanied in many areas by Common Golden-scaled Male Fern (*D. affinis* subsp. *borreri*), Broad Buckler-fern (*D. dilatata*), Lady Fern (*Athyrium filix-femina*) and sometimes by Hard Fern (*Blechnum spicant*), the latter two especially in moister sites and on more shaded aspects. Around the hedgerow, especially on verges and banks, Common Horsetail (*Equisetum arvense*) may also be frequent. In upland districts, various subspecies of Golden-scaled Male Fern may come especially into prominence, with an increase too in the frequency of Hard Fern, and here these pteridophytes may be accompanied, in sheltered hedgerow sites in valleys, by scattered specimens of Mountain Fern (*Oreopteris limbosperma*) and by patches of Wood Horsetail (*Equisetum sylvaticum*). By contrast, in lowland western districts, especially on base-rich clays, the large Robust Golden-scaled Male Fern (*Dryopteris affinis* subsp. *robusta*) occurs widely in the hedgerows of moist, sheltered valleys, where it is usually accompanied by Soft Shield-fern (*Polystichum setiferum*) and Hart's Tongue (*Phyllitis scolopendrium*). The latter, in particular, may also be associated with the sides of adjacent ditches, where the greater shelter and enhanced moisture enables each plant to sometimes reach a large size. Where hedgerows and their adjacent ditches occur in valley sites in sedimentary rocks, these can sometimes be colonised by dense and spectacular stands of the Great Horsetail (*Equisetum telmateia*), usually marking sites of emerging seeping, base-rich water over heavy clay substrates.

The marsh and aquatic element, in the form of two other species of horsetail, the Marsh Horsetail (*Equisetum palustre*) and the Water Horsetail (*Equisetum fluviatile*), can become well represented within hedgerow ditches in many localities. The former is the more common of these, attaining an appreciable frequency in higher rainfall habitats of the west and north and with moderately increasing altitude, although it is certainly present in such habitats at least as far south as Gloucestershire. It seems to be associated mainly with fairly eutrophic drainage, and common associates include Water Mints (*Mentha* spp.), Water forget-me-not (*Myosotis* spp., mostly *M. scorpioides*), Marsh Marigold (*Caltha palustris*), Yellow Flag (*Iris pseudacorus*) and scattered rushes (*Juncus* spp.). Water Horsetail, whilst sharing an essentially western and northern distribution in ditch habitats (and by no means necessarily always associated with traditional hedgerows in the more windswept corners of these islands), occurs in ditch habitats which are shared with *E. palustre*, as well as in ones which are considerably more oligotrophic and in which the water is also deeper, more stagnant and acidic.

The pasture element is represented by the occurrence of the Adder's-tongue (*Ophioglossum vulgatum*). In lowland sites, this species can sometimes reach a considerable size in hedgerows, benefiting not only from shade and shelter but especially from a certain degree of protection from grazing and especially freedom from ploughing, a type of disturbance to which this species seems especially sensitive.

Under the influence of differing conditions of soil type, age and history of the hedge, as well as at differing locations, wide variation occurs in the associated species which form the hedgerow. Associated herbaceous species noted with many of these ferns include Garlic Mustard (*Allaria petiolata*), Hedge Mustard (*Sisymbrium officinale*), Hedge Parsley (*Torilis japonica*), Lesser Celandine (*Ranunculus ficaria*), Buttercups (*R. acris* and *R. bulbosus*), Wood Anemone (*Anemone nemorosa*), Bluebell (*Hyacinthoides non-scriptus*), Ground Ivy (*Glechoma hederacea*), Wild Arum (*Arum maculatum*), Greater Stichwort (*Stellaria holostea*), Red and White Deadnettle (*Lamium purpureum* and *L. album*), Goosegrass (*Galium aparine*), Red Campium (*Silene dioica*), Self-heal (*Prunella vulgaris*), Dandelion (*Taraxacum officinale* agg.), Yarrow (*Achillea millefolium*), Lesser Knapweed (*Centaurea nigra*), Wood Cranesbill (*Geranium sylvaticum*), Herb Robert (*G. robertianum*), Wood Avens (*Geum urbanum*), Violets (*Viola* spp., especially *V. odorata*, *V. riviniana* and *V. reichenbachiana*), Primrose (*Primula vulgaris*), Cowslip (*P. veris*), Bugle (*Ajuga reptans*), and Hedge Bedstraw (*Galium mollugo*). By roadsides in particular, such hedgerows and their ditches are often fringed with a great number of meadow grasses as well as numerous umbellifers, such as Cow Parsley (*Anthriscus sylvestris*), Rough Chervil (*Chaerophyllum temulentum*) and Hogweed (*Heracleum sphondylium*). An assemblage with a very high species diversity is especially characteristic of old hedgerows on the moister, heavier and more calcareous soils of the lowlands of central and southern England. Today, in areas where woodlands have been felled, where pastures have been ploughed up and where marshes and ponds have been extensively drained, the habitats of remaining hedgerows and ditches provide significant refuges for at least some of the species of the former habitats around them. The more mature hedgerows consequently attract appropriate conservation interest, especially in such well-manicured and extensively cultivated landscapes as those of the English shires.

Walls and Stonework

One type of wall, the field and boundary wall, is a common and distinctive feature of very many of our rural landscapes throughout Britain and Ireland, in both lowlands and uplands, almost wherever there was an appropriate availability of local surface stone. Some such walls may be as much as 1,000 years old. Many others were completed in the 12th century, although most have been extensively repaired and reconstructed since. Although such field and boundary walls are occasionally mortared, extensively and traditionally they were of mainly drystone (ie. mortarless) construction. On such walls today, occasional ferns may occur amongst their moss and lichen floras, mainly emerging from deep within the crevices. But their pteridological interest is mainly limited to the sometimes extensive cappings of *Polypodium* which can occur along their crests, especially on old walls in rural areas of the most frequent precipitation, for which they are an appropriate indicator.

Asplenium ruta-muraria *dominating the rupestral community of a wall of mortared, random blocks of Carboniferous limestone. North Yorkshire, July*

By contrast, very many other old walls which were originally built of stonework or brickwork which was mortared with lime-rich cements, occur in a very great range of settings in both the rural and urban areas in our landscape. It is especially walls of these types which may have a considerable pteridophyte diversity colonising between their stone or brick courses today, once the mortar with which they were built is sufficiently decayed.

Although Neolithic Britons constructed some of their huts and tombs of stone at least 5,000 years ago, it was the Romans who probably first imported more sophisticated techniques of stone-cutting and building. More especially, it was the pioneering introduction of cement begun in Britain by the Romans that began the creation of such lime-rich wall ('mural') habitats.

Although the technology for the assembly of such structures appears to have been largely lost with the departure of the Romans, what the Romans built in various forms remained long after their departure.

Further new mortared structures, however, began appearing in the landscape following the Norman conquest at the beginning of the Middle Ages, and these structures took several principal forms. Castles of many types and sizes were constructed through the British and Irish landscape, usually at sites of prime strategic importance—near to towns or trade routes, crossing points of rivers or their highest navigable points, or at the heads of important valleys and passes. Castles of mortared stone were built principally from about the 12th century onwards, often replacing earlier earthen and wooden structures on the same site. Stone was preferred and widely adopted not only because of its lasting qualities, but because of its resistance to the then current methods of attack, whilst high walls also provided better vantage for defence. Their buttressed sides helped further shore them against picking and battering during attack as could thick walls, which were often

Detail of the Rue-like fronds of Asplenium ruta-muraria *growing on an old, lime-mortared, exposed wall. West Lothian, August*

infilled with mortar rubble. Inside, such castles usually had further elaborate stonework, including towers and stairs, stores, living quarters, armories and keeps. Damp stonework would have surrounded troughs, wells and fountains, whilst outside, stone-lined, water-filled moats surrounded many later lowland castles. The construction of such castles on similar general principles continued apace until about the end of the 15th century. After this date, castles themselves became neglected, for they had, by now, usually outlived their primary usefulness as fortifications. Some continued to be added to or modified throughout the 16th and 17th centuries, usually as mansions. Most castles, however, if not already war-damaged and battered, began, after about 1600, to gradually succumb to the inevitable processes of slow and steady dismemberment. Such castles, by the very nature of their original construction as bastions of defence, consumed a very great deal of stone and mortar. Their ruggedness of construction has meant that they have had a particularly lasting pteridological effect, and today, where not restored, often survive as important and relatively ancient mural fern sites in varying states of botanically healthy decay.

Numerous other types of buildings were also constructed of mortared stonework during this period. Ecclesiastical

Fern colonists including Dryopteris filix-mas *and* Pteridium aquilinum, *now take advantage of the exposure of numerous layers of old mortar in the broken edge of a stone-built, former stable-block. West Argyll, July*

buildings, for example, included not only very numerous churches, throughout the length and depths of the countryside, but also many monasteries by the end of the 14th century, and importantly from a pteridological point of view, many of these were surrounded by mortared walls. Towns also became a common feature of the rural landscape by the 14th century, as they had been in Roman times, and there was a great wave of house building between about 1570 and 1640. Towns brought into use not only a great number of new walls, roofs and often leaking gutters, but also roads, and where these crossed rivers, bridges were needed. Stone bridges began to be built in the 12th and 13th centuries, and a great many in the period from about 1350 to 1500. During this period too, and nearer to the sea, a great many strong, stone-built harbours and associated harbour walls were first constructed giving further man-made habitats for ferns to colonise.

Even by the 15th century, brick was not widely used in any of these constructions, especially so in areas where natural building stone was locally abundant. And although brickworks are known to have been in operation in England in areas such as Suffolk from about the latter half of the 12th century, brick did not become a commonplace material for small houses until about the end of the 17th century. It was, however, used more extensively before this for larger houses, and became thus ultimately used too for associated outbuildings and for walled garden walls from about Tudor times onwards. Many of these now dilapidated outbuildings and old walled-garden walls survive today as notable examples of early brickwork that has often not been subsequently extensively maintained or restored. Because they are also frequently habitats which are also in rural settings which may be relatively more free of modern air-pollution than are most walls in larger modern cities, such rural structures in moister districts may bear ferns in particular abundance in their mortared courses, whose current species content and populations may well have resided there little changed over several centuries.

The pteridophyte species of walls are, for the most part, very widely spread throughout both Britain and Ireland, especially in lowland sites. These wall ferns can be grouped approximately into two general habitat categories: those species predominantly of wall crevices occurring mostly in the mortar courses on the sides of walls, and those species whose main habitats are the flatter aspects of wall tops. Although the species of the two sites may merge on a broad fringe, the habitats which they each exploit often display conspicuous differences in the balance of the communities present and are thus here treated separately.

Wall Sides

Wall sides are usually predominantly colonised by mostly small-statured species of ferns, and what each lacks in size is often redressed by the occurrence of sometimes large numbers of individuals. In these habitats, two fern species are almost equally common throughout much of Britain and Ireland. These are Maidenhair Spleenwort (*Asplenium trichomanes*) and Wall Rue (*A. ruta-muraria*). The former occurs on walls from sea level up to at least 2,000 feet (around 610 m) elevation, whilst the latter is more usual at altitudes beneath about 1,200 feet (about 560 m). Throughout much of Britain and Ireland, the usual form of *Asplenium trichomanes* to be found in these habitats is its subspecies *quadrivalens*, which is the more calcicolous of the two native subspecies. Much more locally, in higher rainfall districts of the extreme west of Scotland, I have occasionally seen *A. trichomanes* subsp. *trichomanes* totally replacing it in very great abundance on old walled-garden walls, in sites where excessive leaching, resulting from the high and frequent rainfall, has presumably helped reduce the undoubted potential quantity of available bases.

Asplenium trichomanes *subsp.* quadrivalens *frequently grows well on old lime-mortared walls in districts of high rainfall, here amongst blocks of Lake District slate.* Westmorland, *July*

Both Maidenhair Spleenwort and Wall Rue show a high structural plasticity with exposure in these sites, especially in size. The most luxuriant plants of both are generally confined to the more shaded aspects of walls, although both may occur in very large numbers in a diminutive form even on exposed aspects, especially in cloudier districts. A particularly vivid example of this occurs widely, for example, on many cemented stone walls in the vicinity of the extreme north-east coast of England and that of south-east Scotland. Here, each species becomes locally frequent on walls only in a very thin strip of land lying within a few miles distance of the North Sea. It is my impression that this local abundance corresponds closely with the zone of highest frequency of landward-drift of cold, damp, summer sea-fogs which occur during settled high-pressure summer weather in these districts, when adjacent inland districts (and often the rest of the country) are receiving exceptionally sunny conditions.

Generally less abundant on walls than either of the above species of *Asplenium*, is Black Spleenwort, *Asplenium adiantum-nigrum*. It occurs here and there in wall mortar, mainly in westerly and south-westerly areas and near coasts, in a variety of wall sites including ones of considerable exposure. In the most exposed sites, its fronds can be little larger than those of *A. ruta-muraria*, and are usually held rather closely to

The intricate architecture, squared pinnae and somewhat sinuously-winding fronds of asplenium trichomanes *subsp.* quadrivalens *in wall-mortar. West Argyll, late July*

the wall surfaces. In more sheltered sites it becomes larger and
its frond more spreading. Amongst its wall mortar sites, there
seem to be a large number of localities in which the walls are of
brick, rather than stone, and it seems especially frequent on
brick bridgework and on old, brick-built, walled-garden walls
of large estates. Often it occurs as the sole species of wall fern
present, or may form communities with *A. trichomanes* and *A.
ruta-muraria*. Occasionally, on the Welsh, Devonshire,
Cornish, and Channel Island coasts, I have seen it colonising
the mortar layers of old harbour walls, where the more
common wall ferns are usually absent, and where *Asplenium
adiantum-nigrum* sometimes forms communities with scattered
plants of Lanceolate Spleenwort *A. billotii*, which also occasionally and very locally spreads into these same sites. In such
habitats, both species can range to within the boundaries of the
splash zone of the sea, where they merge with and are largely
replaced by Sea Spleenwort (*Asplenium marinum*) in the more
spray-exposed mortar layers of such old harbour walls.

Also sometimes present on walls, usually in diminutive form,
is Hart's Tongue Fern (*Phyllitis scolopendrium*). It seems characteristic of highly lime-yielding (and presumably rapidly-
degrading) mortar of walls which are sheltered and more or
less permanently damp and shaded. It occurs, for example, on
the footings of many old walled-garden walls, but is especially
characteristic of retaining-walls of all types, from scattered
plants in brick-built city basement stairways in northern
English and Scottish towns to the mill walls of canalised
stretches of river backwaters in northern English mill towns
such as Leeds and Sheffield, to the limestone-block retaining
walls of clear-flowing streams through towns such as Oxford.
In the most shaded and sheltered of these sites, it may also be
accompanied by Brittle Bladder-fern (*Cystopteris fragilis*).

In brighter positions, and especially in oceanic districts of
Britain and Ireland, a widespread and always attractive wall
fern is Rusty-back Fern (*Ceterach officinarum*). Most of its sites
are at fairly low altitude and mainly under about 600 feet (ca.
180 m). It is most common on lime-rich walls, especially those
built of lime mortar (see below) and using natural limestone
blocks, and hence has a patchy distribution generally following
the main areas of limestone outcrops, northward to Yorkshire
and with sporadic local occurrences at least as far north as
central Scotland (to east Perthshire). It reaches its greatest
abundance, however, in wall-mortar habitats in southern
Britain, such as on walls around the outcrops of the Devonian
limestones in south Devon, and on the Carboniferous limestone walls of western Ireland, especially in Counties Clare and
Limerick.

Rusty-back Fern is evergreen and fairly slow-growing, and each year its fronds expand only slowly. It is, however, probably a fairly long-lived species, and on old walls which have been long undisturbed, it is sometimes a highly gregarious plant. It thrives most on exposed and sunny aspects of walls, where plants are clearly tolerant of strong light and sometimes of considerable periods of summer baking and desiccation, and becomes weakened and excluded from excessively dank conditions, such as from walls beneath dense overtopping tree growth. Its overall western and south-western abundance probably reflects a preference of the species for mild winter conditions, as well, perhaps, as reasonable summer sun. It also undoubtedly thrives best where there is year-round high humidity and a long growing season, in sites where mild winter temperatures allow the plant to benefit most fully from its slow-growing evergreen condition.

In its sites over most of Britain, the lobed edges of the fronds are relatively smooth. In parts of south-west England, west Wales and especially over much of Ireland, however, populations of a generally larger form of the plant seem widespread, and these also have more regularly scalloped margins of the frond lobes, and sometimes a particularly curious habit of bearing two annual generations of mature sporangia successively on the same frond—a unique character, as far as I am aware, in any pteridophyte. Preliminary experiments suggest that these characteristics are genetically determined, and support the view of Irish botanists who have long recognised such plants as *Ceterach officinarum* var. *crenatum*.

On brick-built retaining walls of sites such as city stairways, surface acidification plus the progress of regular seepage of often less than base-rich water through the brick and mortarwork from the soil behind, can make suitable habitats for the occurrence of surprisingly acid-loving species, which, if shelter is adequate, can develop to sometimes large size. An exactly similar range of species also turns up in both city and rural areas clustering in surprisingly large and verdant summer patches on damp brickwork resulting from more-or-less permanently leaking gutters on old buildings, from domestic tenement blocks to industrial warehouses and factories. Amongst the unlikely sounding array of species of ferns which may be quite frequent in such sites are Broad Buckler-fern (*Dryopteris dilatata*), Common and Golden-scaled Male-ferns (*D. filix-mas* and *D. affinis* subsp. *borreri*), Lady Fern (*Athyrium filix-femina*), and most surprisingly but commonly, Bracken (*Pteridium aquilinum*). The latter occurs in a most delicate-appearing and initially attractive, virtually permanently juvenile-foliaged form in such sites, looking totally unlike its adult self, and even botanists can often be quite disbelieving to learn of its real identity.

Wall Tops

The second type of habitat offered by walls is the wall top. Tops of newly-built free-standing walls are usually finished with a capping layer of bricks or larger stones, often laid on end. But when derelict, broken wall tops may expose the mortar of their former courses as well as, in thicker walls (such as those of old castles), surfaces of sometimes extensive infilling rubble and mortar which may be quite soft and highly retentive of moisture. Wall tops thus differ from the mortar-course habitats of wall sides in being larger, more variable habitats which are more directly exposed to both light and rain, and which are far more likely to readily accumulate debris to form pockets of rudimentary soils. Arthropods of all types (including insects, arachnids and crustaceans) commonly colonise such developing habitats, and may gradually bring in both additional minerals and deposit nitrogen-rich detritus, adding to the enrichment of the habitat for plants. With time, habitats more suited than the wall sides for the establishment of larger plants begin to form. As with wall sides, shelter and humidity are particularly important physical factors which help determine the success of establishing wall top vegetation. It is typical that both habitats can be rich in pleurocarpous mosses, but these may be particularly extensive on the broken tops of old walls in a state of disrepair.

On wall tops in many places, ferns are especially characteristic of the early seral stages of such colonisation, but particularly in humid, shaded wall sites in western oceanic climates, where they may often persist to become the permanent dominants of these communities.

All of the ferns of wall sides occur also to some extent on wall tops. This is especially so in areas of highest humidity and under conditions of greatest shade. A spectacular example of this can be the extensive capping of walls by Rusty-back Fern (*Ceterach officinarum* var. *crenatum*), which at low altitude near west coasts in Ireland, for example, can form a dense and locally-extensive wall-top capping.

Almost all of the wall mortar ferns can spread, from time to time, to occupy wall top habitats, although they are usually less numerous in these sites than in the greater shelter of the wall sides, and usually occur only as more scattered plants.

The wall-top fern genus par excellence is, however, *Polypodium*. All three native species may be present in wall top sites, depending, to a large extent, on location and on the building material of the wall.

Common Polypody (*Polypodium vulgare*) occurs in such sites almost throughout Britain and Ireland, and is usually a colonist of the most acidic wall tops. It sometimes forms extensive patches, but seldom so extensive as those of the next species.

Western Polypody (*Polypodium interjectum*) is almost everywhere, the most generally abundant wall-top fern, succeeding on a great variety of substrates, but particularly on those which are less acidic than those colonised by *P. vulgare*. *Polypodium interjectum* is present very widely on wall tops almost throughout Britain and Ireland, but with a particular abundance in the west. Here, it occurs fairly frequently along the tops of older walls, sometimes forming a dense capping which, here and there, and especially in cloudier and wetter western counties, can sometimes stretch along the tops of roadside walls as far as the eye can see. Although it is the largest of the three native species of *Polypodium*, it is also the most generally successful in the majority of wall-top habitats, and especially those of free-standing, boundary and roadside walls. In origins, Western Polypody is the allohexaploid hybrid derived by doubling of the chromosomes of the cross between the other two native species: *Polypodium australe* (which is diploid and base-loving) and *P. vulgare* (which is tetraploid and acid-loving). Part of its success in such man-made habitats is probable due to this origin. It succeeds particularly well in wall-top sites not only because of its inherent vigour and apparent edaphic flexibility around conditions of more or less intermediate base status, but also because it displays a very considerably adaptability and plasticity in structural form and frond texture. On the tops of shaded walls, such as along old stone estate-boundary walls, extensive stands of this species may reach their maximum development and luxuriance, with dark green fronds as much as 40–50 cm or more in length. By contrast, on the tops of exposed walls at low altitude near the sea, Western Polypody may occur in a very small and salt-spray resistant form, with fronds often under 10 cm in length and sometimes much smaller, which are of a notably yellow green colour, and in which the markedly thick texture of the lamina resulting from the high ploidy level of this species is of considerable ecological advantage.

The last species of wall fern is probably the strongest calcicole amongst them. This is Southern Polypody (*Polypodium australe*). It too very occasionally occurs on free-standing, boundary walls at low altitude, mainly in southern and western Britain and Ireland. It does so especially on well-broken walls which have exposed extensive old mortar courses, and seems to be somewhat the converse of Black Spleenwort (*Asplenium adiantum-nigrum*) in these sites. It rarely occurs on brick-built walls, preferring usually very old mortared stone walls which also contain a high proportion of base-yielding natural rock in their construction, especially of limestone. I have also seen it on walls made with other rocks, including calciferous Old Red Sandstones, chlorite schists and basic andesitic lavas.

Polyodium australe is, however, the species par excellence of old castles, especially in southern and western Britain, and especially of castles which have fallen into a state of reasonable dereliction exposing the lime-mortar of their original construction and the lime-rich, rubbly fill of their thick wall interiors. In such sites, dense cappings of Southern Polypody in moss-rich associations may come to dominate almost every horizontal surface of the castle walls, over the tops of windows, around high turrets, along old battlements and ledges, and over the broken tops of almost every internal wall. Good examples of castles noted by the author, although there are probably many others, in which extensive growths of Southern Polypody are established, include Berry Pomeroy Castle in south Devon, Carew Castle in Pembrokeshire, and Wigmore Castle in Herefordshire. At the times of visits to the former two sites, teams of workers seemed to be especially employed to go around pulling off this relatively harmless plant. In my view, both this tendency and that for broadcast application to the stonework of such ancient castles of herbicides to rid them of their vegetation as an automatic 'first step' in their architectural preservation, seems totally insensitive to the rarity of these plants and their unique scientific interest in association with our custodianship of such unique and irreplaceable botanical sites. An area of middle ground in which an approach of considerations of structural safety as well as botanical interest are better combined seems highly desirable. For such vestments of plants seem to add considerably to the melancholy charm of such ancient structures as well as to their scientific interest, for their 'ivy-mantled towers' seem seldom so attractive when preserved stark and naked of their adorning vegetation.

In their great variety of wall sites of all kinds, most of the wall ferns discussed above associate with a varying number of flowering plants as well as sometimes extensive patches of mosses. Some of those noted in sites where several wall ferns are present include Ivy-leaved Toadflax (*Cymbalaria muralis*—especially on drier walls), Smooth Hawk's-beard (*Crepis capillaris*), Dandelion (*Taraxacum officinale* agg.), Ribwort Plantain (*Plantago lanceolata*), Wall Pennywort (*Umbillicus rupestris*), Ivy (*Hedera helix*), Herb Robert (*Geranium robertianum*), Pellitory-of-the-Wall (*Parietaria diffusa*),

Mossy Pearlwort (*Sagina procumbens*), the Meadow grasses *Poa trivialis* and *P. annua*, and the mosses *Tortula muralis, T. tortuosa, Bryum argenteum, B. capillare, Hypnum cupressiforme, Mnium hornum, Ctenidium molluscum, Homalothecium sericium, Ceratodon purpureus, Barbula convoluta, Fissidens taxifolius, F. adianthoides, Atrichum undulatum, Encalypta vulgaris, Neckera crispa, Eurynchium confertum, E. striatum* and *Rhynchostegia murale.*

Polypodium australe is a classic fern species of the mortar courses and infill rubble of well-matured and adequately decayed mediaeval castle walls, such as these at Berry Pomeroy Castle in south Devon, August

Hybrid Ferns in Wall Habitats

In certain localities, man-made walls have provided sites upon which hybrid ferns have occurred.

In high rainfall districts, in both northern England, North Wales and in Ireland, *A. trichomanes* has been known to hybridise with other species of wall fern on a very sporadic and occasional basis. The most famous of these is undoubtedly the formation of the Confluent Maidenhair Spleenwort, × *Asplenophyllitis confluens* (*A. trichomanes* subsp. *quadrivalens* × *Phy-*

llitis scolopendrium), which has been known in north-east Yorkshire, the English Lake district and in Co. Kerry, south-west Ireland. In the latter area, the plant was recently refound after a gap of nearly a century. A second hybrid also known from wall mortar sites is that of Lady Clermont's Spleenwort, *Asplenium × clermontiae* (*A. trichomanes* subsp. *quadrivalens* × *A. ruta-muraria*), an extremely rare hybrid known once only with certainty in the mid-19th century from a mortared wall in Co. Down, Ireland, although a much later unconfirmed record of a similar plant from a wall in Westmoreland may also have been of this hybrid. A third wall mortar hybrid is Hybrid Maidenhair Spleenwort, *Asplenium × lusaticum* (*A. trichomanes* subsp. *quadrivalens* × *A. trichomanes* subsp. *trichomanes*)—ie. the hybrid between the two subspecies of *Asplenium trichomanes* itself. This hybrid has been recorded in Merionethshire in North Wales, by the sharp eyes of a local naturalist to whom I am grateful for showing me the plant, where it is distinct from both parents (both of which grow nearby) not only by its inter-mediate form, but also by its considerably enhanced vigour and its tendency therefore to form large local clumps. All these known wall mortar hybrids, seem, however, remarkably rare considering the frequency with which their parents grow together.

Asplenium ×
lusaticum.
Caernarvonshire, July

The Significance of Wall Habitats

The pteridological and conservational interest in wall habitats stems not just from the presence of a wide range of ferns in them, but because such habitats may contain species that do not occur so numerously (if at all) in other sites in specific localities, and because walls provide habitats for fern communities to have developed often in sites whose history can sometimes be relatively accurately documented. A significant part of this interest and history stems especially from the use by man of cements.

Pre-Roman walls, especially those of domestic buildings, were probably cemented, if at all, with the use of clays, whose use elsewhere certainly stretches back to biblical times. Common limes were amongst the first cementitious materials used, from probably Roman times through a very long period of history, until well into the 1800s. The starting point for the manufacture of common lime cements was always calcium carbonate, $CaCo_3$, usually in the form of natural limestone. Such limestone, when heated, gives rise to calcium oxide or quicklime, CaO, which, when it comes into contact with water, is slaked or hydrated, to form calcium hydroxide, $Ca(OH)_2$, or slaked lime. In the presence of water, calcium hydroxide becomes a cementitious material, for it hardens gradually through progressive evaporation of the water and absorption of atmospheric carbon dioxide, CO_2, to give calcium carbonate, $CaCO_3$, or common lime. This reaction is primarily a surface phenomenon, which does not always run to completion in the deeper interstices of mortar courses. Such common lime mortar, although used as the primary cementing agent throughout the greater part of British and Irish building-construction history, is not very resistant to water, even after surface carbonisation. Its relatively soft texture and rapid rate of decay made it, however, highly lime-yielding, and it is consequently on older walls constructed with very considerable amounts of this substance that persist still today, that often carry the largest numbers of the most base-demanding species of pteridophytes.

Portland cement mortars very widely replaced the use of former common lime mortars from the 1800s in most types of wall construction. Their starting points include the firing not only of natural limestones, but also of clays (which are largely complex aluminium sillicates), and their use includes their amalgamation with specific ratios of building sands. The cements produced are more chemically complex, and produce harder, more durable mortars, which include complex oxides, carbonates and silicates of calcium, magnesium and aluminium, including tricalcium silicates, as well as ferric oxide Fe_2O_3, the hardening reaction taking place slowly over a long period of time, but more evenly throughout the mortar. Their hardness slows down their rate of weathering, although with age, even modern cements are somewhat lime-yielding, and on weathered surfaces, ferns can certainly eventually occur.

The Romans used the technique of building construction with lime-mortared stonework very widely through much of lowland Britain. These included such cemented stone constructional features as towns and rural villages, as well extensive country houses or 'villas'. Much of the history of the spread of lime-loving mural ferns, at least in Britain, thus undoubtedly began as long ago as during the Roman occupation, and today, many species of mural ferns are probably greatly more abundant in areas where they may otherwise not have been, through the history of spread of such mortar habitats through historic time. The Irish botanist R. L. Praeger noted how, in Ireland, Rusty-back Fern (*Ceterach officinarum*) had spread very widely over the country in man-made (mostly limestone) walls, greatly beyond its geographically more limited natural range on outcropping limestone rocks, and this perspective also seems true, I think, for most of the wall ferns in both Britain and Ireland.

Ceterach officinarum in lime-rich mortar on the sunny aspect of a wall of Carboniferous limestone blocks. Monmouthshire, September

Such wall habitats, for the most part, show marked genetic contrasts, I suspect, to the habitats of south-western lanebanks. For whilst lanebank sites might well have helped to preserve samples of local genetic diversity of ferns from the localities in which they were originally made, many walls have probably played a somewhat opposite function for pteridophytes. For they have provided widespread mortar habitats, each with a strong element of similarity to others elsewhere in similar situations, but different from wild habitats occurring in most localities. Between different mural localities, over the course of time, ferns have probably enjoyed a considerable spore mobility, and high selection pressure for success of particular ecotypes in these manifestly artificial habitats. I know of no single natural wild sites, for example, in which *Ceterach officinarum*, *Asplenium trichomanes* or *A. ruta-muraria* are as abundant as they are on wall sites, nor any totally wild site in which *Polypodium australe* is as abundant as it is on old castles. In studying and preserving mural fern habitats, we are undoubtedly dealing with a living legacy which was begun by the Romans, but for which many episodes of our history have helped create new and additional dimensions.

Water Mills and Wells

The interiors of stone- or brick-lined wells and the interiors of mill lathes provide local pteridophyte habitats which are somewhat similar to one another. Both are of particular interest because of their very long period of use and widespread former occurrence through these islands.

Wells, as a source of fresh water, have been a traditional focus of activity in village life wherever freshwater supplies could be gained locally by such means. They were certainly in use from Roman times, and perhaps considerably before. The Romans introduced waterwheels as a means of providing mechanical power, necessitating the construction of water-fed mill lathes. In Britain, mills, driven by waterwheels, remained the major source of power, especially for grinding corn and for the mechanical processes of the woollen industry, through Anglo-Saxon times and the Middle Ages. Indeed, in traditional woollen areas of Britain such as the Cotswolds and the Pennines, water driven mills once existed in almost every watered valley. Further mills, or modifications of earlier ones, for the spinning of cotton made their appearance in Derbyshire and Lancashire from about the 1770s, whilst yet others were used during the 19th century for the processing of linen, jute and hemp.

Asplenium
trichomanes *subsp.*
quadrivalens
*luxuriates on old
mortar beside a flowing
millstream. Mid-
Perthshire, August*

Pteridologically, wells and mill lathes have close similarities. Traditional wells usually consisted of a vertical shaft which was stone- or brick-lined, down which a wooden pail could be lowered to fresh water accumulating in its depths. Mill wheels, dependent on moving water, involved somewhat more elaborate structures. Large wooden wheels were each fed by an artificially-channelled watercourse or leat, and the wheel itself set within a large and usually sunken narrow race. Some of the earliest wheels were set horizontally, to drive millstones above

them. Most later wheels were set vertically, and kept in motion by water passing beneath. There were, however, variations on this widespread 'undershot' arrangement, including variants which were 'overshot' or 'breastshot', in which water fell into buckets on the wheel, which was then turned by their weight. The races of these vertical wheels could be narrow and deep, and, like wells, were usually lined with mortared stone or brick. It is these old races, many dating from the 15–18th centuries, which have often remained the more lasting part of mill structures to be seen today.

The environment created within the well or the mill race would have been one which possessed a high degree of shade and shelter. Within this enclosed local humidity, on the well-drained, moist, brick or mortared stone walls, an environment particularly conducive to the success of ferns was created, and in many cases, ferns were probably particularly long-lived and characteristic denizens of such sites, in which they doubtless occurred very widely.

To judge from surviving structures, different ferns probably occurred on different aspects of such sites, with species also differing from place to place.

In milder, western climates, especially in areas such as the Cotswolds, it seems likely that Rusty-back Fern (*Ceterach officinarum*) would have most usually been present in lighter, drier spots near well mouths and on mortared stonework of mill buildings. Nearer to sea-level and to south-western coasts, Sea Spleenwort (*Asplenium marinum*) may well have been an occasional, unusual member of the wellshaft interior vegetation, and is indeed known to still survive in one such site in the Scilly Isles. More commonly, around the lighter and slightly drier upper reaches of both wellshafts and mill races, species such as Maidenhair Spleenwort (*Asplenium trichomanes*) and Wall Rue (*A. ruta-muraria*) would probably have frequently formed a locally abundant, fringing vegetation, with Black Spleenwort (*A. adiantum-nigrum*) present too in appropriate districts. Indeed, a particularly dense stand of Maidenhair Spleenwort still occurs in one Cotswold well of Roman origin.

By contrast, within the darker interiors of both mill races and wellshafts, in sites too dark for the success of Spleenwort ferns, evidence from surviving structures suggests that other ferns were perhaps often abundant. Handsome specimens of Hard Shield-fern (*Polystichum aculeatum*) still occur in many mill races in northern England and the central lowlands of Scotland, as do generally abundant growths of Male Fern (*Dryopteris filix-mas*), Lady Fern (*Athyrium filix-femina*), and Broad Buckler-fern (*Dryopteris dilatata*), in pockets where humus has accumulated. By contrast, in dark, shaded mortar, Brittle

Cystopteris fragilis *grows well in the still, humid atmosphere on a dark, shaded wall of an old mill leat. Blairgowrie, mid-Perthshire, June*

Bladder-fern (*Cystopteris fragilis*) probably was frequently an abundant and widespread denizen of such sites.

However, on a very widespread geographic basis over these islands, the one fern which probably has been most characteristically associated with both mill race and wellshaft habitats for a very long period of time and in very considerable abundance, is almost certainly Hart's Tongue (*Phyllitis scolopendrium*). In such sites, this fern of unusual appearance was probably very well-known by both urban and rural peoples, becoming the centre of various traditions and beliefs.

Although characteristic of very many mill races and wells, specimens of Hart's Tongue within the walls of better-kept wells traditionally probably had a more recurrent and generally traumatic existence than did those within wells which were less assiduously attended. This seems to have been the case in many monasteries and abbeys where, it is clear from surviving records, that the wellshaft interiors were cleared regularly each year of their accumulated festooning plant life. Such clearing was perhaps a necessary part of the process of maintaining the long-term general cleanliness of the well, reducing the risk of leaf-litter, not to mention associated animal life, from falling into the water beneath and gradually tainting or contaminating it. Records show that such work was often delegated to a single person, to whom it was usually allocated along with other

winter tasks such as hedging and ditching, indicating clearly its end-of-growing-season general nature. To judge from the remunerations attaching, such tasks most likely involved a thorough annual 'top-to-bottom' job within the well. Uprooted wherever they occurred within the well, new habitats were doubtless annually recreated in the dark, dank, sheltered wellshaft walls, into which lodgement of fresh spores from nearby or more distant sources would have annually surpassed the ability of the much larger seeds of most competing flowering plants to preferentially immigrate. Under such ideal growing conditions for ferns, the prothalli and then the young heart-shaped fronds of Hart's Tongue sporophytes might well have reappeared in regularly recurring quantity virtually annually and perhaps often in almost pure stands by the end of each successive growing season, their verdure and apparent spontaneous appearance being particularly characteristic through long periods of history of such closely-attended wellshaft sites.

Phyllitis scolopendrium, a colonist of old mill-races. Stroud Valley, east Gloucestershire, late May

Botanically, both wellshaft sites and mill lathes probably helped this species to achieve a considerably wider geographic distribution within these islands than it originally had in purely

natural sites, in river valleys in the south of Scotland, where
Hart's Tongue is not naturally common, local aggregations of
plants of this species have been used by archaeologists to help
locate the hidden sites of former mill workings.

Lime Kilns and Abandoned Lime-workings

A small but interesting aspect of pteridology, which has
received little previous attention, is the local but perhaps widespread association of a few ferns with sites of former lime kilns
and abandoned lime-workings. For around such disused areas,
formerly scattered or dumped lime and lime-waste now often
considerably base-enriches the surrounding patches of rich
grassy turf which have subsequently become established. In
these Adder's-tongue (*Ophioglossum vulgatum*) may now occasionally occur with special frequency, and it may well be that
Moonwort (*Botrychium lunaria*) may have an increased frequency in such sites too.

The lime industry indeed has a particularly long and ancient
tradition in these islands, with the use of lime as a cementing
agent and perhaps also as a fertiliser stretching back to Roman
times. Its use as a cementing agent was certainly essential to the
Mediaeval builder, and surviving commentaries on its agrarian
use in the 15th century refer numerously to 'lyming' and 'guid-
ding' the land. At much the same time or earlier, it also became
widely used as a whitewash to lighten the interiors of houses
and castles, whilst in Scotland at least, but probably also
further afield, the exteriors of churches, castles, houses, walls
and indeed whole towns were regularly limewashed, partly for
aesthetic reasons and partly probably also for hygienic ones.
Such uses required the widespread availability of lime, made
from burning limestone in very many small, rural kilns. These
were scattered probably throughout much of the 'length and
breadth of the land', but more realistically with special concentrations in those areas where demand was highest and where
outcrops of natural limestone rock could be quarried or mined
near to available sources of timber for firing the kilns. Such
lime production probably continued steadily through many
centuries, with its most active era from around 1750 to the
beginning of the 20th century. A survey of the lime industry of
the Lothian counties surrounding Edinburgh, for example,
records a total of over a hundred enterprises, including eight
limestone mines and sixty-three quarries in operation in 1912
(Skinner, 1969).

The characteristic lime-burning installation of earlier centuries was the clamp-kiln, usually of turf, earth and field stones,

and it is of course such structures which have left least identifiable structural remains today. It was the later erection of the
more massive, stone-built draw-kilns that usually survive as
more recognisable landscape features marking sites of past
lime-burning activity, and these were initiated largely in the
late-18th century. Eventually, the pressures of cheap bulk
carriage by rail and more economic lime production centred in
a few giant concerns meant the extinction of much of the small-
scale rural industry. Most of the local lime-producing enterprises had thus closed by about 1920, their sites thereafter
becoming abandoned to nature and to subsequent undisturbed
colonisation by lime-loving, native plant life.

Now derelict, many small scattered lime-burning kilns and
small quarries thus exist, with lime-rich bases, from which the
lime to be burned was once extracted. The lime and lime waste
which inevitably became scattered or dumped about the sites of
either the burning or extraction processes, have usually given
rise to subsequent bright green turfy patches, in which a dense
and often species-rich grassy vegetation has locally
established.

The occurrence of *Ophioglossum* in such sites is usually confined to patches of moister and heavier soils, especially in slight
hollows, and in moister patches of old quarry bottoms. It is not
necessarily confined to workings of purely calcareous limestones, for indeed, in one site of former extraction of soft mag-
nesiam limestone in Co. Durham, vigorous local stands of
Ophioglossum occurred in puddled quarry-bottom hollows of a
pale-coloured, very silty-clay substrata, apparently composed
of degradation of the local magnesium-rich limestone, where
these were most regularly shallowly flooded with seeping milky
water. In another, in north Northumberland, where the base-
source was a more purely calcareous, hard, Carboniferous
limestone, stands of *Ophioglossum* occurred mainly in moist,
entirely grassed hollows, and it is interesting to note that here
one of its most abundant associates were very numerous and
large plants of Cowslip (*Primula veris*)—the establishing
association, undisturbed since the industrial abandonment of
the site, gradually becoming reminiscent of the communities of
old, undisturbed, base-rich pastures of southern England.

The spontaneous appearance of *Ophioglossum* in such moist,
base-rich sites of former industrial workings presumably
marks sites in which establishment anew of *Ophioglossum* has
taken place successfully through original spore immigration,
doubtless coupled with further local establishment from its
own spores as well as subsequent vegetative spread of the colonies formed. It would be of great interest to monitor more of
the details of such sequences, and to consider whether this

plant was likely to have previously been present in the districts in which it now occurs, or whether such sites mark immigration of the plant anew by spores over rather greater distances.

Pit Heaps and Shale Bings

The coal extraction industry in Britain has had a very long history. In some areas, such as in the Forest of Dean in west Gloucestershire, stretching back to Roman times. The modern, great, grey pit heaps associated with the more mechanised aspects of coal extraction, however, which occur through many of our industrial landscapes, are largely a phenomenon of the period of time subsequent to the industrial revolution, and although some may still be in a phase of active addition, many have become derelict during the last century. In addition to these, very similar shale bings, usually pink in colour, are associated with the paraffin extraction industry in such areas as the central lowlands of Scotland, and these were also accumulated mainly in the 19th century, to become largely disused thereafter. These two types of sites have many aspects in common, and have become colonised by an occasional but unusual pteridophyte flora. A third type of massive, mineral-extraction, waste heap—the china clay tips characteristic of the St Austell area of east Cornwall—I have excluded from this account through lack of personal knowledge of known pteridophyte associates.

All of these types of landscape have formed habitats which are very different in their edaphic aspects from most natural habitats. The coal pit heaps consist of the once subterranean debris from around the main productive coal seams, typically including some coal associated with shales, mudstones, ironstones, sandstones, grits, fireclays and sometimes thin-bedded limestones. The shale bings consist mainly of numerous, approximately coin-sized, flakes of roasted shale rock, the organic component of which has been removed in the extraction processing. Both substrates are generally siliceous and acidic ones, and contain many contaminantes, especially quantities of sulphur in pit heaps. Their bare, rocky, soil-less, exposed surfaces are somewhat hostile habitats for plant colonisation, which therefore proceeds only rather slowly.

Three main groups of pteridophytes nevertheless have appeared in these apparently hostile industrial landscapes, which, in recent years, have been recorded with increasing frequency.

The first and earliest of these are horsetails. In a few wetter areas of pit heaps, Marsh Horsetail (*Equisetum palustre*) is occasionally present, but the main horsetail to colonise the sides of the pit heaps themselves is usually Common Horsetail (*E. arvense*). It is very probable that many pit heaps have this species. One which particularly impressed me was in the Tyne valley just west of the city of Newcastle-upon-Tyne. On this large and pyramidal heap, abandoned a quarter century or so before, a very large part of its southern flank was totally covered with a thick and relatively luxuriant sward of Common Horsetail, which produced equally thick swards of cone-bearing shoots every April over very many hundreds of square metres. Beneath the surface, at a depth from about 5 cm down, a densely interwoven mat of rhizomes considerably stabilised the surface, and its extremely high spore production might

Spring cone-shoots of Equisetum arvense *help colonise old coal-mine waste. Newcastle-upon-Tyne, early April*

have provided a considerable innoculum with which other similar sites in the district could have also become colonised, if they were not already. On this site, the colony stabilised a slope of about 30–40 degrees, and the value of this extremely long lived plant, well tolerant of these sites, in promoting the eventual vegetation of their surfaces seems to have been little appreciated. This site was, unfortunately, destroyed by subsequent reclamation.

The second group of pteridophytes of these sites, and especially of their flatter and more long-stable tops, is the occasional occurrence of establishing colonies of Moonwort (*Botrychium lunaria*). Records of this plant occur especially on the disused shale bings of the Forth–Clyde valley of Scotland, where natural Moonwort populations are frequent in the surrounding hills.

The third group of pteridophytes which seem to have become increasingly recorded from such sites in the last few years are the clubmosses. Colonising clubmosses are now known from a number of widely separated sites, not all of which are necessarily very close to known natural populations of these plants. Records from such sites include especially Forked Clubmoss (*Lycopodium clavatum*), Fir Clubmoss (*Huperzia selago*) and occasionally Alpine Clubmoss (*Diphasiastrum alpinum*). In one recently recorded site in the East Shropshire Coalfields, for example, abandoned in the mid 1960s and at an altitude of only about 370 m, all three species occur (Box & Cossons, 1988). Here, *Huperzia selago* occurs on a low bank of clay containing small pieces of coal, with *Lycopodium clavatum* and *Diphasiastrum alpinum* both on a north-west facing low ridge of clay with ironstone nodules. The description of the site is probably typical of many—much of the site is bare ground (pH 4.5–5.0) with a thin mat of algae, several *Cladonia* lichens and a diversity of mosses. Associated plants with the clubmosses include Birdsfoot Trefoil (*Lotus corniculatus*), Autumnal Hawkbit (*Leontodon autumnalis*), Hawkweed (*Hieraceum* sp.), Cat's Ear (*Hypochaeris radicata*), Common Bent (*Agrostis tenuis*), Yorkshire Fog (*Holcus lanatus*), and the mosses *Campylopus introflexus*, *Ceratodon purpureus*, *Pohlia nutans* and *Rhacomitrium lanuginosum*.

All of these cases, though sparse, are of considerable biological interest, for they all presumably represent immigration by species from other either near or distant sites by spores, establishing on the virgin, initially almost competition-free, sites created by the industrial processes, and the toleration of the edaphic conditions encountered by both gametophyte and sporophyte stages of each species. The potential of such sites for further pteridophyte research seems high, and it seems possible that much of the spread of these species to such low competition sites may have become possible by the progressive reduction of urban and industrial air pollution in recent decades (see also Chapter 9).

Canals

Canals and the land immediately around them offer a range of habitats to pteridophytes which are significant in their own right. For not only do the canals stretch widely across rural landscapes, they also penetrate deeply into and through many industrial towns and cities, and it is in these urban areas that the range of structures and habitats around the canals are often most diverse.

The Diversity of Canal Habitats

Although various improvements were made to the river navigations in many parts of Britain between the 12–16th centuries, inland transport of heavy goods such as building stone depended, until the late 18th century, largely on the navigation of existing rivers. With the coming of the Industrial Revolution, the need for a more efficient and cheap means of inland transport of bulky raw materials and finished products to and from industrial centres was answered by the construction of an extensive series of inland canals. These came to link not only the industrial centres of lowland Britain, but even eventually crossed more upland areas such as the Pennines.

Whilst their construction in flat-lying ground may have seemed straightforward enough, to successfully cross the different levels of Britain's rolling countryside, canals were usually constructed to cling closely to the contours of the landscape. Cuts and low embankments were frequently needed to achieve the necessary long level runs and only gradual curves. Cut-and-fill techniques were usually used, re-using material excavated from one portion to make embankments for another. Where more difficult terrain had to be crossed, civil engineers such as Rennie, Telford, Brindley and Jessop were involved in the construction of locks or flights of locks with stone or brick-built sides to the lock-chambers and paired, large, wooden, intermeshing, V-shaped gates; wood, cast-iron or stone-built bridges; brick-lined tunnels, with vertical access and ventilation shafts to the surface above; and occasional aqueducts with strong stone abutments. The canals also required towpaths, and bridges for these at canal junctions; bridges, where important roads crossed the canals; and, in hilly terrain and industrial areas, brick-built retaining walls were numerous. Additionally, the canals required a great number of more local constructions, such as pumping stations, turnpikes, pounds, lock-keepers' cottages, toll offices, house-stables, warehouses and small workshops. Most canals were also hedged, whilst natural springlines were often diverted to feed water into the canals, especially along their summit levels. Indeed, the construction of the canals was the greatest single civil engineering undertaking to occur in the British landscape since the Romans built their road network nearly fifteen centuries before.

By the middle of the 19th century, the newly developed railways began to capture much of the trade for which the canals had been built. Some canals and railways existed alongside each other for a while. The Kennet and Avon canal, for example, linking London and Bristol was only completed in 1810, to become largely displaced by the Great Western Railway when opened in 1835, which also linked these cities. Many canals were, however, purchased by railway companies, and the canals subsequently disused. Canal maintenance was, in most cases, thereafter neglected, and many have gradually fallen into various states of dereliction.

The original construction of the canals created a whole range of new habitats for plants, and the relative shelter of low-lying canal sections (especially where in cuts), the locally enhanced humidity from the standing as well as sometimes seeping water, and the abundance of brickwork with calcareous mortar courses have created sites particularly suitable for the establishment of a range of ferns. Unlike the developing railway system, the canal system was centred mostly in the industrial Midlands and the north-west of England, although there were systems elsewhere too, such as near Exeter, in Scotland and in Ireland. In the City of Birmingham alone, for example, about 25 miles (40 km) of canals still exist. Despite the general air pollution from which such areas have suffered in the 20th century, at least ten species of pteridophytes survive within canal habitats even within this city.

Although air pollution has in the past and probably still does largely prevent most pteridophytes from achieving any degree of urban luxuriance, they persist in the sites largely because canals provide habitats which do not suffer from frequent redevelopment and change, nor from the pressure of grazing animals. The stability and lack of grazing makes the habitat fairly ideal, in certain aspects, for pteridophyte colonisation. Elsewhere along canals in regions of cleaner air, the luxuriance of pteridophytes present generally increases.

Canal Mortar and Woodwork Habitats

The damp mortar of old, undisturbed brickwork along canals provides opportunity for the success of more calcicolous ferns. Mortar of aqueducts, retaining walls and tunnel mouths is frequently damp, but brightly lit, providing habitats in which Maidenhair Spleenwort (*Asplenium trichomanes* subsp. *quadrivalens*) and Wall Rue (*A. ruta-muraria*) usually succeed, whilst the high degree of shelter is also conducive to the persistence to adulthood of occasional larger species. These can include such calcicoles as Hart's Tongue (*Phyllitis scolopendrium*) and occasional Hard Shield-fern (*Polystichum aculeatum*), less calcicolous Common Male-fern (*Dryopteris filix-mas*) or even the generally calcifuge, but surprisingly ubiquitous Lady Fern (*Athyrium filix-femina*). The latter is also known from aqueduct abutments, and young plants of Bracken (*Pteridium aquilinum*) occasionally occur too in these well-lit, moist, wall mortar habitats, where they may persist as semi-permanent juveniles.

Locks, the interiors of brick-lined tunnel mouths, and the undersides of arches of brick-built overbridges, all provide calcicolous habitats which are generally more humid and more dimly lit than those of more-exposed brickwork. Nevertheless, in lighter spots, *Asplenium ruta-muraria* is still often present, sometimes densely so within lock chambers, and *A. trichomanes* is frequently met. Brittle Bladder-fern (*Cystopteris fragilis*) occurs in these habitats mainly away from industrial areas, sometimes hanging pendulously in some numbers from beneath the arches of tunnel mouths or low brick overbridges. Around locks, old woodwork provides habitats where cushions of moss or rudimentary soils accumulate, and in such sheltered moist pockets it is by no means unknown for Lady Fern, Male Fern and especially Broad Buckler-fern (*Dryopteris dilatata*) to grow epiphytically on the old wooden beams of damp lock gates!

Canal Corridor Habitats

In the adjacent vegetation around canals, in the areas that can usefully be called the 'canal corridor', other species of ferns and fern-allies usually occur more generally. Along exposed banks and in derelict areas, Bracken (*Pteridium aquilinum*) is often particularly abundant. Common Horsetail (*Equisetum arvense*) is also often plentiful, and can form extensive colonies along grassy banks as well as in cindery residue along the edges of towpaths. Both Bracken and Common Horsetail seem as abundant, if not more so, in urban areas as rural ones. Clearly

both are able to pioneer a wide range of deep, mostly well-
drained soils, are tolerant of a wide range of conditions of
exposure, and presumably city pollution. *Equisetum arvense* is
often particularly freely fertile in these habitats, sometimes
producing small forests of its pinkish-white, cone-bearing
shoots, each standing no more than a few inches high, for a
week or so in early April. It often grows in canal habitats which
also include various weedy flowering plants, such as Goat's-
Beard (*Tragopogon pratensis*), Greater Knapweed (*Centaurea
scabiosa*), Oxford Ragwort (*Senecio squalidus*), Spear Thistle
(*Cirsium vulgare*) and many grasses. More characteristic of the
rural stretches of canals, though sometimes present also in
urban ones, is Marsh Horsetail, *Equisetum palustre*. Its habitats
are typically moister ones than those of *E. arvense*, and the
species frequently spreads into (or has originally spread in
from) adjacent damp meadows. Its main canalside associates
usually include such plants as Meadowsweet (*Filipendula
ulmaria*), Valerian (*Valeriana officinalis*), Marsh Thistle
(*Cirsium palustre*), Water Avens (*Geum rivale*) and Gipsywort
(*Lycopus europaeus*), showing clear links between its semi-
natural canalside communities and those of marshes or flushes
elsewhere.

Other horsetails occur more locally along canals. Wood
Horsetail (*Equisetum sylvaticum*) is sometimes present in
northern areas, especially in high rainfall districts such as in the
vicinity of the Caledonian Canal. Small stands of Water
Horsetail (*Equisetum fluviatile*) occasionally colonise the still
waters of former passing-bays, to form semi-natural, aquatic,
emergent communities, along with flowering plant colonists
such as Water Plantain (*Alisma plantago-aquatica*), Unbranched Bur-reed (*Sparganium emerseum*) and Yellow Flag (*Iris
pseudacorus*), whilst its hybrid with *E. arvense*, *E. × litorale* is
sometimes also present in such sites. Occasionally seen too is
Great Horsetail (*Equisetum telmateia*), usually colonising
natural seepage lines of base-rich water along English canal
banks, and in at least one of its localities, on a small branch of
the Shropshire Union Canal, its hybrid with *E. palustre*, *Equisetum × font-queri*, occurs too. On the banks of the Royal Dublin
canal in Ireland, *Equisetum variegatum* var. *majus* has long been
known, the canal bank forming one of the plant's classic sites.

Elsewhere in canal corridor environments larger woodland
ferns find suitable niches, especially on the sheltered flanks of
sloping cuts, on grassy banks amongst invading Bramble,
Gorse, Elder or developing scrub woodland, or along the
courses of old canalside hedges. In many cases, these species
occur as scattered individuals, but sometimes larger patches
spreading amongst establishing tree overgrowth clearly mark

significant stages in the succession of the vegetation toward semi-natural woodland. Broad Buckler-fern (*Dryopteris dilatata*) is a particularly early invader of such moist, fairly acidic sites, often accompanied by clumps of Lady Fern (*Athyrium filix-femina*). Other species of *Dryopteris*, notably Male Fern (*D. filix-mas*) and Golden-scaled Male Fern (*D. affinis* subsp. *borreri*) often also occur, and hybrids between the latter two may also be present. Occasionally too, but restricted to more basic pockets and especially to where basic clays have been exposed, Soft Shield Fern (*Polystichum setiferum*) and Hart's Tongue (*Phyllitis scolopendrium*) may also have appeared, whilst in unusually acidic pockets on canal sides both in industrial south Lancashire, and in the heart of industrial Glasgow, specimens of colonising Royal Fern (*Osmunda regalis*) are known.

Railways and their Environs

Although extensive areas of the railway system exist at relatively low altitude, and the habitats around them are thus essentially 'lowland' in character, other parts of the system lie much higher than this (290 m, Shap; 315 m, Beattoch; 400 m, Slochd; 411 m, Carrow; and 452 m, Drumochtes). In total, the lines thus traverse a very considerably greater range of altitudes and landscape types than the canals, and in so doing, have come to add a particularly distinctive corridor of further habitat diversity to our landscape, through a wide range of natural vegetation types.

The success of pteridophytes in the railway corridor is probably partly due to the shelter and enhanced humidity of some railway habitats, such as those within cuttings, partly due to conditions of reduced plant competition, and partly due to the great mosaic of conditions available, offering habitats of widely varying substrates and moisture conditions from place to place. The railway corridor has acted as both a refuge from changing conditions around it, and as a potential corridor along which pteridophytes sometimes meet new opportunities for unusual dispersal, along features which have themselves become integral features of the broader landscape.

The History and Diversity of Railway Habitats

With the invention of the steam railway locomotive in the early part of the 19th century, the great age of railways began. Stimulated by the railway's ability to transport raw materials and fin-

ished products more quickly than could the canals, the
development of the railway system to most parts of Britain proceeded particularly rapidly. By 1843 there were already 2,000
miles (3,200 km) of line, and by 1845, 5,000 miles (8,000 km)
had been laid. Although centred on London, the developing
network reached remote points such as Penzance by 1866, and
Wick and Thurso by 1874, with an independent system in
Ireland, and others in the Isle of Wight and Isle of Man.

The nature of the terrain being crossed and the desire to
create only wide curves and level or only shallow trackbed
gradients largely determined the types and complexity of the
civil engineering constructions needed to traverse our landscape. Britain's rolling landscape is seldom level, and where
lines entered territory such as south-west England, Wales or
Scotland, and crossed the 'grain' of the landscape, innumerable civil engineering constructions were sometimes needed.
These included bridges, viaducts, embankments, cuttings and
tunnels. The Great Western Railway, for example, the longest-
lived of the once-numerous individual railway companies in
Britain, from its inception in the early 19th century to its
absorption into British Railways in 1947, built no less than
twelve thousand bridges and one thousand six hundred
stations along about 3,600 miles of track, which eventually
included not only main lines, but also over 150 more minor, and
mostly rural, branch lines. Today, about 65% of this system
still remains in active use, with the remainder, and especially
many of the rural branch lines and their stations and yards,
disused since the mid 1950s or early 1960s. With track lifted,
these have subsequently fallen into various states of disuse and
dereliction, and where not destroyed, have offered new opportunities for plant colonisation.

In addition to the more major construction works, the
railways too, like the canals, brought with them a wide range of
brick and stone-built structures, as well as the ballasted track
beds themselves. Water for locomotives was needed at stations,
and drainage needed in tunnels and cuttings.

The landscape changes which the railways brought were
thus more fundamental and far-reaching than that of any previous transport system. In their early stages of construction,
considerable scars were undoubtedly created in the landscape.
Gradually these softened as bare surfaces became vegetated.
Over the course of 120 or more years of use, most lines, and
especially the smaller rural branch lines, came to blend closely
into the countryside around them. During this period, few of
the original railway structures were replaced, and most of the
older of those which survive today are thus seldom less than a
century in age. Many of the constructions created have pro-

vided excellent habitats for a variety of plants as well as animal life and where track lengths have been abandoned, recolonisation by plant life has reached a new stage of progression.

Although railway lines which are in active use cannot be directly explored, much about their vegetation can be discerned from careful observation from train windows. From such surroundings, the innermost aspects of railway cuttings can be particularly beneficially seen. Other aspects can be seen from stations. Furthermore, it is often possible to explore more closely many miles of disused trackway on foot, where close inspection of mural and rockwork habitats is possible, as well as of the species colonising the former trackbeds themselves. In almost all types of sites, both the frequency and diversity of the pteridophyte component of the resulting vegetation varies much with the geographic location of the site, being poorest in the relatively drier, eastern regions of England, and where lines cross better-drained soils such as the chalk, and most profuse in wetter western regions of England and especially Wales, Scotland and Ireland.

The railway corridor in a lowland landscape, with well-wooded embankments, sheltered nearby cuttings in Jurassic limestone, and a small stone-built viaduct. Stroud Valley, east Gloucestershire, late May

Trackbed Habitats

The trackbed was always one of the most important and hence assiduously-maintained of all the physical aspects of the railway. Ballasted rails are usually of hard hornfels rock or granite. Although these appear to be somewhat hostile habitats for plants when newly laid, they clearly become subject to-gradual degradation and accumulation of soil and organic debris, making suitably vacant habitats of the ultimate invasion of weed growth. Branch lines, built originally for the carriages of relatively lighter traffic than main lines, were usually laid with only shallow trackbed ballast and were thus always particularly susceptible to the establishment of weeds. Until the 1930s tracks were mostly weeded by hand. Thereafter, weed-killing trains became widely adopted, and these regularly sprayed the trackbed and a short distance either side of it with herbicidal chemicals, usually sodium chlorate.

On minor tracks and sidings, less detailed attention from weedkilling trains enabled many plants to often continue to hold their own, and with the abandonment of substantial areas of rural branchlines, the whole trackbed has often reverted at a surprising speed to a covering of plants.

The most extensive trackbed ballast pteridophyte present during the active use of many railway lines, especially in minor sidings, beneath buffers and in railway yards, is the Common Horsetail (*Equisetum arvense*). This species appears in, and can often retain a particularly permanent hold on, railway track ballast of all kinds, including cinder and clinker. Its extensive vegetative spread results from its ability to achieve considerable underground rhizome growth, from which the green summer aerial shoots can arise, like miniature spruce trees, in very considerable numbers. This horsetail thrives because of the particularly freely-drained texture of the substrate and the lack of competition for it. The lack of competition is itself partly induced by man's attempts at weed eradication, and the ability of this species to survive herbicides, at least in areas peripheral to the main spray concentrations, is notorious.

Although Common Horsetail is certainly the most widespread and frequent member of its genus in railway ballast sites, more locally other species of horsetail may also invade. Where lines traverse hillsides and there is some natural water seepage, layers below the ballast can become moist when original railway drains silt up. In such sites, Marsh Horsetail (*Equisetum palustre*) can be one of the more local invaders, particularly in areas of underlying coal-bearing shales, and extensive colonies of this plant occur, for example, on several abandoned Northumberland lines. In several parts of central and western Scotland, including on the now-abandoned Stirling–Callander line and on the still-active Crianlarich to Fort William line in the West Highlands, Wood Horsetail (*Equisetum sylvaticum*) also occurs in and around the track bal-

last, locally in some abundance, and in these sites it has encroa-
ched, under climates of frequent cloud and abundant light
rain, from surrounding native vegetation.

The moist interstices of the trackbed ballast itself also provides particularly suitable habitats for the success of fern
gametophytes, and in high-rainfall districts, ferns have consequently proved to be amongst the early pioneers of such sites,
even where the ballast itself has been of granite. The most frequently encountered are Male Fern (*Dryopteris filix-mas*),
Broad Buckler-fern (*D. dilatata*), Common Golden-scaled
Male Fern (*D. affinis* subsp. *borreri*) and Lady Fern (*Athyrium
filix-femina*). These species sometimes occur in profusion
within the shelter of former cuttings if the ballast itself has not
been removed, whilst on the more exposed lengths of trackbed,
such as on embankments, Black Spleenwort (*Asplenium
adiantum-nigrum*) occurs in some western districts, whilst
Adder's Tongue (*Ophioglossum vulgatum*) and Moonwort
(*Botrychium lunaria*) have also been reported—both the latter
probably greatly benefiting from the lack of disturbance or grazing of these sites.

Embankments, Cuttings and Associated Structures

Either side of the track itself, within the fenced perimeter of
each line in an area that can usefully be called the 'railway
corridor', exist strips of vegetation of varying width. Where
lines cross relatively level terrain as in much of East Anglia, the
lineside strips are often at their narrowest and have perhaps no
more than 10% of their area which is not flat. In many regions,
however, strips of varying but often much greater width are
regularly necessary to contain a very large number of
embankments and cuttings. Along such lines, a high proportion (often exceeding 50%) of the lineside terrain is thus sloping, and an appropriately wide range of habitats is consequently
present, resulting in widely differing conditions of shelter and
drainage.

The original construction of the railways were usually
carefully engineered to re-use the materials quarried from cuttings to construct adjacent embankments. Cuttings and
embankments are thus usually approximately equally
numerous, and the rock substrate of embankments usually has
an affinity with the native geology of the locality. Under long
conditions of relatively minimal management compared with
both the trackbed itself and with much of the modern countryside around them, and free from grazing by larger animals, a
wide range of semi-natural vegetation has usually become

established on both embankments and cuttings, with even the tops of the most exposed embankments irrigated by water from passing trains.

Where embankment tops are edged with stone or mortared brick retaining courses below the ballast fringe, and where shrub or tree growth is absent, ferns such as Wall-Rue (*Asplenium ruta-muraria*), Maidenhair Spleenwort (*A. trichomanes* subsp. *quadrivalens* and perhaps subsp. *trichomanes*) and Black Spleenwort (*A. adiantum-nigrum*) may occur.

Embankment sides provide especially well-drained habitats, down the slopes of which the edaphic mosaic has often become diversified, and this diversity is often maintained by regular tipping of spent trackbed ballast, creating scree-like patches with a rubble-like or cindery surface. In such sites, Common Horsetail (*Equisetum arvense*) is frequently a rapid invader, and may eventually form large colonies which long persist into later grass-dominated phases of the sites. In wetter, western as well as upland sites, Male Fern (*Dryopteris filix-mas*) and various subspecies of Golden-scaled Male Fern (*Dryopteris affinis*) also occur widely in tipped ballast screes, while over embankment sides as a whole, large stands of Bracken (*Pteridium aquilinum*) occur in many areas. On many embankments, Bracken forms patches within areas dominated by grasses, perhaps marking sites of previous trackside fires.

In cuttings interiors, the environment becomes generally more sheltered than on embankments and edaphically more moist, and in upland areas in particular, bare rock areas, including those of basic strata, are often directly exposed. In lowland areas, Common Horsetail, Bracken, Male-fern and Golden-scaled Male-fern as well as Broad Buckler-fern (*Dryopteris dilatata*) and Lady Fern (*Athyrium filix-femina*) are often to be seen. Where lines cut through more basic rocky strata, especially in south-west England and at low elevations in western Scotland, Hart's Tongue Fern (*Phyllitis scolopendrium*) and Soft and Hard Shield Ferns (*Polystichum setiferum* and *P. aculeatum*) may add further to the diversity, as may Black and Maidenhair Spleenworts (*Asplenium adiantum-nigrum*) and *A. trichomanes* subsp. *quadrivalens*). On moist rocky faces, often supplemented with some moisture seepage, the latter can form particularly massive clumps, whilst it is possible that on less lime-yielding rocks, notably for example in Wales, the rarer subsp. *trichomanes* and perhaps the hybrid between them may also occur. Along one stretch of line of the active former Great Western main line through South Devon to Cornwall, plants of Royal Fern (*Osmunda regalis*) occur around tunnel portals, where there is constantly seeping and dripping water from outcropping sandstone rocks above.

A rarity of very local occurrence where more natural lime-stone rocks are exposed to form relatively dry, tumbled scree in railway cuttings, is the Limestone Oak-fern (*Gymnocarpium robertianum*) associated with a number of other unusual calcicolous species. More widely, where railway cuttings intersect and expose base-rich springlines associated with deep clay soils, local bright green summer stands of the Great Horsetail (*Equisetum telmateia*) may form extensive local patches. Ones I have noted in such sites as far apart as Gloucestershire, Oxfordshire, Kent, Lancashire and Northumberland. In Gloucestershire such stands occur, for example, where the steeply-inclined former GWR line between Swindon and Gloucester descends the western flank of the Cotswolds via the course of the Stroud Valley, and here this species marks the exposures on the cutting sides of Jurassic limestones and underlying clays.

In a great many rocky railway cuttings, species of Polypody are also present. These include Western Polypody (*Polypodium interjectum*) and Common Polypody (*P. vulgare*) very widely, whilst it is likely that in limestone districts at low altitude, *P. australe* may occasionally grow too.

In upland areas, and especially in parts of North Wales, the English Lake District, and the Southern Uplands and Highlands of Scotland, the railway corridor comes more frequently into contact with upland acidic woodland and often

The railway corridor in an upland landscape, with exposed embankments and much surrounding moorland. The greater exposure is to some extent pteridologically ameliorated by the high frequency of rainfall and cloud cover. Near Drumochtes Pass (452 m), Inverness-shire, July

surrounding moorland vegetation, and the pteridophyte flora
of the cutting interiors includes many more northern and
upland species. Amongst these, Common and Golden-scaled
Male Ferns (*Dryopteris filix-mas* and several subspecies of *D.
affinis*) occur widely, as do Broad Buckler Fern (*D.
dilatata*) and Lady Fern (*Athyrium filix-femina*). Wood Horsetail
(*Equisetum sylvaticum*) can be locally common, as can Hard
Fern (*Blechnum spicant*) and Sweet Mountain Fern (*Oreopteris
limbosperma*). Patches of Beech Fern (*Phegopteris connectilis*)
and Oak Fern (*Gynocarpium dryopteris*) sometimes form more
bright green patches on shaded slopes, and Brittle Bladder-
fern (*Cystopteris fragilis*) occurs scantily on wet, shaded, basic
rock exposures.

Further basic sites occur extensively along railway habitats,
both within cuttings and outside them, wherever calcareous
mortar course of railway brickwork exist. Retaining walls and
tunnel entrances provide sites which are often moist and
shaded, but even platform edges and the interiors of the walls
of bridges and viaducts provide enclaves which were kept
especially damp in the days of passing steam trains, and have
subsequently proved particularly appropriate habitats for colonisation by ferns.

Associates of these ferns on railway embankments and in
cuttings are often numerous, and may vary quite locally. On
drier embankment sides, associated flowering plants often
include Coltsfoot (*Tussilago farfara*), Ragwort (*Senecio
jacobaea*), Groundsel (*S. vulgaris*), Ribwort Plantain (*Plantago
lanceolata*), Hardheads (*Centaurea nigra*), Rosebay Willow-
herb (*Epilobium angustifolium*), Creeping Thistle (*Cirsium
arvense*), Toadflax (*Linaria vulgaris*), Tufted Vetch (*Viccia
cracca*), Golden-rod (*Solidago virgaurea*), Bramble (*Rubus fruticosus* agg.), Nipplewort (*Lapsana communis*), Hogweed (*Heracleum sphondylium*), Sorrel (*Rumex acetosa*), Wood Sage
(*Teucrium scorodonia*), Harebell (*Campanula rotundifolia*), Wild
Strawberry (*Fragaria vesca*), and Ground Ivy (*Glechoma hederacea*). On rough earth and rock slopes in more sheltered cutting
localities, additional species noted with fern communities
include Yarrow (*Achillea millefolium*), Red Campion (*Silene
dioica*), Hedge Bedstraw (*Galium mollugo*), Ribwort Plantain
(*Plantago lanceolata*), Herb Robert (*Geranium robertianum*),
Meadow Cranesbill (*G. pratense*), Self-heal (*Prunella vulgaris*),
Garlic Mustard (*Allaria petiolata*), Wild Mignonette (*Reseda
lutea*), Ox-eye Daisy (*Leucanthemum vulgare*), Wood Avens
(*Geum urbanum*), Common Violet (*Viola riviniana*), Primrose
(*Primula vulgaris*), Cowslip (*P. veris*), with trailing Honeysuckle
(*Lonicera periclymenum*) and Ivy (*Hedera helix*) and mosses such
as *Brachythecium rutabulum* and *Plulerozium schreberi*.

Especially in cuttings, *Cystopteris fragilis* readily colonises the mortar of railway brickwork, especially perhaps on the more shaded and sheltered aspects of railway bridges and railway tunnel portals, whilst on many sites of better lit brickwork Maidenhair Spleenwort (*Asplenium trichomanes*), Wall Rue (*A. ruta-muraria*) and Black Spleenwort (*A. adiantum-nigrum*) are frequently present.

Each of these ferns are sometimes in nearly exclusive stands on individual railway mortar sites. One fern-festooned brick bridge known to me on the ex-GWR main line between Truro and Penzance in Cornwall, for example, has dense *A. adiantum-nigrum* only in its mortar courses, whilst the parapets of the former Dowdeswell viaduct in Gloucestershire carried extensive colonies only of *A. ruta-muraria* for nearly its full-length. Such sites might provide interesting areas of study for the dynamics of pteridophyte colonisation.

The Railway Corridor and Adventive Pteridophytes

Railway-inhabiting ferns are not solely confined to species of purely local origin, as is indicated by the intriguing railway distribution of Maidenhair Fern (*Adiantum capillus-veneris*), Font-Quer's Horsetail (*Equisetum font-queri*) and Limestone Oak-fern (*Gymnocarpium robertianum*). Each of these taxa illustrate different and fascinating bio-historic aspects of the railway corridor habitat in relation to more general pteridophyte dispersal.

Maidenhair Fern is a rare native fern in Britain and Ireland, occurring naturally on lime-rich rocks in isolated extreme west-coast sites. It has, however, appeared, in the mortar of some station brickwork, in this case the direct result of former horticultural railway activities. For in the days when railway gangers were engaged in ridding branch lines of their vegetation by hand, signalmen and station staff were often engaged in the pursuit of putting it back again. Generous periods of comparative inactivity which characterised the often rustic life of the rural branch line allowed station staff opportunity to attend to the leisurely culture of flower-baskets and station flower beds. Many stations sported colourful beds of Wallflowers, Sweet Williams and Geraniums. In some places, ferns were grown, including the Maidenhair Fern as a hanging-basket speciality. It is in all probability that it is from spores which escaped from such sources that occasional colonisations by this rare native species have been reported, especially from along platform edges. In such enclaves, plants of this species have sometimes become well-established, especially in

Where standing railway locomotives once discharged steam, Adiantum capillus-veneris *now vigorously colonises the decaying mortar layers of a brick-built disused railway station platform edge. Cheshire, June*

milder, western climates. Such a situation may have arisen many times, and can with certainty still be seen today on at least one now-abandoned railway station platform of the former London and North Western Railway on the Wirral coast, built about 1847 and not finally closed until 1962. Here, it is recollected in local accounts, that during the more active days of this railways there was 'great rivalry between the signalmen on the line in maintaining flower beds around their signal boxes', and at least two boxes were said to be 'outstanding in their show of geraniums and ferns'. Today, in the now abandoned (but still intact) platform edges adjacent to one of these signal boxes, dense stands of Maidenhair fern now perpetuate themselves in almost every mortar crevice along at least 30 feet (ca. 10 m) of platform brickwork, where they show every sign of being permanently established—presumably the progeny of those in the station's former hanging baskets. Their survival here has been aided by the location of the platform in a mild climate, at about 650 feet (ca. 200 m) from the sea.

The occurrence of Font-Quer's Horsetail (*Equisetum* × *font-queri*) on a single railway embankment is, however, more enigmatic in its source. Font-Quer's Horsetail is the rare hybrid between *Equisetum telmateia* and *E. palustre*, and was discovered as an extensive stand in a disused railway embankment in Worcestershire by R. H. Roberts only recently

(Roberts & Page, 1979). Here it forms a single dense stand for about 75 m on both sides of the top of a railway embankment which is capped by a layer of ballast composed of coarse limestone chippings. This hybrid could have formed anew in this site. But the immediate site is not, however, one in which either parent occurs. A more likely possibility is that this unusually vigorous hybrid might have been accidentally introduced to this locality as rhizome fragments along with the fill which was used to originally construct the railway (1866) or with ballast that was subsequently added. The source of the hybrid remains, however, unknown, not having been located anywhere else in Worcestershire or in neighbouring counties.

A third example raises further questions about possible human-aided movement of a pteridophyte along railway corridors. This is the occurrence of Limestone Oak-fern (*Gymnocarpium robertianum*) in railway mortar habitats. This species is of special interest on such sites because of its highly-localised range in native habitats, and its occurrence in a few railway wall-mortar sites in eastern and southern England far from native localities. Such an occurrence raises the possibility of spores becoming formerly transported by trains themselves. In the days of steam, before air-conditioned coaches, it seems very possible that trapped spores may have been transported long distances within passenger railway coaches stopping at platform edges. Perhaps this might have been especially so amongst coach-borne dust, in the days when trains had opening windows and individual compartments each had doors, numerous air-suspended spores may well have flown in and out of compartments at different stations, wafted by gentlemen's long-coats or ladies' long and flowing skirts. For who has ever travelled by such old steam trains, and does not remember the puff of dust from the moquette-covered, horsehair-stuffed seats as you sat on them? Once released, on railway mortar close to the tracks, and especially on platform edges, opportunities for establishment of any transported fern species would have been unique. For in the days of steam locomotives, such areas were always frequently subject to steam exposure from stopping trains, especially from locomotive cylinder glands and steam chests, and from railway passenger carriage heating discharge pipes and faulty steampipe coach connections. Such abundant steam, condensing rapidly in cool air, would have probably regularly coated adjacent brick and mortar surfaces of station edges with new water films, giving ample opportunity for any newly arising fern spores to adhere and later germinate, perhaps sometimes from dust which may well have originated in distant places, containing spores of appropriately distant ferns.

CHAPTER 7

Woodland Pteridophytes

Lying well within the northern limit of tree growth in Europe, and strongly influenced by winter warmth and abundant year-round rainfall from the Atlantic ocean, it is mainly only where altitudes in Britain and Ireland ascend above about 2,000 feet (600 m) that temperature and exposure generally become too severe to support extensive tree growth. Up to this altitude, these islands originally possessed a widely forested landscape. Dense tree stands, mainly of broadleaved deciduous species covered much of the more fertile soils of lowland Britain and Ireland, whilst in the north pine forest was more widespread.

Today, a traveller has only to look for a while from the window of a moving train, passing through almost any part of these islands, or even more emphatically, from a plane flying over them, to appreciate the extent to which our original native vegetation has been decimated by man. Where industry and towns have not claimed the land, then agriculture almost entirely has. The resulting landscape is one composed, in the more fertile lowlands, largely of an infinite patchwork of fields, separated by the occasional enclave of scrub or struggling copse; on the less fertile soils of upland and western terrain, it is mostly bleak hillsides where tree regeneration has long been arrested by constant grazing of stock. Over this landscape, this removal and prevention of regeneration of trees has proceeded almost since man first entered the scene. Remaining patches of self-regenerating natural or semi-natural woodland composed predominantly of native tree species are scarce; those which can be regarded as ancient woodland or 'wildwood', are now rare.

Woodland is, however, the most characteristic of all of the habitats for ferns and fern allies, and certainly the one in which these groups are often the most highly successful and at their most diverse. The inland woodland of the British Isles is dealt with here. The woodlands of the wetter Atlantic fringe are dealt with in Chapter 13.

Woodlands provide particularly suitable habitats for pteridophytes partly because of the generally reduced levels of flowering plant competition beneath the canopy shade, and partly because ferns are able to grow shade-adapted fronds

The profusion of ferns marks an area of enclosed estate woodland, free from grazing. It is very likely that most of our native woodland must once have looked like this. Kirkudbrightshire, early July

which are highly photosynthetically efficient at low light levels in which most flowering plants operate only poorly. In consequence, woodland ferns do not usually join in the great vernal flush of early spring herbaceous growth of the woodland floor, composed of flowering plants attempting to complete the main part of their above-ground cycles before the tree canopy comes into full leaf and light becomes reduced. Instead, most woodland ferns expand their fronds only slowly, when the canopy itself is becoming fully leafy, and the expanding fronds become adapted directly only to the lower light levels that persist through the summer. Perhaps to make up for this, many of the larger species die back only slowly in autumn, and a few have wintergreen fronds. In these species, growth probably remains active in the weak winter light, following loss of deciduous tree canopies.

Other aspects of the woodland environment which are particularly important to fern and fern-ally success include the high degree of shelter from strong winds, the generally high humidity, the enhanced permanency of available soil moisture, and the wide availability of gently-eroding, moist, mineral soil slopes, particularly suited to extensive prothallial establishment. In all of these aspects high environmental constancy characterises the special fern-suitability of most woodland environments.

Under such conditions and in the absence of grazing, the range of pteridophyte species present is largely further

Woodland ferns luxuriate in moist, sheltered sites where protected from grazing. Midlothian, July

determined by the local edaphic conditions prevailing within the woodland floor mosaic, amongst which the distribution of chemical base-status and the physical drainage patterns of the ground, both at macro- and micro-topographical levels, seem of the greatest significance.

Within Britain and Ireland, despite the long period of man's activities to the contrary, a limited number of woodlands of varying type do remain, albeit often as only relict and isolated patches, or in much-modified form. Some of the most important of these are conserved, and from them much yet remains to be learned. Those which are ancient 'wildwood', with a long and continuous history of vegetation cover, are usually of special pteridological significance, whilst additional fern interest also focusses on woodlands which have survived as strips along river and stream corridors on the sides of steep valleys, on woodlands over more local rock-types such as limestones, as well as wet woodlands of all types, especially those around lakes, marshes and springs.

Dry, Lowland, Deciduous Woodland

Woodlands of this type include the great majority of natural and semi-natural deciduous woodlands in lowland sites, present over a very great range of rock types, especially, though not exclusively, of sedimentary origin. Their soils vary from somewhat basic to highly acidic, and are characteristically well-drained.

Such woodlands vary in size from small copses to much more extensive forests. They include vegetation of a great variety of origins, ranging from those which were originally more or less man-made, such as much of the Royal forests of the English Shires, to smaller and more isolated fragments of more natural or semi-natural woodlands, often in remoter regions. In total, they represent, in very much-modified and pteridologically depauperate form, the structural type of woodland which must have predominated over much of Britain and Ireland before its extensive clearance by man.

The tree vegetation of such woodlands, on all but the most basic soils is typically dominated mainly by oaks (especially *Quercus robor* but also *Q. petraea*), usually with an admixture of other trees and some shrubs, including mainly Wych Elm (*Ulmus glabra*), Hazel (*Corylus avellana*), Ash (*Fraxinus excelsior*), Hawthorn (*Crataegus monogyna* & *C. oxyacanthoides*), Field Maple (*Acer campestre*), Wild Cherry (*Prunus avium*), Crab Apple (*Malus sylvestris*), Guelder Rose (*Viburnum opulus*), Birch (*Betula pendula* & *B. pubescens*), Rowan (*Sorbus aucupa-*

ria), and often the introduced Sycamore (*Acer pseudoplatanus*) and more occasional introduced Horse-chestnut (*Aesculus hippocastanum*). Beech (*Fagus sylvatica*) is the forest dominant in those forests over more basic soils, such as the chalk soils of the Chilterns and the exposures of the inferior oolite of the Cotswold ridges in southern Britain.

Some smaller, surviving woodlands of this type, especially of Hazel, may have had a long history of coppicing—the cutting of stems at intervals of every 10–15 years or so, to provide straight, slender, rods for poles, fenceposts and firewood, and bark for tanning. By such rotations, these woodlands may have for centuries been managed sympathetically in a steady state of production. The resulting more or less assured long-term continuation of the general woodland canopy, the maintenance of the forest soils and their texture and the overall woodland environment, seem seldom to have been greatly destructive of the pteridophyte component within them, which has usually persisted and sometimes flourished as an integral and recurring part of the overall regime.

By contrast, in by far the greatest majority of woodlands of this type, and especially in most of the larger ones, there has been a long and extensive pressure of grazing, especially by deer, but also by sheep and sometimes ponies. In these, the grazing has usually served to eliminate most of the pteridophyte diversity over large areas, replacing it instead with an often widespread invasion by Bracken (*Pteridium aquilinum*), with appropriate difficulties in management thereafter.

Non-bracken Pteridophytes

Woodland soils are often covered by a layer of leaf litter, deriving from the tree canopy above. The decomposing litter becomes rapidly incorporated into the soil surface layers by abundant earthworm activity, to give fairly high soil humus levels, holding a certain amount of soil moisture even during dry spells. These activities also leave the soil with an open and uncompacted structure, with a high porosity constantly maintaining conditions of high soil aeration, particularly essential to most pteridophyte growth.

Where grazing pressure is low or absent, the understorey of such woodlands is typically dominated by sometimes large numbers of individuals of a range of large-statured woodland ferns.

Male-fern (*Dryopteris filix-mas*) is often the most frequent fern of well-drained flat ground or of undulating rises on the forest floor. It occurs widely over almost the whole of Britain

and Ireland in low to moderate altitude woodlands. It is particularly characteristic of generally least acidic, often circum-
neutral, woodland sites. In many drier woodlands at low to
moderate altitude, especially in southern Britain, it may form
extensive, nearly single-species, rather open, stands, with individuals varying from an average height of 30–40 cm or so, in
poorer but well-drained sandy banks, to more vigorous plants a
metre or more in height, on more fertile loamy areas.

Athyrium filix-
femina, *a frequent fern
beside streams within
ravine woodland.
Kirkudbrightshire, July*

Elsewhere, frequently associated with *Dryopteris filix-mas*
and occurring through much the same geographic and altitudinal range in Britain and Ireland, is the Lady Fern (*Athyrium
filix-femina*). Although often mixed with *D. filix-mas*, the luxuriant, plume-like masses of *Athyrium*, which can be up to
120 cm or more in height, are especially typical of slightly moister and often more acidic woodland floor niches, and luxuriant
individuals can be frequent in the vicinity of stream-courses
and in moist rocky situations. It becomes most widespread in
the wetter lowland woodland climates of western and northern
areas of Britain and Ireland, and is sparser generally in the
rather drier lowland woodlands of East Anglia and the English
and Irish Midlands. Throughout its range, *A. filix-femina* is a
particularly variable species in details of size and dissection of

the fronds, and in colour of the stipes—the latter can vary from yellow-green through pink to a deep plum-red or purple, although extreme forms seem to occur more abundantly in some localities than in others.

Broad Buckler-fern (*Dryopteris dilatata*) is another large fern which can become very abundant in lowland woodlands, either in mixed associations with *D. filix-mas* and *Athyrium filix-femina*, or as pure stands. Broad Buckler-fern seems more typical of rather more acidic ground than is Common Male-fern, although the two species have a wide range of overlap. Broad Buckler-fern generally becomes increasingly abundant in moister climates where acidic, humus-rich surface layers are especially widespread, and under such conditions, it may extensively dominate the herbaceous vegetation of the woodland floor, even excluding most other ferns from the association.

Common Golden-scaled Male-fern (*Dryopteris affinis* subsp. *borreri*) may also be abundant amongst the major species of ferns forming the forest floor community in many lowland woodlands on neutral to fairly acidic ground, in which it associates with all of the above species or dominates communities of its own. This is the geographically most widespread of the subspecies of *D. affinis*, and the one whose ecology perhaps most closely parallels that of *D. filix-mas*. Like *D. filix-mas*, plants of *D. affinis* subsp. *borreri* have decumbent branching rhizomes. They seem often to be particularly long-lived plants, and hence tend in time to form large, multi-branched, rhizome clumps, with multiple, close-set crowns.

Hard Fern (*Blechnum spicant*) and Wood Horsetail (*Equisetum sylvaticum*) usually indicate damper areas of these woodlands. They are therefore usually absent from much of the general ground floras, except in damper hollows or on damper slopes in the vicinity of streams, where there is a more or less constant water seepage through the ground.

Hard Fern is characteristic of local, moist banks, especially where Greater Woodrush (*Luzula sylvatica*) is present. In some ancient woodlands, *Blechnum* occurs particularly along the banked-up sides of ancient tracks and along ancient woodland banks. In the latter habitats in particular, it is not only usually accompanied by *Dryopteris dilatata*, but occasionally and most unusually too by locally luxuriant growths of Hay-scented Buckler-fern (*Dryopteris aemula*), within the regionally limited southern and western general range of this species (see also chapter 13).

Wood Horsetail occasionally forms large colonies, and especially so in the neighbourhood of local streams passing through an otherwise dry woodland floor. Although it is present in such sites in dry woodlands as far south as Gloucestershire (in the Forest of Dean) and Hampshire (in the New Forest), Wood Horsetail becomes an increasingly frequent component of woodland vegetation in the north of Britain, where it is especially associated with ravine woodland habitats (q.v.). It seems probable, however, that both Hard Fern and Wood Horsetail have been more widespread over Britain and Ireland in woodland habitats than even their present frequency in surviving woodlands would suggest. For both species seem sensitive to both trampling and grazing, and it is probable that where large stands of either of these persist, they are indicative of a relatively long continuum of relatively undisturbed woodland on those sites.

On the tops of boulders or on the boles of tree trunks where pockets of humus accumulates, Broad Buckler-fern may occasionally become epiphytic. More often this niche is filled, however, with more truly epiphytic plants such as Common Polypody (*Polypodium vulgare*) or Western Polypody (*P. interjectum*). Both species have wide ranges through Britain and Ireland, with the latter, as its name implies, becoming progressively more frequent in wetter, western climates. Both species prefer rough-barked trees as substrates, especially

Gracefully arching fronds characterise Dryopteris dilatata *in its many woodland habitats. West Perthshire, July*

oaks. Common Polypody is the more acid-loving of the two species, and hence the most common as an epiphyte in the most acidic woodland habitats. Both, however, have a wide range of ecological and geographic overlap, and where both are present in woodlands, it is not uncommon (especially in wetter, western climates) to find occasional colonies of their hybrid, Manton's Polypody (*Polypodium* × *mantoniae*).

Where *Dryopteris dilatata* is particularly abundant, Honeysuckle (*Lonicera periclymenum*), Wood-sorrel (*Oxalis acetosella*) and Greater Woodrush (*Luzula sylvatica*) may also be common. In woodlands where Birch (*Betula pubescens*) is frequent in the tree layer, *D. dilatata* and often *Blechnum spicant* can occur with Bilberry (*Vaccinium myrtillus*), Heather (*Calluna vulgaris*), Tormentil (*Potentilla erecta*) and Heath Bedstraw (*Galium saxatile*), such associations marking a clear link with lowland heathland communities.

Bracken

Bracken (*Pteridium aquilinum*) was probably not a frequent fern of the original native wildwood of Britain and Ireland. Its spread has taken place steadily from Neolithic times onward, when it makes an appearance rather suddenly in many fossil pollen records, especially above carbon-horizons indicating its rapid rise following deforestation associated with fire-destruction of original forest vegetation (Page, 1976). Before this, Bracken was almost certainly a fern present mainly around drier forest margins and within thin forest glades over poor, sandy soils.

Many dry lowlands, as well as upland forests, today contain very extensive tracts of this fern, especially in glades and along paths and rides, where it can dominate almost to the near-exclusion of other understorey species. Extensive examples of this occur especially in many of the original Royal Forests of the English shire-counties. Many of these occur on relatively acidic as well as sometimes poor soils—the New Forest in Hampshire and Epping Forest in Essex, for example, largely over sands and pebble beds of Tertiary (mainly Eocene) age, the Forest of Dean in west Gloucestershire largely over Devonian Old Red Sandstones and Carboniferous Coal Measure sandstones and grits, Sherwood Forest in Nottinghamshire over Keuper and Bunter Sandstones and associated Pebble Beds of Permian age, and the woodlands around Sandringham in Norfolk on the Greensands of Lower Cretaceous age.

Over large areas of these extensive woodlands, well-drained and mainly sandy, acidic soils thus predominate. The general woodland cover of these forests is one dominated, in many areas, by a rather open Oak–Birch (*Quercus robor, Q. petraea* and *Betula pubescens*) forest community, although other, more scattered, trees of Ash (*Fraxinus excelsior*), Rowan (*Sorbus aucuparia*), Hornbeam (*Carpinus betulus*), Hawthorn (*Crataegus monogyna* and *C. oxycanthoides*), Holly (*Ilex aquifolium*), Crab Apple (*Pyrus malus*) and Elder (*Sambucus nigra*) are also often present, and Ivy (*Hedera helix*) may be frequent. In some, old plantings of Scots Pine (*Pinus sylvestris*) replace the native trees.

Established originally as deer-forests, with deer herds encouraged and protected, with equally heavy grazing by sheep, rabbits, horses and ponies, especially appropriate edaphic and biotic conditions for widespread Bracken encroachment have long been unwittingly managed by man, with the result that particularly extensive stands of Bracken now predominate beneath the generally Oak–Birch woodland canopies of these deer-forests, and almost throughout the glades and rides which penetrate them. Indeed, over very large areas, dense and continuous stands of Bracken fronds about a metre-and-a-half high occur in almost all areas in which appreciable daylight pierces the broken woodland canopy, and such stands, whilst they may have given good cover for outlaws in Robin Hood's day, can be penetrated in summer today only with difficulty.

Such dense and often tall Bracken stands generally occupy all the principal areas between the trees over extensive areas. Fallen dry leaf debris is annually caught and held by the dense Bracken stems and by the numerous fallen Oak and Birch twigs accumulating amongst them. The slow rate of decay of this loose, dry debris, plus that contributed each winter by the Bracken fronds themselves, only slowly turning to a raw, dry, humus mat, adds physically, as well as by its exudates of plant-toxic ('allelopathic') chemicals, to the poor ability of seedlings of other herbs, as well as of trees, to regularly establish within it. The strong, emerging, Bracken fronds are, however, able to annually thrust upward through the dense mat, as do the emerging shoots of Bluebells (*Hyacinthoides non-scripta*).

More occasional other herbs may, however, be present additionally, but usually only in any quantity where such mats are thinner and sparser, such as near to the margins of the stands themselves, or where reduced illumination by shading reduces the density of the overall Bracken frond cover. These typically include such plants as Heath Bedstraw (*Galium saxatile*), Tormentil (*Potentilla erecta*) and Sheep's Sorrel (*Rumex acetosella* within and around the stands, with occasional flowering spikes of Foxglove (*Digitalis purpurea*) emerging above the dense Bracken canopy. Areas of Creeping Soft-grass and Yorkshire Fog (*Holcus mollis* and *H. lanatus*) are often present but are generally confined to areas where the Bracken fronds are more scattered. Bracken is also especially continuous as the marginal society along most of the ancient forest rides, fringed on its lighter side usually by a turf of Wavy hairgrass (*Deschampsia flexuosa*), where Field Woodrush (*Luzula campestris*) also joins the association.

In the densest shade around the boles of the largest Oak trees, where light is usually lowest, is usually a zone where Bracken considerably thins or is totally absent. Such zones, which are typically largely free of leaf debris (which instead blows into and is trapped by the Bracken) may include many small herbs, but is usually covered by a fine grassy turf composed mainly of *Deschampsia flexuosa*.

Although it is difficult for seedlings of higher plants to establish in the densest Bracken litter mat, observations certainly suggest that when grazing is removed, seedlings of plants such as Oak and Rowan nevertheless do appear through it, usually beginning first in places such as those where Bracken is already somewhat thinned by shading, such as (and perhaps even especially) in the relatively light shade cast by the Birch phases of the forest community mosaic.

Inland, Limestone, Valley Woodland

Deep limestone valleys are not common, but occur widely scattered throughout predominantly lowland areas of both Britain and Ireland. Their often steep, rocky sides, can be precipitous, and boulder-strewn slopes may abound, needing appropriate caution in botanical exploration. Sink-holes and caves may also occur. Notable examples occur in the Mendips of Somerset, in Yorkshire, Derbyshire, Shropshire and especially in several sites in and around the Wye Valley fringing the Forest of Dean between Gloucestershire and Monmouthshire (Gwent), from where most of the following examples are taken.

The forest dominants of the lowland limestone woods in these sites usually include varying proportions of larger and smaller trees and shrubs, including Ash (*Fraxinus excelsior*), Beech (*Fagus sylvatica*, native in southern Britain), Oak (*Quercus rubor*), Elm (particularly *Ulmus glabra*), Hazel (*Corylus avallana*), Elder (*Sambucus nigra*), Maple (*Acer campestre*), Dogwood (*Cornus sanguinea*), Hawthorn (*Crataegus monogyna*), Holly (*Ilex aquifolium*), Yew (*Taxus baccata*), Great Sallow (*Salix caprea*), Rowan (*Sorbus aucuparia*), Spindle-tree (*Euonymus europaeus*), Buckthorn (*Rhamnus catharticus*), Wild Cherry (*Prunus avium*), Sloe (*P. spinosa*), Wild Service Tree

(*Sorbus terminalis* and *S. anglica*), Wayfaring Tree (*Viburnum lantana*) and Guelder Rose (*V. opulus*). Lime (*Tilia cordata*), Hornbeam (*Carpinus betulus*), Whitebeam (*Sorbus aria*), and Box (*Buxus sempervirens*) may be present more locally.

Some woodlands of this type have had a history of coppicing. A few may have been quarried or grazed. The steepest valley and gorge sites, however, are generally less accessible to man and stock, and are often less damaged. The tremendous variation of relief has often caused a rich mosaic of moisture seepage and drainage conditions to evolve, and with it a mosaic of conditions of acidity, varying from exposed base-rich, mineral, surfaces to more acidic pockets where quantities of humus may have steadily accumulated from leaf litter and animal activity over long periods. The often diverse flora within these varying habitats suggests that they may be representative, at least in places, of the original wildwood, and where situated in high rainfall districts, such damp and rocky limestone woodlands often possess a very considerable luxuriance of ferns.

In such sites, the forest floor association in all the more base-rich sites is typically composed of a locally dense community of mainly Hart's Tongue Fern (*Phyllitis scolopendrium*) and Soft Shield-fern (*Polystichum setiferum*), often with a smaller admixture of Common Male-fern (*Dryopteris filix-mas*). Scattered tangled clumps of Golden-scaled Male-fern (*D. affinis* subsp. *borreri*) usually mark drier, less basic sites, whilst occasional plants of Broad Buckler-fern (*Dryopteris dilatata*), sometimes with fronds to a metre or more in length, usually mark hollow pockets, such as on the tops of boulders, where appreciable depths of moist, acidic humus has accumulated. This latter species in particular may also be present epiphytically in similar mossy humus pockets on decaying, fallen logs.

In flatter, basic, mainly mineral soil pockets of the forest floor, where more moisture collects, enormous and usually very beautiful, massive, upright shuttlecocks of Robust Golden-scaled Male-fern (*Dryopteris affinis* subsp. *robusta*) frequently join the association. These have stiff, thick-stiped fronds (the largest fronds of any native *Dryopteris*), reaching waist to shoulder high in favourable spots, and the distinctive shuttlecocks themselves may be up to two metres across.

Scattered plants of Hard Fern (*Blechnum spicant*) may occur locally on occasional steep, damp, humus-rich pockets, where inflowing surface run-off water from acidic areas above causes leaching and makes the sites too acidic for Hart's Tongue or for the Shield-ferns to succeed.

On damp cliffs within wooded limestone valleys or gorges, especially around moist, cool, deeply-shaded, sink-holes'

Phyllitis scolopendrium *in rich, western, limestone, valley woodland. Co. Sligo, July*

mouths and caves, communities of Brittle Bladder-fern (*Cystopteris fragilis*) may dominate locally, forming delicate curtains of fine, hanging fronds from the vertical rock surfaces. On aspects of the same cliffs receiving stronger light, Brittle Bladder-fern merges with, and eventually gives way to, sometimes numerous and luxuriant plants of Maidenhair Spleenwort (*Asplenium trichomanes* subsp. *quadrivalens*), fringed along the better-drained and best-lit tops of cliff-faces by often scattered but sometimes large and probably ancient clumps of Wall Rue (*A. ruta-muraria*), in one of its few, purely natural habitats.

Where woodland limestone cliffs emerge out above the woody canopy and become exposed to more or less full daylight, plants of *A. ruta-muraria* are very frequently joined by Rusty-back Fern (*Ceterach officinarum*), forming sometimes massive and also probably very ancient, scaly clumps. Here, *Ceterach officinarum* generally replaces *Asplenium ruta-muraria* in all bare limestone crevice sites most exposed to direct sun and to the most desiccating summer conditions.

Within the woodland, plants of Polypody may clothe whole rock faces with one, or usually many, extensive colonies. The

most characteristic Polypody of limestone woodland habitats is certainly Southern Polypody (*Polypodium australe*). This species reaches its most luxuriant and most extensive in any purely natural habitat where limestone cliffs outcrop in river valley woodland, spreading not only over the cliffs themselves, but also becoming epiphytic and extending 30–40 ft (10 m or more) over rough-barked trees. Moss-covered soil-fragment accumulations around its roots in such habitats show that even in epiphytic sites, these can be quite basic, with a pH range as high as 6.5–8.0.

Western Polypody (*Polypodium interjectum*) is also usually frequent within the same sites, where it may also form extensive clumps, covering tops of cliffs and isolated boulders with a thick, green blanket, or spread luxuriantly over the tops of boulder-fragment slopes across loose cliff bases. It also frequently occurs epiphytically, often extensively ascending rough-barked tree trunks, such as those of oaks, and over the tops of their spreading boughs, especially on trees sited close to stream-courses and along well-lit, more isolated boughs which most directly overhang the moving water. Common Polypody (*Polypodium vulgare*) also occurs in limestone woodland, but in more limited numbers, and is usually restricted to epiphytic habitats, whilst hybrids between the various species of *Polypodium* occur occasionally in limestone.

Cystopteris fragilis, occurring deep in a stream ravine, marking an exposure of Old Red Sandstone conglomerate rock with a lime-yielding cementiferous matrix. Mid-Perthshire, August

This characteristic community of ferns, which is rich in numbers of individuals and luxuriance of the specimens, is associated with a scattered but often diverse assemblage of flowering plants. These may include locally frequent trailing Ivy (*Hedera helix*), twining stems of Old Man's Beard (*Clematis vitalba*) and scrambling Bramble (*Rubus fruticosus* agg.), Stone Bramble (*R. saxatilis*) and Wild Rose (*Rubus arvensis* and *R. canina*); with locally denser patches of Dog's Mercury (*Mercurialis perennis*), Wild Garlic (*Allium ursinum*), Violets (*Viola* spp., especially *V. reichenbachiana* and *V. hirta*) and Wood Anemone (*Anemone nemorosa*), and more scattered Primrose (*Primula vulgaris*), Wild Arum (*Arum maculatum*), Sanicle (*Sanicula europaea*), Wild Madder (*Rubia peregrina*), Wall Lettuce (*Mycelis muralis*), Sweet Woodruff (*Galium odoratum*), Wood Avens (*Geum urbanum*), Wild Strawberry (*Fragaria vesca*), Herb Robert (*Geranium robertianum*), Primrose (*Primula vulgaris*), Bugle (*Ajuga reptans*), Germander Speedwell (*Veronica chamaedrys*), Wood Spurge (*Euphorbia amygdaloides*), Twayblade (*Listera ovata*), Wood Melick (*Melica uniflora*), Wood Millet (*Milium effusum*) and Slender False-brome (*Brachypodium sylvaticum*).

Base-rich Clay Valley Woodland

Clay is the commonest rock type in lowland England, with many rivers flowing partly or wholly on clays of a wide range of geological ages. These include such clays as the Gault, Oxford, Kimmeridge, Lias, Wealden, and the widespread and characteristically red clays associated with the Old and New Red Sandstone systems, such as the red clays of Devon and of several regions of the Welsh Marches. Such clays give rise to moist and sticky, heavy, lowland soils. They are easily eroded by even small and slow-flowing rivers into often steep and slippery-sided valleys, which, because of their general fertility and heavy nature, are usually fringed closely along their sides by pasture land. Too steep to be used for pasture, and hedged against stock, steeper clay valleys often retain valuable woodland fragments, which, in many cases, may have been managed over long periods by coppicing.

Such habitats are particularly characteristic therefore of the low-altitude river and stream valleys of central and western England, but they also occur more sporadically elsewhere, with good examples stretching from Cornwall (eg. Stennack Woods) and Devon (eg. Chudleigh and Slapton Woods) northward on western coasts at least to (Kirkbean Glen) and on the east to the Borders (Pease Dene) and East Lothian

(Thornton Glen). The steeper slopes of these valleys are always slippery after rain, and the habitats particularly easily damaged, and can usually best (and often only) be explored by wading carefully along their stream-beds.

Because clays are comparatively impervious, water usually drains directly across their sloping surfaces, and the patterns of surface erosion may be complex, providing numerous, generally moist, mineral soil surfaces with low plant competition. Such clays characteristically contain a large proportion of extremely fine particles. Since they are the end products of degradation of various more complex rock types, clays are chemically relatively stable, containing large amounts of silica and aluminium and often iron (in a highly oxidised state in red clays). They also have negatively charged particle surfaces, where nutrient cations such as those of calcium and magnesium may be held to a degree which makes them available for plant nutrition but not readily lost by leaching, and although the determinable pH may not always be especially high (varying from pH 5.6 to 8.6, but mostly about 7.0–7.5 in those measured), base-loving species, at least of pteridophytes, usually predominate.

Such clay valleys typically carry mixed deciduous woodland, usually dominated by Oak. Both *Quercus* species occur, but especially *Q. robor*, often with a mixture of other trees which may include Ash (*Fraxinus excelsior*), Elm (*Ulmus glabra*), Hazel (*Corylus avellana*), Field Maple (*Acer campestre*), Wild Cherry (*Prunus avium*), and introduced Sycamore (*Acer pseudoplatanus*) and Sweet Chestnut (*Castanea sativa*).

The pteridophyte community of such woodlands is one often dominated by very large numbers of individuals of Soft Shield-fern (*Polystichum setiferum*) and Hart's Tongue Fern (*Phyllitis scolopendrium*). These generally base-loving ferns may eventually grow into very large size and probably fairly old plants. They both usually predominate on steep, moist ground (the latter usually in the wettest steep sites), and both can usually be found actively recolonising erosion slopes of bare clay surfaces, sometimes in very large numbers. Additionally, in valley-bottom sites, robust Golden-scaled Male-fern (*Dryopteris affinis* subsp. *robusta*) forms, as it does in limestone gorge woodland, sometimes extremely large, upright, basket-like shuttlecocks of fronds. Indeed, the dominant fern association is very similar to that of such limestone woodlands, and it is perhaps the association of especially the two former species with sloping surfaces, where mineral clay surfaces are steadily eroded and virtually continuously re-exposed, that enables such base-loving species to succeed in large numbers. In such sites, they are effectively almost continually pioneering opened

mineral soil surfaces created by steady surface erosion. They thus represent the virtually permanent, early stage of seral colonisation of the bared clay slopes which, were erosion to cease and more stable surfaces with litter accumulation build up, would perhaps ultimately support less base-demanding species.

Indeed, intermixed, in a complex mosaic in such woodlands, often in occasional flatter spots where more litter has accumulated, are usually a smaller number of less base-demanding ferns—the location of these probably marking the least actively-eroding and perhaps most serally advanced spots. These include scattered plants of Common Male-fern (*Dryopteris filix-mas*), occasional hybrids between *D. filix-max* and *D. affinis* subsp. *robusta* (themselves usually producing a large percentage of good spores and self-perpetuating apogamously in these sites), clumps of Broad Buckler-fern (*D. dilatata*) and occasional Lady Fern (*Athyrium filix-femina*) in moister spots and, often fringing moist shoulders of more acidic run-off where Greater Woodrush (*Luzula sylvatica*) appears, are scattered plants of Hard Fern (*Blechnum spicant*).

These woods too can be extremely rich in Polypodies, but here, Western Polypody (*Polypodium interjectum*) is the predominant and often the only species, usually forming large-fronded masses capping the tops of fallen logs and along the horizontal limbs of trees, where these spread across the watercourses. Common Polypody (*P. vulgare*) occurs much more occasionally in such sites, but where it does, its hybrid with *P. interjectum, P.* × *mantoniae* can occur as well.

The most characteristically associated flowering plants of the habitats dominated by *Polystichum setiferum* and *Phyllitis scolopendrium* are certainly, in most sites, dense drifts of Wild Garlic (*Allium ursinum*), with patches of Golden Saxifrage (*Chrysosplenium oppositifolium*) usually marking moister spots of trickling water.

Basic, Spring-fed Woodland

This local and somewhat unusual type of woodland occurs around base-rich seepage lines, springlines and springheads, where calcareous rock aquifers permanently discharge base-rich water over heavy clay soils. The flushed, swampy habitats created are thus rich and wet all year round; their soil is extremely soft, silty and slippery underfoot, and small depressions and footprints usually fill with steadily seeping moisture.

Frequently, the clays themselves, are base-rich ones, and this high base status is usually reflected in their dominant woody vegetation: the trees within or around such swamps are typically mostly of Ash (*Fraxinus excelsior*), Pedunculate Oak (*Quercus robor*) and particularly abundant Hazel (*Corylus avellana*).

Within the field layer around the swamps, scattered plants of Common Male-fern (*Dryopteris filix-mas*) and Robust Golden-scaled Male-fern (*D. affinis* subsp. *robusta*) often occur, the former typically in the slightly drier ground above the wettest parts of the swamps, the latter often along their damp flanks. Below such swamps, where the ground becomes flatter and water flow usually slackens, plants of Narrow Buckler-fern (*D. carthusiana*) are sometimes present, and Lady Fern (*Athyrium filix-femina*) may form scattered clumps. Broad Buckler-fern (*Dryopteris dilatata*) may also occur, but it is usually confined to relatively well drained perches on the emergent roots and boles of standing trees within or around the swamps, or as an epiphyte on old tree stumps and fallen logs, where both Common Polypody (*Polypodium vulgare*) and Western Polypody (*P. interjectum*) may also form local colonies.

Of particular interest is the occasional occurrence below the swamps, of specimens of Hybrid Narrow Buckler-fern *Dryopteris* × *deweveri* (*D. carthusiana* × *D. dilatata*). Where present, these typically occur in habitats of approximately intermediate wetness to those of its two parents, but they can sometimes be vigorous hybrids and occupy every intermediate of soil condition.

Within the swamp itself, however, is usually a single, but vegetatively extensive, pteridophyte. Here, Great Horsetail (*Equisetum telmateia*) characteristically forms one of the most abundant plants. Its distinctive, ivory-white shoots with profuse whorls of bright green branches, usually occur either in a mixed and co-dominant association with a small number of flowering plants, or, more often, form the single vegetationally dominant field-layer plant, in often robust colonies, reminiscent of a miniature version of a Carboniferous swamp.

Throughout the swamps, there is presumably a ready availability of abundant chemical bases from the seeping water, plus siliceous ones from the wet clay substrate itself—a combination which appears to be ideal for the enormous annual biomass of the highly silica-rich shoots of this large species. Other factors probably also of high importance for the success of Great Horsetail in these habitats appear to be a high state of aeration and constant movement of the seeping springwater and the presence of adequate depth of moist clay substrate for its deep and extensive rhizome development.

Equisetum telmateia is the largest native horsetail (and indeed, the largest of the deciduous-stemmed horsetails anywhere in the world). Although its range stretches in a diagonal band across Europe from Ireland south-eastwards to the northern and eastern shores of the Mediterranean, with scattered stations southwards to Madeira, it is an especially European pteridophyte, which occurs elsewhere, in a somewhat different subspecific form, only on the Pacific coast of western North America. This curiously discontinuous distribution, linked only by a probably allied species, *E. mekongense*, in the far east of Asia, is probably indicative of a relict distribution of a former (probably pre-Pleistocene), once more widespread range, which has subsequently become fragmented. Its particular success in Britain and Ireland in the Atlantic north-west of Europe and again in the Pacific north-west of North America is probably no coincidence, for it thrives especially well in these moderately warm, moist climates, forming in both Britain and Ireland, some of the largest and most luxuriant colonies of the species anywhere. Here, it commonly attains 1.5–2.0 m in height, and I have measured shoots in at least one Welsh locality attaining nearly 2.5 m in height, with a basal stem diameter of over 2 cm.

A small but fairly characteristic group of flowering plants is usually associated in smaller or large numbers with Great

Horsetail in these swamps. These usually include some or all of: Lesser Celandine (*Ranunculus ficaria*—occasionally forming a dense carpet), scattered Creeping Buttercup (*R. repens*), Meadowsweet (*Filipendula ulmaria*), Wild Angelica (*Angelica sylvestris*), and sometimes Purple Loostrife (*Lythrum salicaria*), Water Avens (*Geum rivale*), Wood Spurge (*Euphorbia amygdaloides*), Golden Saxifrage (*Chrysosplenium oppositifolium*), Primrose (*Primula vulgaris*), Bugle (*Ajuga reptans*), Wood Bitter-cress (*Cardamine flexuosa*), and Remote Sedge (*Carex remota*). Sometimes plants of Lesser Celandine are very numerous, and form local, solid societies beneath the emerging shoots of the horsetail in early spring. Meadowsweet may locally dominate along better-lit margins of the site. A dense, loose, carpet of mosses is usually present, including *Mnium undulatum*, *Hypnum cupressiforme* and *Hylocomium splendens*.

Ravine Woodlands over Mixed Rock Types

Deciduous woodland fragments exist from place to place along the valley corridors of most of our natural streams and rivers. Whether these be in small ravines near river headwaters or in larger steep valleys and gorges of more mature river reaches, many common factors of site diversity and topographic and environmental conditions unite these sites pteridologically. It is thus convenient to treat those which occur along the whole courses of most rivers together here, pointing occasionally to more upland or lowland aspects of them where appropriate. Only those ravine woodlands which are restricted to the much wetter and more oceanic climates of the extreme Atlantic fringes of these islands differ especially in pteridophyte species content from most, and are thus discussed separately (see chapter 13).

Many of our more precipitous river valleys have been cut or enlarged to their present form where they passed through relatively soft, sedimentary (and hence easily worn) strata, especially in regions where such rocks have risen around the river courses following the release during post-glacial time or the weight of their former heavy overburden of Pleistocene ice. In Britain, deep lowland river valleys are thus especially characteristic of the rivers of the regions stretching from the English Midlands northward to the Midland Valley of Scotland, and in Northern Ireland. Through these regions, the high concentration of many particularly fine examples of deep, wooded river valleys have earned local generic names: 'gorges' in the southern England, 'dales' in the Peak District and Yorkshire, 'denes' in Durham, Northumberland and the Borders, 'dens'

in eastern Scotland, and 'glens' in the rest of Scotland and
northern Ireland (notably those of Antrim).

The Woodland Ravine Environment

Within most river corridor ravine woodlands, environmental
conditions combine in unique ways to make these some of the
most important and diverse pteridophyte habitats within these
islands.

The first important feature in promoting pteridophyte
success in such ravine woodlands is their enhanced shelter,
shade and humidity, the latter of which can be high towards
ravine bottoms near to tumbling watercourses. These factors
are important not just for the levels which they achieve, but also
for their constancy.

Secondly, such sites are usually pteridophyte-rich because
of the very high diversity of edaphic niches available, in the
form of complex rock and soil mosaics. For the erosional forces
of such ravines, often cut into the rock in the form of insised
meanders, have long removed the residual layers of blanketing
boulder clay, exposing instead valley-side successions of very
varying rock strata. The resulting edaphic mosaics include
ones of groundwater conditions, base availability and degree of
erosion.

Of the groundwater conditions, both water seepage and
drainage are usually greatly enhanced on steep valley sides,
with wide variation with almost every break of slope, change of
rock permeability and change of dip of the rock layers exposed.

The mosaic of base availability varies widely, depending on
the base-yielding abilities of each rock stratum exposed or
from which seepage is itself arising. Often sedimentary rock
strata can vary in particularly quick succession. In Northumberland and the central valley of Scotland, for example, where
the rocks exposed are predominantly ones of Lower Carboniferous age, very numerous irregularly successive bands of
shales, mudstones, coals, grits, sandstones, calcareous
sandstones, thin bands of limestone, and sometimes conglomerates can be progressively presented to plant colonisation.

The erosional/depositional mosaic also varies widely with
varying topography, slope, exposure and position on the valley
sides. In sites of little erosion or in ones of steady accumulation,
individual plants may be able to achieve great age or colonial
plants a large colony-size. In sites of steady erosion, newly
exposed mineral-rich surfaces may be available for continual
new fern prothallial establishment, sometimes in large

numbers. A high degree of recruitment of new individuals and constant losses of short-lived old ones, is probably inherent in their pteridophyte populations.

In such diverse and sheltered sites as river valley slopes, there is, through the operation and superposition of all of these mosaics, frequently a high diversity of pteridophyte species, with base-loving and acid-loving species often occurring near to each other, in sometimes confusing proximity.

A final factor in promoting pteridophyte success within ravine woodland is the usually high degree of freedom from disturbance and from grazing of such sites, and especially from the perennial and concentrated grazing of domesticated stock. Indeed, such freedom has probably always largely applied especially to ravine woodlands over long periods. At worst they may have suffered from intermittent extraction of more accessible timber, and sometimes introduction of scattered exotic trees (but, fortunately, not usually of plantations). In many river ravine woodlands it is therefore probable that much of the ground flora vegetation that we see today, if not necessarily the trees themselves, may have a particularly long history of minimal disturbance and change, approaching fairly closely to that of the original wildwood of these special sites.

Typically, such woodlands form very important, surviving fragments of once much more widespread oak woodlands, of which those within ravines often enjoy an especially high species diversity. This diversity extends to their trees as well their herbaceous component. Ravine woodlands are thus often dominated by Oaks (*Quercus robor* and *Q. petraea*), with a wide mixture of other trees and shrubs. A compound list of these can include varying quantities of Ash (*Fraxinus excelsior*), Beech (*Fagus sylvatica*), Rowan (*Sorbus aucuparia*), Birch (*Betula pubescens* and *B. pendula*), Wych Elm (*Ulmus glabra*), Hazel (*Corylus avallana*), Hawthorn (*Crataegus monogyna*), Field Maple (*Acer campestre*), Elder (*Sambucus nigra*), Blackthorn (*Prunus spinosa*), Bird Cherry (*P. padus*) and Guelder Rose (*Viburnum opulus*). Too frequently, introduced Sycamore (*Acer pseudoplatanus*) may be spreading, as may planted Norway Spruce (*Picea abies*) and sometimes Douglas Fir (*Pseudotsuga menziesii*).

Valley Side Habitats

Along the tops of valleys, where they are presently often fenced and where their vegetation consequently now often merges directly into modern pasture, such valleys would have originally merged into the flatter or more gently sloping parts of the original wildwood community. In places, such communities still fringe their tops, often dominated by great stands of Common Male-fern (*Dryopteris filix-mas*), Common Golden-scaled Male-fern (*Dryopteris affinis* subsp. *borreri*) or Broad Buckler-fern (*D. dilatata*), typically with abundant Wood-sorrel (*Oxalis acetosella*) and climbing Honeysuckle (*Lonicera periclymenum*). In the most open spots, such as in the early seral stages of glade vegetation, woodland margin communities are usually present, in which Bracken (*Pteridium aquilinum*) occurs as probably an indigenous element, in communities which also contain such species as Cow-wheat (*Melampyrum pratense*), Golden-rod (*Solidago virgaurea*), Wood Sage (*Teucrium scorodonia*), Foxglove (*Digitalis purpurea*), Bramble (*Rubus fruticosus* agg.), Purging Flax (*Linum catharticum*), Creeping Soft-grass (*Holcus mollis*) and Wavy Hair-grass (*Deschampsia flexuosa*). In spring, there may be large drifts of Bluebell (*Hyacinthoides non-scriptus*).

Descending the slopes of the valleys, the upper shoulders of the ravines, especially in more acidic sites, are frequently marked by the appearance of Hard Fern (*Blechnum spicant*), by itself or in an association with Broad Buckler-fern. These ferns very typically occur amongst drifts of Greater Woodrush (*Luzula sylvatica*), capping the fringes of the slopes and those of upper ravineside shelves, and probably indicative of areas of a lateral and descending movement of fairly acidic groundwater.

Where much more basic and mineral-rich water seeps into the ravines, an altogether different pteridophyte-rich association typically occurs, dominated by often luxuriant stands of the Great Horsetail (*Equisetum telmateia*), marking areas of soft, wet, clay-rich ground, where much of the lateral water percolation may be at or just below the surface.

Depending on the slope of the ravine side and its hydrological properties, both of these communities may continue extensively in downslope directions, or may occur sporadically with changes of slope and water-seepage characteristics in intermittent patches on ravine sides. Usually, however, the widely varying exposures of different edaphic mosaics, ensure other mostly pteridophyte-rich habitats are more frequent.

Where the downslope mosaics continue to be fairly acidic ones, the dominant fern community is usually composed of varying proportions of Broad Buckler-fern, Common Male-fern and Golden-scaled Male-fern, joined by mixtures of Hard Fern and Woodland Lady-fern (*Athyrium filix-femina*). All these species may be present in considerable abundance, while in northern and upland ravines particularly, more scattered plants of both Sweet Mountain Fern (*Oreopteris limbosperma*) and Northern Buckler-fern (*Dryopteris expansa*) may join this richly fern-dominated woodland association. Sometimes Broad Buckler and Male-ferns are totally dominant over large areas, with appreciable numbers of often old individuals occupying most damp, well-drained, rocky or humus-rich niches, and forming a dense, waist-high sward of fronds by midsummer. Sometimes Hard Fern and Wood Horsetail (*Equisetum sylvaticum*) also dominate in large patches, usually on the most shaded, steep, cool, moist earth banks, whilst patches of Lady-fern usually mark areas of greatest acidic surface moisture, and are thus frequently present where seeping water from above accumulates briefly, or in soft, moist soil around the margins of trickling rills. It is especially in these sites, as well as on moist shoulders over which water is dripping, that Sweet Mountain Fern may be present.

Wherever drier boulders outcrop on steep, shaded, ravine sides, these are likely to be capped by one or other species of Polypody, growing extensively amongst shallow humus and moss accumulations. Similar moss-fern communities usually also occur on and around erosion-exposed tree boles and on

Inacessibility to larger grazing animals ensures steep ravine sides are often rich habitats for ferns. Midlothian, October

fallen, decaying logs. On more acidic boulders, such as those of sandstones, as well as on tree-boles and logs in overall more acidic habitats, it is Common Polypody (*Polypodium vulgare*) that is the most common of this group. Often its sites are also marked by occasional plants of Broad Buckler-fern, competing for moist pockets, and succeeding better than the Polypody in those in which raw humus layers become deep. Where there is a slightly better base-status to these sites, Western Polypody (*P. interjectum*) is likely to be present as well. It is unusual, however, to find Southern Polypody in such woodland habitats, except for those in very base-rich habitats, and especially in ones over pure limestones.

Where thin beds of limestones outcrop in ravines, however, it is much more common for these to be marked by fringes of scattered plants of Hard Shield-fern (*Polystichum aculeatum*), and associated with it, on the steep, moist, shaded sides of such bluffs, with a range of small, calciolous fern species. Typically these include Common Maidenhair Spleenwort (*Asplenium trichomanes* subsp. *quadrivalens*), Brittle Bladder-fern (*Cystopteris fragilis*), and, especially in northern districts, Green Spleenwort (*A. viride*). Sometimes on less lime-yielding rock, Delicate Maidenhair Spleenwort (*Asplenium trichomanes* subsp. *trichomanes*) may be present as well. In much larger, generally base-yielding, fissures, there may also be large old plants of Hart's Tongue Fern (*Phyllitis scolopendrium*).

Hart's Tongue Fern may also be present, especially in southern districts (but, more sporadically, as far north as the Borders), in clay pockets or on exposures of shales where they rapidly weather to soft, base-rich clay slopes. Here it is frequently associated with Soft Shield-fern (*Polystichum setiferum*) and, where such clays level out near valley bottoms, it is also very common to find Robust Golden-scaled Male-fern (*Dryopteris affinis* subsp. *robusta*) joining this association.

Usually deep within wooded valleys and ravines, especially in more northern districts, Woodland Oak Fern (*Gymnocarpium dryopteris*) and Beech Fern (*Phegopteris connectilis*) are frequently present. These two species occur chiefly near to ravine woodland bases and above larger outcropping shoulders on lower valley sides or within the angles formed between steep ravine sides and their floors. For here, shallow soil slopes of fine, downwash alluvium sometimes accumulate. These sites, often of moderate base-status, are highly sheltered and humid and their soil usually deep, soft, moist, and well-drained, and especially suitable to the vegetative spread of the thin subterranean rhizomes of each of these species. Either Beech or Oak Fern consequently usually dominate this habitat, although each may extend in lesser form to more minor soil pockets else-

where or spread vegetatively to other habitats nearby. Despite their English names, these two species are by no means confined to habitats within just strictly Beech or Oak woodland, but are generally characteristic of such sites in northern deciduous ravine woodlands (especially in Britain, although are rare in Ireland), and it seems likely that the occurrence of colonies of either species are indicative largely of sites with a particularly long history of continuous former woodland cover.

Gymnocarpium dryopteris *which is probably a valuable indicator of ancient deciduous woodland ground flora in the absence of excessive grazing. Mid-Perthshire, June*

Valley Bottom Habitats

Towards the bases of steep woodland valleys, where their slopes begin to level out, habitats usually grade through alluvial earth banks to damp and often seepage-irrigated valley floors. Steep undercut rock faces may occur on the outside of river and stream bends, whilst sands and shallow gravel fans frequently flank their inner shores. Swampy patches may form where water is temporarily impounded, and fallen, semi-rotten trunks of trees straddle streams where they fell or where winter storms have lodged them. Outcropping boulders of all sizes can be common, whilst numerous small waterfalls along stream-courses help maintain a cool and slightly turbulent humidity in the sheltered valley depths.

The particular suitability of these sites for pteridophyte growth, is reflected in the vegetational dominance which pteridophytes usually achieve, as well as in the size and sheer luxuriance of most individuals present. Indeed, almost all the pteridophytes seen previously are likely also to be encountered here, usually as large-statured individuals, whilst several other species of more restricted ecological range, also join the association.

Especially, though not exclusively, in northern and upland ravines, on slopes of only moderately acidic, sloping soil alluvium and spreading into damper, more peaty hollows where there is some mineral-flushing, extensive colonies of Wood Horsetail (*Equisetum sylvaticum*) may occur. This horsetail can be very abundant in these upland habitats, its numerous, upright shoots looking individually like forests of miniature spruce trees, but with branched branches so numerous and fine that en masse the plant appears to cover the ground with a fine, green, mist.

In shallow valleys, semi-open riverside banks with occasional outcropping rock faces and sandy spits, may carry their own riverside flora of species characteristic of inland rocks and of disturbed sandy ground. Scattered plants of Black Spleenwort (*Asplenium adiantum-nigrum*) may grow in exposed crevices of occasional sunny rock faces, surrounded by patches of Wild Thyme (*Thymus praecox*) and English Stonecrop (*Sedum anglicum*). *Dryopteris filix-mas* and *Athyrium filix-femina* may occur here too, as well as in adjacent sandy banks, where rather thin stands of *Pteridium aquilinum* are usually also widely, and probably entirely naturally, present.

Along sandy banks raised slightly above the levels of the water, but which are variously drained, different species of horsetails are very frequently present. In both lowland and upland regions. Common Horsetail (*Equisetum arvense*) is a very common component of the vegetation here, and like Bracken, is probably an entirely natural component of damp, sandy banks. From these, it frequently spreads by shallow, subterranean, rhizome growth into spits of shifting sand, where it perhaps adds a certain amount of stability to otherwise mobile sand surfaces as one of the first vascular pioneers.

Equisetum arvense and sometimes also *E. sylvaticum* may be joined in northern England, but especially in northern Ireland and in Scotland, by stands of Shade Horsetail (*E. pratense*), streamside clumps of Dutch Rush (*E. hyemale*), occasional Variegated Horsetail (*E. variegatum*), and very locally (such as in the Antrim glens), Mackay's Horsetail (*E.* × *trachyodon*).

Equisetum pratense, *from the woodland shown below, is an indicator of ancient streamside woodland in Scotland. Mid-Perthshire, July*

Hazel woodland on base-rich, streamside sand. This woodland is ancient, confirmed by its rich ground flora, with dense patches of Equisetum pratense, Paris quadrifolia *and* Convallaria majalis. *Mid-Perthshire, late June*

Both these latter two horsetails usually occur as scattered but sometimes locally extensive waterside colonies. *E. pratense* is particularly characteristic of sandy, seepage-irrigated, banks sloping gently down to flowing stream water, where there is some regular stream innundation and scouring of the site in winter, helping minimise the vascular plant competition within it. Its shoots are nearly as delicate in appearance as those of *E. sylvaticum*, with which, in the field, it can easily be confused at first sight, although its equally slender whorled branches, are not themselves usually further branched. *E. hyemale* also usually grows within the immediate neighbourhood of flowing streamwater, in sites which are also at least partly winter-scoured, but seems more frequently to inhabit more substantial clay banks than does *E. pratense*, from where it may ascend along lines of local groundwater seepage, to bank levels appreciably above streamwater flooding.

Associated with these pteridophytes in rather open river-bank habitats are usually a dense tangle of species characteristic of moist, sandy and slightly flushed ground, grassy places, and those of disturbed habitats.

Valleys with predominantly mixed rock strata in which such a great diveristy of pteridophytes abound, are very often also sites in which a great number of small and scattered herbs also grow in association with the fern communities, some of which are of more unusual occurrence. Those most frequently noted include Woodrush (*Luzula sylvatica*), Stone Bramble (*Rubus saxatilis*), Ivy (*Hedera helix*), Bluebell (*Hyacinthoides non-scripta*), Wood Anemone (*Anemone nemorosa*), Dog's Mercury (*Mercurialis perennis*), Wild Garlic (*Allium ursinum*), Honeysuckle (*Lonicera periclymentum*), Wood-sorrel (*Oxalis acetosella*) and Primrose (*Primula vulgaris*), with more scattered plants of Sweet Woodruff (*Galium odoratum*), Wild Arum (*Arum maculatum*), Herb Robert (*Geranium robertianum*), Wood Cranesbill (*Geranium sylvaticum*), Common Violet (*Viola riviniana*), Pale Wood Violet (*V. reichenbachiana*), Wild Strawberry (*Fragaria vesca*), Wood and Water Avens (*Geum urbanum* and *G. rivale*), Sanicle (*Sanicula europaea*), Ground Ivy (*Glechoma hederacea*), Yellow Pimpernel (*Lysimachia nemorum*), Wood Forget-me-not (*Myosotis sylvatica*), Pignut (*Conopodium majus*), Self-heal (*Prunella vulgaris*), Bugle (*Ajuga reptans*), Enchanter's Nightshade (*Circaea lutetiana*), Red Campion (*Silene dioica*), Hedge Woundwort (*Stachys sylvatica*), Common Hemp-nettle (*Galeopsis tetrahit*), Greater Stitchwort (*Stellaria holostea*), Wood Melick (*Melica uniflora*), Wood Millet (*Milium effusum*), Wood Brome (*Festuca altissima*), Slender False-brome (*Brachypodium sylvaticum*) and Hairy Brome (*Bromus ramosus*). Very numerous bryophytes are also present.

In northern England and in Scotland, both *E. pratense* and *E. hyemale* frequently occur within the same valleys, and these are usually in areas where the sands and clays probably most often contain a particularly rich mixture of both available silicates and adequate chemical bases. In Ireland, *Equisetum* × *trachyodon* occurs extensively on rather similar, flushed, calcareous, clayey riverbanks, in glens in which *E. pratense* also occurs. In Scotland, extensive stands of *Gymnocarpium dryopteris* and *Phegopteris connectilis* frequently occur within the same valley woodlands, as do these horsetails, and these valleys are frequently those where flowering plant associates such as *Convallaria majalis, Paris quadrifolia, Listera ovata, Adoxa moschatellina, Sanicula europaea, Anemone nemorosa* and *Conopodium majus* seem to occur in particular close association with these ferns and horsetails, and often in quantity. It seems likely that the sites of such colonies of each of these horsetails, as with those of Woodland Oak Fern *Gymnocarpium dryopteris* and Beech Fern *Phegopteris connectilis*, may well mark valley woodlands which have a particularly long history of constant conditions and ancient woodland cover.

Native Pine Forest

Pine Forest Origins and Environment

Scots Pine (*Pinus syvlestris*) is the world's most widely-distributed species of pine, with a present natural range which forms a far-northerly band extending from Scotland across northern Europe and northern Asia to eastern Siberia. In Britain and Ireland, fossil pollen of this very hardy species of tree is known widely in the Post-glacial, its forest usually expanding into the open birch–hazel vegetation which formed the first Post-glacial woodlands during the period up to about 6,500 yrs BP ('before present').

The majority of the pine forest was largely over heavily lime-deficient, often waterlogged, sandy, gravelly, rocky or peaty soils resulting from the wide extent of poorly base-yielding native rocks, especially in Highland Scotland. Such rock had also been subjected to extensive Pleistocene glacial action and resulting dislocation of the drainage patterns caused by Late-glacial dumping of moraines, the spreading in valleys of extensive fluvio-glacial outwash fans of acidic sands and gravels and the further damming of the drainage systems by extensive subsequent development of peat. The acidity of the habitats over very many areas made them relatively unsuitable for the wide development of broadleaf forests, except, perhaps, for birch, which still today occupies an important place amongst the mosaic of pine.

The extent of the area which became dominated by Scots Pine and the diversity of ecological sites in which it established are, in part at least, the result of the unusual conditions of ecological isolation encountered by this conifer in Post-glacial Britain. Scots Pine (*Pinus sylvestris*) is one of only three native conifers in Britain and Ireland (the others being the Yew *Taxus baccata* and the Juniper *Juniperus communis*). Yew is confined

Native pinewood at the margin of a quiet loch. East Inverness-shire, July

principally (as a native) to alkaline soils, and is thus not a serious competitor for Scots Pine, whilst native Juniper usually forms only a shrub. The success of *Pinus sylvestris* in many habitats of the Highland landscape was in part assisted not only by the lack of extensive broadleaved competition for these sites, but also by the lack of other competing native conifers. In the absence, for example, of such genera as *Abies* (the Firs), *Picea* (the Spruces) and *Larix* (the Larches), all of which are present in mainland Europe but which failed to gain a foothold in Post-glacial Britain before it became an island, a wide range of variants of *Pinus sylvestris* have been able to survive here, which would probably have been eliminated from many habitats in competition with those other conifer genera had they also been present. In consequence, variants of Scots Pine have evolved in northern Britain and especially in Scotland, which have come to occupy virtually the whole range of habitats which are more typically occupied by species of other conifer genera elsewhere in Europe. Forest dominated by pine thus came to extend over many separate facets of our more acidic, upland landscapes.

Whether *Pinus sylvestris* was a Post-glacial immigrant from the continent or whether native insular populations may have survived in our islands (or both) is not known with certainty. It must, however, have been here before Britain was cut off from Europe by the Channel, for this would provide an almost insuperable barrier to conifer migration, except for bird-distributed species such as Yew. One important factor assisting its rapid spread within these islands (rapid for a conifer) is the unusual seed-release time of the cones of at least the native British populations—the cones, instead of shedding all their seed in autumn, usually do not do so until the following January–March. At such times of year, during severe winters, they often fall on to the surface of frozen snow. In such a situation, they are then readily caught by winter winds and 'ski' over the snow surfaces, very greatly increasing their dispersal distances compared with the situation which would arise were they to drop their seed before the snow came, merely to become entangled within the local shrubby undergrowth.

In Ireland and England (and especially in the northern Pennines), *Pinus sylvestris* appears to have become extinct as a native plant, perhaps with the widespread extension of waterlogged soils, from about 5,000 yrs BP onwards. In Scotland, however, it survived, and here the former extent of pine, which has been reconstructed from pollen analytical data, can be shown to be one which covered some very extensive tracts of the Highlands. A former pine or pine-birch forest probably once stretched fairly continuously from near the west coast eastwards across the Great Glen to Grampian in the north, and from the Clyde westward north of the Highland Boundary Fault to the Tay in the south. Today, although only small fragments of this former forest remain, those which persist, such as at Sheldaig and Loch Maree, Glen Affric and the Rothiemurchus and Abernethy forests give some remaining impression of the probable appearance of the former native pinewood and its constituent species (see map on p. 222).

Unlike plantation woodland, the mature Scots Pine trees within much of these remaining native pinewoods are typically widely spaced and of highly individual and of often massive and craggy form. Between them, adequate light normally reaches the ground for a dense understorey to exist, especially of dwarf shrubs of Heather (*Calluna vulgaris*) and Bilberry (*Vaccinium myrtillus*). Birch (*Betula pubescens* in wetter and colder sites and *B. pendula* often in rather drier ones) typically forms patches amongst the pines. A number of other trees and shrubs often occur within the woods more locally. Along streams where bare rock is exposed, Mountain Ash (*Sorbus aucuparia*) usually forms a scattered fringe, and shrubs of Juniper (*Juniperus communis*) may occur in a patchy and scattered form. In this mosaic of communities, interrelationships and successions are probably continuously taking place, whilst with changes in soils, topography, altitude, aspect and drainage, many variations in the herbaceous members of the community occur, including in their fairly widespread pteridophytic components.

Pinewood Ferns and Horsetails

Along streams and small rills in the pinewoods, several ferns are usually present, partly resulting from the heightened humidity and shelter of these sites, and partly resulting from the reduced competition of the numerous regularly eroding surfaces. These habitats typically have an acid-loving flora of species tolerant of high ground moisture and sometimes of deep shade.

Occupying the most freely-drained sites along the streamsides, such as along gravelly shoulders and around outcropping boulders, are usually numerous plants of Broad Buckler-fern (*Dryopteris dilatata*). Broad Buckler-fern is a highly variable species, especially in size and plant habit, especially in pinewood sites. Typical specimens usually have a frond length of about 50–80 cm, but may be as much as 150 cm, and I have occasionally seen plants of this size forming dominant ground-flora patches in old pinewood sites, stretching away from streams, with nearly continuous waist-high or shoulder-high swards, with long fronds arising from massive old stocks, especially where grazing has been successfully excluded. More typically, however, numerous, somewhat smaller, plants of Broad Buckler-fern form a streamside fringe, where their fronds adopt a habit of gracefully arching downslope.

Most larger and well-established plants of Broad Buckler-fern are characterised by a dark-based stipe and numerous, dark-brown, lengthwise striped scales. Smaller specimens may occur, however, in which this characteristic scale colour is much less distinctive and may even be lacking, and, not uncommonly in pinewood sites, plants of this form may also have thin, creeping, rather than thick, ascending rhizomes. Such plants seem especially characteristic of extremely acidic sites and of crevices in rock faces and pockets where raw humus accumulates on the tops of boulders. Plants somewhat intermediate between this type and more typical terrestrial plants also occasionally occur as epiphytes in humus pockets in old pine forks at the bases of branches, especially in areas where humidity is highest near lochsides or at the edges of streams. It is possible that some of these forms may be genuinely genetically different and await further studies to be made on their taxonomic and ecological inter-relationships.

In similar pinewood sites to *Dryopteris dilatata* may occur Golden-scaled Male-fern (*Dryopteris affinis*), whilst on somewhat moister, steeper, more shaded streamside slopes there are often Lady Fern (*Athyrium filix-femina*), Hard Fern (*Blechnum spicant*) and sometimes Narrow Buckler-fern (*Dryopteris carthusiana*).

Dryopteris affinis and *Athyrium filix-femina* usually occur as scattered plants, both along streamsides and in pockets within the forest, especially around boulders. Both can be quite variable, *Athyrium* varying in details of colouration, especially of the stipe, and *Dryopteris affinis* in habit and details of frond dissection. The subspecies of *D. affinis* probably most frequently represented is subsp. *borreri*, and it is possible that in ancient pinewood sites, as with *Dryopteris dilatata*, much of the variation seen within theses two species may have a wide and ancient genetic base.

In somewhat moister stream-side sites and on damp, shaded banks, especially in well sheltered, moist and ungrazed pinewood, Hard Fern (*Blechnum spicant*) may occasionally become an abundant and luxuriant fern forming large, old clumps, often reaching 60 cm or more in diameter. These bear enormous tufts of spreading, dark green, large, irregular rosettes of foliage, from the centres of which, as the growing season progresses, the nearly erect, fertile fronds may arise in great abundance.

Unlike almost all the other ferns of native pinewood, the fronds of *Blechnum* (or, at least, its vegetative ones) are evergreen, unrolling through late May and June, and persisting on the plant for twelve months or longer. Its fertile fronds arise during June and July—later than the vegetative ones, and from the centres of the vegetative rosettes. They shed their sooty black spores mainly through August and September, then die away fairly rapidly—long before the vegetative fronds which initially preceded them in seasonal development. Such rapid shedding of the fertile fronds from the plant seems to stress the highly specialised role of these fronds—almost solely for spore production and dispersal. Each pinna is extremely narrow, with the leafy portion reduced to its inner, sorus-bearing parts, the whole fertile frond thus having a herringbone-like appearance, which is emphasised still further by its usually stiffly erect habit, raising the sori and their spores higher into the more turbulent layers of moving air of the forest than would be achieved were the spores to be produced on the backs of the spreading vegetative fronds of the plant. The vegetative fronds, freed from the need to produce spores by this pronounced frond dimorphism, can be orientated in a fairly spreading and presumably good light-catching direction, which, with their dark

Dense drifts of Phegopteris connectilis *on a steep, wooded slope. Easter Ross, July*

green colour and evergreen habits, enables the fern to succeed in particularly dimly-lit, moist sites, in evergreen forest.

Elsewhere within the pinewoods, sometimes in moist hollows, several colony-forming pteridophytes are usually present, including Woodland Oak-fern, Beech Fern and Wood Horsetail.

Woodland Oak-fern (*Gymnocarpium dryopteris*) may occur widely, mainly in the more sheltered moist but not stagnant hollows amongst the ground flora, typically forming large, bright-green patches in summer. Beech Fern (*Phegopteris connectilis*) is more occasional, but also forms patches in similar habitats, with its triangular, slightly pubescent-surfaced fronds, usually all pointing in a similar direction. In pinewood, both species perhaps mark sites of locally greater mineral exposure and modestly higher soil base-status and effective incorporation of mineral matter into the humus. In such areas, where shelter and ground-moisture are good, individual frond size of both species can be large, with their fertile fronds, usually slightly later to arise and with smaller blade size, standing slightly higher than the purely vegetative ones. Such colonies of both species appear to compete well with other herbaceous vegetation for these sites.

Wood Horsetail (*Equisetum sylvaticum*) may also form extensive pinewood patches, especially in sheltered and slightly moister hollows than those occupied by Oak or Beech Fern, and perhaps indicative of sites of modest mineral and base flushing. Under favourable conditions, luxuriant colonies can grow locally, with their numerous, upright shoots reaching heights of up to about 50 cm and sometimes more, each bearing regular whorls of bright green branches which are themselves regularly and gracefully branched. Its shoots, forming shoots which consequently have something of the appearance of miniature conifer trees themselves!

Associated with almost all of these ferns and horsetails is usually a dense ground cover of herbaceous flowering plants typical of the pinewood understorey. Heather (*Calluna vulgaris*) is nearly always present, but in the moister hollows and pockets which are usually richest in pteridophytes, Heather usually gives way to a dominance of Bilberry (*Vaccinium myrtillus*), sometimes with Cowberry (*V. vitis-idaea*), Bearberry (*Arctostaphylos uva-ursi*), and, in local, moister spots, Bog Whortleberry (*Vaccinium uliginosum*) and Cross-leaved Heath (*Erica tetralix*). Patches where Woodland Oak-fern and Beech Fern grow may also be marked by the presence too of Wood Anemone (*Anemone nemorosa*) and often Wood Sorrel (*Oxalis acetosella*), Common Violet (*Viola riviniana*) and Germander Speedwell (*Veronica chamaedrys*).

More generally in the moister hollows of pinewood, these ferns are associated with other, scattered flowering-plant species, several of which are particularly characteristic of, or exclusive to, the pinewood community. These include such mainly northern elements as Cloudberry (*Rubus chamaemorus*), Crowberry (*Empetrum nigrum*), Cow-wheat (*Melampyrum pratense*), Hairy Woodrush (*Luzula pilosa*), Wavy-hair Grass (*Deschampsia flexuosa*), and mosses such as *Thuidium tamariscinum*, *Dicranum majus* and species of *Polytrichum*, and the more restricted and largely pinewood-specific Twinflower (*Linnaea borealis*), One-flowered Wintergreen (*Moneses uniflora*), Serrate Wintergreen (*Orthilia secunda*), Common Wintergreen (*Pyrola minor*), Intermediate Wintergreen (*P. media*), Chickweed Wintergreen (*Trientalis europaea*), Lesser Twayblade (*Listera cordata*) and Creeping Lady's Tresses (*Goodyera repens*).

The pinewoods also contain a mosaic of Birch, and sometimes Alder (*Alnus glutinosa*) is present in moister hollows and near margins of standing water. Although the *Calluna–Vaccinium* shrub layer is usually dense beneath the drier Birch communities, in wetter hollows often marked by Birch and Alder, the understorey may give way locally to one of a

Sphagnum–Juncus bogmoss–rush community. It is in such sites that Narrow Buckler-fern (*Dryopteris carthusiana*) may be present, chiefly at low altitude in valley bottom sites amongst the pinewoods. Such sites are discussed more fully under the heading of Wet Birch–Alder Woodland.

A final fern (apart from Bracken—see below) worthy of mention here, is Oblong Woodsia (*Woodsia ilvensis*). This small fern is extremely rare today and more often thought of as an alpine than a pinewood fern. This is a species which, I suspect, however, may have originally been associated with rocky cliffs and screes in native pinewood vegetation, and that it is from such former habitats that at least some of its present scattered localities and populations have survived.

Pinewood Clubmosses

Two species of clubmosses may have been specially associated with native pinewood in Britain in the past, and at least one of these, Interrupted Clubmoss, still occurs in these habitats today.

Interrupted Clubmoss (*Lycopodium annotinum*), survives somewhat occasionally in pinewood habitats. Additionally, it also persists in areas of nearby moorland within central and northern Scotland (and especially in the Cairngorm region), from where it again expands into (or has persisted in) a very limited range of man-made, older, open-canopied coniferous tree plantation woodlands. It occurs in these only in a limited range of edaphically suitable sites and where the canopy is usually mixed and to a large extent mimics that of the original native pinewood. Its occurrence in such sites is probably associated with long periods of lack of disturbance (ploughing, grazing, burning, etc.) and in such old enclosed estate plantings, also with freedom from heavy grazing (although it is not taken by rabbits).

Interrupted Clubmoss is a relatively large and leafy moss-like plant, with aerial shoots which arise from long (50 cm or more), tough, flexuous, surface-creeping, rooted perennial stems, which give rise to ascending aerial shoots at intervals. The aerial shoots are often around 10 cm high, sometimes more, but as they gradually lengthen they recline and become prostrate in their basal portions, themselves often producing roots and eventually giving rise to fresh side branches. The ascending shoots, which are also perennial, have numerous, stiffly-spreading, small, triangular leaves densely clothed around them, and are rather harsh to the touch. Each aerial shoot grows in length only gradually over several years, the end

of each summer's growing period being marked by constrictions or 'interruptions' to the growth, formed by smaller and tighter leaves marking the winter resting season and giving rise to the plant's common name. Cones, which are normally without any stalks, are eventually borne one per shoot from the ends of some of the longer, erect, aerial shoot tips.

An important indicator of former pinewood sites, the bright green shoots of Lycopodium annotinum *may form locally extensive carpets. Mid-Perthshire, July*

Interrupted Clubmoss is entirely northern in its modern range. On the Continent, it spreads very widely through central and northern Europe, more as a mountain valley-bottom species than as a strict Arctic–Alpine one, and is widely distributed even at low altitudes in Scandinavia. From here its range spreads eastwards across northern Asia, mostly north of latitude 50°N, and thence at a rather similar latitude across North America, almost entirely within Canada. In this range, the species is particularly characteristic of moist conifer forest understorey, largely of northern birch and especially spruce forests over peat. Under such conditions it has been shown to be extremely tolerant of cold soils and low mineral nutrient availability, being a very efficient energy producer under severe climatic conditions, and growing with only extremely low amounts of essential elements such as potassium (Callaghan, 1980).

In Britain, apart from in a few, extremely rare and scattered localities in North Wales and in northern England, Interrupted Clubmoss has almost all its principal localities in Scotland, north of the Highland Boundary Fault. Here, its main headquarters are, like the range of *Pinus sylvestris* centred in the Cairngorm Mountains. Most of its sites are in damp, sheltered, pockets in heather moorland on peat over fluvio-glacial moraine, and damp peaty mountain slopes, hollows and streambanks, over predominantly acidic rocks. Its habitat pattern and range thus suggest *Lycopodium annotinum* to be largely a relic of former pinewood sites in Scotland. Such a view also accords with its world range, which is that of northern boreal forests, and its edaphic requirements, which are those of birch–conifer vegetation and especially vegetation of spruce *Picea* (with which, elsewhere, it is very widely associated). Indeed, in Scotland, *Pinus sylvestris* includes within its ecological range the habitats that would have been spruce forest here too, had spruce been present in the native flora of Britain in Post-glacial times.

Also very much associated with the boreal coniferous zone at high northerly latitudes of the world is Ground Pine (*Diphasiastrum complanatum*). Although older texts ascribed this species to the British flora, a more recent view is that all its reported British sites are probably that of a hybrid between this species and Alpine Clubmoss (*Diphasiastrum alpinum*), referred to as Hybrid Alpine Clubmoss (*Diphasiastrum* × *issleri*). Within our islands, *Diphasiastrum* × *issleri* also appears to have its main headquarters north of the Highland Boundary Fault, again especially in the Cairngorm area, but with far-flung and widely scattered outlying single stations in England, notably in east Gloucestershire (in a heathland enclave on an outcrop of Fuller's Earth in the Cotswolds) and in Worcestershire (in a local *Calluna* dominated vegetation pocket over Precambrian granite in the Malvern Hills).

Outside Britain, where it is now presumed long extinct, its parent, *Diphasiastrum complanatum*, like *Lycopodium annotinum*, occurs widely through the forests of central and northern Europe, and especially in Scandinavia, spreading across northern Asia to Kamtchatka and across North America from Alaska to Newfoundland. As with *Lycopodium annotinum*, the range of *Diphasiastrum complanatum* thus very closely parallels that of the northern boreal and especially coniferous or mixed coniferous-broadleaf forests. In such habitats, on somewhat better-drained ground than *Lycopodium annotinum*, it may form enormous colonies running through the fairly bare litter of the forest understorey. If it were a pinewood relict in Britain, as seems likely, and that its hybrid has survived it, then such overseas habitats today help give some impression of at least one additional species component that might have been indigenous to the pinewoods of Britain, and perhaps also Ireland, at a former phase of Post-glacial time.

Pinewood Bracken

Bracken (*Pteridium aquilinum*) is familiar to everyone, at least as the subspecies which occurs so widely on our hillsides, which is *P. aquilinum* subsp. *aquilinum* (see also chapter II). This fern also occurs in areas of drier, better-drained native pinewood and in birch-pine communities in Scotland. Thus in Blackwood of Rannoch and in Glen Affric, *P. aquilinum* subsp. *aquilinum* forms extensive patches in glades beneath the open forest canopy.

Of more special interest here, however, is the occurrence of another Bracken, which appears to be specific to pinewood habitats in Scotland, where it was discovered only recently (Page, in press). This is Northern Bracken (*Pteridium aquilinum* subsp. *latiusculum*). It is however, not a new species to science, for it occurs widely in northern Europe (especially in Scandinavia), with a range which stretches across far northern

Another indicator of former pinewood sites is the bright-green, red-scaled, early-flushing Pteridium aquilinum subsp. latiusculum, *which is extremely rare in these islands. East Inverness-shire, late June*

Asia to Japan and across northern North America, especially in
the eastern states (Page, 1976).

Pteridium aquilinum subsp. *latiusculum* is thus the northern
pinewood Bracken of the world, following closely in its distribution the northern boreal conifer forests, in which it is
closely associated with the well-drained sandy and gravelly
soils that normally carry a forest of pines. It is thus wholly
appropriate that in Scotland, its sole known site is in the vicinity
of the native pinewoods of the Rothiemurchus area of Strath-
spey, although it could well be present elsewhere in relict pine
communities in Scotland.

I first discovered the original native colony of this plant near
to Loch an Eilean in 1983, and have kept it under close observation since. It thus does not appear in my taxonomic book, which
was completed before this date (Page, 1982). Subsequently, I
have found one other large stand of it only a few miles distant
from the original locality, whilst there are also colonies of pure
P. aquilinum subsp. *aquilinum* in the area, plus one colony,
discovered independently by A.F. Dyer in 1987, which is clearly
intermediate between the two, and almost certainly represents
a hybrid. Several other colonies of *P. aquilinum* subsp. *aquilinum* in the vicinity of the pinewoods also show some degree of
morphological features of subsp. *latiusculum* in their fronds,
and it seems probable that these represent introgressants
between the cross and subsp. *aquilinum*. These are of
additional evolutionary interest, for introgression (the back-
crossing of hybrids with their parents in each direction to produce a whole spectrum of morphological intermediates), is, as a
whole, a very rare phenomenon in ferns.

The colonies of Northern Bracken (*Pteridium aquilinum*
subsp. *latiusculum*) are morphologically very distinctive—
sufficiently so, indeed, that I initially spotted the first one while
driving a Landrover and the second from the window of a
moving high-speed train! What makes them especially so is
that they have a strongly different appearance from one
another in spring. When colonies of common *P. aquilinum*
subsp. *aquilinum* have their fronds in an early unfurling state,
with the first pinna-pair just expanding laterally, and the rest of
the frond still standing as a fist-like bud in the middle, so that
the whole frond is posed like the head and wings of an eagle,
those of *P. aquilinum* subsp. *latiusculum* are already fully
expanded. Their blades too, instead of having the slightly
drooping pose of those of the pinnae of subsp. *aquilinum* at this
stage, have a turgidly straight and slightly ascending orientation. These differences make the two subspecies especially
distinctive and easier to spot in about late May or early June
than later in summer when both have their fronds fully

expanded. This difference in early season appearance is brought about partly by a slightly earlier start to the expansion season made by subsp. *latiusculum*, but especially by its mode of opening. In subsp. *latiusculum* the whole frond and all its pinnae expand rapidly and nearly simultaneously, in contrast to the prolonged and slow expansion of subsp. *aquilinum*, which also has a strongly sequenced opening of pinna-pairs successively up the frond, not shared by subsp. *latiusculum*.

There are many other differences between the two subspecies. When the fronds are expanding, the rachis and pinna midribs of subsp. *latiusculum* have many more cinnamon-red hairs than have those of subsp. *aquilinum*, giving the crozier tips and the young segments an overall more reddish appearance. As the fronds expand, the blade angle of subsp. *latiusculum* always inclines steeply at the first pinna pair, so that this subspecies holds the whole blade more horizontally from this point than is the habit of subsp. *aquilinum*, where the blade curves backwards from vertical only rather gradually and ponderously along the length of several pinnae as the blade gradually expands. When fully expanded, the fronds of subsp. *latiusculum* are always much smaller, than those of nearby subsp. *aquilinum* (often only half of two-thirds the size), and the stipes of subsp. *latiusculum* are not only shorter than are those of nearby subsp. *aquilinum*, but are also usually only about half the diameter, and much less succulent and very much more woody from their earliest stages. The fully expanded blades of subsp. *latiusculum* are very much more regularly triangular than are those of subsp. *aquilinum*, and are more upward-dished in overall 3-dimensional pinna arrangement (more reminiscent of the blade shape of *Dryopteris aemula*). The ultimate segments of the pinnae are also more widely spaced, more elongated and less variably shaped than are those of subsp. *aquilinum*, giving the blade an altogether more regularly dissected appearance throughout, conspicuous even from a distance.

At the end of the season too, there appear to be some differences between the two subspecies in their dying-down behaviour. In autumn and early winter, the fronds of subsp. *latiusculum* seem to become much more cinnamon red in overall colour than those of nearby subsp. *aquilinum*, and they remain standing erect on their slender, woody stipes for very much longer into the winter (and in most seasons observed, still partly stand crisp and dry in the following early spring, when those of nearby subsp. *aquilinum* have long-fallen, and are soggy and rotting).

As well as a smaller frond size and these morphological and behavioural differences, Northern Bracken appears to form considerably more open stands than is typical of common Bracken, with a much lesser frond density, and apparently considerably less ecologically aggressive vigour. Consequently the stands have a rather more open appearance, with more light penetrating to the ground below, where a more or less complete grassy sward with a high diversity of ground-flora seems to more easily persist.

It thus seems very likely that *Pteridium aquilinum* subsp. *latiusculum* exists in Scotland as a relic fern of the ancient Caledonian pinewood association, to which it has very probably been exclusive. As pinewood of this type has been very much more widespread over both Britain and Ireland in the past than at present, it is very probable that this Bracken has also been more widespread with it, and may, indeed, in Post-glacial history, have been, at one time, our most widespread Bracken. A lack of aggressive behaviour, compared with subsp. *aquilinum*, would seem to be a characteristic of it, and it is easy to believe that it could well have retreated ecologically as its pinewood association has retreated, whilst subsp. *aquilinum*, which is larger and far more vigourous, has taken over most of its former sites instead. The evidence from the existing colonies of subsp. *aquilinum* within and around the pinewoods today, indicative of some introgression, is of interest in perhaps suggesting that as subsp. *latiusculum* retreated and subsp. *aquilinum* expanded in the past, perhaps there may have been a moving front between the two subspecies, migrating in a general northward direction over Britain and possibly Ireland, along which some degree of introgression might always have been of frequent occurrence. How many such introgressants may have occurred and still survive in enclaves of the former range of subsp. *latiusculum* is as yet unknown, and will make a fascinating further study. One possibility is that at least some of the widespread variation seen in subsp. *aquilinum* today, over virtually the whole of our islands, plus its inherent vigour, may be in part due to incorporation in the past of genes from subsp. *latiusculum* on a broad and moving front.

Pteridophyte Changes in the Pinewoods

I have emphasised several times the relict nature of both the pinewood itself and its pteridophytes, an aspect true, indeed, to a large extent of the whole pinewood community. Some of this loss of pinewoods has been a long process, due to gradual climatic amelioration and success of competing trees, through a long period of Post-glacial time. Such changes, as well as increasing wetness, have probably been naturally responsible for driving the pinewoods north from England, and for the total elimination of native pine throughout Ireland. But a large amount of the diminution of the forests of pine which remained into historic time in Highland Scotland has disappeared at the hand of man.

The effect of man has been either directly by his activities, including felling and burning or, worse still, by changes in grazing pressures brought about by modifications to the natural animal populations of the forests, resulting in diminution or elimination of natural forest regeneration.

Substantial tracts of pine woodland survived well into recent historic time. The name of one of the existing remnant pinewoods—Rothiemurchus—reflects such a pinewood history, for its gaelic spelling: *Rath a mhor ghuithais* means 'plain of the great pines'. Interestingly, for our purposes, another surviving pinewood, referred to in English as the Blackwood of Rannoch means 'pinewood of the ferns'— perhaps indicating a long history of association between ferns and pinewood that probably long pre-dates the results of modern, heavy grazing pressure by introduced sheep and deer. For these herald the demise of most ferns and the dense spread of common Bracken in their place—almost certainly a more recent phenomenon than the particular significance of ferns referred to in the origin of this place-name.

For although there were grazing animals present before sheep as well as most deer (and indeed rabbits) arrived, the numbers of these were originally kept in check by natural predators, the more significant of which were also eliminated by man. Man shared the early Post-glacial forest in Britain with many larger mammals, which included not only wild boar, wild horse, wild ox (auroch), hares, beaver, reindeer, elk and red deer (the only present native deer), but also with predatory wild cat, fox, polecat, marten, badger, brown bear, wolf wolverine and lynx, all associated essentially with these forests. It is interesting to read, in this connection, that although the elk was hunted into extinction before the Romans came, wild boars persisted until the 17th century, and although the last wolf was killed in England in the 15th century, both wolverines and wolves persisted in the Scottish forests as late as the 18th century. Doubtless such animals perhaps helped keep a check on Scotsmen felling the forests, as well as on the grazing animals removing the seedlings!

The more direct effects of man are perhaps more easily quantified, although, in my view, have been the lesser in permanent effect. It is possible that as long ago as the Paleolithic, between the later Ice Ages, man penetrated as far as the Highlands, but the first conclusive evidence of settlement

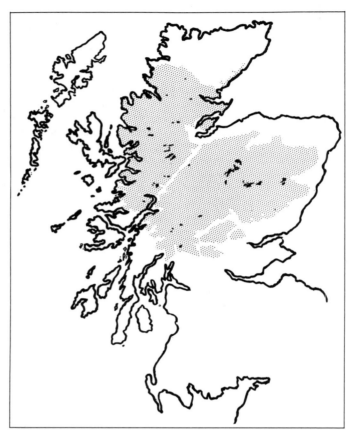

Fig. 11
*Past (stippled) and
present (black) areas of
native pinewood in
Highland Scotland.
(After O'Sullivan,
1977)*

comes from the Mesolithic, following retreat of the last glaciation. The Mesolithic settlers probably arrived from Ireland,
and their localities remained close to the sea shore, where there
were shellfish as well as land berries and perhaps smaller mammals. Although it was probably as long ago as between about
4,000 and 3,000 BC that Neolithic man first began to introduce
rudimentary farming and used fire, it was not until the iron-
smelting industry was established extensively in Scotland, from
as late as the 17th century onward, that felling of the larger trees
of many, accessible, remaining pinewoods probably took place
for charcoal to fuel furnaces (Millman, 1975).

Although such activities would very probably have successively removed a long-established stock of many parent seed-
trees over large areas, they would be unlikely to have done so in
a manner which totally prevented all seed production. Without
the added devastation of persistent grazing pressure removing

all regenerating seedlings, such forest, involving mixtures of pine, with perhaps Birch, Rowan and some Oak, would have almost certainly widely regenerated by now. We can do nothing about reversing the explosive over-exploitation of the past, but the satisfactory reduction of grazing pressure still remains very much within man's power. The modern forests thus reflect only in fragmentary form the diversity and abundance of plant species that these magnificent forests once had.

CHAPTER 8

Wetland Pteridophytes

Throughout the world, pteridophytes are generally absent in temperate, saltwater wetlands, but are present in some diversity and frequency in the temperate, freshwater habitats of pools, fens, lakes and some types of marshes.

Almost all of these freshwater, wetland, plant communities have in common that they typically form particularly rich sites for a wide variety of wildlife of many kinds, making the best of them of special scientific interest and hence of particular conservation value.

The Seral Nature of Freshwater, Wetland Habitats

Although the plants present in such sites—especially flowering plants, pteridophytes, bryophytes and algae—are mostly adapted to conditions where water levels are generally high, they vary widely in species and the adaptations which they show, especially to differences in physical and chemical aspects of the habitat present. These include depth and quality of water, and its movement, scouring action and rate and depth of silt deposition.

Many of these factors differ profoundly between different types of wetland habitat and often almost equally profoundly within different aspects of single sites. The plant communities of freshwater wetlands are thus often complex as well as diverse. Those we see are also frequently in a state of progressive natural change from one community to another, in a predictable and orderly manner, as many of the physical and chemical aspects of the environments, as well as consequent biotic ones, themselves change with time.

Such progressive change is referred to as seral, and the process a sere. Typically, unless freshwater seres, and especially water-margin ones, are interrupted by some external factor, maintaining them at a certain seral stage, the more 'dryland' vegetation at the margins of the communities gradually encroaches, with the wetland area progressively reducing. The ultimate stages in such progressions are usually towards native woodland.

Dryopteris affinis *subsp.* affinis, *showing the strongly yellow green colour of the flushing fronds in spring. Mid-Perthshire, May.*

The lakeland habitat of Pilularia globulifera. *Loch Tummel, Mid-Perthshire, September.*

The walls of an old castle, a habitat which can provide one of the most extensive habitats anywhere for Polypodium australe. *Berry Pomeroy Castle, South Devon, July.*

The pink flushing fronds of Osmunda regalis *are linked by natural gossamer. South-west Scotland, May.*

Characteristic 'bracken-brown' fronds of Pteridium aquilinum *glistening with winter hoar-frost. Forest-of-Dean, West Gloucestershire, December.*

Etched by winter frost, the fronds of Polystichum aculeatum *well-demonstrate their wintergreen quality. Central Scotland, February.*

The hanging alpine gardens of cushion plants in high cliff gulleys provide a habitat for Cystopteris montana. *Mid-Perthshire, August.*

Dryopteris filix-mas *under winter snow. West Wales, January.*

The spectacular shoots of Equisetum telmateia, *thrusting upwards in spring. Midlothian, May.*

The beautiful, slightly hispid fronds of Phegopteris connectilis *pointing regimentally downslope in a northern forest. Mid-Perthshire, July.*

Red-brown, overwintering clumps of Dryopteris aemula *caping mossy boulder crests in winter mist near sheltered western coasts. West Argyll, February.*

The bold green fronds of Blechnum spicant *covering a sheltered, moist bank in acidic woodland. Dart Valley, Devon, July.*

Cliffs and montane screes abutting ancient native woodland of Pine and Juniper and containing colonies of Woodsia ilvensis *in what is probably their original native habitat. Inverness-shire, July.*

A detail of a frond of Dryopteris affinis *showing the dark-coloured pinna-rachis junctions which distinguish this species from D.* filix-mas. *Mid-Scotland, late May.*

Geological junctions of limestones overlying impervious clays providing seapage-line, valley-bottom sites which later in the year will be clothed with shoots of Equisetum telmateia. *Cotswolds, East-Gloucestershire, early April.*

A dense Equisetum fluviatile *stand fringing the shallower margins of a sheltered pool. Northumberland, July.*

Polystichum setiferum *dominating the woodland floor fern community over heavy red, Devonian clay. South Devon, July.*

The delicate fronds of Thelypteris palustris *in fen reed-swamp glistening with morning dew. East Norfolk, July.*

Extensive patches of Bracken Pteridium aquilinum, *forming islands of dense vegetation on all the better drained aspects of this landscape. These may further expand and coalesce under the constant pressure of heavy upland grazing. The diversity of other ferns becomes richer along the more grazing-inaccessible embankment of the disused railway line. Glen Ogle, Perthshire, August.*

Oreopterus limbosperma *showing its distinctive white-scaled croziers. West Lothian, May.*

Polypodium interjectum *forming a dense colony over a decaying fallen forest tree trunk, in the moist western climate of the Welsh Marches, September.*

The history of the site is thus often also important, for in our much modified landscape, man has in many ways influenced these natural vegetation progressions, whilst creating other sites where such progressions, and the species associated with them, can begin anew. In more recently abandoned sand and gravel extraction pits and in abandoned, newly flooded, quarry workings, for example, as well as on the margins of some ponds, some of the early seral stages of pondside vegetation succession can sometimes be seen. By contrast, and equally important, in the longer-undisturbed aspects of lakeside reedswamps, fens and some marshes, the mature aspects of such vegetation succession are typically present.

Various pteridophytes are characteristic of different stages in such vegetation seres.

Late seral stage of reed-swamp vegetation with Equisetum fluviatile *becoming displaced by rapidly advancing flowering plant growth. Slapton Lea, south Devon, early August*

Ponds, Flooded Mineral Workings and Wet Heathland Hollows

Traditional small ponds of all types are very widely spread through Britain and Ireland, and have long been characteristic of rural farms, villages and traditional village greens. A few of our ponds are probably natural, such as glacial kettleholes, Irish turloughs and perhaps many former wet heathland hollows and East Anglian meres. But most of our ponds were dug by man, created at many different times through history for many different purposes, which include marl ponds, retting ponds, mill ponds, duck ponds, fish ponds, eel ponds and even leech ponds in southern Britain. Indeed their uses were many. Perhaps the most important is one for which they were not specifically intended: for how many of us do not in large part owe our interest in wildlife to our experience as children, freely dipping for tadpoles and other water life in the local village pond? In Britain, in particular, the rate of loss of such traditional ponds has clearly accelerated enormously during the middle of the 20th century, with many becoming systematically drained or wantonly infilled with rubbish, to be claimed for modern industry or agriculture, the latter seemingly so often to add a mere few extra yards to an already extensive and manicured field.

In places, however, some traditional ponds remain, and in appropriate sites, some of these continue to provide habitats where a small number of highly distinctive species of pteridophytes occur. Alternative natural habitats for a few of the more pioneering of these also include wet heathland hollows.

In addition to these, other sites have from time to time appeared in our landscape through a variety of causes. One of the most frequent of these is as a result of mineral extraction workings in the form of quarries, sand-pits or gravel works, which have been abandoned to nature and have subsequently become partly or wholly flooded. A few ponds are known to have originated as wartime bomb craters (Rackham, 1986).

Floating Azolla Communities

Although not a native plant, the small, free-floating Water Fern (*Azolla filiculoides*), introduced from tropical America, is widely spread in these islands, forming sometimes dense communities completely clothing the surfaces of small ponds and the quiet corners of larger lakes. It is most abundant in southern counties, though in Britain, has been known to establish as far north as Edinburgh.

This small fern, whose plants usually measure only 1–2 cm in size, has a minutely-scaly, somewhat moss-like habit. The central, thread-like rhizome bearing the minute, scale-like leaves, branches freely, and by gradual breakup, multiplies vegetatively extremely rapidly, to form very numerous, separate, plants, floating freely across freshwater surfaces.

In habit, *Azolla* is very much the fern equivalent of Duckweed (*Lemna*), though its rapid spring and summer growth to form a myriad of individual plants can be even more densely blanketing of the water surface than even can Duckweed. *Azolla* achieves a fine covering to the water surface, which is green in early summer and may turn deep red in autumn in well-illuminated sites. This growth can be so smooth and velvet like, that it can create the impression of a very fine, level lawn, and if exuberant enough, can totally mask the fact that there is water beneath—a situation brought particularly vividly to mind by a visitor to a neighbouring estate in north Cornwall who remarked mistakenly to the owner, who was suffering from a sudden abundance of *Azolla* 'I see you've converted your pond into a bowling green.'

Each year the dense summer growth of *Azolla* dies back or sinks in winter. In more northerly localities, the plant appears to survive only through mild winters, and to be killed off by severe ones. In more southerly sites, it appears to more regularly overwinter, to begin rapid vegetative coverage of the water surface in the following spring. It is possible that *Azolla* may spore in Britain and Ireland in favourable years. Much of its mobility between isolated ponds and lakes in these islands, however, is probably by movement of appropriate initial innocula of whole plants to new sites, either as deliberate introductions, or by carriage between ornamental ponds on other transplanted aquatics, or through conveyance of small vegetative fragments on bird's feet or feathers. For in appropriate waters, even small pieces will grow.

Azolla appears to be most successful in relatively eutrophic waters, and its prodigious rate of growth and biomass production results from an interesting cryptogamic symbiotic association between this minute fern and a species of blue-green alga called *Anabaena azollae*. This unusual association (somewhat analogous to the fungus–alga association of the lichens) enables both partners to succeed better than they can (if at all) in isolation from each other, and in the case of the fern–alga association, for the whole system to be an extremely efficient fixer of atmospheric nitrogen. *Azolla* thus adds greatly to the fertility of the ecosystem in which it is present. It is precisely for this reason that in Asia it is so widely introduced into rice paddy fields, where it greatly increases the yield of the rice.

Pillwort Sites

With the cessation of construction of new ponds, it is only in certain aspects of the older ones, where dense vegetation has not established, that the more pioneering species of pteridophytes such as Pillwort (*Pilularia globulifera*) are likely to be present. Although Pillwort can very occasionally be found in abandoned sand and gravel extraction pits and in flooded quarry workings, it is an especially characteristic species of the shallow, silty margins of ponds.

Pillwort is a fern of very distinctive and unusual appearance. It bears simple, bright green, rather grass-like growth, formed of ascending, filiform fronds, about 3–8 cm or more in length and about 1 mm diameter. These arise at short intervals from the sides of greenish-cream coloured, far-creeping, cylindrical rhizomes, each of which can give rise to further groups of fronds in a close-crowded succession. The many, slender, upright fronds can be distinguished from those of other plants by their slightly wavy appearance and by the characteristic watchspring-like (circinnate) coiling of the emerging young frond tips. The fully-expanded fronds each also have a slightly wavy appearance, and extensive patches of the plant (which can sometimes be several square metres in area) can have the appearance of a mass of slightly curly hair.

Pilularia grows on shallow, muddy shorelines which are submerged during winter and more or less exposed during the summer. In many of its sites, other vegetative competition is minimal, but it sometimes grows on shorelines of ponds where other characteristic marginal species are thinly scattered or

Pilularia globulifera in lake-head silt. Loch Tummel, Mid-Perthshire, early September

occupy other aspects of the pond, whilst a few unusual species may also be present. A species list from one of its more extensive New Forest sites includes, for example, Marsh St. John's Wort (*Hypericum elodes*), Marsh Bedstraw (*Galium palustre*), Lesser Spearwort (*Ranunculus flammula*), Bog Pimpernel (*Anagallis tenella*), Shore-weed (*Littorella uniflora*), Ludwigia (*Ludwigia palustris*), Starwort (*Callitriche* sp.), sedges, including *C. demissa*, and rushes including *Juncus bulbosus*), *J. articulatus* and *J. foliosus* (R. P. Bowman, personal communication).

The biology of this rare plant is very poorly known, and is certainly in need of closer study. Colonies are potentially perennial, but nevertheless die back substantially in the winter months. Especially in warm summers, established colonies may produce their characteristic bean-like sporocarps in great numbers along their rhizomes. These contain the spores internally, which are embedded in a jelly-like matrix.

Although spore-establishment of new plants may proceed rapidly after the spores become liberated, the wall of the sporocarp is tough. It is possible that such sporocarps may retain viable spores over prolonged periods, and this would be biologically advantageous should detached sporocarps become carried around ponds (or perhaps between ponds by water fowl?), to become buried in mud and exhumed by later erosion, perhaps after many years.

One part of Britain in which appropriate natural ponds still survive in much the form in which they may have been present over a long period, is in the New Forest area of Hampshire, and, appropriately, Pillwort is probably more extensive in Hampshire today than in any other single British or Irish county.

Overall, however, this species provides a particularly vivid example of the rates of change and loss of such habitats, as well as probably of other harmful effects, which may include groundwater and atmospheric pollution. For Pillwort was widely known in pond margin sites perhaps throughout Britain (but perhaps always less so in Ireland?) throughout the Middle Ages, and was still known in some abundance a century or so ago. At this time, it was also widely spread across central and northern Europe, to which it is entirely restricted, and in Britain was known in a total of 69 vice-counties with a further 10 in Ireland. Today, it has become extinct in at least 40 vice-counties, and it has simultaneously diminished over Europe in general, where it is considered now to be a Red Data Book species, whose survival is threatened. As well as habitat loss, it seems very likely that some more general overall factor such as air pollution may have been additionally responsible for this. Therefore, in both a national and European context, all the

remaining sites in Britain and Ireland are of considerable
international conservation significance.

Marsh Clubmoss Sites

In other low-competition habitats around open-water areas,
suitable habitats for the establishment of various clubmosses
occur. Of special interest amongst these is the occasional
appearance of Marsh Clubmoss (*Lycopodiella innundata*).

Marsh Clubmoss is a species of the margins of nutrient-poor
water. Its more natural habitats are typically in small pools,
generally associated with lowland heath habitats, and it is also
known from damp sandy and peaty depressions on wet heaths,
and occasionally in similar sites in abandoned mineral-
extraction workings. It is also sometimes found on the marshy
edges of lakes, in silty patches on the margins of valley bogs and
has occasionally been reported from wet dune slacks and even
from old tank-track ruts. Many of its sites are ones which
become heavily inundated with rainwater or surface run-off in
winter especially where such flooding also results in an annual
winter deposition of peaty silt.

The sites of Marsh Clubmoss are mostly on sandy or peaty
substrates, and are usually highly acidic ones which are base-
and mineral-deficient. It thrives in habitats which remain wet
in summer and can be flooded to a depth of several centimetres
in winter, and for which competition of other plants is generally
low. In such sites, plants pioneer open, silty, peaty or sandy
surfaces, and in favourable sites, can form nearly pure stands,
with established colonies sometimes covering several square
metres. Each patch is probably most often developed by steady
vegetative growth and fragmentation from one or a few individuals. In vegetatively luxuriant colonies, normally only a fairly
small number of stems produce cones. It seems possible that
different stems bear cones in different years, and that it may
take several years of steady growth before the same shoot bears
a cone again (Page, 1982).

In habitats which remain relatively open, plants probably live
for many years, and individual colonies have been known to
survive for over 30 years. Patches may, however, change considerably in size and vigour from year to year. On their shallow,
silty substrates with rapidly fluctuating water levels, plants are
presumably greatly influenced by short-term changes in
weather patterns, both directly and by the influence these have
on surface run-off and rates of erosion and deposition of silt. It
is perhaps therefore not surprising that even established colonies of the plant have the repute of easily disappearing.

Just as it may disappear from former sites, so it may appear in new ones or reappear in old ones in which it has not been known for many years, even when there are no other known populations nearby. It seems probable that such new colonies establish mainly from prothallial growth, the prothalli perhaps arising from spores which have lain submerged and dormant in muddy layers for considerable periods.

In most of its sites, associated species are typically sparse. In damp, peaty hollows such as those of heathland habitats, some of the more typical of these are the Sundews (*Drosera anglica* and *D. rotundifolia*), Bog Asphodel (*Narthecium osssifragum*), Deer-grass (*Trichophorum caespitosum*), Common Spike-rush (*Eleocharis palustris*), White Beak-sedge (*Rhycnospora alba*), Black Bog-rush (*Schoenus nigricans*), Few-flowered, Star, Great Pond and Moor sedges (*Carex pauciflora, C. echinata, C. pilulifera, C. binervis*). Lesser Butterwort (*Pinguicula lusitanica*) and Dorset Heath (*Erica ciliaris*) may be present in southern English sites.

Marsh Clubmoss appears to be very much more rare today than it was a century ago. It appears to have suffered badly not only from drainage and fragmentation of its former habitats, but like *Pillularia*, also from atmospheric pollution, against which such a plant so directly dependent on incoming rainwater and immediate surface run-off for its modest mineral supplies can have little defence.

Lakes and Reservoirs

Areas of standing freshwaters in the form of natural lakes or artificial reservoirs are of frequent occurrence throughout these islands, either in wholly lowland terrain or as freshwater lakes, lochs or loughs in valley sites in more mountainous regions. Even at higher altitudes, many small areas of standing water in the form of small pools, tarns or lochans may also be present, as may more upland reservoirs. To some extent, the pteridological flora of artificial reservoirs may approach that of more natural lakes, especially in their deep bottom communities, although their more marginal ones, by contrast, are typically in a considerably less advanced state.

Quillwort Communities of Deep Lake Bottoms

In both man-made reservoirs and natural lakes, tarns and lochans, quillwort communities may be present wherever suitable water and lake bottom conditions occur.

The Quillworts (*Isoetes*) are pteridophytes, related to the clubmosses, of which two of our native species are adapted to a wholly submerged existence, rooted to the bottom of lakes. Although I have referred to these lake-bottom habitats as deep ones, I have used this term to distinguish them from the fringing reed-swamp communities of lakes, which are ones of generally shallower watersites. In practice, the depths of the quillwort communities vary widely with the clarity of the water, from as little as a metre or so below the normal lake levels to (usually) depths of 3–6 metres or more.

Both our aquatic species of quillwort are widely spread in such freshwater habitats throughout these islands, especially in Scotland, North Wales and western Ireland, plus parts of western north-western and south-western England, with Common Quillwort (*Isoetes lacustris*) the more frequent and Spring Quillwort (*I. echinospora*) sharing a similar but less abundant range.

Both are species of the bottom communities of standing freshwater sites, and in appropriate habitats within this range, either or both species may be present. Because of their somewhat obscure habitat, they are seldom seen *in situ*. Their presence in a lake can, however, best be detected by examination of downwind lakeshore driftlines during the late autumn and winter months, when large numbers of their isolated quills can be washed up, as well as occasional, whole plants, as the sometimes abundant components of thick drifts of strandline debris.

Isoetes lacustris and *I. echinospora* both form spiky rosettes of numerous, slenderly-tapering, bright green, quill-like leaves, with those of *I. lacustris* usually stouter, somewhat stiffer and often much larger than those of *I. echinospora*. *I. lacustris* thrives especially well in large, deep-water, glacial lakes and tarns, larger than *I. echinospora*, and generally at higher elevations. It also occurs more often in deeper water, and although the two species have a wide range of ecological overlap, *I. lacustris* is generally the more abundant. *I. lacustris* sometimes forms submerged, meadow-like swards in the deeper bays of upland lakes, usually as pure stands.

Both species seem mainly restricted to water of low calcium content, and of usually poor (oligotrophic) nutrient status, and their distribution within lakes is typically somewhat patchy, being determined largely by suitability of a range of factors, including clarity of water, water depth, degree of water movement, suitability of substrate and degree of silting. Both species are confined to water which is clear, and probably where there is a slight current and some wave action. *I. lacustris* grows chiefly in water of a slightly higher base content, however, than *I. echinospora*. *I. lacustris* most frequently colonises unsilted, coarse to fine, consolidated sandy or gravelly lake bottoms and generally more stony habitats than *I. echinospora*, but is also occasionally present on deep nekron mud. *I. lacustris* also more commonly extends into more mesotrophic waters than does *I. echinospora*, presumably through a greater competitive ability against flowering plant growth resulting from its slight advantage in size.

Indeed, for their preferred sites, flowering plant competition is usually low, for the quillworts typically occupy a water zone deeper than that of the very similar-looking rosette plants of Shore-weed (*Littorella uniflora*) and Water Lobelia (*Lobelia dortmana*), which are often present in the same lakes. Other associates noted in sites of *I. echinospora* (but many of which are probably common to lakes of both species) include Awlwort (*Subularia aquatica*), Starwort (*Callitriche intermedia*), Alternate-flowered Water-milfoil (*Myriophyllum alterniflorum*), Perfoliate Pondweed (*Potamogeton perfoliatus*), Reddish Pondweed (*P. alpinus*), Floating Scirpus (*Eleogiton fluitans*), Floating Bur-reed (*Sparganium angustifolium*), locally Pipewort (*Eriocaulon septangulare*), and often the Stoneworts *Chara vulgaris* and *Nitella opaca*.

Both species are perennials and are heterosporous, each plant producing microspores and megaspores in the sporangia of different quills. Liberation of the spores is achieved by rupture of the sporangia, as older quills are eventually shed

Winter, strandline accumulation of naturally-shed quills of Isoetes lacustris *in a small mountain lake. Caernarvonshire, March*

from the outside of each rosette towards the end of the actively-growing season. In their shallower sites in larger lakes, wave-action by autumn and winter storms may play a significant part in promoting extensive quill shedding. But in smaller lakes where the fetch is less, and in sites in larger lakes which are at greater depths, it is possible that plants may depend more heavily on natural decay plus the stimulation of depradation by fish or ducks to remove old leaves, thereby releasing the spores around these animals into the water. How both types of spores can be dispersed between isolated lakes (and occasionally even into newly-constructed reservoirs in areas where quillworts were not present before) requires further research. Whilst it is possible that microspores which dry at the water margin may become wind-dispersed, other methods are probably important for the large megaspores. Both spore types may be carried internally by birds such as ducks, as well as by fish which eat the foliage, whilst the megaspores of *I. echinospora*, which have particularly rough protuberances, may be capable of clinging externally to water fowl feathers, particularly downy body feathers, thereby becoming transported rapidly from lake to lake along bird migration routes.

Nevertheless, great size and some growth-form differences exist, especially in *I. lacustris*, between specimens from different lakes, and it is possible that in some of its sites, a considerable degree of genetic isolation may exist. The existence of Late-glacial and early Post-glacial sub-fossil records of *Isoetes lacustris* from Irish lake sediments in Co. Cavan and Co. Kerry underlines that at least this species has had a long history within the lakes of these islands, with adequate time for locally differing forms to have evolved, in an analogous manner to the natural fish populations of similar isolated waters.

Lakehead Pilularia *Sites*

At the edge of a few lakes and lochs, colonies of Pillwort (*Pilularia globulifera*) occur. These are usually confined to lakehead sites, at the water-inflow end of large lakes, where incoming muddy silts accumulate to form extensive, rather bare, regularly inundated shallows. Such shallowly lakehead sites seem especially characteristic of many of our narrow ribbon lakes. Under such conditions, Pillwort may colonise to form large and diffuse stands, creeping extensively over the insubstantial silty surfaces.

As in ponds, *Pilularia* grows mainly in habitats which are largely competition-free, and especially where reed-swamp is absent. It is especially characteristic of habitats which are regularly flooded in winter, when new, shallow silt and mud accumulations are brought in or where old ones are re-distributed, and where the plant can therefore continually pio-neer new, bare sites. It usually grows in habitats which are circumneutral to rather acidic in character, which remain more or less permanently damp throughout the summer, and which warm rapidly whenever there is sunshine. It can, however, survive periods of quite long immersion, and sometimes occurs in water up to about a metre in depth. Even in such sites, run-ning observations suggest that there may, however, be con-siderable fluctuations in the success of the plant from year to year, as well as in its reproductive vigour. In some years, especially warmer ones, plants may succeed in forming exten-sive, turf-like patches, whose rhizomes ultimately carry pro-fuse crops of sporocarps. In other years, especially in generally cool and cloudy summers, seasonal growth of colonies may be spasmodic and limited to small isolated patches, only regenerating in a modest way from the small, overwintering rhizome fragments.

Although it mainly inhabits sites for which there is little competition, other associates occurring around its lakehead sites usually include a range of submerged aquatic and emergent marginal species, including Water Mints (*Mentha* spp.), Pennywort (*Hydrocotyle vulgaris*), Shore-weed (*Littorella uniflora*), Bog Pondweed (*Potamogeton polygonifolius*) and Bladderworts (*Utricularia* spp.).

Plants are perennials, but die back considerably in the winter. In addition to reproduction by spores released from the sporocarps, and the possibility of long-term perannation of the species in submerged muddy layers, longshore distribution of *Pilularia* during periods of winter immersion may occur, ena-bling this rare species to re-appear in new areas where winter flooding has caused silt to become deposited.

Much research is, however, yet needed on the ecology and dynamics of the populations of this rare fern. In addition to the other possible causes of its loss (see under 'ponds'), the ever-present danger of habitat loss of such shallowly shelving, lake-head, shoreline habitats should be borne especially in mind in sites in which water levels are threatened to be artificially raised to form only steep-banked reservoirs.

Fringing Reed-swamp Communities

In still, deep, silty areas of ponds and lakes, dense reed-swamp communities may occur which include areas of Water Horsetail (*Equisetum fluviatile*). This horsetail is present in a range of freshwater habitats from moderately acidic to more basic ones, and is perhaps most vigorous in mineral-rich eutrophic waters. It is well adapted to pioneering sites either where there is a fairly constant accumulation of deep subterranean silts, or, where standing waters occur over deep clay substrates.

Although large stands of Water Horsetail are especially characteristic of large lake waters, fairly pure stands may occur in smaller bodies of water in appropriate circumstances, including in flooded quarry bottoms, brick pits and in ponds on clay substrates. Indeed, in a survey of one Cheshire parish, Brian *et al.* (1987) reported the presence of *Equisetum fluviatile* in 28 (about 18%) of marl-pit ponds, in which most ponds had a pH of 6.0–8.9. Such marl-pits are very numerous through Lancashire, Cheshire and in the lower Dee valley of Clwyd.

In larger lakes, Water Horsetail occurs widely throughout both lowland and upland Britain and Ireland. In such habitats, its nearly pure, bright, grass-green stands sometimes form extensive patches and fringes of dense, tall shoots between open water communities such as those of White Water-lily (*Nymphaea alba*) and reed-swamp communities behind. Its shoots often persist, in much sparser form, through the subsequent reed-swamp communities, including those which extend out over the water surface in the form of rafts of floating vegetation. In many cases, these overly deep layers of soft, silty peat, and such vegetation, which appears solid on the surface, can be insecure to walk on. In such communities, the shoots of Water Horsetail may continue to emerge through the floating mass, with short, thin shoots at the surface arising from rhizomes sometimes situated nearly a metre below the water surface.

Indeed, in most lake communities, the aerial shoots of Water Horsetail arise from thick, often deep-seated, far-running rhizomes, which, in such communities, usually penetrate and ramify extensively through layers of submarine clay, mud and/or silt, under highly stagnant and anaerobic conditions. This horsetail seems extremely tolerant of growth in such deoxygenated sites, where the channels of its roots spreading from the rhizomes usually show abundant evidence of local ferric oxidation. The internodes of its aerial shoots have exceptionally large central cavities, and, uniquely amongst the deciduous-shooted species of horsetails, these large central cavities continue through each internodal segment of the rhizome. These large air chambers appear to be responsible for conveying air downward to the submerged parts of the plant, with the nodal diaphragms separating them presumably acting as the equivalent of downward pumping stations for air *en route*. It is of interest to note that in winter, when the aerial parts of the shoots of this species die down, the lengths of the shoots which are under water usually long remain whole to water level, thus maintaining active air contact between the rhizomes and surface atmosphere above.

Other species which are common associates of *Equisetum fluviatile* in its open reed-swamp communities, or which form neighbouring communities around it into which the shoots of the horsetail persist, include White Water-lily (*Nymphaea alba*), Flote-grass (*Glyceria fluitans*), Broad-leaved Pondweed (*Potamogeton natans*), Various-leaved Pondweed (*P. gramineus*), Bogbean (*Menyanthes trifoliata*), Marestail (*Hippuris vulgaris*), Bur-reeds (*Sparganium* spp.), Water Plantain (*Alisma plantago-aquatica*), Yellow Flag (*Iris pseudacorus*), Sweet Flag (*Acorus calamus*), Purple Loosestrife (*Lythrum salicaria*), Common Club-rush (*Schoenoplectus lacustris*), Common Spike-rush (*Eleocharis palustris*) and Common Reed (*Phragmites communis*). Such habitats, on a warm summer day, can be especially rich in insects, notably in dragonflies and damselflies.

Towards the inshore end of reed-swamp communities containing Water Horsetail, the natural seral succession may eventually proceed to a fen carr stage. With the shallower water and the increased shading cast by the woody overgrowth of the carr, the taller members of the reed-swamp community usually become weaker and thinner, and under these conditions, Water Horsetail may again become a frequent and vigorous member of the community. In the increased shelter and shade, its shoots, in contrast to those of open water sites, are usually especially freely-branched.

Occasional other pteridophytes may also enter the vegetation at this stage, notably Narrow Buckler-fern (*Dryopteris*

Dryopteris carthusiana *is characteristic of wet woodland. Forest of Dean, West Gloucestershire, late June*

Fringing reed-swamp community, with intermixed reeds and Water Horsetail. Mid-Perthshire, September

carthusiana) in damper pockets, with occasional Woodland Lady-fern (*Athyrium filix-femina*) on moist hammocks and scattered plants of Broad Buckler-fern (*Dryopteris dilatata*) on fallen, mossy logs and around the drier boles of established trees. Hybrid Narrow Buckler-fern (*Dryopteris × deweveri*), the hybrid between Narrow and Broad Buckler-ferns, sometimes occurs in these sites, and occasionally (though today much more rarely than formerly), clumps of Royal Fern (*Osmunda regalis*) may also be present.

Other species associating with *Equisetum fluviatile* in typical lake-margin carr associations include struggling survivors of several of the reed-swamp associates, plus a rich range of other species, amongst the most frequent of which are usually Marsh Pennywort (*Hydrocotyle vulgaris*), Water Mint (*Mentha aquatica*), Marsh Bedstraw (*Galium palustre*), Greater Skullcap (*Scutellaria galericulata*), Lesser Spearwort (*Ranunculus flammula*), Water Forget-me-not (*Mysotis scorpioides*), Marsh Speedwell (*Veronica scutellaria*), Marsh Marigold (*Caltha palustris*), Ragged Robin (*Lychnis flos-cuculi*), with shrubs of Sweet Gale (*Myrica gale*) and trees of Alder (*Alnus glutinosa*), Alder Buckthorn (*Frangula alnus*), Eared Willow (*Salix aurita*) and Sallow (*S. atrocinerea*).

Horsetail-rich fen carr communities are widespread in undisturbed lake-margin habitats in our islands. It closely approaches those of the fen carr communities of the East Anglian fens (see below), from which it differs pteridologically principally in the abundance of Water Horsetail and the (usual) absence of Marsh Fern (*Thelypteris palustris*), the presence of the horsetail probably indicating edaphic conditions in which there is a heavier (and especially slightly siliceous) mineral component in the deep accumulating silts.

Fens

Fens differ from marshes in that their vegetation is mainly developed over organic-rich peat soils, and that, in due course, their own vegetation contributes further to this same peat formation. The peat accumulation results from high water tables in which anaerobic conditions occur; differing from bogs in that fens are fed by calcareous ground waters. The peat produced is consequently a less acidic one, and under the constant influence of percolating base-rich water, bears a different, taller and more luxuriant vegetation than do bogs.

Because the formation of fens is directly related to the presence of constantly high water tables fed by calcareous waters, fens tend to occur at low altitude in areas of shallow land depressions. Sometimes such fens are small, occurring in very local depressions fed by calcareous springs, or at the margins of reed-swamp communities on the shallow sides of base-rich ponds and lakes. Such habitats are very widely scattered and often local in occurrence. Others, however, occur where expanses of such low-lying ground over calcareous soils are large, over the whole of which fenland vegetation may dominate. The best examples of the latter, and hence of fenland habitats generally, are or have been in historic time in the Vale of York, in the Somerset levels and in the original fenland regions of east Norfolk adjacent to the Wash, and in the vegetation surrounding the Norfolk Broads.

Much of the once large fenland areas of the Vale of York, the Somerset levels and the Norfolk Fenlands have been extensively drained and claimed for agriculture. Areas of the smaller fenlands fringing the even wetter area of the Norfolk Broads have proved less easy to drain, and hence some of the latter are well preserved. These still display, in places, the floristic and pteridophyte-richness of fenland, and have an interesting and well-documented history which emphasises the seral and dynamic state of fenland vegetation everywhere, and of the varied plant and animal habitats within it. Those of the Broads are therefore extensively used here to illustrate the varied habitats of fenland ferns in general.

Origin of the Broadland Fens

The fenland areas fringing the Broads of north-west Norfolk are one of the largest remaining areas of fen within these islands. The origin and history of the development of these sites in relation to their modern pteridophyte richness and the seral nature of the vegetation in which they occur, is one of particular interest to consider in outline.

The origin of the Broads combines the activities of man with those of natural processes over a long period of historic time. For the fens of the Broads almost certainly originated largely as a result of peat digging and extraction from medieval times onward, in sites which were naturally predisposed, through their hydrological conditions and glacial history to the extensive seral development of fenland vegetation.

The glacier fronts of the last main advance of the Pleistocene glaciations (the Weichselian glaciation) did not advance as far south as the present-day East Anglian region, although the area was nevertheless substantially influenced by general periglacial climactic conditions. It was also affected profoundly by post-glacial sea level and consequent fluvial changes, greatly altering the distributions of land and estuarine conditions. Perhaps during and certainly after the last ice advance, layers of peat began to accumulate in the broadland valleys, no doubt in places forming directly over still older, interglacial, peats which were able to persist beyond these margins of the glaciation. These, at times, may have been covered by clays from invading seas, and they subsequently persisted into the post-glacial period as deep, peat accumulations. This is probably particularly true of the great extents of low lying land along the broad, shallow river valleys of the region.

About 6,000 years ago, the North Sea formed, and it is likely that during the times of Neolithic and Mesolithic cultures,

about 7,000–5,500 BC, the Broads area was part of a large estuary, an area of high deposition.

From about AD 900 , for several centuries, it is believed that the great peat accumulations along the low-lying valleys were gradually shallowly excavated by man, through generations of hand-digging. The peat turves of this mainly brushwood peat were of high quality for burning purposes, especially as once cut, they could be readily dried for such use in the relatively dry

The succession of fen vegetation around the remaining open water of Upton Broad, East Norfolk. (Cambridge University Collection: copyright reserved)

climate of the region. They were probably much prized as a source of heat through the relatively severe winters of this part of Britain, where firewood was not abundant, and where such timbers as Oak were anyway considerably prized for boat and domestic dwelling construction. During these centuries, Norfolk and Suffolk are known to have been amongst the most densely populated parts of Britain, and peat turves are recorded to have been removed in their thousands not only to domestic dwellings, but also to the Medieval monasteries of the region as well as to the Cathedral Priory at Norwich. The submerged remains of some of the stone trackways along which the single-wheeled carts laden with peat were manoeuvred, are known in places.

The cutting of so much peat created broad, shallow depressions near to the many slow-flowing and meandering rivers of the area, where the peat accumulations were best and deepest. The areas from which peat was cut, some to a depth of about 15 feet (nearly 4 metres) but often much shallower than this, may well have caused some drying out of adjacent ground as a result of these activities, with subsequent contraction of surrounding areas of peat. The original areas from which the peat was extracted were probably far larger than the areas of the present broads, as once they became flooded, have been subject to progressive marginal encroachment of fenland vegetation ever since.

Peat cutting is believed to have continued steadily in this way until about the 13th and 14th centuries. After this time, gradual steady changes in the levels of land in relation to sea (of the order of several metres) caused widespread flooding of the workings by impounding of river waters. In some places, where still practical, a few further, now much smaller and shallower depressions were created by continued local peat extraction, mainly around old workings, from about the 16th century onwards. But from such dates, most major areas of peat extraction became progressively unworkable, and diggings subject to extensive flooding.

As areas of peat diggings became flooded and abandoned, so silt began to accumulate within them again. Water in the Broads then, as today, would mostly have come from surface run-off and from springs of groundwater, the latter especially feeding some of the Broads more isolated from the main river systems. Accumulating areas of silt then provided the basis for vegetation to establish new hydroseres around the margins of the former workings. In the eutrophic water conditions resulting, a rich macrophyte flora would have probably very rapidly established, with Yellow and White Water Lilies (*Nuphar lutea* and *Nymphaea alba*) colonising the open waters and reed-swamp (mainly of Common Reed *Phragmites communis*) extending into open water from the landward margins.

Amongst this vegetation, it seems very likely that Marsh Fern (*Thelypteris palustris*), Fen Buckler-fern (*Dryopteris cristata*) and Royal Fern (*Osmunda regalis*), and perhaps other pteridophytes, would have played a very significant pioneering role in the initial silty, developing fenland habitats. It is probable that each of these species were previously, naturally present as more minor elements within existing waterside margins within the district of the diggings. With peat-digging abandonment, the frequency of each probably showed a particularly early, explosive spread, as each newly abandoned area became progressively first available for plant colonisation. Thereafter, it seems likely that each species has steadily diminished in numbers and increased in isolation as more aggressive reed-swamp seres have come to dominate most of the fenland habitats.

From about 1700 onwards, the resulting dense reed-swamps began to be managed, with large areas of the reed annually harvested by man. The cut reed was used for thatching (often the traditional method of building a watertight roof, until slates and tiles became available, but still important in some rural areas today). *Phragmites* reed-beds were cut annually, mostly in midwinter, when the leaves had died down and only the hard, dry flowering stems were left. This 'Norfolk Reed' proved a particularly durable material for thatching, a roof once thatched or re-thatched with this material then having an expected life of about half a century. Although *Phragmites* was preferred for this purpose, Saw-sedge *Cladium mariscus* was also cut from the areas of reedbeds where this species dominated, for it provided the preferred most pliable material for the final waterproof joint along the crest of each roof.

Such abundant annual produce could only be removed from the areas from whence it was cut, by way of the water channels themselves. For this, large flat-bottomed boats were used, which could be rowed or punted ('quanted') by the marsh-men through the still, shallow waters, to numerous timber-built landing-places ('staithes'). At these, the load could be transferred to horsedrawn wooden wagons. The importance of boat transport meant that numerous new narrow waterways ('dykes') were also constructed, through which the heavily-loaded boats of reed, or those of more mixed 'marsh hay' destined for cattle fodder, could be navigated—boat cargoes which contemporary accounts indicate probably looked, from a distance, more like floating haystacks.

Today, the area of the Broads thus consists of a series of reed and alder-carr fringed lakes, some completely isolated, but many interconnected by man-made channels and by meandering, slow-flowing waters, the whole the result of human activity which initially created conditions suitable for extensive seral fen vegetation to expand, and then maintained and further diversified some of the habitats and interconnections within it. This has occurred by traditionally managing the fens as an annually renewable, self-sustaining, resource, without destroying the habitats concerned, and allowing a rich and now ancient vegetation to form.

Ferns of the Norfolk Broads' Fens

Fringing fenland communities exist in areas where naturally high water tables occur over extensive areas of generally calcareous (mostly chalk) strata, joined and fed by rivers (including the Bure, Ant, Thurne, Yare and Waveney) draining from slightly higher, base-rich ground. The water of the Broads is thus calcareous, base-rich and also rich in dissolved nutrients (eutrophic).

The resulting vegetation surrounding the open waters is a floristically rich and often luxuriant one, which from place to place shows every intermediate of habitat from open water to ultimate woodland. The different habitats are not separate, isolated and permanent ones, but are each of temporary status and in a constant state of change from one to another, as accumulating peat levels constantly build towards drier, more terrestrial habitats.

Each of the different seral stages of fenland development have their own characteristic vegetation, each with its particular pteridophyte components. It is thus convenient to group the pteridophyte communities into an approximate sequence from open water through reed-swamp communities to those of ultimate fen woodland. Many of these can be examined by careful exploration with a rowing boat combined with observation from the broadwalks provided in the several excellent and well-explained nature reserves established in the area.

Fenland Reed-swamp Communities

Characteristic of the early seral reed-swamp phase of the colonising vegetation is Marsh Fern (*Thelypteris palustris*). Plants are colonists, particularly near to the advancing front of actively-growing reed-swamp, where floating vegetation mats form over dykes and ditches. In such mats, the strong-growing creeping rhizomes become anchored just at or above water level, extending forward sometimes a metre or so into the open water and giving rise to scattered fern fronds well ahead of the extending reed-swamp front.

Within the more established reed-swamp, plants of *Thelypteris palustris* occur either as bright green clumps of many, adjacent, small fronds, or, more usually, as somewhat scattered and usually tall and straggling fronds densely intertwined within the tangle of reedy vegetation. Within dense reed-swamp patches, the soft and rather delicate fronds, with their thin and very widely-spaced pinnae, probably benefit from considerable shelter and physical support from the surrounding reeds. Fronds may reach their maximum size of any habitat here, with the lower-growing sterile ones to about 80 cm height and the more slender, taller-growing, fertile ones to around 150 cm (of which approximately half the length is made up of the long, slender, stipe).

In these habitats, the long, dark, slender rhizome of Marsh Fern creeps, occasionally forking, over considerable distances amongst the bases of the reeds, where it may add 30 cm or so in length each growing season. These rhizomes extend near to the surface of floating mats accumulating soft, silty mud, or descend to 2–3 cm or so below the surface of lightly-compacted, recently-decomposing, reed-swamp litter. The actively growing rhizome tips seem to always strike somewhat upwards, generally maintaining a level slightly above the most wholly waterlogged conditions. The roots, however, may, and frequently do, descend into more anaerobic and stagnant, sulphurous and methane rich submerged layers below. Such habitats may consist mostly of floating vegetation with entrapped silt, which can be soft and deep, and can be dangerous places to explore, except with the aid of a boat.

Within the dense reed-swamp, other additional pteridophytes present may include Fen Buckler-fern (*Dryopteris cristata*), Narrow Buckler-fern (*D. carthusiana*), and the hybrid between these two species, Hybrid Fen Buckler-fern (*D.* × *uliginosa*).

Fen Buckler-fern (also formerly widely known as Crested Buckler-fern, for reasons that seem not obvious and have never been clear to me) is a medium or large sized fern which is characterised by having bipinnate, very narrow-outlined fronds up to about 30–60 cm in height (occasionally to 100 cm) and broad, blunt-tipped pinnae. Its light-green coloured fronds usually stand strongly erect in small numbers in quite close clusters, the fertile being the taller with the longest stipes, and bear the narrowest, most widely-spaced pinnae. Most of the pinnae are tilted at their bases, so that they are each held in a nearly horizontal plane. Its rather stout, pale green or rather

Dryopteris ×
uliginosa *in reed-*
swamp, its typical
habitat. East Norfolk,
September

straw-coloured stipe, which is darker chestnut brown only
towards its extreme base, has a sparse basal covering of broad,
often rather limp, very pale brown scales. Plants are variable in
appearance mainly only with size, but nevertheless, its hybrid,
which can approach it closely in appearance and is sometimes

fairly strong and vigorous, can at times be quite difficult to distinguish. Hybrid plants differ from *D. cristata*, however, in their somewhat broader general frond outline, more acutely tapering and more lobed pinnae, more pointed, more separated pinnules with the basal ones usually distinct and pinnae-like lobed, and with their edges more conspicuously toothed with distinct, spinulose-tipped teeth.

In East Anglia, both *Dryopteris cristata*, *D.* × *uliginosa* and *D. carthusiana* seem mostly confined to rather more base-poor spots in the reed-swamp communities than is Marsh Fern, although there is a general overlap of habitats between them. They also seem to have more of an affinity with patches that are more heavily silted with mineral mud. There is some evidence of temporary increase in the abundance of *D. cristata*, for example, following periods of extensive flooding of the reed-beds and consequent widespread, silty depositions, such as occurred after the widespread Norfolk floods of 1952.

The somewhat greater acidity of the preferred habitats of these *Dryopteris* species and their more mineral-rich character is also emphasised by the occurrence of *D. cristata* on small islands in reed-swamp and other fenland habitats where there is *Sphagnum* and young colonising Birch amongst dying remains of old Birch trees; habitats which may mark a transition zone between reed-swamp and old fen carr.

Common associates of the ferns in such reed-swamp habitats usually include many prominent aquatic macrophytes, such as frequently dominant Common Reed (*Phragmites communis*), Saw Sedge (*Cladium mariscus*), Lesser Reed-mass (*Typha angustifolia*), Reed-grasses (*Glyceria maxima* and *Phalaris arundinacea*), Blunt-flowered Rush (*Juncus subnodulosus*) and various sedges (*Carex* spp., including *C. paniculata*, *C. pseudocyperus* and *C. appropinquata*), with more scattered Fen Bedstraw (*Galium uliginosum*), Yellow Loosetrife (*Lysimachia vulgaris*), Hemp Agrimony (*Eupatorium cannibinum*), Brooklime (*Veronica beccabunga*), Ragged Robin (*Lychnis flos-cuculi*), Water Mint (*Mentha aquatica*), Marestail (*Hippuris vulgaris*), Marsh Helleborine (*Epipactis palustris*), Marsh Willowherb (*Epilobium palustre*), Marsh Marigold (*Caltha palustris*), Marsh Cinquefoil (*Potentills palustris*), Hog's Fennel (*Peucedanum palustre*), Marsh Pea (*Lathyrus palustris*), Marsh Pennywort (*Hydrocotyle vulgaris*), Water Violet (*Hottonis palustris*), Bur-reed (*Sparganium amersum*) and Great Water Dock (*Rumex hydrolapanthum*).

Indeed, of almost any native habitat in these islands, it is this phase of reed-swamp vegetation which so leaves the over-riding impression of teeming with life. For on a warm summer day, sitting amongst such reeds in a small boat, one is easily aware of only the sounds of lapping water, the splash or plop of the occasional water bird, frog or fish, and the gentle rustle of the reeds with every sign of breeze, amongst, between and over which, an almost endless pageant of insect diversity makes its bizarre and varied way.

Fenland Fen Carr

The natural progression of the reed-swamp phase of fenland development is into a fen carr vegetation. Such a change is associated with the building of the peat to such levels that moisture-tolerant tree vegetation is able to establish, and a luxuriant and often species-rich woodland is formed.

Common Reed (*Phragmites communis*), which is typically the dominant plant of the reed-swamp stage, usually persists for long periods into the fen carr, typically with abundant Saw Sedge (*Cladium mariscus*). Their annual biomass helps the peat levels to continue to build, and in the shallow waters, silt also usually accumulates. Although flushing of the peats with base-rich groundwater continues, patches rising above groundwater levels usually come more under the influence of rainfall, and become more acidic. Leached of their minerals, such patches often bear Bog-moss (*Sphagnum*) patches. Under the fairly dry climate of East Anglia, further development of truly bog condi-tions does not, however, take place, although such ultimate bog development has probably been the eventual fate of many former post-glacial fens in wetter parts of these islands.

The landward edge of the reed-swamp at the beginning of the carr stage of fen vegetation is typically marked by the pres-ence of establishing Sweet Gale (*Myrica gale*) within the reed-swamp, and by Alder (*Alnus glutinosa*) and Common and Grey Sallow (*Salix cinerea* & *S. atrocinerea*), especially beginning on decaying mats of silty reed-swamp peat, and rapidly developing to form an Alder woodland. Other species which invade through the carr phase include Alder Buckthorn (*Frangula alnus*), Bird-Cherry (*Prunus padus*), and ultimately Birch (*Betula pubescens*) or Ash (*Fraxinus excelsior*) in light gaps, Holly (*Ilex aquifolium*), Hazel (*Corylus avellana*), Guelder Rose (*Viburnum opulus*) and Oak (*Quercus robor*), finally giving rise to an oak woodland. The wetter initial phases are usually referred to as a swamp carr woodland, and the later as fen carr, before ultimate Oak woodland development.

Marsh Fern (*Thelypteris palustris*) often forms a discon-tinuous fringe around the waterward edge of the carr. Here its clumps are often not larger than about 20–40 cm across, but in occasional patches, large, billowing masses of its frail-looking, bright green fronds in early summer may mark larger patches a metre or more in diameter. From these, its long, slender, creeping rhizomes often sprawl distantly through extensive carr-reed-swamp edge, as well as into the carr itself. It also sometimes vigorously colonises the edges of eroding carr margins, where old Alder trees bend directly over open water.

Within the carr itself, marsh Fern initially often grows somewhat thinly in the dense competing vegetation, only to become more generally abundant again when the herbaceous vegetation becomes thinner with increasing closure of the overhead canopy. In this way, plants can quite vigorously colonise the barer patches of silty ground amongst established shading alders, especially along slow-flowing incipient stream edges, although in the deepest Alder shade they tend to adopt a somewhat etiolated form.

It is often in the swamp carr phase that Narrow Buckler-fern (*Dryopteris carthusiana*) often makes its most frequent appearance, here largely replacing *D. cristata* of the more open reed-swamp. In this vegetation too, Broad Buckler-fern (*D. dilatata*) usually also makes its first appearance in the sere. In the wetter edge of the swamp carr, *D. dilatata* usually colonises especially the high, fairly dry edges of large sedge tussocks, especially those of *Carex paniculata*, whilst in the later stages of the fen carr woodland, it becomes more terrestrial, especially on the slightly better-drained ground around tree boles or in the company of dense moss growth on logs of fallen, decaying timber.

Additionally, mostly confined to these carr stages of the sere is Royal Fern (*Osmunda regalis*). Plants of this fern, characterised by their large, bright green summer-fronds, first begin to make their appearance on the waterward edge of some of the carrs, where the tree canopy of Alder and Birch itself sweeps down to the water's edge. Later in the swamp carr and sometimes in the fen carr stage, it often forms particularly large and spectacular old clumps, with metre-long fronds forming spreading shuttlecocks and the whole plant looking remarkably different from the much more open-grown, clumps of this plant in the west. Indeed, the habit of these swamp carr *Osmunda* plants is most reminiscent of those of Swamp–Cypress swamps of eastern North America, and indeed, the whole environment of the interiors of some of the carrs is reminiscent of this type of community.

Willow Epiphytes

A minor, but unusual wetland pteridophyte habitat within freshwater wetland areas (as especially those originating as fen carr) is the occasional occurrence of colonies of epiphytic Polpody ferns.

Although such willows occur widely in lowland river valley floodplains and in many former fenland habitats, such as in many parts of Cambridgeshire, the presence of Polypody on them is mainly restricted to willow communities in wetter western climates, and of these, those of the Somerset levels— occupying the broad, flat basin between the Quantock Hills and Mendip area of Somerset—provide a good example.

Since the Middle Ages, drainage of the former fenland areas of the Somerset levels has created farmland with a pattern of flat, low-lying, wet, water meadows 'fenced' by deep drainage ditches. Today, the willows characteristically stand in ground of naturally high water tables. They occur somewhat sentinel-like at edges of ponds and marshes and especially along low-land stream-banks and the courses of small, muddy rivers, and sometimes in somewhat regimented rows along deep, wet ditches forming modern field boundaries. In many places, the old willows have clearly had a long history of pollarding, and it is through their ability to be pollarded that the frequency of willows in these habitats has been long promoted by man.

The willow was used as rods for basket making and to make hurdle fences, and by thatchers for thatching rods ('brortches') as an alternative to hazel for this purpose. Willows were grown or encouraged for these uses, and pollarding, like coppicing, was a very widely adopted technique for the production of appropriate materials continuously throughout the life of a tree. Whereas in coppicing, trees were cut to ground level from where they sprouted new shoots, in pollarding, original trees were cut at about six feet from the ground and allowed to shoot from there. New willow shoots arising were thus out of reach of grazing animals around them, and adjacent fields could thus be used for pasture without damage to the willow crop.

Such willows provide especially suitable habitats for epiphytic *Polypodium* ferns. Colonies of *Polypodium* present are usually those of Western Polypody (*Polypodium interjectum*), although it is possible that Common Polypody (*P. vulgare*) is sometimes present too. On occasional unpollarded willows, such *Polypodium* colonies may occur on the lower, larger spreading branches of old willow trees. More commonly, however, on pollarded willows fringing grazed water-meadow fields, Western Polypody colonises the available parts of the flat top of the older pollarded trees, from where rhizome growth usually enables it to spread on to the upper parts of the bark, whole colonies sometimes forming a crown to the tree.

The association of *Polypodium* with such willows probably in large part results from the especially favourable physical characteristics of this particular habitat. For such willows can be long-lived trees, giving ample time for large *Polypodium* colonies to gradually establish. Further, old trees of willow have thick, furrowed bark, providing ideal sites for initial prothallial success, whilst established fern colonies (also free of grazing) are able to obtain and retain a firm anchorage on such rough substrates, whilst benefiting considerably from the increased humidity of their location near to more or less constantly standing or slowly-flowing water.

CHAPTER 9

Pteridophytes of
Grasslands and Rock
Outcrops

Grasslands and outcrops of rocks of all types form inland habitats in which several well-adapted pteridophytes sometimes succeed. Such sites have in common that they include habitats which may be either relatively natural ones or, especially in the case of grasslands, have had their ranges very widely extended by man. Sites of each type occur almost throughout Britain and Ireland.

Grasslands

Grasslands of various kinds are a traditional feature of considerable parts of the British and Irish landscape. Species-rich grasslands with short, grazed turf are especially associated with the downland scenery of limestone areas, as well as with the chalk downs of south-eastern England, while more acidic grasslands occur widely through our uplands. Exposed, drier grasslands as well as upland acidic ones are, however, except in local pockets, usually less pteridophyte-rich than are sometimes those of the more traditional grasslands of hedged fields which occur widely over sometimes heavy but often moister and more low-lying soils of our more rolling landscapes. These typically become more verdant moving southwards and westwards, with some of the richest consequently occurring in western and south-western England and in Ireland. It is therefore upon these meadow and pasture grasslands that I have particularly focused this section, although this is not to imply that the pteridophytes of these habitats are not also sometimes able to occur in suitable niches in other grasslands elsewhere.

Most of these meadows and pasture grasslands were formed either more or less directly out of clearance of the original forest cover, or by later amalgamation of small arable fields. They were initially created for, and have subsequently been largely maintained by, grazing animals, being used either directly as pastures, or as hay-meadows for the annual removal of grass for hay. Many have consequently remained as more or less permanent grassland throughout long periods of time, with the constant management regimes allowing a vegetation type to develop, adjusted to the particular conditions. The native plant species of these grasslands have probably mostly derived from the original native grassland habitats of cliff-top turf and fixed dune-pasture. From these, on moist and fertile soils, rich floras of very many small herbaceous species have consequently established, usually studded intimately into the close matrix of a thick, grassy sward. The whole shows a richness in species diversity achieved only slowly, over many a century.

At least four pteridophytes have come to occur in such semi-natural grassland communities, either as meadow or pasture species, or both: Field Horsetail (*Equisetum arvense*), Marsh Horsetail (*E. palustre*), Adder's Tongue (*Ophioglossum vulgatum*) and Moonwort (*Botrychium lunaria*).

The two horsetails occur widely in pasture and especially in hay meadows. In each of these habitats, although Field Horsetail is generally typical of the better-drained and hence drier ground and Marsh Horsetail of the somewhat wetter hollows, both species have a wide edaphic tolerance, and they not infrequently occur close together.

Both *Equisetum arvense* and *E. palustre* are highly variable in form and may adopt a different appearance in different habitats. In fertile ungrazed hay meadows, where each is in competition with a dense, tall-growing sward of closely surrounding vegetation, the summer shoots of both species are very similar in appearance. Both typically grow tall and are abundantly-branched. The cones of *E. arvense* are borne on separate, colourless, short-lived, fleshy, fairly low-growing, unbranched shoots which appear above the surface of the ground about the first week of April. By contrast, those of *E. palustre* do not mature until about June, and are held high amongst the surrounding vegetation, which has grown up by this time, borne from the very tips of ordinary vegetative shoots.

The turf of semi-natural grasslands in appropriate sites can also be ideal for the success of Adder's Tongue (*Ophioglossum vulgatum*) and Moonwort (*Botrychium lunaria*). Both these ferns seem to have been widely known as regular and sometimes abundant members of grassland communities in the lowlands of Medieval England, and it has probably been because of their curious appearance and seasonally spasmodic occurrence, that both have long been the mystically-endowed subjects of various rural legends. The normal modes of transport in those days— on foot or by horseback—probably helped ensure a frequency of encounter with these plants by journeying country folk in a way that is seldom matched today from passing cars. It is also true, however, that the plants themselves seem also to have widely disappeared from many of their former sites, and in others are much less abundant than they appear previously to have been.

Ophioglossum vulgatum still survives however, in some undisturbed sites, and its present habitats are probably mostly those which have persisted over a very long period of human history in these islands. It is especially typical of old, level, low-lying, unploughed, moist, grassy meadows, developed over deep, often heavy and usually markedly basic soils, and of old, moist, water-meadows and pastures in the rural lowlands of central and southern England, which have evolved a good species diversity. In such habitats, luxuriant stands can sometimes still occur. It generally inhabits slight hollows which fill with rain, and it can consequently sometimes be characteristic of the damper, greener turf of the furrows in old ridge-and-furrow pasture. In other fields, it seems more a feature of the edges of the fields, in the longer, more luxuriant and moister grass near to the shade of the hedgerows and sometimes larger bushes and brambles. Perhaps in these areas it not only marks areas which are moister, but also ones which have avoided former ploughing, or where grazing pressure has been least. One of its most frequent and characteristic associates in such sites is the Cowslip (*Primula veris*), and, indeed, an old Somerset legend prescribes that to find the Adder's tongue, you must look first for the Cowslip.

Ophioglossum vulgatum stands become increasingly rare in grasslands above about 500 feet (ca. 160 m). In its lowland pasture sites, however, *Ophioglossum* is usually subject to a moderate grazing pressure, and its long-term survival in such turf, for such a grazing-sensitive species, is probably assisted by its relatively rapid spring growth in locally large numbers coupled with its colonial habit. Plants, however, do seem to readily disappear under heavier grazing pressure, especially in years when grass is late and the fern grows up far quicker than does most of the surrounding sward. During such seasons it is possible that localised grazing effects may particularly adversely affect it and be responsible for its apparent failure to appear in such habitats in some years, even though it may have been abundant there under a different set of seasonal circumstances in only the previous season.

By contrast, Moonwort (*Botrychium lunaria*) is a less gregarious species than Adder's-tongue, seldom forming such dense or numerous colonies, and occurring more often as rather more scattered individuals throughout lightly-grazed, grassland turf. As with *Ophioglossum*, plants of *Botrychium* occur on meadow and pastureland soils which vary from circumneutral to ones of strongly basic character. Plants usually grow under less damp and better-drained conditions than are typical for Common Adder's-tongue, and in rare lowland sites where the two grow nearby one another, Moonwort usually occupies the better-drained hummocks and knolls. Moonwort grows, however, through a wider range of altitude than does Adder's-tongue, ascending from the lowlands to about 1,400 feet (ca. 425 m) in Devon to 2,300 feet (ca. 700 m) in the northern Pennines and to around 3,350 feet (1,020 m) in Perthshire—well above the altitude of most enclosed fields, and ascending to natural sub-alpine communities on damp, grassy, basic rock ledges (see chapter 12). Lowland sites that are typical habitats for *Ophioglossum* and *Botrychium* are often ones in which early-morning mists frequently lie low over the ground in spring and autumn, whilst even in summer, heavy overnight dew may lie thickly on the grass. Lowland sites of alluvial water-meadows, old herb-rich grassland and calcareous clay pastures, in which *Ophioglossum vulgatum* and sometimes *Botrychium, Equisetum arvense* and *E. palustre* occur, are usually also characterised by a great variety of flowering herbs and grasses.

Adder's-tongue and Moonwort in the History and Conservation of Old Pasture

In both *Ophioglossum* and *Botrychium*, the long-lived sporophyte generation (the generation of the plant that we see) is unusual amongst pteridophytes, for the aerial shoots are partly able to manufacture their plant materials through the process

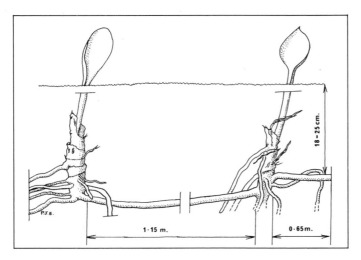

Fig. 12 Ophioglossum vulgatum *in grassland turf, showing characteristic underground root connections which enable the plant to gradually, vegetatively spread through grass turf communities (P. J. Edwards)*

of photosynthesis using their own green tissue (autotrophic) and are partly dependent on a fungal association with the roots to augment their supply of nutrients (mycotrophic). In the case of the shorter-lived gametophyte generation (which gives rise to the sporophyte, and which we usually do not see), the whole generation takes place within the soil and is wholly dependent on such mycotrophic fungal associations. In both genera, the materials supplied by the mycorrhizal fungal associates are probably largely derived from the steady soil breakdown of dead organic material deriving from many of the other plants in the neighbouring grassland sward, perhaps especially the grasses. Such steady states of dynamic equilibrium are probably built up only gradually over long periods of time, but can be rapidly destroyed by sudden external disturbance.

Both *Ophioglossum* and *Botrychium* consequently seem to be particularly easily killed in agricultural grassland by break-up of their colonial structure, especially through sudden ploughing and re-seeding of old meadow and pasture grasslands, although these species, and especially *Ophioglossum*, seem able to persist through slower, natural, grassland changes.

In many lowland meadow and pasture sites, old enclosed small pastures remain locally which show from their still-visible shallow ridge-and-furrow structure, a distant derivation from once-cultivated land. In many cases, such ridges were probably originally created to help improve land drainage, and have been retained for this purpose. Their surface has probably not been subject to subsequent ploughing since the days of its former arable abandonment, whilst the turf that has evolved has been subject to year-round grazing at low stock densities ever since. Such grazing has long been by horses as well as by sheep and cattle, and even by rabbits, introduced to Britain by the Romans.

Many of the pastures and hay meadows sited in the bottoms of broad, flat valleys such as those of the upper Thames valley of Oxfordshire and the Windrush Valley of Gloucestershire, are probably even older. Such sites occur on deposits resulting largely from erosion of surrounding Jurassic and Cretaceous sedimentary strata, upon which, during Pleistocene times, rivers accreted extensive terraces over former clay vales, only to later start down-cutting through them again to expose rather poorly-drained alluvial clay flood plains of neutral to basic character, upon which further deposition of sediments has taken place. In such sites, where broad expanses of calcareous gravel terraces now step down to flood plains of ample alluvial flats, the regular winter flooding has for centuries deposited annual films of fine, fertile silt, resulting in a vigorous flush of plant growth each summer and a herb-rich grassland vegetation in which especially Adder's-tongue and sometimes Moonwort grow and have probably long occurred. Within these 'water meadows', archaeological evidence shows that the history of human involvement has been both an ancient and more or less continuous one. For certainly since pre-Roman times, these rich Thames flood-plains have had intensive agricultural settlement. There are Iron Age, Bronze Age and Neolithic occupation horizons. There is also evidence of drainage channels of Roman age and of grazing by horse and cattle since pre-Roman times, followed by Pagan-Saxon settlements during the 5th and 6th centuries. Pollen spectra suggest that species-rich grasslands have from these times or earlier, been important aspects of the vegetation, with wet grassland grading more locally into marshes. Such grassland habitats thus appear to have had a particularly long history. Through much of this time there has probably been a considerable continuity of use, with meadow grasslands managed as pasture or as hay meadows over many centuries, whilst they have been subject only to a changing strip ownership. There thus seems every reason to believe that many of the unusual, as well as more common, plant species now associated with these, including these rare ferns, have had a particularly long and continuous history of establishment and association with constant regimes of similar management.

This is just one example for which there is archaeological evidence that helps us to date more precisely than for most grassland sites, the probable antiquity of their use and vegetational history. But for most meadow and pasture sites for which there is good botanical evidence of an ancient vegetation, varying but always long and unchanging management histories seem likely to have been the case. Today, very much of the widespread demise of both *Ophioglossum* and *Botrychium* from agricultural lowland sites over the last century, but especially in more recent years, is very probably in large part due to extermination of whole colonies through insensitive ploughing up of such ancient pasture and meadow grassland swards, thereby destroying the steady natural plant progression and species diversity, built up over centuries.

Rocks, Quarries and Mines

Outcrops of inland rocks of all geological types occur either as natural rock exposures or as ones which man has made through mineral extraction activities in the form of rocky quarry faces and the spoil-heaps, and other outcast rock debris, associated with underground mine workings.

Natural rock outcrops at low altitude are, of course, wide-spread, and are small and local or sometimes large and extensive. They include everything from occasional rocky bluffs and single groups of outcropping old, hard rocks such as the granite tors of south-west England, to more extensive cliffsides along river valley sides and the great outcrop areas of cliffs and horizontal pavements of limestone areas. Whether small or large, most form features of prominent relief and hence form especially notable and often characteristic aspects of our landscape.

Rocks exposed in mineral extraction activities are also wide-spread, with ones of different type and different mineral occurrence showing concentrations in particular regions. They include the faces of abandoned quarry workings and spoil heaps of extracted rock, which is often that surrounding the particular mineral (especially coal or metal ore) being extracted, or the waste rock debris found unsuitable for use (such as slate debris) or from spent extraction processes (especially in metalliferous ore mining and extraction). The rock deposits resulting are also features of usually fairly prominent relief, and also are often characteristic features of the landscapes of the regions in which they occur. Many such sites have particularly long histories, with mineral extraction in many places dating back to Roman times or even earlier. Many reached the peak of their production after the industrial revolution, subsequently becoming worked out in an economic sense, now variously abandoned to nature. Such sites include heaps of rock debris, bare rock faces (especially in quarries), pits, water courses, settling-ponds, adits, shafts, and buildings in various states of disrepair, usually constructed out of the same local rock, with often now-decaying courses of mortar added. All, are often somewhat difficult and often dangerous sites to examine, and caution and discretion must always be exercised in their more detailed exploration.

From the pteridophyte standpoint all such sites have in common that they are usually ones of reduced plant competition. Especially in wetter, western climates where rainfall is most frequent and humidity and frequency of cloud-cover high, they may be especially rich in pteridophyte colonists, and the value of such derelict sites for pteridophyte conservation (as well as the industrial archaeological value that they may have) seem seldom to have been appreciated by conservationists, with fascinating and scientifically valuable old quarries too often used to dump modern rubbish and irreplaceable old mine areas suddenly infilled and levelled, to give one more agricultural field.

Natural or man-made rock habitats mainly differ from each other physically in the amount and mobility of the rock areas exposed, and the degree of surface weathering which the rock surfaces have undergone. The most significant differences in the component of colonising ferns and fern-allies are, however, not usually so much dependent upon the naturalness of the site, but on the make-up of rock exposed. Consequently, different geological types of rock often tend to have characteristic assemblages of pteridophytes, which are similar whether the rock exposure be a natural or man-made one. Often, though not always, in any particular locality, the rocks exposed by man's activities are similar in general type to rock exposures occurring naturally in the same vicinity, and the same species of pteridophytes are typically present— sometimes reaching their greatest profusion on the man-made ones. In a few cases, deep, subterranean rock brought to the surface may differ profoundly to that naturally exposed, and in such cases rich growths of ferns result from species immigrating sometimes from considerable distances, such sites consequently adding greatly to the interest and diversity of the local flora.

In discussing the distribution and adaptations of species of pteridophytes to rock outcrops of all types, it is thus convenient here to group both natural and artificial rock outcrops together into one general treatment, and to classify the habitats concerned into three broad categories of rock type exposed. The categories discussed below are those of acidic to neutral rock outcrops, basic rock outcrops, and ultrabasic and metalliferous mineral rock outcrops.

Acidic to Neutral Rock Outcrops

For pteridophytic purposes, rocks of acidic to neutral type can be defined as those which are poorly base-yielding, and hence include a high proportion of fairly hard rock types, usually with a high silica content (see also chapter 3). Examples include especially granites, granodiorites, gneiss, quartzites, quartz-dolerites, slates, grits, sandstones, greywacke, many mudstones and some conglomerates and breccias.

The pteridophytes present on such sites include a range of often quite widespread species, including, in the sites of greatest acidity, Parsley Fern (*Cryptogramma crispa*), Hard Fern (*Blecnum spicant*), Woodland Lady-fern (*Athyrium filix-femina*), Broad Buckler-fern (*Dryopteris dilatata*), Yellow Golden-scaled Male-fern (*D. affinis* subsp. *affinis*), and, in slightly more neutral habitats along with all of these Common Male-fern (*D. filix-mas*), Common Golden-scaled Male-fern (*D. affinis* subsp. *borreri*), and Black Spleenwort (*Asplenium adiantum-nigrum*). Sometimes Common Polypody (*Polypodium vulgare*) and, especially in western districts on more neutral rocks, Western Polypody (*P. interjectum*) are present, and colonies of Woodland Oak-fern (*Gymnocarpium dryopteris*) and Beech Fern (*Phegopteris connectilis*) sometimes occur in sheltered pockets where there is an accumulation of humus amongst loose rock debris. Lanceolate Spleenwort (*Asplenium billotii*), Hay-scented Buckler-fern (*Dryopteris aemula*), Wilson's Filmy-fern (*Hymenophyllum wilsonii*), Tunbridge Filmy-fern (*H. tunbrigense*) and Killarney Fern (*Trichomanes speciosum*) are characteristic of such rocks in extreme Atlantic districts (see chapter 13).

In most lowland rocks, smaller specimens of the more common of these predominate in small fissures of natural rock exposures (such as of Black Spleenwort and stunted specimens of Broad Buckler-fern, but occasionally also Lanceolate Spleenwort) on Dartmoor tors.

Often along woodland margins or elsewhere, acidic rocky habitats occur in which Bracken (*Pteridium aquilinum*) is often dominant. These include especially sites in which Birch and other trees may be scattered, but in which Bracken is abundant in exposed grassy areas, often with light soils and some rocky habitats amongst them. Frequently these are sites which have been variously disturbed, burnt or grazed, and where shrubs of Gorse (*Ulex europaeus* or sometimes *U. gallii*), Broom (*Sarothamnus scoparius*), Hawthorn (*Crataegus monogyna*) and occasional Rose (especially *Rosa canina* and *R. arvensis*) usually occur. Honeysuckle (*Lonicera periclymenum*) is often abundant, as are patches of Wood Sage (*Teucrium scorodonia*), associated with a number of other, mostly small, scattered herbs.

In larger and more distinctly rocky habitats, where dampness, humidity and shade increase, such as on acidic river cliffs, the damp sides and ledges of quarries, and in acidic mine workings, the presence of Bracken usually diminishes or disappears on the shallow substrates available, and instead the larger-statured Lady, Buckler, Golden-scaled and Male-ferns usually predominate, and may gradually build large clumps. Screes of slate debris in quarries and around mines usually carry characteristic communities in which smaller, clump-forming species, and these species may also fringe the sides of abandoned quarry workings, such as where loose rock debris collects at the backs of dark slate staircases, like enormous steps. Here are to be found especially Parsley Fern, Black Spleenwort and Common or Western Polypody, whilst Hard Fern and Woodland Lady-fern are often very characteristic of damp, shaded ledges on acidic quarry sides and in old slate mine workings. They may be especially frequent in clefts and cracks of cool rock faces around sources where dripping or emerging water slowly trickles from innumerable springs, the seepage paths below them often marked by stains of minerals and local growths of mineral-tolerant algae. In slate workings, similar fern communities also frequently fringe the mouths of black mine-tunnel entrances to former subterranean faces.

In the bottoms of old quarry workings are occasional, still, deep pools of often acidic and mineral-charged water. Steeper rock slopes descending to such pools are frequently sites where also dense fringing fern communities of Male-fern, Woodland Lady-fern, Hard Fern and Broad Buckler-fern may occur.

In all of these sites, ferns abound because they pioneer the relatively bare faces of exposed rock, areas that are free from compeling species of plant. Other associated plants are usually few. Amongst those noted are most often scattered plants of Heather (*Calluna vulgaris*), Bell-heather (*Erica cinerea*), Bilberry (*Vaccinium myrtilus*), Foxglove (*Digitalis purpurea*), Wild Thyme (*Thymus praecox*), English Stonecrop (*Sedum anglicum*), Wood sage (*Teucrium scorodonia*), Stone Bramble (*Rubus saxatilis*), Red Campion (*Silene dioica*), Birdsfoot-trefoil (*Lotus corniculatus*), Lady's Bedstraw (*Galium verum*), Hawkweed (*Hieracium* spp.), trailing Ivy (*Hedera helix*), Red Fescue (*Festuca rubra*), sometimes Thrift (*Armeria maritima*), cushions of mosses and often abundant crustose and fruticose lichens, whilst Starworts (*Callitriche* spp.) may thrive throughout many parts of the still, deep pools.

On the shallower edges of such pools, it is not uncommon to find bright green stands of horsetails—especially Water Horsetail (*Equisetum fluviatile*) in the water, Marsh Horsetail (*E. palustre*) near the margins, and Common Horsetail (*E. arvense*) in the debris of the drier parts of the quarry floor. In at least one former roadstone (quartz-dolerite) quarry in Northumberland, Shore Horsetail (*E.* × *litorale*) is also present.

Basic Rock Outcrops

For pteridophytic purposes, basic rocks are those which are not necessarily always geologically exceptionally high in base content, but are ones which, on weathering, are nevertheless able to yield a sufficiently steady, if sometimes small, supply of bases sufficient to neutralise the otherwise acidic tendencies of the edaphic environment. In large part, such bases are usually of lime, calcium carbonate, although other basic chemicals may also be involved. As well as the geological base-yielding tendencies of the rock, the rate of release of basic chemicals present, and hence their effect on the environment, will also depend on the state and depth of weathering of the exposed rock surfaces, the degree of ease with which the chemical structure of the rock decomposes to water-soluble form, and the climatic and hydrographic circumstance of the rock outcrop itself. These include the role of that rock type in forming subterranean aquifers, and the depth of appropriate rock through which any emerging water may have percolated.

In practice, even various metamorphic and igneous rocks may have outcrops which carry locally base-loving (basicolous) floras, but as such exposures often related more closely to mineral-bearing and ultrabasic rocks of the next section (see below), they are more conveniently considered there.

Among sedimentary rocks, local outcrops of calciferous sandstones and sometimes shales and clays (the latter especially through their ability to loosely bond cations of potassium, magnesium and calcium) can be quite basic, whilst the most base-yielding (notably lime) and the regionally most extensive of all basic rocks are limestones. It is also these which contribute most substantially to a distinctive landscape type. I have thus concentrated this discussion principally on this group of rocks, whilst the pteridophyte floras of exposures of clays and shales are discussed more fully in the woodland and coastal sites, where their most frequent exposures best demonstrate their resulting pteridophytic floras (see chapters 7 & 5, respectively).

Inland limestones of course, also vary greatly in their type and hardness as well as chemical content, and, in Britain and Ireland, occur in rocks of many different geological periods, including those of the Cambrian, Ordovician, Silurian, Devonian, Carboniferous, Permian, Jurassic and Cretaceous.

The main, pteridologically significant, landscape features formed by the outcrops of the more massive limestones are the physiographic features associated with outcrops of limestone pavements. (Limestone gorge woodlands and those of base-flushed slopes are discussed separately in chapter 7, and limestone outcrops at low altitude in extreme western, Atlantic climates, which have pteridophyte species not found elsewhere, are included separately in chapter 13.)

In the higher areas of gently uplifted old, hard, limestones, the form of the resulting topography becomes much more diverse, for such features as surface sink-holes, dry valleys, bare rock crags, and great exposures of bare limestone pavements rimmed by terraces of white rock scars, maybe notable features of a high proportion of the landscape.

Of these, it is limestone pavement habitats which are of greatest pteridological significance, their importance lying largely in the degree and depth of their dissection into a microkarst topography. For most such flat-surfaced limestone exposures have been substantially influenced by long periods of subaerial erosion, cutting into and widening original fracture lines into a deeply-incised network of very many deep, often criss-crossing, steep-sided fissures (grykes), with massive, flat-topped pavement-like slabs of solid limestone blocks (clints) between them. These narrow grykes, sometimes up to a metre in depth but maybe only 15–30 cm wide, provide local habitats of shelter, enhanced humidity and good grazing protection within overall sites which are otherwise very exposed

Fissuring of limestone pavement produces characteristic grykes, often rich in ferns. North Yorkshire, July

and subject to strong daytime illumination. Within these dark, damp retreats, only a small amount of soil usually accumulates, and with this limitation, plus the dankness and darkness within, usually prevents excessive rank flowering plant competition establishing in either the depths or on the sides of the grykes. Such conditions are, however, ones which are usually well tolerated by various pteridophytes and, within these extensive and relatively competition-free habitats, it is usual to find several species of calcicolous ferns.

Indeed, the habitats within the grykes vary considerably depending on the aspect of the individual fissure, its depth and the texture of its sides. Different ferns have different optimal abilities at exploiting different combinations of these features, typically resulting in an approximate zonation of ferns and occasional associates from top to bottom, although it is rare to have all the species of limestone pavement ferns within one fissure.

Around, the tops of grykes, in the most exposed and highest illuminated spots, the most frequent fern is Wall Rue (*Asplenium ruta-muraria*), occurring here in one of its few, truly natural habitats. It is usually absent from gryke sites where the rock profile is a smoothly rounded one, but in grykes where the shoulders contain many small fissures and miniature ledges, good niches for the establishment of this species exist and in such sites plants may form a locally extensive, green fringe, with larger plants usually on the more shaded aspects and more compact ones on all the more sunlit ones.

A little deeper into the grykes, also especially in those sites richest in good niches for fern establishment, are likely to be the sinuously wandering, somewhat tentacle-like displays of fronds of Maidenhair Spleenwort (*Asplenium trichomanes* subsp. *quadrivalens*). These usually have a wide zone of overlap with those of Wall Rue, with the deeper Wall Rue plants within the grykes also those with the largest and most pinnately divided fronds.

Deeper in recesses, if larger ferns are absent, a common denizen of dark, shaded and moist rocky depths, and clinging precariously to their more sheltered and shaded sides, are sometimes numerous, delicate plants of Brittle Bladder-fern (*Cystopteris fragilis*). This species is present in most limestone pavement sites that offer sufficiently deep and moist recesses, whilst in northern localities, it may be joined by Green Spleenwort (*Asplenium viride*), and in southern and western localities especially by Hart's Tongue fern (*Phyllitis scolopendrium*).

Phyllitis is certainly one of the larger gryke ferns. Another is Hard Shield-fern (*Polystichum aculeatum*), which occurs especially in northern localities fairly widely, but sometimes sparsely, scattered in grykes, usually wherever larger, moister and well-sheltered niches are available to accommodate it. Nevertheless, although much of the lengths of its shining fronds may be contained within the grykes, those of old and large specimens usually outgrow their habitats, with much of their frond tips eventually projecting into the open, where they suffer either from sun or wind-scorch or are grazed level with the pavement surfaces, especially by sheep.

More rarely, a second species of the same genus, Holly Fern (*Polystichum lonchitis*) is also present in limestone gryke sites, from North Yorkshire northwards, though is never very common in these sites, perhaps suffering too much from their relatively low altitude, high summer temperatures, and their likely high degrees of summer drought in the better-illuminated sites.

Much more tolerant of summer drought, however, are the two remaining more exposure-resistant ferns of inland (non-Atlantic) limestone pavements. These are Limestone Oak-

The mealy fronds of Gymnocarpium robertianum, *especially characteristic of limestone pavement grykes. Mid–Perthshire, August*

fern (*Gymnocarpium robertianum*) and, unique to certain (mainly northern-Pennine) limestone pavement sites, Limestone Buckler-fern (*Dryopteris submontana*). Both appear well adapted to tolerating conditions of high light and of perhaps moderate summer droughts. Unlike the species of *Polystichum*, both are winter-deciduous and both have a bluish, somewhat mealy frond-texture—presumably adaptations to raising the albedo of their upper frond surfaces for light-reflectance purposes, on the often brightly lit, white limestone surfaces.

Limestone Oak-fern is a colonial species, whose long, slender rhizome extends along the bottoms of grykes, as well as often through loose, natural rock rubble slopes around the edges of the main areas of pavement, or on associated cliff slopes. Most of its localities are at fairly low altitude (250–900 ft, ca. 75–275 m), although scattered plants occasionally occur higher. In most of the limestone pavement sites in which it is present, it is usually confined to shallower fissures of around 30–40 cm depth. The blades of its fronds are of somewhat similar general appearance to those of Woodland Oak-fern, but they usually have less tripartite-looking blades, which are also of firmer and more mealy surface texture. It is a local plant within our islands, with its main limestone-pavement headquarters in the Peak District and North Yorkshire Dales, but with solitary sites of extremely limited extent also in Scotland, as far north as Sutherland and in extreme western Ireland. In almost all of its pavement sites, plants grow half-hidden within the grykes, its blades only emerging at, or somewhat below, the level of the general pavement surface.

More exposed at or slightly above the general pavement surface may be plants of Limestone Buckler-fern (*Dryopteris submontana*). This species has much bigger fronds (usually about 25–35 cm long) than Limestone Oak-fern. It is mainly confined to a limited area of the limestone country of the northern Pennines on the Lancashire–Cumbrian–North Yorkshire borders, with rare outlying stations in North Wales and the north-west English Midlands. In the Pennines it occurs especially on exposures of the Great Scar limestone, from near sea-level to about 1600 feet (ca. 490 m). Here, it often grows near to sites for Limestone Oak-fern, but is usually restricted to those grykes of somewhat greater (about 30–60 cm) depth, so the two species seldom directly compete.

Plants of Limestone Buckler-fern have fairly rigid fronds, which, like those of Limestone Oak-fern, have a distinctly mealy and farinose texture, and when lightly bruised, fronds have a balsam-like fragrance. It is a probably long-lived and usually gregarious fern, which thrives in moist, well-drained niches in open or only very lightly shaded sites, with free air

movement about its fronds. In deeper fissures, it usually grows with only the tips of its fronds emerging at the surface of the grykes, but may emerge more fully into the open, where low growths of surrounding woody vegetation (usually Yew, Juniper and Hawthorn—see below) give the necessary local shelter and good protection from grazing.

Although communities of ferns can largely dominate most of the deeper and more shaded fissures in very many limestone pavement sites in which gryke systems are well developed, a small but distinctive contingent of flowering plants are usually associated with them, especially on the margins of the main fern sites. At the surface, small, greatly wind-pruned and often partly-grazed old shrubs of Yew (*Taxus baccata*), Juniper (*Juniperus communis*) Hawthorn (*Crataegus monogyna*) and sometimes Blackthorn (*Prunus spinosa*), may add further site protection, whilst within the fissures, other plants more closely associated with the ferns can include Herb Robert (*Geranium robertianum*), Wood-sorrel (*Oxalis acetosella*), Wood anemone (*Anemone nemorosa*), Herb Christopher (*Actaea spicata*),

The grey-green fronds of Dryopteris submontana *are usually well-hidden within deep grykes of limestone pavements, but here grow more fully exposed within a grazing-protected enclave amongst surrounding Hawthorn and Juniper bushes. West Yorkshire, July*

(*Sanicula europaea*), Common Dog-violet (*Viola riviniana*), Lily-of-the-Valley (*Convallaria majalis*), Wall Lettuce (*Mycelis muralis*), Dog's Mercury (*Mercurialis perennis*), Blue Seslaria (*Seslaria albicans*), Red and Sheep's Fescue grasses, and dense growths of mosses, especially of *Ctenidium molluscum*. In its single Irish site (Co. Mayo), *Gymnocarpium robertianum* is associated with Wood Bitter-Vetch (*Vicia orobus*). In more open grykes with deeper soils, many of these flowering plants may come to dominate and oust the ferns—a feature especially of *Mercurialis perennis*.

Much of the limestone pavement scenery we see today is the result of its geological history since the Pleistocene, the markedly tabular profiles of limestone pavements being largely worn to their present shape by the scouring action of ice during the last glacial advance. Amongst both the ferns and the flowering plants, the number of species present today of woodland affinity within the depths of the limestone grykes is high, indicating perhaps, in part, the similarity of the factors of shade and shelter of the grykes to those of woodland, and perhaps also that in some cases, woodland vegetation cover may have been more widely present. However, in the case of Limestone Oak-fern and Limestone Buckler-fern, both of these species seem well and specifically adapted (especially in their light-reflecting farinose surfaces) to growth in well lit, well-drained, lime-rich environments. These species today seldom, if ever, penetrate far into limestone woodland habitats, and it seems likely that this has also been true of their ecology in the past. Both would thus seem likely to be Post-glacial survivors which have largely persisted in, and perhaps at different times contracted to and spread from sites in which dense tree overgrowth has never been a major vegetational feature.

Finally, where cave systems occur through limestone masses, which man has long artificially illuminated for tourist display purposes, such as in those of the Carboniferous limestone caves of the Cheddar Gorge in Somerset or the Devonian limestone caves of Torbay in south Devon, it seems common for guides to point to, and comment upon, the apparently wondrous occurrence of dense growths of green ferns clinging tenaciously to bare rock faces around the sources of artificial underground illumination (including those of tungsten filament lamps), often very far from the surface above (usually the only bit of popular biology in the tour!). This is something I have hardly ever seen commented upon in pteridological literature. But it seems to me that the occurrence of ferns in just such deeply subterranean enclaves is probably of quite common occurrence, though nevertheless remarkable for that, almost wherever man has created appropriate condi-

tions for photosynthesis. The fern species involved as the colonist is nearly always Hart's Tongue (*Phyllitis scolopendrium*), although I have sometimes also seen Brittle Bladder-fern (*Cystopteris fragilis*). And although much tourist intrigue and speculation seems to be raised as to 'how the ferns got here so far away from the surface', the occurrence of such sites demonstrates well, I think, the very high mobility of fern spores, even through cave systems, either naturally through the passage of steady cave-system air-movements or augmented by whatever may be constantly carried into the depths of such caves on the clothing of myriads of passing tourists every year.

Asplenium trichomanes *subsp.* quadrivalens *has one of its few, purely natural habitats, within limestone pavement grykes. West Yorkshire, July*

Ultrabasic and other Igneous and Metamorphic Rock Outcrops

For pteridophytic purposes, ultrabasic (sometimes called 'ultramafic') rock outcrops are the most important ones of this category, but are most conveniently discussed along with a number of igneous ones, and especially those of metal-mining districts, which often bear somewhat similar pteridophyte floras.

Ultrabasic rocks, despite their name, are ones which are geologically not necessarily exceptionally high in calcium content, but are ones which contain especially little silica, that present being typically bound into magnesian or iron (sometimes calcium) silicates. As well as high magnesium and iron, these rocks are often also exceptionally rich in various heavy metal elements which tend to be toxic to most plant life, including cobalt, nickel and chromium. There are no ultrabasic rocks which are of sedimentary origin (although magnesian limestones also contain high magnesium). All are either volcanic in origin (such as peridotites) or are metamorphic rocks which have been locally heavily influenced by volcanic activity (especially serpentines). Peridotite is a hard, fine to coarse grained, dark coloured igneous rock, rich in pyroxine and olivine minerals. Serpentines are hard, locally metamorphosed rocks of various colours (sometimes including grey, red and green), which are also rich in pyroxine and olivine. Where ultrabasic rocks are present (always quite locally in these islands), the hardness of each typically results in their exposure forming features of prominent topographic relief, whilst their curious combination of low calcium and high magnesium plus metal elements toxic to many plants, makes them of unusual botanical significance.

Various other igneous rocks may have outcrops of high pteridological interest due to locally base-yielding abilities. Examples of these include exposures of volcanic extrusive basaltic, andesitic and rhyolitic lavas (low, intermediate and rich in silica respectively, the first two rich in plagioclase and pyroxene minerals), especially when they occur in the form of soft, water-permeable tuffs. Well-weathered exposures of volcanic intrusive rocks such as dolerites (also geologically low in silica and high in plagioclase and pyroxene minerals) in the form of dykes and sills, though usually harder than tuffs, may also carry locally base-loving pteridophytes. Such basicolous enclaves are often especially noteworthy where they outcrop locally in otherwise extensively acidic regions, in sites which are steep enough to prevent acidic humus accumulating and where seepage water may influence them.

Of special pteridological significance, however, are other native volcanic rocks which may carry combinations of basicolous pteridophyte floras and those similar to ultrabasic ones. These include exposures of rocks which are especially rich in various metal elements, such as lead, zinc, tin and copper. Such metalliferous rocks usually occur in the form of veins or 'lodes' of volcanic rock intruded into other surrounding 'country' rocks. They are thus also always of very local occurrence within these islands, and their natural exposures few. Significantly, however, man has usually added considerably to these, for the economic value of such veins, and their local concentration, has usually made them sources of considerable mining activity, with deeply subterranean rocks long being brought to the surface (often especially actively during the 19th century), with the waste rock heaped or scattered. Rock spoil around disused mines usually still contains botanically significant quantities of metalliferous minerals left from the extraction process, often in the form of metal carbonates of sulphates with high levels of arsenic, and fairly easily degraded by weathering. The toxicity of such sites to many plants, often in combination with lime or other bases, determines a pteridological similarity of many to those of ultrabasic rocks. Left abandoned and available for plant colonisation, the old workings of many former metal mines, including the rubble heaps, engine houses, mineshafts, adit entrances, settling ponds and associated artificial water conduits and streams, have usually thus become colonised by vegetation of considerable pteridological interest.

The principal areas of exposure of ultrabasic rocks in these islands occur in fairly small and widely scattered sites, from the Lizard Peninsula of Cornwall to the Isle of Rhum in the Inner Hebrides and in the Shetland Islands. Those of the principal metalliferous ore outcrops are widely scattered from the tin mines of Cornwall to the copper and lead mines of North Wales and the strontium mines of Ardnamurchan in the western Highlands, while outcrops of other lavas are often very local and are largely concentrated in the more mountainous regions of these islands.

Taking these types of rock in reverse order, the outcrops of largely non-metalliferous rocks, and especially of lavas, are pteridologically mainly notable for forming local and sometimes rich enclaves for a variety of small, mainly mural, ferns. Those rocks, which are fairly hard and acidic also produce only acidic habitats, and in appropriate regions, where these form screes, such sites may be marked mainly by the presence of Parsley Fern (*Cryptogramma crispa*). Those which are usually somewhat softer or form more fissured rock faces may, espe-

Asplenium
trichomanes *subsp.*
trichomanes *on base-
poor igneous rock.*
Mid-Perthshire, June

cially in northern and mountain areas, support scattered populations of the rare Alpine and/or Oblong Woodsia (*Woodsia alpina* and *W. ilvensis*), and although these are by no means restricted to such volcanic rocks, these species seem to sometimes occur on them on quartz dolerite, basaltic lavas, trachite and pumice tuffs. All are rocks which are probably somewhat low in lime-yielding abilities, although it is possible that the always local occurrence of these ferns may be on sites which are both siliceous and perhaps to some extent influenced by some degrees of base-flushing from other rocks nearby. Other sites of such rocks, especially where of softer texture and perhaps modestly more basic, may, especially at lower altitude, bear more extensive populations of Black Spleenwort (*Asplenium adiantum-nigrum*) and Delicate Maidenhair-Spleenwort (*A. trichomanes* subsp. *trichomanes*).

Where such lavas are perhaps a little more base-yielding, such as on doleritic, andesitic and rhyolitic tuffs, they are much more often marked by the occurrence of enclaves of Wall-rue (*Asplenium ruta-muraria*) and Common Maidenhair Spleenwort (*Asplenium trichomanes* subsp. *quadrivalens*) in appropriate habitats, the former mostly only in lower altitude sites. Where such rocks have exposures in more mountainous and northern areas, Green Spleenwort (*A. viride*) is frequently associated with the most lime-rich habitats, where it usually to a large extent replaces *A. ruta-muraria* in them. Where such rocks are exposed at lower altitudes, especially in western climates, Rusty-back Fern (*Ceterach officinarum*) and Southern Polypody (*Polypodium australe*) may also occur, and indeed, do so as far north and eastwards as one site on andesitic agglomerates in Clackmannanshire (Fife).

In some sites of outcrops of lavas of all types, pteridologically fascinating mixtures sometimes seem to occur in such habitats, suggesting that either complex edaphic mosaics are present or that the lime-yielding abilities of the rock are not the most paramount factor. In two sites in eastern Scotland, for example, almost all of these species seem to occur together, on warm, south-facing exposures, in one site on Lower Carboniferous volcanic extrusive basalts and related volcanic tuffs and ash beds within the city of Edinburgh. In the other, in Mid-Perthshire, the site is on naturally exposed faulted and sheared blocks of Lower Devonian hypersthene-andesites and volcanic conglomerates associated with the formation of the Highland Boundary Fault. In each of these sites too, it is notable that an additional spleenwort, more often associated with rocks of high metal ore content is also present—Forked Spleenwort (*Asplenium septentrionale*)—see below.

The rock of metal-bearing lodes often also includes many base-yielding veins, and hence where exposed, also frequently (though not always) forms habitats for basicolous and usually calcicolous species. Sometimes, many non-spleenwort pteridophytes are present. Common Male-fern (*Dryopteris filix-mas*) occurs quite widely in such sites, often accompanied by scattered Hard Shield-fern (*Polystichum aculeatum*) and sometimes abundant patches of Brittle Bladder-fern (*Cystopteris fragilis*). In others, populations of Lady Fern (*Athyrium filix-femina*) may be very common, and this species, plus Common Horsetail (*Equisetum arvense*) appear to be, in west Cornwall, among the few plants able to tolerate the highly toxic slurry deposits generated in old tin-mine settling ponds. In southern Scotland, and perhaps elsewhere, Marsh Horsetail (*E. palustre*) may vigorously colonise and sometimes dominate the tailings of old lead-mine workings.

However, it is the spleenworts which dominate most of the rupestral habitats of most old metal-mining areas in these islands. In the more basic sites, Wall-rue (*Asplenium ruta-muraria*) and Common Maidenhair-Spleenwort (*A. trichomanes* subsp. *quadrivalens*) are again the two most usual species, with Green Spleenwort (*A. viride*) joining them and sometimes becoming exceptionally abundant (notably so, for example, on the strontium mine tailings of Ardnamurchan). In what are

Ceterach officinarum, Asplenium trichomanes *subsp.* quadrivalens *and* Cystopteris fragilis *in the mortared slate walls of a former lead mine pump room. The succession from exposed,*

probably the less basic sites, the composition of the flora usually shifts towards a different trio of spleenworts, usually becoming dominated by Black Spleenwort (*Asplenium adiantum-nigrum*), accompanied by more scattered Delicate Maidenhair-Spleenwort (*A. trichomanes* subsp. *trichomanes*) and especially the highly local Forked Spleenwort (*A. septen-trionale*). Habitats of this type are notable in the lead and copper mine sites of North Wales, where sometimes these species becomes so abundant that they spread to form the vegetation on adjacent drystone walls of the local rock, where they are often joined by Rusty-back Fern (*Ceterach officinarum*) in many areas of former metal ore mining.

Forked Spleenwort is a small fern which may eventually build to form more massive clumps than do most other native species of *Asplenium*. It has distinctive, narrowly wedge-shaped forked fronds (actually extremely irregularly, sparsely and obliquely pinnate), and its characteristic habitats are on steep rock faces of dark coloured, often highly siliceous, rock. It is intolerant of shade, and its habitats are also most always of southerly exposure, in sites where they normally receive considerable direct sunshine, and can warm rapidly on sunny mornings following cold night temperatures. Such thermal situations presumably enable this very southern and continental evergreen fern to achieve adequate temperatures for brief periods of active growth even during severe winter weather, and the thermal capacity of the great bulk of hard, dark coloured rock of most of its sites may well be of ecological relevance in this species' success in our oceanic climate on the edge of its geographic range (for it is, for example, on basalt in Midlothian, on gabbro in Galway and on epidiorite in the Highlands). Further, the relatively massive clumps of old colo-

light, wall-top species to darker, more sheltered and moister bottom species is especially typical. Merionethshire, September

Asplenium septentrionale on dark-coloured, well-jointed, intrusive igneous hypersthene-andesite rock associated with the Highland Boundary Fault. Mid-Perthshire, June

nies of this fern undoubtedly serve to absorb and hold a certain amount of moisture, enabling the plant to make a remarkably quick recovery following long dry spells. Its habitats are almost invariably steep ones, and these sites plus the curious structure of the fronds seem to ensure that the plants do not become waterlogged. For its fronds orientate to arch outwards and downward from often near-vertical rock faces, their winged stipes appearing to draw excess water readily away from the numerous crowns of dense clumps, whilst the curious forked structure of the blades, with many downwardly directed acute points, act as very many drip-tips from which small water droplets are shed rapidly. The plant would seem, in our wet and humid climate, not only to be highly susceptible to waterlogging, restricting it from all but the most freely-draining of sites, as well as sunshine-requiring and demanding of rock with a high thermal capacity, but it is known too to be susceptible to depradations of invertebrates such as slugs, snails and woodlice. Perhaps it is precisely this susceptibility, which in large part also confines it to habitats in which highly toxic metalliferous elements usually so abundantly surround it.

Finally, turning to ultrabasic rocks, almost all the above species of spleenworts seem able to occur in these habitats within our islands, with a somewhat notable exception in my experience of *Asplenium viride*. This absence is curious for although we regard this species as a positive indicator of moist, highly lime-rich rock sites, it appears to be regarded in Scandinavia as an indicator of ultrabasic ones. This seems to be one way in which our pteridophyte flora differs ecologically as well as in species content from that of continental Europe. We apparently also lack, in our ultrabasic sites, another species of spleenwort widespread in, and also characteristic of, this rock type in Europe, called *Asplenium cuneifolium*.

Indeed, this latter species was thought for a few years to occur in British sites on ultrabasic rock, for specimens of spleenworts looking very similar to those of European *Asplenium cuneifolium* were found and recorded as such by many botanists in sites from as far apart as the Lizard, western Ireland, the Isle of Rhum and Aberdeenshire (Grampian). All however proved to be curious forms of our native Black Spleenwort on chromosomal investigation undertaken by Dr. A. Sleep of Leeds University. This surprised everyone, and thus the name *A. cuneifolium* was deleted from the inventory of the British and Irish flora.

The interesting question remains, however, as to 'what, why and how' are the reasons for structurally distinctive forms of Black Spleenwort on every one of our native serpentine sites in Britain and Ireland, but not in Europe. Experiments I have carried out show that propagation from spores and culture of the progeny from native sites produces offspring which always maintain the distinctive appearance of the 'serpentine form' of *A. adiantum-nigrum*, as it has become known. They continue to do this whether they are grown in their own serpentine soil or in a standard greenhouse potting mix, except that they seem to grow less well away from their own soil. Interestingly, under experimental greenhouse conditions, the simultaneous reciprocal experiment shows that non-serpentine *A. adiantum-nigrum* also breeds true when the prothalli are similarly allowed to cross amongst themselves, and whilst it grows better than does the serpentine form in the same standard greenhouse potting mix, it fares very badly when planted into the serpentine soil. Each thus appears to be a genetically adapted form, specific to its appropriate 'wild' soil type, to which I conclude that

The bluntly-segmented serpentine-form of Asplenium adiantum-nigrum *on coastal serpentine rock. Lizard Peninsula, west Cornwall, September*

each is physiologically very specifically adapted on a genetic base, and that this adaptation is simultaneously reflected in the adoption of a distinctive frond morphology.

Geographically, whether this distinctive form of *Asplenium adiantum-nigrum* 'hopped' from one native (and widely separate) ultrabasic rock site to another within our islands I am inclined to think is less likely than the independent parallel evolution of similarly-adapted forms, wherever the more widespread population of *A. adiantum-nigrum* encountered serpentine conditions (for 'normal' *A. adiantum-nigrum* is fairly variable anyway). It is my suggestion that the stimulus for this multifold parallel evolution was the pteridological vacancy of these sites in our rather species-reduced flora, and especially in the absence of genuine *A. cuneifolium* to occupy them or the inclination of *A. viride* to do so.

A last post-script to all these rock sites is that, in addition to the species of spleenworts which are prevalent, a number of very rare, but nevertheless distinctive hybrids are also known from some. These include Alternate-leaved Spleenwort (*Asplenium × alternifolium*) which is *A. septentrionale × A. trichomanes* subsp. *trichomanes*), Caernarvonshire Spleenwort (*A. × contrei*) which is *A. adiantum-nigrum × A. septentrionale*), and Murbeck's Spleenwort (*A. × murbeckii*) which is *A. ruta-muraria × A. septentrionale*). All of these are discussed in somewhat more detail in Page (1982), but their uniting ecological factor is their occurrence in these islands at all. I put this down to not only the complex mix of parents that can sometimes be present on these unusual volcanic rock types, but also, as with the new forms of *A. adiantum-nigrum* on ultrabasic ones, to the general availability of all of these unusually low-competition sites for the success and survival of such novel forms, sufficient at least to attract botanical attention. What we are seeing in these sites are not plants worthy of mere note for their Victorian curiosity value. They are instead, to me, some of the incipient stages of pteridophyte evolution happening today in a comprehensible and accessible ecological setting. What better argument for their careful conservation?

Pteridophytes of Heath and Moorland CHAPTER **10**

The terms 'heath' and 'moorland' refer, in general, to vegetation of a single principal type. Such vegetation is typically dominated by large numbers of woody, much-branched, small-leaved, evergreen, low-growing shrubby plants of the Ericaceae family. The dwarf shrubs typically form a canopy about 10 to 30 cm or so in height, and this canopy may either be a fairly dense and continuous one, or a very patchy one, interspersed with a mosaic of more open pockets and even bare ground.

In popular terms, the word 'heath' is often used in relation to such communities which are mostly on mineral-soil substrates in lowland regions, such as the various heathlands or former heathlands of southern England, whilst 'moorland' has more popular connotations with rolling, remote, windswept, heather-clad, upland and especially northern sites, often developed over deep, peaty substrates. The latter may either be relatively well-drained (especially on steep slopes), or have moister pockets of wet heath, and these, in turn, in the wettest and poorest-drained situations merge into separate communities of upland bogs. The general similarity of the plant communities within the non-bog portions of each of these sites, whether they be lowland or upland ones, has led to the widespread adoption for them of the somewhat unwieldy technical term 'dwarf-shrub heath association'.

As a matter of convenience, the communities of all of them are referred to here by the more traditional term of 'heath' (or 'heathland'). The lowland and upland variants are distinguished as necessary by the terms 'lowland heath' *versus* 'upland heath' or 'upland moorland'.

Derivation of Heathland Communities

All such heathlands today are characteristic of generally base-poor and acidic soils. Their parent materials range from wind-blown, stabilised, siliceous sand, through an extensive range of fluvio-glacial and other gravelly deposits to glacial tills. Heathlands are especially widely developed in regions where generally acidic rocks such as sandstones, grits, granites and gneisses underlie the habitats. On such substrates, heaths especially evolve in areas where there is high atmospheric humidity throughout the year, and in the wetter upland regions, such conditions have been responsible for the widespread development over such substrates of peat. Under such climatic conditions, heathlands then develop where some factor has prevented the initial establishment of woodland vegetation, or has removed pre-existing larger shrubs and trees and prevents their re-establishment. The heathland vegetation created is, however, one which is very tolerant of high and persistent winds, and appreciable periods of winter snow-lie, experienced especially by upland moorlands, seem generally beneficial to heathland existence (Gimmingham, 1972).

A vital factor in heathland development is hence the absence of trees, and hence the full exposure of the dwarf shrub layer, and the plants growing amongst it, to the full force of the elements. In a few places where tree growth was probably always difficult or absent, such as on exposed cliff-top sites in highly maritime, coastal regions, as well as in the sub-alpine zone above the tree line in our mountains, such communities are very probably the natural and original ones to have developed in our flora. In these sites, such communities and the species within them, presumably link more or less directly back to open communities which were more widespread in the early post-glacial, before the extensive establishment of forest cover. However, the very great bulk of our modern heathland communities in Britain and Ireland are to a very large extent man-made and man-maintained communities, where man has reversed the natural situation and again removed the forest cover. Their history, however, may, in many cases, be a long one, stretching back as a continuum of heathland communities to the days when man first cleared large areas of the primaeval forest cover. The very great bulk of the widespread heathland communities we see today, however, thus appear to owe the bulk of their floristic content either to spread of species from these former, more localised, original heathland enclaves, or to survival of species which already formed a part of the plant understorey association of the former woodlands themselves. The latter is perhaps especially true in the case of the understorey vegetation of the original, once relatively widespread, natural pinewood vegetation. It is significant in relation to the pteridophytes of heath and moorland vegetation today, that the communities include some (especially the clubmosses) which are mostly typical of naturally open sites, and a substantial component (especially the ferns) which are probably largely fragmented survivors from former forest cover.

In practice, today, although man has been almost entirely responsible for the removal of the original forest vegetation, the usually small numbers of seed trees persisting still occasionally achieve a limited recolonisation of the heathland surface, as can occasionally be seen especially by pioneering birch. Such instances probably reflect an early seral stage of colonisation, providing a habitat into which, were other seed tree species available, such as oak or pine, a more permanent woodland canopy might eventually begin to return. A particularly interesting comparison here is that usually presented by the vegetation of small islands in upland lochs, which, where free from grazing, continue to carry a woodland cover, even in extremely exposed sites. These contrast abruptly with the stark upland moorlands around them. Overall, however, the natural succession back to woodland which might eventually occur on most heaths and moorlands, is seldom able to advance very far in the face of widespread and long-established persistent grazing pressure by sheep and deer, and of moorland burning by man for the purposes of creating and maintaining an artificial vegetation climax, especially, for example, for grouse-moor.

Pteridophytes occur widely through heathland habitats, especially in higher-rainfall western locations, and in such sites, form important parts of the vegetation of both lowland heath and upland moorland the great majority of heathland pteridophytes are essentially similar in both lowland and upland sites.

Bracken Heaths

Undoubtedly, by far the most abundant and widespread pteridophyte of well-drained heathland communities is Bracken (*Pteridium aquilinum*). This fern has come to ecologically dominate extremely large areas of both lowland and upland heathlands throughout Britain and Ireland, where its fronds vary in density from thin, open, low-growing stands in exposed sites to often tall, dense and almost impenetrable thickets.

Established colonies of Bracken are tolerant of a wide range of climatic conditions, including exposure to full daylight, to which they adapt with vigour. Its colonies can be especially extensive over well-drained, sandy soils, such as in the 'Breckland' area of East Anglia at low altitude, or on the outcrops of sandstones and grits in upland areas such as the fells of the Pennines. Indeed, in such upland areas, including many of the moorland areas of North Wales, the northern Pennines and

Scottish Highlands, large stands of Bracken may cover whole hillsides, forming dense, nearly continuous blankets across their lower slopes. From here, almost unbroken stands of the plant often ascend to the altitude of the former tree line, their waist-high or even head-high patches pale, verdant green in spring, glossy, deep green by mid summer and yellow-green eventually becoming a rufous, 'bracken' brown in autumn.

In heathland habitats, the associates of Bracken are usually mainly Heather (*Calluna vulgaris*), Bell Heather (*Erica cinerea*), Bilberry (*Vaccinium myrtillus*), and grasses such as Wavy Hair-grass (*Deschampsia flexuosa*), Common Bent-grass (*Agrostis tenuis*) and Sheep's Fescue (*Festuca ovina*). When in dense, solid stands, however, Bracken excludes most other species from beneath its own frond canopy, with such associates reduced to isolated patches or much weakened individuals. Other species which may and sometimes do survive in Bracken stands that are not too dense, include Foxglove (*Digitalis purpurea*), Heath Bedstraw (*Galium saxatile*), Sheep's Sorrel (*Rumex acetosella*) and sometimes Bluebell (*Hyacynthoides nonscripta*). The latter seems especially indicative of the former woodland derivation of some of the Bracken heath sites, and is one species that often responds to artificial control of Bracken by profusely flowering.

In the original native wildwood of these islands, Bracken was present, probably as an already widespread but seldom very extensive fern, thriving mostly along natural forest margins and in glades. In the denser and moister forest, its growth was probably always largely checked in extent by natural forest shade and more vigorous growth of other ferns. Bracken owes its present day success partly to its own innate abilities, and partly to a very long history of interference with former forest and subsequently heathland habitats by man. For not only are the heathland habitats in which Bracken so largely occurs of man-made origin, but the progress of Bracken into them has largely resulted from the long and steady history of forest clearance, woodland and moorland burning, and grazing of domesticated animals, especially with sheep. Combined together, these factors have long served to remove most of Bracken's natural competitors, constantly create conditions for the progressive vegetative spread of old colonies and promote events suitable for the periodic establishment of new ones.

The long history of Bracken's spread goes back to the beginnings of forest clearance in Mesolithic and Neolithic times. For sub-fossil spore evidence indicates great local increases in the frequency of Bracken spores around areas of early human habitation, where it showed a quick response to forest opening, especially by burning and the subsequent use of such areas for grazing stock. Such historic heathlands as the East Anglian Brecklands and many Scottish and Irish moorlands are believed to have originated during Neolithic settlement, when lighter, well-drained soils were especially utilised for shifting cultivation, both in the lowlands and up to about 300 m. Once the forests were removed, steady increase of grazing pressure through historic time, has itself been responsible for largely preventing effective natural forest regrowth, allowing especially long periods of time for established Bracken colonies to slowly expand and spread.

At much later dates, depopulation of rural areas has also probably contributed to Bracken's renewed vigour. For, in the Scottish Highlands, for example, before the depopulation resulting from the Highland clearances, Bracken was regularly cut (see chapter 1). With the cessation of cutting, its natural vigour was no longer checked, whilst the disturbed soil of abandoned homestead sites and areas of abandoned cultivation such as 'lazy beds' (which formerly grew especially potatoes), with their increased drainage, also provided yet further habitats into which Bracken could expand.

Throughout our heathlands and moorlands, disturbance of ground and especially fire-burn sites have long offered appropriate habitats in which Bracken could invade anew. Simultaneously, constant pressure of grazing, especially by sheep, has probably been in large part responsible for promoting steady encroachment of the fronts of existing Bracken colonies. Some of the problem of the ever-increasing rates of spread of Bracken in the 20th century probably result from the combination of upland moorland burning and from the tendency to also try to maintain constant sheep stocking-rates on the hillsides, with sheep grazing ever smaller Bracken-free areas and creating a vicious circle of ever-increasing events.

The biological assets of Bracken which have enabled it to so successfully take such widespread opportunities include ability to exploit edaphically poor habitats, considerable sporophyte longevity and effective vegetative spread, and fire-adaptation both in sporophyte survival and in gametophyte establishment phases.

Fires benefit established Bracken colonies, for the deep-seated rhizomes are frequently at depths of 10–50 cm and occasionally more. At such depths, many Bracken rhizomes usually remain undamaged even by hot surface fires, which may cause the wholesale removal of all competing vegetation. Thus after a fire has passed through, new Bracken fronds are usually amongst the first plants to emerge, gaining some benefit from the temporary release of minerals and often subsequently becoming more dominant (Page, 1976).

Fires also benefit the establishment phases of Bracken, however, enabling it to appear in sites in which it was not present before. For sites especially suitable for Bracken invasion by spores seem to result from the complete temporary removal of other plant cover, the sterilisation of the site by a fire, and the release of quantities of potash from the burn.

That such fire-site establishment has long been an integral part of the strategy of Bracken's spread, seems indicated by its especially unusual edaphic requirements. For as a mature plant, most Bracken colonies are strongly calcifuge, though, as young, establishing sporelings, they are markedly calcicolous. As plants establish, so they appear to undergo a complete pH metamorphosis, from calcicolous to calcifuge, a situation which appears to be an adaptation to pioneering fire-burn habitats. For in these, the release of potash minerals results in an initial high pH, which becomes rapidly leached from the system as the plant establishes and as its rhizome penetrates deeper soil layers (Page, 1986). As far as I am aware, such a pH-metamorphosis in early life is unique in the vascular plant kingdom.

Ferns of Moist Heathland Slopes and Margins of Rills and Streams

Hard Fern (*Blechnum spicant*) is one of the most regularly occurring smaller ferns of heathland communities in all the wetter climates of Britain and Ireland. Spreading clumps of this fern are generally very widespread amongst Heather in many areas of heathland, but especially so on damp valley sides in upland moorland in wetter, western districts. In such sites, it survives well amongst Heather, probably because of its low, rather flat, vegetative frond profile which is relatively little disturbed by the wind. In western communities especially it grows through a great range of altitude, from near sea level to about 2,000 ft (600 m), and sometimes much higher, with outlying specimens sometimes occurring as high as 3,900 ft (1,200 m). Despite its generally low-growing profile, plants nevertheless usually reach their greatest abundance in heathland habitats in the vicinity of stream courses, where plants may become locally abundant especially on steeply sloping, moist, peaty erosion banks and here usually achieve a larger and more luxuriant form of growth with larger, more arching fronds.

Of usually larger stature but also of very frequent occurrence in moist heathland communities is Sweet Mountain Fern (*Oreopteris limbosperma*). This species, with fronds sometimes reaching 90–120 cm in height and about 20 cm broad, is wide-

Oreopteris limbosperma *in a sheltered upland site of seeping acidic groundwater. Glen Orchy, Argyll, September*

spread in mainly upland heathlands in North Wales, the English Lake District, and especially in the central and western Scottish Highlands, where it too can reach an altitude, in upland heathland, of over 3,000 ft (ca. 915 m), although most of its stations are much lower than this.

Oreopteris limbosperma is a strongly calcifuge fern, which also has a particularly high moisture requirement, associated with a very high and fairly uncontrolled rate of water loss through its large and leafy, soft-textured fronds. In heathland, it thrives mostly in locally sheltered pockets, where its fronds are protected from strong winds. Within such sheltered sites, it is confined to habitats where the groundwater is moving, for which it is a good marker, and avoids areas where the groundwater becomes more stagnant. It thus occurs only where there is a trickling surface or subterranean run-off of peaty water constantly providing moving, moist, aerated and acidic conditions around its roots. In sites which provide this right combination of conditions, it can be a fast-growing and gregarious species, and plants can form extensive patches on the flanks of moorland valleys marking areas of appropriate shelter and hydrological conditions. It can also occur numerously along the fringes of streams and ditches down the steeper aspects of moorland valleys, where frequent plants may form long, somewhat regimented, meandering, lines, marking the many courses where tumbling moorland streams have cut deep, narrow, often hidden, clefts down to the base rock surface, through the thick layers of peat.

Several other ferns also occur on heathlands generally, but become more frequent and luxuriant in the shelter of the flanks of valleys and near to flowing streamcourses. Woodland Lady-fern (*Athyrium filix-femina*) often less numerously adopts much the same distribution patterns and habitats as *Oreopteris limbosperma*, following stream-courses and seeking the shelter of shallow, heathland stream valleys, although this species is less tied to high rainfall areas than is *Oreopteris limbosperma*. At altitude in central and western Scotland, this species is widely replaced, especially on damp, heathy ledges inaccessible to sheep and deer grazing, and within high mountain corries (see Chapter 12) by Alpine Lady-fern (*A. distentifolium*). At low elevations, Woodland Lady-fern occurs more often than *Oreopteris limbosperma* in the neighbourhood of standing water, in thick Heather stands around small lochans. It is particularly frequent in these sites in the north-west of Scotland and in the Scottish Islands, as well as in the higher rainfall areas of western Ireland, and in each of these areas plants are often joined in these heathland habitats fringing open water by striking, robust plants of Royal Fern (*Osmunda regalis*), reaching its best development on islands and at the feet of steep, inaccessible banks, where it is best protected from grazing pressure by both deer and sheep.

Also very widely occurring in heathland habitats, especially in the shelter of the flanks of valleys, are various members of the Golden-scaled Male-fern (*Dryopteris affinis*) complex, and sometimes, especially where direct mineral soils are exposed along streamside erosion banks, also Common Male-fern (*Dryopteris filix-mas*). Plants of *Dryopteris affinis* can be locally common, especially on steeper, well drained, sheltered and often rocky-peaty banks, where they often form large and probably ancient clumps. In most heathlands, the subspecies of *D. affinis* present seem most usually to be *D. affinis* subsp. *affinis* or subsp. *borreri*, but subsp. *stilluppensis* may occur on a more scattered basis in these sites too.

In the shelter of heathland streambank sites, all of these species are frequently joined by a wide mixture of other ferns, often including many juvenile specimens of Broad Buckler-fern (*Dryopteris dilatata*) or sometimes Northern Buckler-fern (*D. expansa*), and colonies of Woodland Oak-fern (*Gymnocarpium dryopteris*), Beech Fern (*Phegopteris connectilis*), and several horsetails and clubmosses (see below), which may form large patches. Occasional plants of Common Polypody (*Polypodium vulgare*) may be present on rocks, and Parsley Fern

(*Cryptogramma crispa*) may occur too where acidic rock scree, such as those of slate, impinge on heathland habitats.

Associated with many of these ferns in their more sheltered heathland valley and stream-side sites are a number of flowering plants, which are in some cases also indicative of former woodland cover. These include Wood Sorrel (*Oxalis acetosella*), Wood Anemone (*Anemone nemorosa*), Violets (*Viola* spp., especially *V. riviniana*), Slender St John's Wort (*Hypericum pulchrum*), Autumnal Hawkbit (*Leontodon autumnalis*), Self-heal (*Prunella vulgaris*), Purging Flax (*Linum cartharticum*), Honeysuckle (*Lonicera periclymenum*), Golden-rod (*Solidago virgaurea*), Sheep's Sorrel (*Rumex acetosella*), Heath Bedstraw (*Galium saxatile*), Tormentil (*Potentilla erecta*), Wild Angelica (*Angelica sylvestris*), Lesser Twayblade (*Listera cordata*), Alpine Lady's-mantle (*Alchemilla alpina*), Eyebrights (*Euphrasia* spp.), Harebell (*Campanula rotundifolia*), Woodrush (*Luzula sylvatica*) and mosses such as *Dicranum scoparium*, *Rhytidiadelphus squarrosus*, *Thuidium tamariscinum*, *Pleurozium schreberi*, *Polytrichum commune* and *Leucobryum glaucum*. In streambank sites poorly accessible to grazing animals, seedlings of Birch (*Betula pubescens*), Rowan (*Sorbus aucuparia*) and Willow (*Salix aurita*) may still occur.

A rich moorland fern mix marking a rare grazing-free moorland pocket along a small rill. Cairngorm, east Inverness-shire, July

Nearly all of the species of ferns which today have their principal heathland sites most commonly confined to sheltered valleys and stream-course sides, were probably very much more widespread in the greater shelter, shade and humidity of the former woodland cover which the heathlands have replaced. Perhaps largely as a consequence of loss of the forest canopy, few, if any, seem as abundant on lowland heaths today, although they have persisted better in the generally higher rainfall areas and mostly cloudier climates of upland ones.

Heathland Horsetails

The fern-ally Horsetail genus *Equisetum* is well represented in some heathland habitats, mainly in sites where damp mineral-soil banks are directly exposed, or where there is a certain degree of base-rich and mineral rich seepage through peat from surrounding or underlying rocks such as those descending to heathland streams.

Horsetails present in heath and moorland habitats typically include Wood Horsetail (*Equisetum sylvaticum*), Common Horsetail (*E. arvense*) Marsh Horsetail (*E. palustre*) and Water Horsetail (*E. fluviatile*), all of which are widespread, especially in wetter, western climates. All tend to occur in patches amongst Heather-dominated heathland vegetation, commonly up to an altitude of about 1,500 ft (ca. 455 m), but sometimes as high as 3,000 ft (ca. 915 m). In addition, in a few heathland habitats, mainly in northern England and Scotland, Dutch Rush (*E. hyemale*) is occasionally present in base-rich moorland flushes, usually below 2,000 ft (ca. 610 m).

Wood Horsetail, distinguished particularly by its regular, horizontal branched whorls of very numerous fine green branches, occurs amongst grassy and Heather-dominated heathland vegetation mainly in high rainfall districts, and is especially characteristic of upland and northern heathland vegetation.

As with several of the ferns of moist heathland, Wood Horsetail is almost certainly a survivor from the former forest cover of heathland sites, with the role of the shade-casting and humidity-retaining original woodland canopy now to a large extent replaced by overall climatic conditions of frequent cloud cover and regular precipitation.

In heathland valley sites, especially near to the margins of streams, Common Horsetail (*Equisetum arvense*) can occur widely, and where the slopes are marshy with surface run-off and rich groundwater seepage, Marsh Horsetail (*E. palustre*) may also form local extensive patches.

A dense stand of Equisetum hyemale *fringes a moorland stream where it is protected from grazing by a nearby wall. Allendale, Northumberland, early July*

A dense stand of Equisetum sylvaticum *on a flushed streamside slope in woodland. Peebles-shire, late May*

Equisetum arvense is mainly a species of drier, rocky heathland slopes, especially of those exposed by surface erosion or slumping of land, and it frequently vigorously colonises erosion slopes on the sides of heathland stream valleys. It is also present more sporadically in other rocky and gravelly areas of heath and moorland vegetation, and in these, especially in wetter and cloudier, western climates, there is often an especially wide range of ecological overlap between it and *E. sylvaticum*, these two species often growing closely together.

Equisetum palustre becomes more frequent in wetter pockets and in small run-off rills, especially in the shelter of valley bottoms. Here it very frequently adopts a fairly sparsely-branched or even simple and unbranched form. It may form fairly pure stands in peaty silts, where it is frequently joined by scattered shoots of Water Horsetail (*E. fluviatile*), especially in areas of very permanent run-off, where there are anaerobic accumulations of deep, soft, mobile silt. In such sites in western Scotland and the Scottish Islands, where *Equisetum palustre* and *E. fluviatile* are particularly abundant, especially in acid flushes and in shallow, nutrient-poor, silty rills of slow-flowing water, or where this becomes locally arrested into shallow, peaty mires, these two horsetails are usually associated with sparse growths of many moisture-loving and sometimes bog-dwelling flowering plants.

Equisetum Hyemale *Flushes*

In northern Britain, *Equisetum hyemale* occurs sparingly through local and often discontinuous patches of moorland flush vegetation, especially in sites where basic, shallowly-sloping flushes occur in the vicinity of, and drain into, adjacent mountain streams or larger rivers, often surrounded by extensive areas of acidic upland moorland terrain.

More usually, however, they are associated with other species characteristic of such flushed habitats on the lower mountainsides, including Meadowsweet (*Filipendula ulmaria*), Wild Angelica (*Angelica sylvestris*), Water Avens (*Geum rivale*), Bugle (*Ajuga reptans*), Globeflower (*Trollius europaeus*), Ragged Robin (*Lychnis flos-cuculi*), Moschatel (*Adoxa moschatellina*), Lesser Celandine (*Rannunculus ficaria*) and Dog's Mercury (*Mercurialis perennis*).

Many of the moorland flush sites of *Equisetum hyemale* today appear to link these habitats with those of riverbanks in upland woodland valleys and ravines. The discontinuously scattered occurrence of this species in many moorland flush habitats, plus the presence of its hybrid in yet others where the parent is

now absent, would also seem to indicate a somewhat relict nature of the distribution of this horsetail in these bleak moorland sites. Further, the large extent of some of the extant colonies of this slow-growing species, especially in Scotland, seems to strongly contrast with the present rather diminutive size and sparse scattering of the annual shoot growth that this plant now makes within them. For such a slow-growing species, it seems most likely that such large, sparse patches are indicative of long periods of former more vigorous vegetative growth in sites which were once stream-side flushes occurring beneath an ancient upland woodland cover.

Equisetum hyemale flush. Northumberland, June

Heathland Clubmosses

In both lowland and upland habitats, several species of clubmoss occur widely throughout the heathlands of Britain and Ireland.

Stag's-horn Clubmoss Communities

Stag's-horn Clubmoss (*Lycopodium clavatum*) is particularly widespread in drier heathland areas, and is one of the most likely species to be encountered. It is also one of the largest of the native clubmosses. Its long, perennial, creeping and trailing stems run sometimes for a metre or more through and over the surrounding heathland vegetation, and bear very numerous and crowded conspicuous, silver hair-pointed, tightly over-lapping leaves. Its main stems fork from time to time, and give off frequent spreading then upcurving, branching, lateral shoots which, when fertile, end in conspicuously forked, yellow-green cones, standing erect on thin wiry stems to a height of about 10 cm or so above the general ground surface. The silver, incurved, hair-like tips to all of its leaves, give the plant a generally hoary, somewhat frosted appearance, different from that of any other native clubmoss, and from ancient times, this species appears to have long been a favoured item by country lore in the making of garlands for rustic personal adornment.

Stag's-horn Clubmoss grows mostly in areas which are dominated by Heather, but usually too where there are also abundant mosses and often Bilberry. In regions of high rainfall it seems especially characteristic of terrain where the substrate is thin and rocky, whilst in areas of rather drier climate it can densely colonise and spread from the peaty humus of shallow

Lycopodium clavatum *community in unburned heather moorland. Mid-Perthshire, July*

mossy hollows. Sometimes, in the latter sites particularly, it can occur in small and dense patches, forming a compact, matted turf, and many such sites may be ones of characteristically long spring snow-lie. Stag's-horn Clubmoss is undoubtedly a species of both lowland and upland heathland areas. It commonly occurs in the latter in areas which are also rich in other clubmoss species, notably Fir Clubmoss (*Huperzia selago*) and Alpine Clubmoss (*Diphasiastrum alpinum*), although with a maximum altitude of around 2,700 ft (ca. 820 m), it does not ascend as high as do the latter species.

Stag's-horn Clubmoss has, however, in the historic past, clearly also been widely known in lowland heath areas. Although its disappearance from many of these may be partly due to collection of material, its general demise seems more recent and most likely the result of widespread air pollution. Additionally, in both lowland and upland habitats, it, like all the other clubmoss species, is particularly sensitive to destruction by fire. In heathland habitats which are managed by fire on a rotational basis of every 15–20 years or so, the species seems to be just showing signs of return from neighbouring unburned patches, when it is destroyed again. The areas in which it is most likely to occur are therefore in old, unburned patches of Heather, where there is a good, patchy, mosaic structure to the vegetation, and where the Heather itself is also most richly colonised by epiphytic lichens.

Fir Clubmoss Communities

Fir Clubmoss (*Huperzia selago*) is a species of quite distinctive appearance, its closely-grouped tufts of thick and prickly-looking ascending shoots, lacking a long, creeping phase, look like small shoots of native Juniper (*Juniperus communis*).

Fir Clubmoss has a generally more upland heathland distribution than does Stag's-horn Clubmoss, although the two species have a wide range of overlap in which they can occur near one another, Fir Clubmoss ascends in heathland communities to the sub-alpine zone at about 3,500 ft (1,065 m) or more, becoming generally scarce below about 2,000 ft (ca. 610 m), except on low altitude heathlands, where it can occasionally descend to nearly sea-level.

In upland heathland communities, it is mostly a species of rocky ledges or of peaty hummocks around boulders and of sites where the growth of Heather is low and thinned by the presence of shallowly underlying rocks. In lowland heaths, its sites seem also to be mainly on shallow rocky substrates or on more open patches over undisturbed gravelly exposures. All its sites seem particularly freely-drained ones, and it is tolerant of highly exposed situations, with both considerable winter cold as well as summer sun.

Fir Clubmoss has, however, become very rare or extinct in many of its former lowland heathland sites, in most of which it has not been known this century. The complete reason for this demise are unknown, although as well as general loss of habitats, air pollution has probably here too played a very central role. Once established, however, the species has a potential to reproduce prolifically and rapidly by bulbil establishment, with new plants up to 1–2 cm tall or more resulting from rooting of wind-blown bulbils, shed late in the previous season. Questions surround the comparative efficiency and frequency of its reproduction by spores, about which very little is known.

Alpine Clubmoss Communities

Alpine Clubmoss (*Diphasiastrum alpinum*) is a low-growing, much-branched, rather stiff moss-like plant of generally compact habit, with erect, scaly branches, somewhat resembling the twigs of a cypress tree, which arise from running shoots in tight, erect, even-topped clusters.

It shares a very similar geographic and altitudinal range with Fir Clubmoss, and occurs in rather similar habitats. It is a fairly frequent species at altitude, especially in heathland habitats in the Scottish Highlands and in the mountains of North Wales, where it can occasionally be sufficiently common to form the dominant plant in local patches of a closely-grazed 'Lycopodium turf'. Most of its habitats, however, are in heather dominated communities where there is only a thin vegetational covering over rock, and in wetter climates in upland sites, usually on steep and well-drained slopes.

Like Fir Clubmoss, Alpine Clubmoss is clearly tolerant of conditions of severe exposure. Many of its sites, especially where it occurs in shaded hollows on north-facing slopes with Bilberry, Stiff Sedge (*Carex bigelowii*) and *Cladonia* lichens, may mark patches of long spring snow-lie.

Over upland heathlands and related habitats generally, Alpine Clubmoss ascends to well above true heathlands, to areas of mountain-top, broken rock detritus at around 4,000 ft (ca. 1,220 m). Such a British distribution corresponds closely with its range in Europe outside these islands, where it is a truly Arctic-Alpine species, with centres discontinuously in the Alps and in the arctic fringe of Europe, from Iceland through Scandinavia to northern Russia, from where it extends around the northern latitudes of both Old and New Worlds. In accor-

Diphasiastrum alpinum in unburned heather moorland. Mid-Perthshire, August

dance with a range confined to the higher latitudes, or mountainous areas of the lower latitudes, in Britain Alpine Clubmoss becomes infrequent, even in heathlands, below about 1,500 ft (ca. 460 m).

Scattered plants clearly belonging to this genus, however, but of much more lax and less compact form, can be occasionally found in more sheltered habitats at much lower altitude. These occur on various Scottish (and possibly North Wales and English Lake District) mountain sites, often amongst dense Heather communities. The exact identity of many of these lower mountainside individuals remains currently unresolved. In older Floras, many were hitherto referred to *Diphasiastrum complanatum* (under its former name *Lycopodium complanatum*), which is now believed to be a continental European but not a British species. They may be low altitude ecotypes of Alpine Clubmoss. They do, however, show some structural similarities with Hybrid Alpine Clubmoss (*Diphasiastrum × issleri*), which itself is thought to have originated as a hybrid between *Diphasiastrum alpinum* and *D. complanatum*.

True plants of *Diphasiastrum × issleri* are known with more certainty from lowland English heathland localities, where they were formerly recorded under the names *Lycopodium complanatum* or *Lycopodium alpinum* var. *decipiens*. One of the classic sites for this plant was on a local lowland heathland in east

Gloucestershire, where it was known last century (though sadly not this century) growing on sandy ground amid *Lycopodium clavatum*, on 'banks at the head of a ferny valley'. Although the habitat still exists, both clubmosses no longer grow there, and general atmospheric pollution may again be amongst the causes. What is possibly the same plant has, however, been more recently refound in the Malvern area of Worcestershire, in a locality almost bare of trees, in acidic soil sites overlying Precambrian granites. It is of interest to note that where *D. complanatum* currently occurs in continental Europe as well as in north America, it is a species generally of the understorey community of deciduous, oak woodland over well-drained, acidic soils. It might well be expected therefore, that its hybrid might also inherit some of these habitat preferences. In the Malvern Hills area, there is some evidence from associated ground flora species surviving in the district, that the lower parts of these hills indeed formerly bore just such oak woodland vegetation.

Marsh Clubmoss Communities

Marsh Clubmoss (*Lycopodiella inundata*) is a small and somewhat curious-looking plant, consisting of usually numerous, scattered, bright green, horizontal axes pressed tightly to the substrate (often underwater in winter), clothed with numerous, crowded, stiff, cylindrical, upcurving leaves. The short sections of green stem (often only 2–4 cm long) represent annual growth increments which persist through the winter of their first year and normally die thereafter, as a new length of shoot is added in front of them. Occasional strong shoots also give rise from their dorsal surface to usually a single, 2–3 cm high, radially symmetric, leafy, stiffly assurgent cone shoot.

Lycopodiella inundata is a somewhat rare clubmoss, of widely-scattered stations in Britain and Ireland. It is characteristic of lowland heathland areas, occurring in upland heathlands usually only where they descend to valley bottom sites. As indicated in its name, it is a species of damp, periodically flooded ground, especially in wet heathland hollows, and is the only species of clubmoss in Britain and Ireland tolerant of very wet, acidic ground. It occurs usually only in small patches in open hollows in heathlands and in upland valley bottoms, especially over sandy or rocky substrates, or occasionally over eroded deep peat hags, where there is an annual deposition of fine, silty peat on the surface layers. It has been recorded most widely from damp sandy and peaty depressions on lowland heaths, and in such vegetation is known to have occasionally

established anew in certain man-made habitats, including depressions bared by removal of heathland turf and in old tank-track ruts. In all of these habitats, it benefits from the effect of winter innundations and new silt accumulations in helping maintain the open nature of the habitats and their freedom from dense plant competition (although its patches may be surrounded on all sides by dense heathland, and especially wet heathland, vegetation). In some high-rainfall Welsh and Scottish localities, its wet heathland sites verge on to ones of upland blanket bog.

Like the other clubmosses in lowland sites, *Lycopodiella inundata* seems to have been very much more widely known last century than it is at present, especially in many sites in central England. Its colonies, even when well established, have the reputation of easily disappearing, and in Britain this has already happened to a very considerable extent. It has a wide range outside Britain and Ireland at mid-latitudes across Europe and the north temperate zone. It is, in this region, a particularly interesting example of a northern outlier of a group of species of very similar habitats and general appearance, which are mostly characteristic of warmer latitudes in warm-temperate and sub-tropical bogs.

Lycopodiella inundata in a wet, silty, heathland hollow. Loch Torridon, Wester Ross, August

Interrupted Clubmoss Communities

Interrupted Clubmoss (*Lycopodium annotinum*) occurs in various heathland sites, ascending to about 1500 ft (ca. 460 m), almost exclusively in Scotland, although it has been formerly known and is now very rare or possibly extinct in a few scattered localities in the English Lake District and North Wales. *Lycopodium annotinum* has long running and trailing stems, which give rise to numerous groups of generally ascending side branches, each with numerous, bright green, stiffly-spreading leaves which are rather harsh to touch. These bear distinct but stalkless terminal cones, and the vegetative portions of the stem are interrupted by conspicuous annual constrictions, marking the end of each season's growth.

Interrupted Clubmoss occurs in sites of predominantly, but not exclusively, acidic rock, on a variety of heathland aspects from those of damp Heather slopes, stream-banks through upland heathland, and occasionally in more low-lying wet heaths. Its habitats are essentially centred in the Cairngorms area of Scotland, and, as with the occurrence of *Diphasiastrum* × *issleri* in more southern British localities, the habitats of *Lycopodium annotinum* seem to be closely linked with ones of former woodland or forest cover.

In the case of *Lycopodium annotinum*, however, the forest cover with which it was orginally associated was almost certainly, and possibly exclusively, that of Scots Pine (*Pinus sylvestris*). Today, *L. annotinum* occurs widely through central and northern Europe and northern Asia, following very much the northern boreal coniferous forest zone, where it is associated with both pine and spruce. At least in Scotland, its presence seems to be a particularly good indicator of the past distribution of the former extent of native Scots Pine element of these northern boreal forests.

Pteridophytes of Lower Mountain Habitats

Relatively small mountain masses, such as those of Britain and Ireland, situated as they are on islands, have their altitudinal zones of vegetation sometimes highly compressed. Species which might be restricted to very high altitude on much larger mountain masses are thus able to occur at much lower elevations on our mountains, which, because of their small area and low altitude, thus offer a considerable range of habitats in which truly montane pteridophytes are present.

I have grouped into this chapter those pteridophyte habitats which are more characteristic of our lower mountain elevations: upland slopes and screes; base-rich upland springs and flushes; base-rich upland streamside sands and gravels; and Juniper shrub-woodland. Those pteridophyte habitats which are more characteristic of our upper mountain elevations are included in chapter 12.

Upland Slopes and Screes

The steep slopes of our upland regions present an almost infinite array of aspects, exposures, soil depths, and conditions of soil drainage and mineral flushing. Virtually all the many topographic variations are also constantly subject to the almost ceaseless forces of natural erosion, continually wearing down the very fabric of the mountains themselves. Much of the rock is eventually pulverised to sand and gravel, and is ultimately washed downslope and away from the mountain sources by the carrying capacity of the very many outflowing streams. More dramatic in extent, however, are some of the intermediate stages in this process, notably where steadily falling rock yields bare cliff-faces, with a myriad of frost-hewn, angular blocks forming vast boulder-fields in the form of steeply-sloping screes below the eroding high-mountain sources of the debris. These steep talus-slopes often contain boulders sorted by their size. The most massive block-boulders, sometimes as big as a car, are frequently lodged precariously upon each other towards the bottom of the slopes, with progressively smaller and usually more loosely-resting stones becoming more numerous upwards towards the scree fan tops.

Clearly the dynamics of such sites demand that there is a constant addition of new boulders to the slope, which arise and tumble downslope until they each find a position of temporary rest. Most, but not all, such new boulders are probably added in winter. But any sensible exploration of such sites at any time of year should be done not only with the dynamics of the site in mind, but, more practically, also with appropriate consciousness of the ease with which it is possible to dislodge already stationary boulders from the slope. If more than one person is exploring, individuals are likely to be safer strung out across such fans, rather than one below another—dislodged stones can cause considerable damage.

Significance of Scree Habitats

Such scree slopes, especially if loose and mobile, are however greatly suited to colonisation by sometimes numerous ferns. The general wetness and cloudiness of the mountain environment, the frequency with which deep, moist, scree-recesses occur, the freedom from established vegetation competition, and the ease with which fern spores can become blown into such sites, are all factors particularly favouring pteridophyte success. Exposure to the elements, however, is usually a severely limiting factor to their growth, and it is for this reason that most of the ferns present stay well-hidden for all their lives amongst the many deep, dark, irregular spaces that make up much of the volume of the scree itself. Such screes thus can look bare and barren from a distance, yet harbour very large numbers of conspicuous, bright green, ferns that cannot be seen until one is close-to and often on top of them. The very numerous scree crevices and caves beneath the myriad of temporarily lodged boulders, contain sufficient local shelter, shade and humidity for the success of both the gametophyte and the sporophyte stages of the fern life-cycle. Especially successful are the many smaller statured species, able to cling at all angles to the resulting bare rock-faces. But within the bottoms of deeper fissures, the enhanced moisture plus the tendency towards accumulation of wind-blown debris and some plant humus also allows opportunity for a few larger fronded species tolerant of the mountain environment to establish and thrive as well. One of the major factors in their abundance is the relative freedom from grazing by large herbivores that their inaccessibility within deep crevices also creates.

Upland acidic scree. Applecross peninsula, Wester Ross, August

When old block-boulder screes become stabilised through the failure of new rock debris to become regularly added to them, they pteridologically deteriorate as they gradually adopt a shallower angle of repose. In such screes, flowering plants have usually had time to slowly invade and establish, and tend to eventually displace many of the ferns. In the more acidic screes, it is often *Vaccinium* and the many grasses that gradually spread. In the more base-rich screes of central Perthshire (Tayside), an almost blanketing carpet of Alpine Lady's-Mantle (*Alchemilla alpina*) may eventually cover almost all of the fissures, and indeed sometimes much of the exposed boulder surfaces themselves. Whilst, however, screes are continuing to receive an ample supply of new rock fragments from eroding cliffs above them, the whole slope is constantly sustained at its naturally highest angle of repose. The instability allows considerably reduced opportunity for extensive flowering plant invasion, and, instead, ferns are able to sustain their populations by constantly re-pioneering the fresh rock slopes accumulating. The more active the accumulation of rock debris, the more active the dynamics of this colonisation probably are, so that the number of individual plants of all ferns which are present as juveniles is likely to be greater the more

Polystichum lonchitis
which only survives
within its range in the
northern mountains
where protected from

unstable the scree. A few genera present, and especially the Spleenworts (*Asplenium*) and Bladder-ferns (*Cystopteris*), probably mature quite rapidly, and most specimens present in such sites are usually mature and freely fertile. Others, however, and perhaps notably the Lady-ferns (*Athyrium*) and the larger Male, Buckler and Shield-ferns (*Dryopteris* and *Polystichum*) take longer, and thus seem to often occur in screes in a condition too juvenile to be fertile. In such sites, these populations are probably mostly maintained from spores blown-in from occasional larger individuals, often lower in the screes themselves, or from the same species well established in cliff-ledge sites nearby. In such screes, numerous juvenile plants of Hard Shield-fern (*P. aculeatum*) can, for example, look somewhat similar to the much rarer Holly Fern (*P. aculeatum*), and immature *Athyrium* very much like mature *Cystopteris fragilis*. Indeed, large accumulations of actively growing but partly hidden juvenile *Athyrium* and *Dryopteris* growing together, with nearby *Cystopteris*, can be a source of considerable mountainside debate, if not sheer taxonomic disbelief.

grazing by steep, rough, boulder-strewn slopes. Mid-Perthshire, July

Within screes, many of the smaller ferns grow especially closely associated with bare rock faces. Plants growing more or less directly on such freshly-cleaved mineral surfaces have, in turn, a high dependence on that particular surface for most mineral supplies. The intimacy of contact between rock and fern through all stages of each plant's life-cycle, helps ensure that the species of ferns present in screes and their diversity are particularly closely influenced by the geological nature of the accumulating rock itself. In consequence, where the rock type of screes is poorly mineral-yielding (and especially poorly

Dryopteris filix-mas *in sheltered mountain scree with little grazing pressure.* Caernarvonshire, June

base-yielding), all the habitats are typically acidic ones. Where
the rock type is more richly mineral-yielding (and especially
base-yielding), more of a mosaic of base-rich and base-poor
sites is usually present, depending on the degree of leaching
and presumably on the grain and orientation of the rock with
respect to the plant. A greater diversity of habitats is consequently present.

Acidic Scree Fern Diversity

On poorly base-yielding rock, the range of ferns present is in
general poorer than where the rock is more richly yielding in
minerals, but its species are nevertheless distinctive.

Poorly base-yielding rock is typically indicated in the screes
of the mountains of Britain and Ireland by the absence amongst
the fern communities present of the genera *Cystopteris*, *Polystichum* and of most species of *Asplenium*. Instead, such screes
usually have a fern flora dominated by a few more acid-loving
ferns. These typically include members of the genera *Athyrium*
and sometimes *Blechnum* and *Oreopteris*, but especially some of
the more acid-loving species of *Dryopteris*. Also particularly
characteristic of acidic screes is the Parsley Fern, genus
Cryptogramma, whilst members of a few other fern genera are
sometimes also present.

In the lower parts of mountain valleys, where large boulders
accumulate to form the lower fans of acidic mountain screes,
the fern flora can be quite diverse. Screes formed from a wide
range of rock types varying from considerably acidic to about
circum-neutral in character, frequently harbour a number of
acid woodland relics. These can include occasional plants of
Broad Buckler-fern (*Dryopteris dilatata*), Woodland Lady-fern
(*Athyrium filix-femina*), Common Male-fern (*Dryopteris filix-
mas*), Golden-scaled Male-fern (*D. affinis*), Hard Fern
(*Blechnum spicant*), and sometimes Woodland Oak and Beech
Ferns (*Gymnocarpium dryopteris* and *Phegopteris connectilis*).
Fronds of Sweet Mountain Fern (*Oreopteris limbosperma*) frequently emerge in small groups in often somewhat twisted and
etiolated form through rocky chinks towards the light. Their
presence usually indicates sites where the fallen rock forms a
fairly shallow layer over former acidic watercourses, and where
the moving water can often still be heard trickling below.

Occasionally, within the lower peripheries of such screes,
there may also be scattered horsetail shoots, which, according
to the degree of drainage of the ground, most typically include
Common Horsetail (*Equisetum arvense*), Wood Horsetail (*E.
sylvaticum*) and Marsh Horsetail (*E. palustre*). In such sites

where bases are limiting, although silica availability may be high, horsetail shoots nevertheless remain usually small and scattered, compared with their generally much more luxuriant growth in sites of better base enrichment. Clubmosses, notably Stag's-horn Clubmoss (*Lycopodium clavatum*), Alpine Clubmoss (*Diphasiastrum alpinum*) and Fir Clubmoss (*Huperzia selago*), may also occur, mostly around the peripheries of many of the more acidic screes or very occasionally upon mossy or heather islands within them. Interrupted Clubmoss (*Lycopodium annotinum*) additionally forms sometimes extensive, bright green marginal patches, mainly on the granites of the Cairngorms in the Grampian Mountains of Scotland.

Diphasiastrum alpinum. Perthshire, July

Acidic Scree Male-Fern Communities

The generally large-statured species of the Male-fern genus *Dryopteris* are often the most prominent ferns of many more acidic screes throughout virtually all the mountain areas of Britain and Ireland, often reaching their most frequent and luxuriant in acidic scree habitats in the higher rainfall districts of the extreme west. These large plants typically either form a fringe around the lateral and sometimes lower scree margins, or form patches within the more semi-stable areas of the scree slopes themselves. In such sites, the slightly increased stability of the rough rock surface seems to create sites where small pockets of humus accumulate within the many crevices and hollows between the larger boulders, giving these eventually large ferns an opportunity to establish and slowly develop. All the species which occur on screes tend to be long-lived ferns, which gradually build up large and usually fairly exposed rhizome clumps. They consequently tend to develop best perhaps on those aspects of screes which generally offer the best local shelter from the strongest winds, although, in many sites, such shelter can often seem extremely modest.

Although the Common Male-fern (*Dryopteris filix-mas*) can frequently occur on screes, in the more exposed and more acidic habitats, it is more often replaced by members of the Golden-scaled Male-fern (*Dryopteris affinis*) group, in the lower and central parts of the screes, and by the Mountain Male-fern (*Dryopteris oreades*) in the upper, more mobile parts of mountain screes. The latter is generally (although not always) small in stature, and eventually builds rather smaller clumps than does the Golden-scaled Male-fern. All the species are deciduous, the fronds dying down, but usually long remaining attached to their parent clumps, during the winter months. New fronds appear during May and early June each

Dryopteris × mantoniae *locally dominating a scree that has little grazing pressure. Caernarvonshire, June*

Dryopteris oreades *in a high cliff gulley. Westmorland, June*

year, and the simultaneous flushing of so many fronds together at this time of year, can give the whole of the hillside a characteristic colouration. This is particularly true of the Golden-scaled Male-ferns, whose expanding fronds are typically a vivid golden-yellow colour when expanding, and which, when present in large numbers, give a characteristic splash of bright colouration to the mountainside landscapes during the early summer months.

As well as the presence of the three distinctive species of the Male-fern group on such screes, the taxonomic situation is made more complex by the existence of *D. affinis* as probably at least three different subspecies on such screes, and by the even greater complication that all of the subspecies of *D. affinis* can probably also hybridise with *D. filix-mas* and with *D. oreades*, whilst the latter two can presumably hybridise with each other as well. This potentially complicated biological situation is made even more so by the fact that the subspecies of *Dryopteris affinis*, which are cytologically and hence genetically different from one another, are all also apogamously-breeding populations. This means that their prothalli do not have to be fertilised to complete their life-cycles, and the breeding system is thus analogous to that of Blackberries (*Rubus* spp.) in the flowering plants. (The prothalli do, however, still continue to produce active and viable male gametes, which is how they can still hybridise.) The breeding system ensures that, without outbreeding genetic exchange, each separate population of each subspecies is free to gradually accumulate its own genetic differences over the course of time, resulting in the accumulation of local structural differences to the plants from place to place even of the same subspecies. To add a final twist to the knife, the apogamous ability of the parent subspecies is, to a certain degree, passed on and inherited as a genetic dominant in the hybrids between any of the subspecies of *D. affinis* and either of the other two Male-fern species with which they cross. This results in their hybrid offspring, which anyway have an intermediate morphology, also being able to breed true, and, further, potentially hybridise back to their sexual parent (ie. either *D. filix-mas* or *D. oreades*). This is probably the single most complex biological situation as yet known in any of the British pteridophytes, which is still probably far from yet fully unravelled! It is still consequently a topic of active research and considerable taxonomic debate, and much more study at population biology level is needed of some of the sites where both parents and possible hybrids appear to exist in quantity.

Acidic Scree Parsley Fern Communities

Somewhat less taxonomically complicated, but also closely and almost exclusively associated with acidic mountain screes, is the simple, yet beautiful Parsley Fern (*Cryptogramma crispa*).

Good examples of screes in which *Cryptogramma crispa* is extensively developed occur especially widely in the mountains of North Wales and the English Lake District, with more local stations in the Scottish Southern Uplands and throughout the Scottish Highlands. It is surprisingly uncommon in Ireland. It succeeds on screes of a wide range of generally poorly lime-yielding, often siliceous, rock types, including sandstones, gritstones, shales, lime-free basalts and granites. In North Wales, the English Lake District, and in parts of southern and central Scotland, it is often at its greatest abundance on screes of slate, including those created by human mining activity. In such sites it can be locally but frequently the dominant plant, adding numerous splashes of conspicuous colouration to an otherwise often sombre landscape.

Cryptogramma crispa is a relatively small fern, with dimorphic (ie. separate vegetative and spore-producing) fronds, the vegetative ones up to about 15–20 cm tall and of arching habit, the fertile ones up to about 25 cm tall and standing more erectly from well-established plants. The blades of all the fronds are finely cut, closely resembling leaves of Parsley in appearance, but those of the fertile fronds have somewhat narrower segments. All the fronds emerge during late May to mid-June, and the fertile ones shed their sooty-black spores through July

Cryptogramma crispa
amongst large block-
boulder scree.
Caernarvonshire, July

and August. Following expansion, all the fronds are of a vivid
and conspicuous bright light-green colour, which slowly
deepens throughout the summer. The fronds die down rapidly
following the first severe frost of autumn, drying to a bright
rusty-brown colour by late September or October. The dead
fronds remain, however, firmly attached to the plant which
bore them, often persisting well into the following summer and
thereafter decaying only slowly. The short decumbent or partly
ascending scaly rhizomes branch freely in older plants to eventually build up large hummock-like masses, with their very
numerous crowns grouped closely together, the whole tightly
woven to the shape of the boulders and crevices over and
amongst which they steadily spread. One advantage of the long
period of old frond retention may well be that in not blowing
away in this windy and stony habitat, the humus that the
decaying fronds eventually form tends to become incorporated
around the expanding edges of the fern mound which originally bore them.

Indeed, Parsley Fern is unusual amongst scree-inhabiting
ferns in forming clumps which spread amongst and even over
the tops of the component boulders of the scree, often more
densely than it does in the crevices between them. Plants of
Parsley Fern pioneer these sites, often over much of the more
mobile portions of appropriate mountain screes, its prothalli,
about which little field study has as yet been made, presumably
colonising sheltered crevices or thin moss cushions. In such
sites, associates of *Cryptogramma* are usually rather few, and
confined mainly to scattered plants colonising the root-bound
masses of humus accumulated by older clumps of the later
seral stages.

Plants of *Cryptogramma crispa* appear to demand conditions
of particularly free drainage beneath their rhizomes, and good
summer air-movement around their fronds. In mountainous
regions where screes abound, *Cryptogramma* occurs through a
considerable range of altitude, descending occasionally to as
low as about 300 ft (ca. 100 m) in a few places, and ascending
occasionally to around 4,000 ft (ca. 1,200 m) in others, but is
normally most abundant on mountain flanks between about
1,000–3,000 ft (ca. 305–915 m). It does, however, seem to be a
relatively oceanic species, avoiding climates of very severe and
especially dry winter cold. It seems tolerant of long winter
snow-lie, and at its higher-altitude sites above about 3,000 ft
(ca. 915 m), becomes mostly confined to fern-beds where a
thick blanket of snow adds to the protection of plants against
both winter cold and wind desiccation.

Elsewhere in Europe it is present in most of the higher
mountains, particularly in those of Scandinavia. Outside

Europe, related forms, though perhaps not the same species, occur discontinuously in the Himalayas and far east of Asia, and in northern and western North America.

In Britain, Connoly & Dahl (1970) showed *Cryptogramma crispa* to be limited southward in its range by the occurrence of high summer temperatures, and excessively hot summers may well be the most important factor excluding it from more lowland and more continental sites. Its preference for site conditions enjoying good year-round drainage probably make it also particularly dependent on a steady moisture input directly from precipitation, whilst climates with a generally high frequency of cloud-cover and a normally high enough humidity to reduce water loss during summer are perhaps also factors helping confine this species to the most oceanic mountains. Its rarity in Ireland certainly remains enigmatic, although the regular absence of winter snow-cover of long duration seems a factor which should not be overlooked.

Base-rich Scree Habitats and Fern Diversity

In Britain, it is unusual to find many areas of true limestones contributing to the rocks of high-mountain screes. But other rocks which contain numerous base-rich (and especially lime-rich) veins do occur at altitude.

In North Wales, the northern Pennines (especially in Teesdale) and in the English Lake District, areas of base-yielding rock occur locally. These are mostly formed of such rocks as volcanic tuffs with rhyolitic or andesitic lavas, which are, however, mostly of quite local occurrence. In Upper Teesdale, the rocks responsible include the sugar limestones, and although the resulting basicolous flora is a fairly rich one, the relatively soft texture of the rocks does not lend them to the formation of many screes.

Amongst the more extensive and certainly more famous base-yielding upland rock which are hard enough to form high mountains but cleave readily enough to give rise to scree slopes are the mica schist rocks which outcrop fairly widely throughout the central Highlands of Scotland. Here, biotite-rich and chlorite-rich mica schists form extensive high and mountainous tracts of land and along this chain are many famous botanical alpine localities, from Ben Lui in the west through the Breadalbane ranges and Ben Lawers, to Glen Clova in the east. Most of the species referred to below can be found within this, the most famous of Britain's upland botanical regions.

Even in such regions where basic rocks outcrop to form extensive screes, the tendency under the high mountain rainfall for leaching to continually create acidic as well as basic habitats in all pockets in which the supply of basic minerals is not continuously maintained, ensures that a complex mosaic of base-loving and acid-loving species usually co-exists. Almost all the pteridophyte species of acidic screes can thus occur locally in pockets in and around basic screes, adding to the richness of the species diversity seen. A notable exception, however, seems to be Parsley Fern, which rarely, if ever, occurs away from its truly acidic rock sites. In the most extensive and notable base-rich sites, however, a richness of specifically base-loving ferns typically predominates.

The pteridophyte (mostly fern) diversity of base-rich screes is thus almost always greater than that of purely acidic ones. Amongst the additional groups of ferns present are an increase in the diversity of Buckler-ferns (*Dryopteris*), Spleenworts (*Asplenium*), and the appearance of Bladder-ferns (*Cystopteris*) and Shield-ferns (*Polystichum*).

Base-rich Scree Buckler-fern Communities

One especially large-statured species of fern which is prominent on base-rich screes, is the Northern Buckler-fern (*Dryopteris expansa*). Its frond outline is not dissimilar to that of the much more usual Common Buckler-fern (*Dryopteris dilatata*), with which it has long been confused. *Dryopteris expansa* generally differs from *D. dilatata* most clearly in the field in having a frond dissection which gives it overall, a more delicate and lace-like appearance. This seems to result from a greater evenness and regularity of the spaces between the pinnae and the pinnules than is characteristic of *D. dilatata*. It also has a flatter, usually yellower-green blade colour, and scales at the stipe base which are not so markedly striped (if at all) as are those of *D. dilatata*. They also tend to be more ginger-coloured overall.

Northern Buckler-fern has a frond length reaching up to 70–80 cm or so, although specimens with fronds around half this size are far more frequent. As beholds such a normally large-fronded species, *Dryopteris expansa* is a fern which is most characteristically developed along the lower fringes of high screes, where the boulder size is largest and most stable, and hence where crevices are the largest and deepest. It does, however, ascend much higher in screes where boulders are particularly angular and hence even if fairly small, still have plenty of deep gaps between them. In smaller fissures and crevices, plants usually reach only a small size, and in the upper parts of such screes, most specimens seen tend to be juveniles.

It is quite characteristic that much of the plant remains well-hidden, deep within the larger scree crevices, with often only the tips of the fronds protruding at the surface amongst the broken boulders. Where they emerge too far, they are very readily grazed, and it is this factor, as well as shelter, that is very probably responsible for currently confining this fern to the protection of deep scree crevices on mountains, an area of very low grazing pressure.

Base-rich Scree Spleenwort Communities

Species of *Asplenium* may occur in particular abundance in scree crevices of all sizes, and are usually present virtually wherever there is a base-yielding tendency to the scree-forming rock. Particularly widely spread in such sites is the Common Maidenhair-spleenwort (*Asplenium trichomanes* subsp. *quadrivalens*). This fern requires moderate light, and it thus usually avoids the deepest recesses. On base-yielding rock, plants can be very numerous, growing directly on the rock surfaces, especially in all the more directly illuminated aspects of the scree crevices. In such areas plants vary greatly in size. Small plants in all stages of development frequently occur, sometimes with their prothalli still present. Larger ones, often clustering around the upper edges of scree crevices, press their somewhat sinuously-curving fronds fairly closely against the rock faces about them, or, where the light is somewhat lower (and especially during particularly cloudy summers) arch their fronds more towards the light gaps between the boulders. Common Maidenhair-spleenwort occurs in screes over a wide range of altitudes, from valley bottom sites, ascending usually to well over 2,000 ft (ca. 610 m), above which plants become more infrequent.

Looking somewhat like Maidenhair-spleenwort, but differing from it especially in plant habit and in the green, not black, stipe to each frond, is Green Spleenwort (*Asplenium viride*). This spleenwort is a very strong calcicole, present only in screes where appreciable quantities of lime are available to it and is a particularly good indicator of such sites. It also is more of an alpine species than Common Maidenhair-spleenwort, usually beginning to appear in most lime-rich screes on British or Irish (and especially central Scottish) mountains only above about 1,000 ft (ca. 305 m), from where it ascends to altitudes of well over 3,000 ft (ca. 915 m). Very occasionally and locally, such as on the limestones of Wester Ross, the plant descends, along with other calcicolous alpines, nearly to sea-level (see chapter 12).

Asplenium viride *as most usually seen, lurking in a sheltered dark retreat beneath large scree boulders of mica-schist rock. Mid-Perthshire, July*

Asplenium viride is, however, a truly Arctic–Alpine fern in its overall distribution, which ranges widely throughout the higher mountains of western and central Europe, including those of Scandinavia, and on a world-wide scale is present, in most of the highly-disjunct montane regions of the northern hemisphere, including the Urals, western Siberia, Japan and in north-eastern and north-western North America. Elsewhere in Europe, *A. viride* is known to hybridise with *A. trichomanes* subsp. *trichomanes* to form the hybrid *A.* × *adulterinum*. This hybrid, through the doubling of its chromosomes, has become fertile in Europe, and in this form is quite widespread in both the Alps and Scandinavia. Indeed, its widely discontinuous stations suggest that it might well have originated independently many times within this range. Curiously, this hybrid has not been found in Britain or Ireland, although the appropriate parents occur.

Green Spleenwort and Common Maidenhair-spleenwort have a wide altitudinal overlap in their scree habitats in Britain and Ireland, with the two species frequently growing alongside each other, and jointly recolonising new scree boulder surface within the fissures, in often large and frequently intimate mixtures. Mature plants of Green Spleenwort have fronds which generally arch and cascade from the rhizomes, arching rather stiffly downslope and spreading well away from the rock-faces, with their pinnae all regularly rotated towards the light, instead of spreading close to the rock faces and spreading in all directions upon them as more commonly does Common Maidenhair-spleenwort. Green Spleenwort also differs in being much more shelter-demanding than is Maidenhair-spleenwort, and is probably also more tolerant of deeper shade and higher humidity, enabling it to often retreat far further and deeper into the crevices and recesses beneath large, wedged, boulders. In such sites, the spreading fronds of Green Spleen-wort, with their pinnae typically all turned perpendicularly to the incident light, clearly endows Green Spleenwort with an efficient light-catching ability in the unusual depths of these dank, dark recesses.

Base-rich Scree Bladder-fern Communities

Base-rich mountain screes with large boulder-size and hence numerous crevices, are also especially suitable habitats for the widespread occurrence of Brittle Bladder-fern (*Cystopteris fragilis*). This small and fragile fern grows in mountain screes through a particularly wide range of altitudes, commonly ascending to about 2,800 feet (850 m), but with outlying stations occurring as high as about 3,900 feet (1,200 m). It occurs fairly frequently on basic rocks throughout almost all the mountain regions of Britain and Ireland. Like Green Spleenwort, the presence of Brittle Bladder-fern is usually indicative of a high lime-yielding ability of the rocks to which it clings. Also like Green Spleenwort, plants of Brittle Bladder-fern frequently grow attached to rock surfaces of all angles deep within the deepest recesses of tumbled boulder scree, where they frequently hang in an inverted position. In such sites, its wiry root system probably often ramifies deep into the smallest cracks, where it doubtless comes into particularly intimate contact with richly mineral-yielding naked rock surfaces.

The small plants of *Cystopteris fragilis*, usually with fronds which are fully fertile under about 12 cm in length, and sometimes when as small as 4 cm, begin shedding their sooty black spores as early as late June in mountain scree habitats, where they are normally the first species of the season to do so. Thereafter, its spore-sheding season is prolonged by the production of a regular succession of steadily maturing fronds, the last of which persist until they are cut-back by the first severe frosts in about mid-September. Like the more robust and evergreen *Asplenium viride, Cystopteris fragilis* is highly sensitive to shelter and humidity, whilst tolerant of very low light levels in the deep scree recesses. Indeed, in many of the mountain habitats of Brittle Bladder-fern, it and Green Spleenwort frequently grow closely together.

Unlike *Asplenium viride* however, *Cystopteris fragilis*, in its montane (and especially scree) habitats in Britain and Ireland, is a very variable species in both the size and form of its fronds. Specimens with widely varying degrees of blade dissection and pinnule shape exist. In some specimens, the ultimate segments of the frond are extremely attenuated, while in others, they are less so. In a few, the shape of the ultimate segments can be quite rounded, and occasionally, local plants from basic montane screes in some parts of Scotland, the frond morphology is very similar to *Cystopteris dickieana* (see Chapter 5).

Although some, but not all, of the size variation is environmentally influenced, much of the structural variation in upland *Cystopteris* appears to be genetically determined. Members of the European *Cystopteris fragilis* group are known to be of a complex genetic base, involving at least three levels of ploidy (of which at least two are known for certain in upland Britain). In many cases, the differences seen in the frond form in the field may well correspond to plants possessing different levels of ploidy. But in some cases, and especially those where plants occur with a frond form approaching that of *Cystopteris dickieana*, it also may well be that true *C. dickieana* has been present more widely in our mountains in the past, and that introgression between *C. fragilis* and *C. dickieana* may have formerly taken place unusually extensively in the maritime climate of our montane habitats, leaving only occasional enclaves of plants still with a *C. dickieana*-like frond form to survive on a local basis to this day. (Only in coastal habitats in Scotland, where *C. fragilis* does not survive the effects of salt spray, does *C. dickieana* seem able to persist in a relatively pure form in these oceanic islands—Page, 1982.)

Base-rich Scree Shield-fern Communities

Often growing in our mountain screes with *Cystopteris fragilis*, are the two British species of *Polystichum* characteristic of basic mountain screes: Hard Shield-fern (*Polystichum aculeatum*) and Holly Fern (*P. lonchitis*). *Polystichum aculeatum*, like *Cystopteris fragilis*, is present in almost all upland areas of Britain and Ireland where appropriate habitats exist; through an altitudinal range of from just above sea-level to around 2,500 ft (ca. 760 m), with its main montane sites usually occurring between about 800–1,750 ft (ca. 240–530 m). By contrast, *P. lonchitis*, more like *Asplenium viride* in its range, is confined mostly to the central and north-western Scottish Highlands, with a few highly local and generally disjunct stations mainly in northern England, north-west Wales and in the extreme west of Ireland.

Polystichum lonchitis reaches its greatest abundance between about 1,200 to 1,800 ft (ca. 360–550 m), with individuals ascending occasionally to as high as 3,500 ft (CA. 1,070 m). and thus occurs at generally higher altitudes than does *P. aculeatum*.

These two native montane species of *Polystichum* thus have a wide range of altitudinal overlap. In mountain scree habitats in central Scotland, *P. aculeatum* tends to be most abundant in those more basic screes which reach to lower altitudes, where it is associated with their lower and middle portions, in areas where block-boulder size is typically large. In these sites, its fronds indeed seldom reach the surface. Thus, although at fairly low elevations, the plant is very frequently not easily seen by observers, except by climbing over and amongst the large block-boulders themselves, and searching down into the deeper crevices.

At higher elevations on screes, *Polystichum aculeatum* becomes generally more infrequent, although as average boulder-size decreases, those plants present tend to be more

Polystichum × illyricum. *West Sutherland, August*

out into the open. It is in these regions that there is usually a wide zone of overlap, between about 1,200–1,750 feet (365–530 m), where *P. aculeatum* and *P. lonchitis* may grow alongside one another. Above these elevations, there is usually a fairly rapid diminution in plants of *P. aculeatum* present, and a steady increase in those of *P. lonchitis*. Between these extremes, and usually in the middle reaches of screes containing both species, there occasionally occur specimens of the hybrid between the two, *Polystichum* × *illyricum*.

Young specimens of *Polystichum lonchitis* and *P. aculeatum* can at first look very alike, and it is only as they become steadily larger that the differences between these two species become more obvious. In general, all plants of *P. lonchitis* have a narrower and much more linear outline than have those of *P. aculeatum*, whilst the margins of *P. lonchitis* are always very much more setose, with long, colourless spines (hence the species name). The fronds of *P. lonchitis* are usually about 15–30 cm long, and may be fertile when quite small. Occasional plants occur in a few localities in Tayside, however, which every year bear large fronds in excess of half a metre.

Each year, the new frond growth of *Polystichum lonchitis* usually begins at an appropriately late date for the high altitudes at which it normally grows, not usually starting into expansion until about mid-May in most years. The new fronds thereafter grow only slowly, so that they do not usually become fully unfurled until late-June or early-July each year. The fronds, however, thereafter typically have a very long life and an unusually long spore-shedding season, with most being fertile and shedding their sooty-black spores from late-July or early-August, right through until at least April of the following year. The fronds themselves then persist in a green condition to the end of the second season and sometimes into a third.

Outside Britain and Ireland, both these species of *Polystichum* are fairly wide-ranging. What may be the same or a closely-allied species to *P. aculeatum* occurs also in a few localities in the far east of Asia, but it is mainly a European species with a more continuous range through central Europe to just south of the Caspian Sea. It is, however, scarce in much of the western part of this range, especially in Scandinavia, western France and the Iberian peninsula. It is absent from Iceland, and in the west thus seems widespread only in Britain and Ireland. *Polystichum lonchitis*, by contrast, has a range which spreads discontinuously right around the northern hemisphere, but is particularly widespread in a decidedly Arctic–Alpine pattern through the central European mountains (and especially in the Alps) and through western Scandinavia in northern Britain and western Ireland and in Iceland.

Fern Associates in Base-rich Scree Habitats

All these pteridophytes usually succeed best where angiosperm competition is not great, but species of flowering plants noted in association with such scree fern assemblages include typically a mixture of alpine calcicoles and relict woodland species, including especially Alpine Lady's Mantle (*Alchemilla alpina*), Alpine Meadow Rue (*Thalictrum alpinum*), Mountain Avens (*Dryas octopetala*), Northern Bedstraw (*Galium boreale*), Yellow Mountain Saxifrage (*Saxifraga aizoides*), Purple Saxifrage (*S. oppositifolia*), Starry Saxifrage (*S. stellaris*), Opposite-leaved Golden Saxifrage (*Chrysosplenium oppositifolium*), Alpine Scurvy-grass (*Cochlearia alpina*), Moschatel (*Adoxa moschatellina*), Mountain Sorrel (*Oxyria digyna*), Wood-sorrel (*Oxalis acetosella*), Wood anemone (*Anemone nemorosa*), Common Dog-violet (*Viola riviniana*), Herb Robert (*Geranium robertianum*), Wild Strawberry (*Fragaria vesca*), Purging Flax (*Linum catharticum*), Harebell (*Campanula rotundifolia*), and mosses such as *Ctenidium molluscum*, *Plagiothecium undulatum*, *Tortella tortuosa*, and *Rhytidiadelphus loreus*.

Base-rich, Upland Springs and Flushes

Where the many erosion surfaces of mountain slopes intersect subterranean water-bearing aquifers, water emerges at the surface of the ground in the form of fast-flowing springs or slower-flowing flushes. Spreading out across the surface of the mountain below their point of origin, the emerging water strongly influences the species component of the vegetation which it contacts. The upwelling water will have been little influenced by the process of surface humification and acidification which may characterise the upland soils around it, since it issues directly from the rock layers of the mountain. Instead, where the underlying rock is a mineral and lime-yielding one, the emerging water will be to a larger or smaller extent mineral and base-rich, resulting in a flushed slope at the soil surface which can be a calcareous one, even on mountain slopes which are otherwise acidic in character. Such sites are usually of considerable botanical interest, containing species of flowering plants, pteridophytes and bryophytes which are particularly characteristic.

Base-flushed vegetation can be conspicuous on mountainsides even from a distance, as it usually includes species (such as grasses, sedges, saxifrage clumps and especially bryophytes) which give the flushed areas an overall, verdant colour, which usually contrasts with the typically darker hues of other vegetation around them. They also include sites of a wide range of wetness, varying from relatively dry flushes, where only a little active seepage may be apparent at the soil surface, but which is nevertheless sufficient to influence the vegetation, to wetter ones where free surface water is more obviously flowing. In the extreme, they may emerge as locally gushing springs, with narrower or wider zones of vegetation which are influenced by them stretching down the hillsides.

In relatively dry flushes, the surface vegetation is usually sufficiently mature and stable to form a more or less complete vegetation cover, and in such sites, grasses usually predominate. The main pteridophytes of interest are usually the scattered occurrence of Moonwort (*Botrychium lunaria*), occasional shoots of Lesser Clubmoss (*Selaginella selaginoides*), and the presence of several horsetails. Amongst the latter, although Common Horsetail (*Equisetum arvense*) may be present in a diminutive form, most characteristic is the presence of Wood Horsetail (*E. sylvaticum*) and especially Shade Horsetail (*E. pratense*). In thick swards of grassy vegetation, shoots of these horsetails can be small, widely scattered and hence inconspicuous, and as a result are probably very much under-recorded. It is almost certainly the combination of high base status and simultaneous availability of silica, that enables these horsetails to gain such a successful and tenacious hold on such sites, even in the face of severe angiosperm competition. The horsetails usually extend even into adjacent sites which are quite rocky, and it is in such habitats in Perthshire (Tayside), that the hybrid between them, Milde's Horsetail (*E.* × *mildeanum*), occasionally also occurs.

In rather wetter, and hence more characteristic, base-rich mountain flushes, the numerical abundance of pteridophytes, as well as bryophytes, usually increases. This is largely through the increased openness of the habitat, with a resulting competition from flowering plants. This is because the surface of such flushes is one where there is a constant movement of shallow, well-aerated water moving downslope and there is consequently a high rate of shallow surface erosion, surface movement of sand and silt particles, and constant redeposition. The resulting instability of the wet surface seems to make it a less accessible surface for angiosperms to successfully colonise, although several pteridophytes are able to maintain a better hold and hence to thrive in the relative absence of flowering plant competition. The pteridophytes present are thus those that are able, through vegetative growth, to constantly repioneer the fairly mobile surfaces, and are thus those which also succeed well in sandy and gravelly fans beside mountain streams—especially Lesser Clubmoss (*Selaginella selaginoides*) and several horsetails, including Marsh Horsetail (*Equisetum palustre*) and Common Horsetail (*E. arvense*) but notably Variegated Horsetail (*Equisetum variegatum*).

Selaginella selaginoides occurs very widely in sites in all the main mountain regions of Britain and Ireland, but is especially widespread in these habitats throughout the mountains of Highland Scotland. It seems indicative of highly calcareous sites, and to be able to grow in surprisingly wet habitats when the water surrounding it is also moving and well aerated. Within such flushes it particularly occurs on small, stony, micro-hillocks, which raise it subtly higher above the most mobile bottoms of the flush, and on small islands of thin, low-growing vegetation within such flushes and around their periphery—usually just above the normal waterline, where these sites provide it with moderately more stable and less regularly inundated substrates. Here it grows with its very moss-like, foliar shoots spreading gradually amongst the low terrestrial herbage. It probably also reproduces abundantly via spores, and usually many separate plants of this clubmoss follow the course of very similar habitats away from the primary sources of such springs and flushes, along the moist, seeping banks of the streamlets and rills leading from them, its shoots generally appearing between luxuriant cushions of Yellow Mountain Saxifrage (*Saxifraga aizoides*) and frequently in the neighbourhood of plants of Butterwort (*Pinguicula vulgaris*).

Equisetum arvense and *E. palustre* occur usually as scattered shoots, the former mainly around the edges of the flushes. Even here, however, such conditions often seem surprisingly wet for *E. arvense*, although it is probably aided by the naturally high degree of aeration of the constantly passing water. Even so, the diminutive size usually achieved by the shoots of *E. arvense* in these conditions means that it is easily overlooked and eminently confusable with *E. palustre*, which is usually growing closely alongside it.

Equisetum variegatum usually occurs within the same soft, wet silty places within the flush itself, though its slender, unbranched, dark bluish-green shoots are usually not so easy to spot as are those of the other horsetails, and can also prove difficult to separate from unbranched shoots of *E. palustre* (those of *E. variegatum*, besides being evergreen, have bi-angulate, main stem ridges). Once present in flushes, spread of this and the other species of horsetail probably mainly takes place, unlike that of *Selaginella*, by vegetative growth. Its shallowly-creeping slender rhizomes extend extensively through any sand and gravelly layers beneath the immediate surface silt, and often spread successfully beneath any larger stones that may be present in the flushes, doubtless helping give colonies a greater tenacity of occupation of the site against the physical forces of steady sand and water downslope-scouring.

Other plant species usually present in such flushes usually include a number of reed-like flowering plants within the water itself and several insectivorous ones generally on the higher islands of vegetation, as well as a fairly large bryophyte component throughout. These include Few-flowered Spike-rush (*Eleocharis quinqueflora*), several carices (including *Carex demissa, C. dioica, C. panicea, C. flacca, C. nigra, C. lepidocarpa* and *C. capillaris*), Common and Pale Butterwort (*Pinguicula vulgaris* and *P. lusitanica*), Common Sundew (*Drosera rotundifolia*), Yellow Mountain-Saxifrage (*Saxifraga aizoides*), Purple Saxifrage (*S. oppositifolia*), Starry Saxifrage (*S. stellaris*), Grass of Parnassus (*Parnassia palustris*), and the mosses *Tortella tortuosa, Cratoneuron commutatum, Ctenidium molluscum, Philonotis fontana, P. calcarea, Scorpidium scorpioides, Drepanocladus revolvens* and *Pohlia gracilis*. More locally, in Teesdale, Alpine Bartsia (*Bartsia alpina*), Bird's-eye Primrose (*Primula farinosa*) and Spring Gentian (*Gentiana verna*) grow in nearby, better-drained habitats.

Seasonal Aspects of Mountain Flush Pteridophytes

A notable aspect of such upland flushes, which may be significant in relation to the success of evergreen pteridophytes such as *Equisetum variegatum* and *Selaginella selaginoides* within them, is the early start to the growing season which such species are able to make, despite the altitude of the sites. Exploration of such mountain-sides in about early April can readily show that it is nearly always from such flush areas of the hillsides that winter snow first disappears. Even before the snow begins to disappear, the springs themselves and the flush areas and rivulets trickling from them, hollow out snow-caves beneath the winter blanket. As the cave roofs get progressively thinner, so the dark silty muds accumulated during winter become exposed to the early spring sunshine. At such times of year, it is not uncommon, for example, to find a great activity of mating frogs and resulting frogspawn in the outflow rills of such mountain springs, whilst crisp and compacted layers of snow still lie deeply on the adjacent land about them. Within such flushes there is thus opportunity for an early onset of a daytime temperature rise, perhaps sufficient to activate plant growth, and possibly especially benefiting the evergreen species. From this point of view, the pteridophytes of such flushes are rather the opposite of the late-starting species of mountain snow-patch vegetation, a feature which is doubtless of significance in allowing these essentially montane species to descend to low altitude in certain places.

Base-rich, Upland, Streamside Sands and Gravels

Above the upper limits of tree growth and below the higher flanks of the mountains, a myriad of fast-running rills, cascades and small streams of fast-flowing water tumble and funnel into progressively larger streams and wider upland river-courses. The watercourses characteristically cut down along their lengths to firmer bedrock surfaces, sometimes deeply through the softer, overlying sediments and peats surrounding them, whilst along the immediate flanks of the watercourses are exposed smaller lines of seepage, run-off and damp slopes of local surface erosion.

The tumbling water also has considerable erosive properties, steadily loosening, fragmenting and pounding the rock over which it travels into fragments, the smaller of which, from pebbles down to sand grains, are continually transported away by the fast-flowing waters to new sites further downstream.

As the dendritic drainage patterns of the mountain streams funnel progressively together to form more major streams, so some shallowing of the initial steepest slopes of the valley sides allows more meandering watercourses to form across upland valley bottoms. Silts, sands, gravels and pebbles continue to be carried by such streams, and, as current speeds change, their suspended matter is variously deposited along the stream lengths. Larger and heavier items are released from suspension first, and patches of water-worn gravels and sands of well-sorted particle sizes consequently accumulate along the stream-courses, especially in the slacker waters around the inner angles of meander bends and in numerous backwater eddies.

Valleyside Rills

On the valley sides, the eroding surfaces of the edges of the rills and mountain burns form wet, mobile and insubstantial substrates which are typically somewhat devoid of plant competition. Pteridophytes appear to benefit from this situation and usually invade and pioneer such sites. Waterside ferns thus form an important component of the vegetation of most of the edges of the valleyside rills and burns.

In such sites, especially frequent as water-margin ferns are Hard Fern (*Blechnum spicant*), Lady-fern (*Athyrium filix-femina*) and Sweet Mountain Fern (*Oreopteris limbosperma*), but a little back from the wettest edges there may also be Oak Fern (*Gymnocarpium dryopteris*) and Beech Fern (*Phegopteris connectilis*). The first three are especially characteristic of the more acidic areas. But as the clear and cool flowing waters originate both from immediate surface drainage, and from springwater which has passed through mountain rock and dissolved at least some of its minerals, over appropriate rock substrates many of the areas of moisture seepage can be base-rich ones.

Relatively base and mineral-rich sites are usually marked by the presence of several horsetails, often in diminutive form, including Marsh Horsetail (*Equisetum palustre*), Common Horsetail (*E. arvense*), Wood Horsetail (*E. sylvaticum*) and Shade Horsetail (*E. pratense*), with the moister margins of such rills often marked by clumps of Yellow Mountain Saxifrage (*Saxifraga aizoides*), and scattered plants of Lesser Clubmoss (*Selaginella selaginoides*). Oddly, the better-drained knolls in the immediate vicinity of watercourses, even in otherwise quite base-rich sites, sometimes make habitats for tussocks of the normally more acid-loving Fir Clubmoss (*Huperzia selago*).

Valley Bottom Streams

The water levels of the valley bottom streams, with their small catchment areas, can rise and fall rapidly with changes in levels of recent precipitation: the water-scoured fringing streamside sites are, at times, submerged, and at others, dry. Once deposited, the various sand and gravel beds thus remain continually scoured by the shifting currents and changing water levels, especially in winter and spring, and hence their location and contents are re-sorted and redistributed from season to season and from year to year.

As with the valleyside rills, and perhaps even more so, these streamside sand and gravel fans are consequently usually fairly free of plant competition, and although several of the valleyside species continue to occur (especially in habitats where shelter is high and grazing pressure is low), the gravel fans are sites which, in regions of base-rich rock, are colonised by Variegated Horsetail (*Equisetum variegatum*) and Lesser Clubmoss (*Selaginella selaginoides*). The horsetail is especially characteristic of the most water-scoured fans of semi-mobile sands and gravels themselves, whilst the clubmoss is mainly a species of the gravel fans' more stable landward margins.

Equisetum variegatum, which is mainly a species of these

sites, is worthy of further discussion here. Its presence is, however, easily overlooked in these sites for its shoots are very thin and widely scattered, and even in localities in which it has been seen in a previous year, it can take a certain diligence to find it again in a subsequent year (by which time it or its gravel fans have often moved anyway).

Equisetum variegatum is, as a sporophyte, a potentially very long-lived perennial, and so long as the habitat persists, it would seem likely that established colonies would be able to persist and spread by gradual rhizome extension more or less indefinitely. Its winding, wiry, black, subterranean rhizomes,

Equisetum variegatum *var.* majus *in streamside gravel. Northumberland, June*

scarcely thicker than the 1–2 mm diameter shoots, spread widely through the gravelly or sandy substrates beside the streamwater, occasionally branching and very frequently passing beneath larger boulders, enabling this horsetail to gain considerable stability against erosion and hence permanency of occupation of sites in which it succeeds in once establishing.

However, streamside erosion of existing colonies usually sooner or later exposes portions of rhizomes, and these, or even stems, can become detached and rapidly transported by fast-moving currents. Experimentation with such isolated fragments shows that so long as they are in water which is moving and well-aerated, they retain a high longevity and a ready ability to take root if they are deposited on new beds of sand or gravel. By such means colonies very probably spread along the lengths of flowing streams.

Once colonies of *Equisetum variegatum* are well-established, however, they may succeed in entering adjacent denser riverside vegetation swards by rhizome growth, and in these sites too, occasional plants of *Selaginella selaginoides* also usually occur. Here, a turfy denser, and floristically richer community may include many base-loving species. Some are similar to the associates of *Equisetum variegatum* in sand-dune slacks, including Thrift (*Armeria maritima*), Sea Plantain (*Plantago maritima*), Ribwort Plantain (*Plantago lanceolata*), Daisy (*Bellis perennis*), Hairy Hawkbit (*Leontodon taraxacoides*), Common Violet (*Viola riviniana*), Self-heal (*Prunella vulgaris*), Mouse-ear Chickweed (*Cerastium holosteoides*), Eyebrights (*Euphrasia* spp.), Thyme-leaved Speedwell (*Veronica serpyllifolia*), Bird's-foot Trefoil (*Lotus corniculatus*), Clovers (*Trifolium* spp.), Red Fescue (*Festuca rubra*), Sharp-flowered Rush (*Juncus acutiflorus*) and various sedges (including *Carex flacca, C. capillaris, C. demissa* and *C. lepidocarpa*), sometimes diminutive shoots of Marsh Horsetail (*Equisetum palustre*), and the mosses *Dicranum scoparium, Ctenidium molluscum, Tortella tortuosa* and *Cratoneurum commutatum*.

Several more characteristically mountain species may also occur in these habitats. In northern England, in sites in Teesdale, these can include Northern Bedstraw (*Galium boreale*), Salad Burnet (*Poterium sanguisorba*), Bird's-eye Primrose (*Primula farinosa*), Blue Sesleria (*Sesleria albicans*), Alpine Bartsia (*Bartsia alpina*), Kobresia (*Kobresia simpliciuscula*) and nearby Alpine Penny-cress (*Thlaspi alpestre*), Alpine Cinquefoil (*Potentilla crantzii*), and Shrubby Cinquefoil (*P. fruticosa*), whilst in the Scottish Highland Mountains these most frequently include Yellow Mountain-Saxifrage (*Saxifraga aizoides*), Alpine Lady's-mantle (*Alchemilla alpina*), Alpine Meadow Rue (*Thalictrum alpinum*), Mountain Avens (*Dryas octopetala*), Mountain Sorrel (*Oxyria digyna*), Mountain Bistort (*Polygonum viviparum*), Thyme (*Thymus praecox*).

In Britain and Ireland as a whole, *Equisetum variegatum* is a variable species on a genetic and ecological basis, and this contrasts with the variation seen in most other horsetails, which experimental evidence shows to be mostly environmentally induced (Page, 1982). In most of our mountain areas in which *Equisetum variegatum* and *Selaginella selaginoides* occur in upland river-side sands and gravels, substantial lengths of their streams are, and have perhaps always been, above the altitudes of dense native forest vegetation. Both species were probably widespread and characteristic species of the exposed and open gravelly outwash habitats at all altitudes through Britain and Ireland in the early post-glacial (see chapter 4). The ability of Variegated Horsetail to clonally maintain itself through dispersed fragment establishment may well have been significant in early post-glacial spread along steadily flowing, shallow watercourses, in which base-rich shingle banks probably frequently abounded. It is also possible that today's bare mountain streamside sand and gravel sites are ones which have probably enjoyed a general continuum of habitat persistence and site occupation by such species since that time.

Juniper Shrub Woodland

The genus *Juniperus*, the junipers, is widely spread through mostly temperate latitudes of both Old and New Worlds, where its many different species form everything from low, shrub communities to ones of tall forest trees. In Britain and Ireland, our single native Common Juniper (*Juniperus communis*) is itself of extremely variable form. Its plants can, to a fair extent, mimic the range of form of the genus, with different individuals, even within single populations, varying from bushes to plants of much taller, more columnar habit. Such taller trees are typical of rather rare sites where the canopy is neither excessively wind-pruned, nor artificially grazed. Although all such native juniper vegetation is often referred to as 'scrub', this term does little justice to these sometimes large, venerable and often ancient conifer communities which are somewhat akin to a dwarf woodland, and whose understorey species may include several pteridophytes. The alternative term 'shrub woodland' might therefore be a more appropriate term for such juniper vegetation as a whole.

Such juniper communities are widely spread, if usually localised, throughout Britain and Ireland, where they occur from coastal cliff-top valley sites nearly at sea level, to habitats

at considerable altitude on some of our mountains. Indeed,
they are perhaps most common at these two extremes of their
altitudinal range, and hence of somewhat bi-modal distribution. They occur mostly in rather open sites, where other
overtopping vegetation is not dense or has been always largely
excluded by some other factor. Some of their communities are
consequently on unusual soils such as on limestone or ultrabasic ones, whilst junipers also often form an important
component of glade vegetation or of open understorey in
natural pine forest. Juniper communities are perhaps most
characteristic, however, of sites which are at, or just below, the
natural tree line, and it is in such areas that they are sometimes
extensive.

Juniper Pteridophyte Communities

In their study of the vegetation of the Scottish Highlands,
McVean & Ratcliffe (1900) indicate three ferns especially
associated with the mainly higher-altitude communities in the
Scottish Highlands, namely Common Male-fern (*Dryopteris
filix-mas*), Golden-scaled Male-fern (*Dryopteris affinis*) and
Sweet Mountain Fern (*Oreopteris limbosperma*). Casting the net
geographically and ecologically wider, however, it is certainly
possible to add several more pteridophytes to this list. Several
other woodland species may be locally common amongst juniper patches, especially in northern England and in Highland
Scotland, including Woodland Lady-fern (*Athyrium filix-
femina*), Broad Buckler-fern (*Dryopteris dilatata*), Hard Fern
(*Blechnum spicant*), Beech Fern (*Phegopteris connectilis*),
Woodland Oak-fern (*Gymnocarpium dryopteris*) and Wood
Horsetail (*Equisetum sylvaticum*). Where junipers occur over
rocky communities, Black Spleenwort (*Asplenium adiantum-
nigrum*) may grow in the rocky fissures, and in some of the
ultrabasic juniper sites, such as on the Lizard Peninsula of
Cornwall and in Aberdeenshire, these include the morphologically curious 'serpentine-form' of this species. In other rocky
areas, where clearly some basic strata are present, other small
spleenworts, including Maidenhair Spleenwort (*Asplenium
trichomanes* subsp. *quadrivalens*) and Green Spleenwort (*A.
viride*) may be present on rocky outcrops shaded and protected
from grazing by the junipers, as well as clumps of Brittle
Bladder-fern (*Cystopteris fragilis*) in sheltered rocky niches.

Where areas of wetter seepage occur amongst the junipers,
Lesser Clubmoss (*Selaginella selaginoides*) and Marsh Horsetail
(*E. palustre*) may be frequent, while even Dutch Rush (*E. hye-
male*) may also be a rare member, such as in the upper Deeside

juniper communities of Morrone in the Upper Deeside area of Aberdeenshire. By contrast, in Cumbria, much-grazed juniper patches in limestone pavement sometimes give shelter to plants of Hard Shield-fern (*Polystichum setiferum*) and to the always local Limestone Buckler-fern (*Dryopteris submontana*).

A very wide range of small herbs may be associated with such fern–juniper communities, and are frequently reminiscent of those of woodland, even in higher altitude sites. Flushed areas within the mosaic of juniper which are rich in *Equisetum palustre* and may have additional *E. hyemale* or *E. variegatum*, are usually locally rich in various sedges, including *Carex echinata, C. nigra, C. lepidocarpa* and *C. pulicaris*, as well as Cross-leaved Heath (*Erica tetralix*), with Yellow Mountain-Saxifrage (*Saxifraga aizoides*) near springheads.

The richness of the juniper communities both in ferns and other woodland plants results in part from the shelter of the micro-topography created by the juniper bushes, but very largely too from the protection from constant grazing that the bushes create (although the bushes themselves are to a large extent grazed by deer).

CHAPTER 12

Pteridophytes of Upper
Mountain Habitats

There is a continuous gradation between the habitats of our
lower and higher mountain habitats. I have grouped into this
chapter those pteridophyte habitats which are more characteristic of our higher mountain elevations: high mountain basic
cliffs and ledges; high cliff-gullies; high mountain corries,
snow patches and fern beds; and the habitats of ridges, plateaux and high summit peaks.

High Mountain, Basic Cliffs and Ledges

Almost any ascent of our higher mountain ranges is likely to
bring the scrambling botanist sooner or later to the feet of any
of the very numerous rock face outcrops which rise abruptly as
steep mountain cliffs. In North Wales or in Scotland especially,
abrupt broken lines of such cliffs often mark the steepest parts
of the profiles of the sides of U-shaped, glaciated valleys. They
frequently rise directly above screes or above the tops of the
steep, rock-strewn, boulder slopes which may form much of
the lower valley sides, whilst other cliffs may occur at much
higher elevation, as parts of the walls of hanging valleys or of
corries.

The rugged and often inaccessible profiles of such cliffs
typically contain numerous small fissures and ledges, as well as
small gullies, down which cool mountain water continually
seeps. Although the often slippery and wet rocky surfaces are
usually particularly unsuitable for climbing, partly through
their often rotten structure, and partly through the floristic
damage that can be caused to the precarious footholds which
their plant life obtains, some examination of their flora is
usually possible. Access to their upper levels is usually best
restricted to binoculars, whilst with appropriate care and
caution, portions of their feet can usually be explored a little
more closely.

The unusual degree of success of ferns and some fern allies
in these sites seems largely due to the constant involvement of

several inter-related factors. Very important factors are probably the steepness of such sites, their constant erosion, and the generally small size of the ecological niches concerned. The steep rock faces themselves are normally in a constantly dynamic state of backcutting through steady surface erosion, whilst the shallow ledges and tight fissures seldom allow large quantities of humus to build up, and hence are usually too fragile and insubstantial to allow the successful anchorage of too many large and rank competing plants. Another factor is the generally cool, subalpine situation, which also tends to limit the size of the competition. The exposure of the sites, especially to passing cloud, and the shade of those on north-facing aspects, which are always the most fern-rich, is a further factor. These features help ensure the constancy of the air humidity, and such shaded but airy conditions suit pteridophyte growth particularly well. Another factor is the free-draining abilities of the habitats, where run-off from rock surfaces above never accumulates, but nevertheless provides an almost constant source of seeping moisture, which may be rich in minerals. Such sites are particularly easily reached by the minute, wind-blown, spores of pteridophytes, and newly exposed, damp rock surfaces are thus prime sites for rapid pioneering by invading pteridophyte prothalli. Once sporophyte plants have gained a

Fern-rich, high, mountain cliff ledges and gullies, where larger grazing animals cannot climb. Trotternish, Isle of Skye, July

foothold, the fine, fibrous roots of most species, without secondary lateral expansion in thickness, are then able to penetrate deeply through any tiny cracks and fissures, gaining a relatively tenacious hold, sometimes in the very steepest of locations. Lastly, the relative inaccessibility of these habitats from grazing by mammals of virtually any size is often a vital factor in permitting such exposed ferns, once established, to persist indefinitely and reproduce.

As a result of the interplay of almost all of these factors at many sites, pteridophytes often contribute in very large proportion to the high montane or 'alpine' plant communities of such damp rock faces and ledges. In doing so, the intimacy of contact between fern and rock is always an especially close one. Under the wet, and often cool and shady conditions of these montane sites, there is normally a rapid leaching away by surface run-off of any basic minerals in solution as these are released from the eroding rock surfaces. As a result, there is always a strong tendency towards constant habitat acidification, except where sites are steadily and constantly neutralised by an ensured supply of freshly-yielded basic rock minerals. Thus where only acidic rocks occur, the habitats are always acidic ones, and the flora is limited to those species able to tolerate such conditions. Where more basic rocks such as mica schists outcrop, which have lime-yielding veins mixed amongst other, more siliceous ones, an intimate mosaic of widely differing conditions of surface acidity and base-availability can be present on a very local scale, reflected in a rich and sometimes bewildering mix of acid-loving and base-loving species growing in particularly close proximity.

Mountain Cliff and Ledge Pteridophyte Diversity

The pteridophytes present on such montane cliffs usually involve an intimate mixture of species of two general habitat types.

Firstly, there are the true alpines themselves, more or less restricted to these habitats, and these are often the species which outside Britain and Ireland share similar, largely Arctic–Alpine geographic ranges elsewhere, especially in Europe. In Britain and Ireland, some of these are exclusively montane in occurrence. Others, however, although predominantly montane, include several which have an essentially bi-modal habitat distribution, involving not only habitats of high montane sites but also ones at low elevations, near to the coast.

Secondly, there are species in these high montane habitats which are woodland relicts. These are species usually more

Polystichum lonchitis *on a nearly-inaccessible high cliff-ledge. Mid-Perthshire, July*

typical of upland, woodland ravine vegetation, which have geographic distributions which are generally northerly ones, but which are usually not strictly of Arctic–Alpine range. They have outlying cliff-ledge montane stations largely because such factors as the shade, moisture and humidity of these sites much resemble the woodland ravine ones, and partly because of the general lack of other extensive vascular plant competition for these habitats. They are thus able to associate quite often with alpines, especially on larger ledges in the more sheltered and shaded montane spots. Their occurrence in montane sites is often associated with flowering plants of similar woodland affinities, and in many cases, their presence may mark patches, long isolated by grazing, of what well may be whole relict associations of former woodland communities.

The most truly alpine pteridophytes likely to be encountered in such sites (although many also occur in other rocky sites at other altitudes), are typically *Botrychium lunaria, Asplenium ruta-muraria, A. septentrionale, A. trichomanes, A. viride, Athyrium distentifolium, Cystopteris fragilis, C. montana, Dryopteris expansa, D. oreades, Polystichum lonchitis, Woodsia alpina, W. ilvensis, Diphasiastrum alpinum, Huperzia selago, Lycopodium clavatum, Selaginella selaginoides, Equisetum pratense* and *E. variegatum.* Amongst the additional pteridophytes which may occur in and around such cliffs, but which are better classed as woodland relics, can be added *Athyrium filix-femina, Blechnum spicant, Dryopteris affinis, D. dilatata, D. filix-mas, Gymnocarpium dryopteris, Phegopteris connectilis, Polypodium interjectum, P. vulgare, Polystichum aculeatum, Equisetum arvense, E. palustre* and *E. sylvaticum.*

Of the more truly alpine species, those with a generally bimodal distribution (though it may differ, in degree and exact alternative habitat occupied elsewhere, from species to species) include *Botrychium lunaria, Asplenium ruta-muraria, Cystopteris fragilis, Dryopteris expansa, Selaginella selaginoides* and *Equisetum variegatum.* In some Perthshire (Tayside) habitats last century, and in at least one current alpine site on Skye, plants which may be the otherwise coastal *Cystopteris dickieana* also occur, whilst on a few inland cliffs as far inland as central Perthshire, *Hymenophyllum wilsonii* is also known.

Cliff-ledge Woodsia Communities

An interesting pair of ferns are the species of Woodsia, Alpine Woodsia (*Woodsia alpina*) and Oblong Woodsia (*W. ilvensis*). The former especially seems to be a truely alpine species. The latter is alpine too, but allies this distribution with its occurrence in rocky habitats within and around pine forests, and I have a suspicion that this may well have once formerly been its most characteristic location in upland northern Britain.

Woodsia alpina is a small or very small fern (with fronds generally about 3–8 cm in length, or occasionally larger), looking like a diminutive form of Brittle Bladder-fern (*Cystopteris fragilis*), but of generally more compact, rosetted habit, with more robust stipes and a frond which is clothed on its underside with rather sparse, long zig-zag hairs and a few short scales on the rachis. The sori have a cup-shaped indusium, with the upturning edges divided into numerous, long, filiform projections, which incurve over the sorus when young.

Woodsia ilvensis plants are usually of similar size or slightly larger than *W. alpina*, and have similar sori, but the fronds are generally of slightly more robust appearance, with more oblong pinnae which are more oppositely set and have scales along their midribs.

Both are rare Arctic–Alpine species, with *W. alpina* confined to alpine habitats between 1,900 ft (ca. 580 m) and about 3,000 ft (ca. 915 m) or possibly higher, whilst in alpine habitats, *W. ilvensis* occurs from about 1,200 ft (ca. 365 m) to about 2,300 ft (ca. 716 m). There is thus clearly a wide range of altitudinal overlap between the two species, especially above about 1,900 ft (ca. 580 m), and the two species sometimes occur side

Woodsia alpina in a nearly-inaccessible cliff-ledge crevice. Angus, August

by side. The habitats of both typically include small fissures on mountain cliff ledges, especially on sheer, precipitous rocky faces, where there are 'rotten' rocks on steep, craggy mountains. In such sites, both species usually occur in exposed places, with a range of aspects, including south-facing ones.

Both species of *Woodsia* occur most often as gregarious, small colonies. Both species are restricted to habitats where there are relatively low maximum summer temperatures, and both seem to thrive most in sites of moderately high rainfall. Although in both species, the fronds are able to cleanly absciss from the rhizomes along regular, predetermined abscission-zones (a feature unusual in ferns), they appear nevertheless to be severely limited in their occurrence by severe drought spells, from which surviving plants may take many years to fully recover. The rocky niches of both, however, are ones where the local rock-face relief probably provides at least some degree of shelter from the most severe winds and driving rain, although it is probable that both species also require a fair degree of free air-movement around their rather woolly-surfaced fronds, which, in winter, may become encrusted in ice.

In their rocky habitats, plants of both species occur on a range of mostly volcanic and hard, sedimentary rock types, which, for at least *W. ilvensis*, include basalts, pumice tuffs, Silurian grits and slaty shales. In these sites, competing species are normally few.

Plants of Alpine and Oblong Woodsia seem potentially long-lived, but are very slow-growing. In Britain, they are clearly on the oceanic edge of their natural ranges, for both species are of high, northern, circum-boreal range with, in Europe, their chief headquarters in Iceland, Scandinavia and the Alps. In their very few, geographically outlying stations in northern Britain, they are each in probably a particularly delicate balance with their environment, and this is a balance which small changes in circumstance could clearly easily upset. Undisturbed in the past, both species have sometimes formed colonies of numerous clumps over nearby cliff faces, and in the case of *W. ilvensis*, they formerly occurred in places such as Teesdale and in the Moffat Hills of southern Scotland, where they survived up to the period of the coming of the railways in the mid-19th century. Their subsequent history of extermination by botanical collection in such areas has been documented by Rickard (1972) and Mitchell (1980).

Although it has been traditional to rightly blame Victorian botanical collectors for the sudden demise of the Woodsias in historic time, biologically such collection has probably been a final blow to a long period of natural decline, each species being relict in the British flora from once far more numerous and widely ranging populations in post-glacial time. Their remaining sites have probably become progressively smaller and more isolated from each other over very many centuries. Even before botanical collection, in their increasingly local patches, numbers of individuals must have already fallen close to a size where they were genetically considerably impoverished as well as substantially inbred, probably contributing significantly to their lack of vigour. Although both species, today, are specifically protected from collection by law, doubt must nevertheless surround their ability at some sites to be able to again form viable breeding populations, and more positive conservation measures may eventually be needed.

Other Cliff-ledge Pteridophytes

On more base-rich cliffs and ledges, rare ferns such as both species of Woodsia may persist, and are often joined by a number of much more base-demanding ones, including Brittle Bladder-fern (*Cystopteris fragilis*), Maidenhair Spleenwort (*Asplenium trichomanes* subsp. *quadrivalens*), Green Spleenwort (*A. viride*), and Holly Fern (*Polystichum lonchitis*). These species are, however, especially characteristic of adjacent base-rich mountain scree sites, and are discussed more fully under that habitat. Two additional pteridophytes of interest in these sites, however, which are usually at their best high-montane development on moist, base-rich cliff ledges are the occurrence of Lesser Clubmoss (*Selaginella selaginoides*) and Moonwort (*Botrychium lunaria*).

Lesser Clubmoss seems to thrive most on base-rich cliffs where the height of surrounding vegetation is low, so that the plant itself is not densely shaded by tall, competing, herbage. It occurs on cliff ledges mostly where the soil is shallow and where the surface is moist from seeping moving water. This small plant, with its thin, weak and often rather straggling-looking vegetative growth of seldom more than a few centimetres in length, twisting irregularly amongst the bases of other plants, looks very moss-like, and, indeed, is seldom noticed at all until it cones. It is possible that it may grow for years in such

Selaginella
selaginoides *on a
mountain cliff ledge.
Mid-Perthshire, July*

a state, and, although it is widespread and perhaps much more common in such habitats than generally appreciated, very little is known about its natural history. Once it cones however, the plant becomes rather more conspicuous and readily identifiable. The tall, erect, foxtail-like cone shoot, although often only 4–6 mm broad and usually only 3–6 cm high on most plants, can occasionally reach up to 10 cm. Modest as such a height may sound, it is, in practise, a relatively enormous cone shoot for the flimsy vegetative body of the plant, and it is possible that each cone might well represent the culmination of many years of steady vegetative growth.

Plants also appear to need to make an early start in the growth of the large cone shoot. In its alpine habitats, *Selaginella* seems to achieve this by making considerable cone growth headway beneath regular coverings of winter snow. Although light must be weak under such conditions, temperatures are probably not too severe, and it may well be that the mycorrhizal association which has been demonstrated to occur with this species may be of particular importance under such conditions.

Moonwort (*Botrychium lunaria*) occurs mostly in pockets of short, alpine grass turf, but, in contrast to *Selaginella*, the niches occupied by *Botrychium* are often in cliff-ledge pockets where deeper soils accumulate, and where other vegetation is more dense. Such Moonwort habitats are similar to its low altitude ones, because they provide close-knit, turfy communities in which the plant does not become too heavily overtopped by tall, surrounding vegetation. Indeed, the presence of a grassy sward is almost certainly important for the success of this plant's subterranean mycorrhizal association, with which its fleshy, spreading, white roots are intimately associated. Even in the alpine zone, it is not strictly confined to cliff habitats, for it is likely to occur at such altitudes (especially from about 2,200 to about 3,000 ft, 670–915 m), wherever appropriate grassy swards are present. Experience suggests, however, that except for in montane areas where grazing pressure is unusually low, the largest and most spectacular specimens of this fern usually group themselves in pockets of turfy vegetation on steep rock ledges. One reason for this is possibly a requirement for well-aerated soil structure and the good drainage that cliff ledge habitats necessarily provide. However, it is also in these inaccessible habitats that, each season that they appear, the aerial parts of the plants seem to last the longest—sometimes long after most of their spores have been shed, in late August or early September, especially in cool summers. A second reason for their success in these sites is therefore, almost certainly, the substantial freedom from grazing which such inaccessible rock ledges provide.

High, Cliff Gullies

Botrychium lunaria
in mountain cliff-ledge
vegetation, where it is
inaccessible to grazing.
Isle of Skye, July

High on mountain cliffs, scattered local gullies may occur, where steadily seeping water crosses steeply sloping cliffs and ledges. Here, such water may trickle and drip down cool, narrow, shaded, loose-rock clefts. Often in remote and nearly inaccessible high cliff reaches, the fragmented rock surfaces of such damp gullies are usually loose, soft and slippery and, presenting little secure foothold, consequently remain fairly undisturbed by man or by any grazing animals. Their somewhat recessed sites are also ones which can be unusually sheltered for their altitude, and in their shade and shelter, especially when on northerly-facing aspects, a habitat of seeping groundwater through steep and scarcely balanced rocks and insubstantial sodden moss cushions may locally survive beneath a pervading atmosphere of cool, moist humidity.

Under such ideal habitat conditions, as well as under their usually complete freedom from grazing, pteridophytes in such sites may be particularly prolific. The precariousness of their physical setting, as well as the fragility of the terrain itself, dictates that these are not suitable sites for direct exploration.

Acidic Rock Gullies

Where the rock type is a poorly-base yielding one, the pteridophyte component is usually limited to the sometimes abundant occurrence of a relatively small number of typically acid-
loving ferns and occasional clubmosses. In appropriate
districts, and especially in the mountains of North Wales, those
of the English Lake District and the Scottish Southern
Uplands, these may include luxuriant growths of Parsley Fern
(*Cryptogramma crispa*) and Lady-fern (*Athyrium*), with more
scattered Hard Fern (*Blechnum spicant*), Mountain Male-fern
(*Dryopteris oreades*), small specimens of Broad Buckler-fern
(*D. dilatata*) and occasional Fir Clubmoss (*Huperzia selago*).
Other clubmosses sometimes also stray into these habitats
from adjacent upland and moorlands, including Alpine
Clubmoss (*Diphasiastrum alpinum*) in all our mountains, and
interrupted Clubmoss (*Lycopodium annotinum*) in those of
central and northern Scotland. In the latter region too, the
species of *Athyrium* present may include both the Woodland
Lady-fern (*Athyrium filix-femina*) and the Alpine Lady-fern
(*Athyrium distentifolium*), as well as occasional hybrids between
them. The occurrence of *A. distentifolium* is of special interest,
but as it is much more typical of the habitats of the high mountain corries, it is discussed more extensively under that habitat,
below.

Basic Rock Gullies

Where more richly base-yielding rock is present, such as on the
mica-schists of the central Scottish Highlands, the species of
ferns and fern-allies of these sites become even more varied
and the whole community a rich and usually luxuriant one.
Here, smaller numbers of many of the species of more acidic
habitats may still grow, although *Cryptogramma crispa* is usually
absent and *Blechnum spicant* infrequent. But in their place,
many smaller, base-demanding pteridophytes usually succeed
in large numbers. Some of these, at least, are more typically
plants of woodland and upland streamside habitats which have
outlying stations in these rocky recesses, whilst others are true
alpines. Merging into these sites from surrounding rocky
fissures and adjacent cliff-ledge communities are often particularly luxuriant growths of such ferns as Green Spleenwort
(*Asplenium viride*), Holly Fern (*Polystichum lonchitis*) and Brittle
Bladder-fern (*Cystopteris fragilis*), often with more scattered
Northern Buckler-fern (*Dryopteris expansa*), Moonwort (*Botrychium lunaria*) and Lesser Clubmoss (*Selaginella selaginoides*).

A magnificent old clump of Asplenium viride *in a basic, high-cliff gulley, where grazing animals cannot go. Mid-Perthshire, September*

The variation in the frond form of populations of *Cystopteris fragilis* in these sites is sometimes especially noteworthy, for in some areas of Scotland, and perhaps elsewhere, plants can occur with a frond form approaching that of Dickie's Fern's *Cystopteris dickieana* broader, more crowded pinnae, seen only in its restricted habitat south of Aberdeen.

With many of these ferns, a number of scattered flowering plants and bryophytes usually also grow, which include woodland species along with ones of more strictly alpine affinity. For here, with the ferns, grow plants such as Wood Anenome (*Anenome nemorosa*), Common Dog-violet (*Viola riviniana*), Globe-Flower (*Trollius europaeus*), Wood-sorrel (*Oxalis acetosella*), Meadowsweet (*Filipendula ulmaria*) and Water Avens (*Geum rivale*), alongside alpines such as Mountain Avens (*Dryas octopetala*), Alpine Lady's Mantle (*Alchemilla alpina*), Moss Campion (*Silene acaulis*), Mountain Sorrel (*Oxyria digyna*), Alpine Scurvy-grass (*Cochlearia alpina*), Alpine Bistort (*Polygonum viviparum*), Yellow Mountain Saxifrage (*Saxifraga aizoides*), Purple saxifrage (*S. oppositifolia*), Mossy Saxifrage (*S. hypnoides*), Starry Saxifrage (*S. stellaris*), Alpine saxifrage (*S. nivalis*) and mosses such as *Ctenidium molluscum, Bryum alpinum, Fissidens* spp., and several thallose liverworts.

Most of these ferns, and the majority of the flowering plants, are mainly confined to the firmer, rockier fringes of the gullies, whilst the areas of most sodden, rotting, mobile rock and dripping water in the gully centres, often offer better scope to luxuriant growths of cushion-forming mosses and to additional pteridophytes whose creeping, semi-submerged rhizomes enable them to gain at least a fragile footing in the insubstantial substrate. Such ferns and fern-allies typically include, in appropriate sites in most of our mountains, Oak Fern (*Gymnocarpium dryopteris*), Beech Fern (*Phegopteris connectilis*) and Wood Horsetail (*Equisetum sylvaticum*). In the Scottish Highland mountains, however, these are also joined by sometimes luxuriant growths of Shade Horsetail (*Equisetum pratense*) and, especially typical of these sites, and virtually restricted to them and to similar other steep, damp, rocky, mountain patches, are colonies of the beautiful Mountain Bladder-fern (*Cystopteris montana*).

Cystopteris montana is a colony-forming fern of particularly delicate-looking appearance. The finely-divided, 3–12 cm long blades of its fronds are broadly triangular in shape, of rather translucent-green colour and of a crisp, pellucid texture. They are rather upward-dished, and are held in a nearly horizontally-inclined position relatively high (especially for an alpine plant) on tall (10–15 cm or more), pale straw-green coloured stipes. Frequently all the pinnae curve gently towards the tip of the frond in a slightly sickle-like manner, whilst the lower-most pair of pinnae, which are set oppositely, are very much more extensively developed and more compound and asymmetric than are those above, with the more developed and more divided side of each directed towards the frond base.

All the fronds of a colony usually point in a similar, downslope direction, giving each colony a very orderly and neatly-regimented appearance. Colonies of the plant usually thread their rhizomes through or beneath the cushions of the many surrounding species of moss-like and cushion-like habit (including both mosses and frequently saxifrages such as *Saxifraga aizoides*). Such cushions, the frequency of which is notable amongst its associates, probably help act as additional reservoirs of moisture for the fern during occasional dry summers.

Mountain Bladder-fern is a strictly alpine species in Britain, with a distribution limited to the central and west-central Scottish Highland mountains. Its sites seldom descend below 2,300 ft (ca. 700 m), and mostly it occurs much higher than this. Overall, its sites are somewhat sparingly distributed, and

The delicate frond of Cystopteris montana *in a grazing-free high-cliff gulley. Argyll, August*

are usually confined to northward-facing slopes, where the maximum summer temperature probably usually does not exceed about 27–28°C. Elsewhere in Europe, the species has a much-fragmented, truly Arctic–Alpine range, where it is also mostly occurs at high altitude. On a world-wide scale, its range crosses northern Asia discontinuously to Eastern Siberia, thence to the mountains of northern North America and those of southern Greenland.

Within the British Isles, it is very probable that *Cystopteris montana* is a relic from habitats which might well have been more widespread in the early Post-glacial. Today, in Britain, suitable conditions for Mountain Bladder-fern certainly seem to occur only over very limited areas. Large stands of it are rare, and it is possible that in most of its sites, each colony represents a single clonal individual, underlining that in Britian at least, this species may have already naturally achieved a very limited genetic base.

Its communities, in such high cliff-gullies, though remote and often inaccessible, do, however, give something of a glimpse of the type of success which our native pteridophyte flora can achieve in alpine sites in which grazing by animals and disturbance by man are both at a minimum. If any habitat in our much-modified islands is a truly natural and ancient one, it is, to me, sites such as these.

High Mountain Corries, Snow Patches and Fern Beds

High on many of our mountains, well above the levels of the cliffs of the lower valleys, occur the bleak, remote heights of the mountain corries. These enormous, ice-carved, quarry-like, armchair-shaped depressions often occupy much of the upper parts of many of our higher mountains. Such corries usually have steep, often precipitous, hard rock walls, which rise in height away from the corrie mouths. The junction between wall and corrie floor is often strewn with rugged slopes of massive, angular, tumbled, ice-hewn boulders. The floors are often comparatively flat, or shallowly depressed, and their entrance at the corrie mouth is usually marked by a low raised lip, inherited from the rolling outward-movement of the original Pleistocene ice which once ground its way out from within the corrie basin and gave the corrie its charatectic 'bowl' shape.

The Mountain Corrie Environment

Today, instead of ice, summer streams of trickling water fed by condensing cloud and frequent light rain usually glisten down the back walls and rock faces of the corries, to accumulate through dendritic veins of small streams into quiet mountain pools ('lochans' or 'tarns') of clear, oligotrophic water, set in the depressions of the corrie floors. Indeed, apart from the ever-present sound of trickling water, the cloud-wrapped corries can seem particularly silent and sometimes rather eerie places, the silence occasionally punctuated only by the distant crashing of a tumbling boulder echoing around the corrie's inward walls.

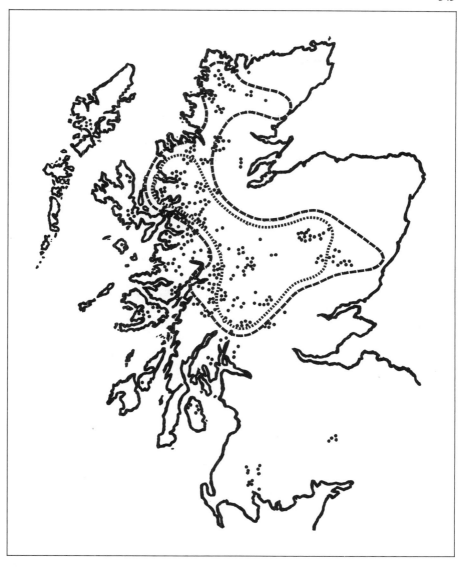

The origin of the corries, through ice-plucking at the mountain head of the former Pleistocene glaciers, seems often to have been most vigorous on more northerly aspects, with the result that the great majority of our mountain corries retain particularly shaded orientations. Their climates today are ones which are cool almost all year round, with frequent cloud and light rain or snow interrupted by occasional clear spells and

Fig. 13
Distribution of corries and Asplenium distentifolium *(dashed line) and* A. flexile *(dotted line) show a very similar pattern. (After Linton, 1959)*

Mountain corrie, corrie lake and scree. Note the flat corrie floor, with the corrie lake, impounded by a bare rocky lip, and the outflow stream. Cader Idris, Merionethshire. (Cambridge University Collection: copyright reserved)

cold nights. Permanent air movement ensures that the environment is always fresh and never dank.

Snow falling throughout the winter may accumulate deeply across the corrie floors and especially so within their hollows. Here, the deepest drifts typically melt only slowly in spring. Melting is usually hastened more by the arrival of warm spring rain than by large quantities of sun. Snow nevertheless lasts longest in those hollows where it regularly accumulates most deeply through the winter, forming snow-patches which may well last well into early summer before they finally melt (or, in some summers, the deepest of which occasionally do not!).

In a few mountain corries, occasional base-rich enclaves occur. Rarely are these limestones, more often they are the result of the local presence amongst more massive, hard, old, acidic volcanic or metamorphic rocks of softer, more base-yielding lavas. In such local sites there may be small enclaves, especially around the side and back-walls of corries, of base-demanding alpine ferns, usually marked by the presence of Brittle Bladder-fern (*Cystopteris fragilis*) and numerous plants of the small Maidenhair Spleenwort (*Asplenium trichomanes* subsp. *quadrivalens*) and Green Spleenwort (*A. viride*). Although the latter is generally a northern species, it is of interest that in such high altitude sites as these, the plant occurs in Britain as far south as the mountains of South Wales (especially in the Brecon Beacons) and in Ireland, in widely spaced and discontinuous stations as far south as west Cork and south Kerry.

Much of the habitats of the greater parts of the floors of most such corries are, however, fairly acidic, resulting from the frequent combination of predominantly acidic underlying rocks and the downward leaching effects of the very frequent rainfall. In consequence, in most of our mountain areas, the corrie bases, where not occupied by tarns, contain very much of an upland moorland flora, with thin, poor, rocky soils and more peaty pockets.

Rock-wall Base and Corrie Floor Communities

The tumbled rock-wall bases of the corries may provide scree-like habitats suitable for the presence of various species of *Dryopteris*, but especially for Golden-scaled Male ferns (*Dryopteris affinis*, probably including subspecies *borreri*, *stillupensis* and perhaps *affinis*), Mountain Male-fern (*D. oreades*) and, in the least acidic habitats, Northern Buckler-fern (*D. expansa*). As well as on the corrie wall bases, the various species of *Dryopteris* usually occur where there are rocky hummocks and outcrops on the corrie floors themselves.

In the heathy habitats of the corrie floor, most of the pteridophytes typical of the upland moorland community are likely to be present. Sometimes in more base-rich sites, Marsh Horsetail (*Equisetum palustre*), Wood Horsetail (*E. sylvaticum*), Shade Horsetail (*E. pratense*), and Common Horsetail (*E. arvense*) may all occur, whilst plants of Hard Fern (*Blechnum spicant*) occur widely scattered through the heathland community, and Sweet Mountain Fern (*Oreopteris limbosperma*), occurs mainly along the borders of small rills. Several species of clubmoss also typically form an integral part of the vegetation association of the heathy community of the corrie floor. These include scattered Fir Clubmoss (*Huperzia selago*) over the shallower soils, Alpine Clubmoss (*Diphasiastrum alpinum*) on steep, acidic slopes, and Stag's-horn Clubmoss (*Lycopodium clavatum*) amongst hummocks. In such sites in North Wales, *Diphasiastrum alpinum* may be particularly abundant, occasionally becoming the locally dominant plant, and forming a veritable turf. In corrie bases in Scotland, especially in the Cairngorms area, areas of damp peaty slopes are particularly

Huperzia selago *in a high mountain corrie. Aberdeenshire, July*

characterised by the presence of sometimes extensive, bright green colonies of Interrupted Clubmoss (*Lycopodium annotinum*).

Cryptogramma crispa occurs in many corrie sites throughout appropriate, mostly western, districts, and is thus to be found in them chiefly in North Wales, the English Lake District, and in Scotland, especially in the west. It is a relatively oceanic species, avoiding climates of very severe (and especially dry) winter cold, but also avoiding conditions of high maximum summer temperatures (Connolly & Dahl, 1970). It is, however, tolerant of long snow-lie and at its higher altitude sites (above 3,000 ft, ca. 915 m) is mostly confined to sites where a thick blanket of winter snow adds considerably to the protection of the plants against both cold and winter dessication. Under such conditions, especially in the vicinity of corries, plants of *Cryptogramma crispa* may ascend to over 4,000 ft (1,220 m) in altitude.

The fronds of the clumps of *Cryptogramma crispa* are typically retained attached to the parent clumps after they die in autumn, and they persist attached to the clumps beneath the winter snow. Their eventual rotting, beside adding to the humus of the parent plant, may also act in a thermally protective capacity at these altitudes, as seems especially the case also with Alpine Lady-fern.

Within the lowest-lying portions of the corrie floor, the presence of upland tarns of clear, acidic water, usually allow opportunity for a fringing reed-swamp (especially on the shallower, downwind shore) of Water Horsetail (*Equisetum fluviatile*) to develop, usually of low-growing, aquatic quillworts, Common Quillwort (*Isoetes lacustris*) or Spring Quillwort (*I. echinospora*) are likely to occur—the latter especially in more western sites in Scotland, North Wales and far-western Ireland.

Alpine Lady-fern Communities

Alpine Lady-fern (*Athyrium distentifolium*) begins to become an increasingly frequent member of many fern communities above about 1,500 ft (ca. 500 m), with its greatest frequency usually occurring between about 1,800 to 3,600 ft (ca. 550–1,100 m). It is fairly widespread through the higher elevations of the Scottish Highlands, with outlying stations as far east as south Grampian and as far west as Wester Ross. Its main headquarters, however, are in the Grampian Mountains. In these regions, its generally calcifuge habits make it particularly characteristic of acidic rock areas such as granites and gneisses, although it can also extend, usually less abundantly, on to more basic surface layers. As far as is known, it is absent from any of our more southerly mountains such as those of the English Lake District or North Wales, and not present in Ireland. One factor confining it to higher elevations at northerly latitudes appears to be a requirement for a low summer maximum temperature of perhaps not above about 27°C, coupled with adequate year-round precipitation. Elsewhere in Europe, it is a species of strongly Arctic–Alpine range, present in the Alps, Pyrenees and higher central European mountains, as well as through the Scandinavian mountains and in the Faeroes and in northern Iceland.

In our Scottish mountains, *Athyrium distentifolium* occurs through a range of rocky habitats, and although these are not always in corries, it has a high frequency in these sites; its distribution in the Scottish mountains closely follows that of the corries (see map on p. 345). It grows, especially in shallow, rocky depressions and in moist pockets on boulder slopes. It is an unusually large-fronded fern to occur at such high altitudes, with its rather soft-textured and finely-divided fronds sometimes standing as much as 70 cm high in summer. In high mountain habitats, the plant comes very much into its own where the topography is such that there is enhanced local shelter, and in high corries that have sheltered corners, dense, almost pure stands may grow.

Its sites are also ones where regular accumulations of appreciable winter snow cover the plant for long periods each winter, usually lasting well into spring. Such snow cover probably helps protect large colonies from excessive damage by winter wind-blast and severe winter cold, as well as from winter desiccation. Its occurrence in sites of long snow-lie also helps ensure that plants receive ample irrigation during spring snow-melt. Its habitats, almost always on gradients, are ones which never accumulate stagnant moisture, and instead are charac-terised at such times by a steady, trickling throughflow of fresh spring meltwater, presumably bringing an abundant annual supply of fresh mineral downwash. The sudden rise in air-temperature around the plant following spring snow-melt is probably the main factor responsible for triggering the begin-ning of the expansion of spring frond growth, enabling maxi-mum advantage to be taken by the plant of the short montane growing season, once steadily milder springtime weather has finally arrived at these high-altitude sites.

In the lower part of the range of *Athyrium distentifolium*, at about 2,000 feet (ca. 600 m), there is usually a small region of overlap with the more lowland Woodland Lady-fern (*Athyrium filix-femina*). The hybrid between these two species is known elsewhere in Europe, and I have recently found specimens answering its description in the eastern Highlands of Scotland, usually as scattered plants in regions where the two parents grow nearby in some quantity. It is perhaps not surprising that the occurrence of such plants appears to correspond approxi-mately with the position of the upper margin of forest vege-tation of former times.

In its sites in more base-rich areas, scattered plants of *Athy-rium distentifolium* may be associated with many of the other ferns and flowering plants more characteristic of such sites, and especially with Mountain Buckler-fern (*Dryopteris expansa*) and Mountain Male-fern (*Dryopteris oreades*). However, in its more typical acidic habitats, where it forms large snow-bed patches, the associates of *A. distentifolium*, and those too of *A. flexile* and *Cryptogramma crispa*, are often rather few. Most typical of such sites, however, are often scattered plants of Bil-berry (*Vaccinium myrtillus*), Heath Bedstraw (*Galium saxatile*), Stiff Sedge (*Carex bigelowii*), and patches of Alpine Lady's-mantle (*Alchemilla alpina*), whilst there may be also Crowberry (*Empetrum nigrum*) and nearby grasses, including Wavy Hair-grass (*Deschampsia flexuosa*) and Sheep's Fescue (*Festuca ovina*).

As with *Cryptogramma crispa* (see above), the fronds of the clumps of *Athyrium distentifolium* are typically retained attached to the parent clumps after they die in autumn. Ratcliffe (1977b) records that following spring snow-melt, the dead overwintering fronds which have persisted beneath the snow, give a characteristic red-brown colour to patches of *Athyrium distentifolium* at these altitudes on the hillsides. The over-winter persistence of large quantities of lying fronds results from a normally heavy frond-fall at the end of the previous season. The slow rate of decay of the fronds results in the gradual accumulation of a dense, acidic, raw humus around the plant clumps. It seems possible that as in the case of *Crypto-gramma*, these dark-coloured fallen fronds of *Athyrium disten-tifolium* help form a heat-absorbing and heat-retaining blanket, assisting with the normal thermal balance of the plant, especi-ally during days of early spring sunshine interspersed with chilly nights.

Flexile Lady-fern Communities

At much higher altitude, in the upper part of the range of *Athy-rium distentifolium*, especially well-above about 3,000 ft (ca. 900 m), there is a very much wider altitudinal overlap with another species of the same genus. This is with Flexile Lady-fern (*Athyrium flexile*). Occasional intermediates between *A. flexile* and *A. distentifolium* may also occur within this region, usually as scattered individuals. But for the most part, plants of *A. flexile* are quite distinctive, especially between the altitudes of about 3,400 and 3,750 feet (1,040–1,140 m), to which *A. flexile* is chiefly restricted. Plants are usually smaller than those of *A. distentifolium*, but considering their high elevation and exposed habitats, nevertheless achieve a respectable size, with fronds mostly about 8–20 cm long, and occasionally as much as 30 cm. Plants differ in appearance from *A. distentifolium*, and indeed from any other native fern, however, in several unusual features. One of these is that the stipe is quite thick and rigid for the size of the frond. Further, a little way above its base, the stipe, which starts off at a steeply ascending angle, also bends abruptly to grow thereafter in a rather stiffly horizontal direc-tion. As a result, the whole of the blade of the frond is held rather stiffly horizontally, close to the surface of the ground. It is this 'flexing' of the stipe near its base into a nearly horizontal position which gives the plant its botanical and common names, whilst the resulting blade usually also adopts a slightly sinuously left-and-right curving habit when viewed from above, emphasised further by the narrow outline of the blade and the gradually-tapering tip. Fronds as small as 7–10 cm long can be fully fertile, in contrast to those of *A. distentifolium* and *A. filix-femina*, which are seldom fertile at this size, and when fertile, particularly distinctive from any other native fern is the habit of *Athyrium flexile* of becoming fertile only over the central and basal part of the frond, or on a few of the basal pin-nae only.

Athyrium flexile is a Scottish endemic. It is a fern of high altitude rocky sites, especially of sombre and rather shaded ones, such as rough rocky slopes in the shelter of massive, cool, north-facing corries. Like those of *A. distentifolium* at lower altitude, the habitats of *A. flexile* are mainly ones where snow normally accumulates deeply during the winter months, and where, because of the shade, there is usually a particularly long, late-spring snow-lie. Its curious structural adaptations appear to be ones which especially fit it for survival in the quite extreme, semi-exposed, often wind-buffeted and short growth-season habitats in which it grows. Following the long period of winter dormancy, spring frond-expansion takes place nearly simultaneously throughout the plant. As with *A. distentifolium*, expansion of the new-season's fronds is probably first triggered in *A. flexile* by increase in warmth, following a substantial period of winter cold, rather than by a change in daylength alone. Despite a fast frond-expansion rate, the tips of the fronds seem to scarcely finish uncurling before the short high-altitude growth-season is again at its end. The restriction of the fertile areas to only the basal region of the frond enables the maturation of their sporangia to begin as soon as the basal pairs of pinnae have expanded, long before the tip of the frond has finally uncurled. The vegetative functions of the plant probably maximise only later in the season, once the spring growth of fronds is well under-way, with the stiff stipe and rachis angle holding the blades of each frond at a low repose, presumably allowing the plants to achieve a blade-orientation and moderately large and photosynthetically-effective frond size whilst maintaining a low wind-profile.

Athyrium flexile shares with *A. distentifolium* the feature of having circular sori, although those of *A. flexile* are usually smaller and more distant, and both also have the same chromosome number of $n = 40$ chromosome pairs. Due to these similarities there is a theory, requiring scientific verification, that they are the same species. Yet *A. flexile* shows many aspects of distinctness beyond its unusual appearance. Plants seem to breed true and to maintain their appearance in cultivation, and in the wild have a distinct altitudinal range, where they occur in similar habitats on a number of remote Scottish mountains. If *A. flexile* is a local high-montane derivative of *A. distentifolium*, then it is certainly one which has become effectively established and spread, whilst maintaining its own distinctive structural and ecological identity in doing so.

Ridges, Plateaux and High Summits

Above the altitude of the maximum height of the former tree-line on our mountains, at around 2,000 feet (ca. 600 m), is a very appreciable amount of upland terrain in all the main mountain masses of Britain and Ireland. In the Scottish Highlands in particular, when the windswept panorama is viewed from high up, it can be seen that the rounded tops are not merely those of a succession of isolated mountains rising separately from the lowlands. Rather, much of land at high altitude forms part of an extensive, broken range of high plateaux of fairly level ridges and summits. It is into these that subsequent erosion has carved the upland valleys and the more sheltered high mountain corries. Between these features, there remains, however, much land of bleak and exposed rocky ridges, plateaux and mountain summits, clothed mainly with a thin, low vegetation.

These high upland areas have a generally similar, rather arctic-like, mountain climate. Rainfall is generally heavier and more frequent in the west, where the climate is also slightly milder. Coverings of fine snow are characteristic of much of the winter months, and such snows generally lie longest in the east. Winds are almost always strong, whilst sun insolation is also characteristically high.

The vegetation at first can present a somewhat bleak prospect, its thinness, lowness of stature and the percentage of bare, rocky ground generally rapidly increasing with altitude. The vegetation mostly consists of a very low-growing dwarf

High summit rocks of bare appearance hiding pockets rich in clumbosses and Lady-ferns. Wester Ross, August

shrub-heath association, dominated by Heather (*Calluna vulgaris*), merging gradually into that of the moorlands below. Slight hollows where snow accumulates and lasts longest are typically dominated by species of *Vaccinium*, forming brighter green summer vegetation patches.

The diversity of vegetation in these habitats is low, but the associations which are formed are nevertheless interesting ones, including several mountain flowers especially adapted to these extreme conditions and a proportionately large pteridophyte component, especially of clubmosses.

The fern most usually present, as widely scattered small, very prostrate plants, is Hard Fern (*Blechnum spicant*). Sometimes associated with it at surprisingly high altitudes (to about 3,900 ft, 1,180 m) are small plants of Beech Fern (*Phegopteris connectilis*), often half-hidden amongst the heather, or in the shelter of rocks and in slight hollows. Also usually in sheltered hollows amongst boulders, are occasional plants of Alpine (*Athyrium distentifolium*) and Flexile Lady-fern (*A. flexile*), their sites especially marking late snow-beds.

Amongst the clubmosses are to be found often frequent spreading plants of Interrupted Clubmoss (*Lycopodium annotinum*) in the lower part of the zone (which itself largely replaces Stag's-horn Clubmoss *Lycopodium clavatum* which is rarer at these altitudes), and usually abundant growths of Alpine Clubmoss (*Diphasiastrum alpinum*) and Fir Clubmoss (*Huperzia selago*).

Huperzia selago *and* Diphasiastrum alpinum *on a steep, high mountain slope. Mid-Perthshire, August*

In all the habitats, soils are typically moderately to highly acidic, thinly peaty ones, often covering boulders or solifluction terraces and in the sites where clubmosses are present, the clubmosses are usually extremely thin. Further the pteridophytes present not only seem extremely tolerant of wide temperature fluctuations, but especially of frequent cold night-temperatures, and, in the case of Alpine Clubmoss and Fir Clubmoss, also of high daytime sun and almost constant high wind-exposure. All, however, appear to be both grazing and fire-sensitive.

Associated with all of these plants, in such extensive upland granitic areas as the Cairngorms, for example, is a dominant, low-growing woody community of predominantly berry-bearing dwarf shrubs, containing such species as Heather (*Calluna vulgaris*), Bilberry (*Vaccinium myrtillus*), Cowberry (*V. vitis-idaea*), Bearberry (*Arctostaphylos uva-ursi*), Crowberry (*Empetrum nigrum*), Cloudberry (*Rubus chamaemorus*), Mountain Azalea (*Loiseleuria procumbens*), Bell Heather (*Erica cinerea*), Least Willow (*Salix herbacea*) and sometimes Black Bearberry (*Arctous alpina*). Especially in more-sheltered *Lycopodium annotinum* pockets, there may also be Alpine Meadow Rue (*Thalictrum alpinum*), Boreal Fleabane (*Erigeron borealis*), Dwarf Cornel (*Cornus suecica*), Intermediate Wintergreen (*Pyrola media*), Three-flowered Rush (*Juncus triglumis*), Alpine Poa (*Poa alpina*) and Spiked Woodrush (*Luzula spicata*). In more windswept *Huperzia selago* sites, where much bare rock and sometimes damp gravels are exposed, these clubmosses may be associated with Moss Campion (*Silene acaulis*), Three-leaved Rush (*Juncus trifidus*), Stiff Sedge (*Carex bigelowii*), and Viviparous Fescue (*Festuca vivipara*), as well as usually abundant grey carpets of Woolly Hairmoss (*Rhacomitrium lanuginosum*) and *Cladonia* and *Cetraria* lichens.

Such habitats of the high mountain ridges, plateaux and high summit tops represent, in our islands, the nearest vegetation type to that of the arctic fringes. The presence of pteridophytes forming a constant and sometimes fairly numerous component of their low-growing vegetation, underlines the wide adaptability of ferns and fern allies to these extremes of temperature conditions on a world scale.

CHAPTER 13

Pteridophytes of the Atlantic Fringe

Included within this chapter are a number of habitats in which ferns and fern-allies are especially extensively developed under the mild and moist oceanic climates of the Atlantic fringe of these islands. These include communities which are seldom, if at all, represented far inland from western coasts, and many of which are unique not only within Britain and Ireland, but also to our islands within Europe as a whole. They are the most fern-rich habitats in the British Isles.

Atlantic Cliff-Top Grassland, Ledges and Rough Slopes

Grassland and scrub vegetation of various kinds characterises the rolling, exposed habitats at the tops of hard or soft cliff shorelines. The habitats are ones of predominantly shallow, rocky soils, and on Atlantic coasts especially, of almost constant exposure to strong winds and salt-spray. The exposure helps ensure that any woody shrub growth attains only a low, wind-pruned profile, becoming taller only where wind-speeds are lessened in hollows, and here, pockets of deeper soils may also locally accumulate. Grazing, especially by rabbits, is often a pronounced feature of the cliff-top vegetation, whilst adjacent cliff-ledges are usually sites for many nesting seabirds.

Despite the exposure, several species of pteridophytes can be present in these habitats, largely because of the reduced competition from other vegetation, resulting from the severe winds and salt-spray, and because of the shallowness and often general instability of the cliff-top slopes themselves. It follows that great caution for personal safety must always be exercised in exploring any of these sites. In precarious places, such exploration is always best done by remaining firmly on adequate cliff-top paths, from where much can often be learnt using field-glasses from a firm and stationary position!

On and beneath the exposed shoulders of Atlantic cliffs, many small ferns may make a scattered appearance. Especially in the local shelter of moist cliff-top clefts and in sloping recesses beneath wind-pruned shrubby cliff-top canopies, scattered plants of Black Spleenwort (*Asplenium adiantum-nigrum*), Common Male Fern (*Dryopteris filix-mas*), Soft Shield-fern (*Polystichum setiferum*) and Hart's Tongue Fern (*Phyllitis scolopendrium*) may occur even on quite exposed western coasts. Lanceolate Spleenwort (*Asplenium billotii*) can occur too more locally and usually amongst outcropping boulders on the coasts of Wales, Devon and Cornwall and in the Channel Islands, and in the latter region, Guernsey Spleenwort (*A.* × *sarniense*) may also grow. In more acidic, moist spots, Lady Fern (*Athyrium filix-femina*) and Broad Buckler-fern replace several of the above, whilst in the most cool, Atlantic, situations, highly western and drought-sensitive acid-loving species, include Hay-scented Buckler-fern (*Dryopteris aemula*), Wilson's Filmy-fern (*Hymenophyllum wilsonii*), and bright green fringes of Royal Fern (*Osmunda regalis*), give additional local diveristy, especially where small streams of acidic water trickle and seep over cliff faces (see also chapter 5). Where such water is less acidic, Dutch Rush (*Equisetum hyemale*) can occur very locally, and in shady recesses and around springs of calcareous water, Maidenhair Fern (*Adiantum capillus veneris*) grows in some cliff-top sites. Here, such species can be brought into close proximity with cool, moist, sea-sprayed rocks bearing colonies of Sea Spleenwort (*Asplenium marinum*). All undoubtedly benefit from the freedom from grazing of such inaccessible maritime sites.

Common Horsetail (*Equisetum arvense*) and Bracken (*Pteridium aquilinum*) occur sparsely on larger ledges, but are more widespread on many cliff-tops. Indeed, Bracken is often the most abundant pteridophyte of cliff-tops, thriving especially in shallow hollows over sandstone cliffs, where deeper, moister, but nevertheless well-drained soil accumulations allow adequate soil depth for extensive rhizome networks to establish. In such sites in summer, dense knee- to waist-high stands of Bracken fronds (but much smaller than this with greatest exposure) may dominate whole patches of cliff-top slopes, extending in dense drifts down shallow cliff recesses facing the sea. Bracken stands often also spread as continuous and sometimes tall blankets back from many cliff tops. The plants are sometimes so tall, that on the Isle of Ulva, off Mull in western Scotland, it has been picturesquely described that in summer, only the tips of the horns of the Highland cattle can be seen above it (Fraser-Darling, 1947).

On cliff-top slopes associates of Bracken may include scattered Male Fern (*Dryopteris filix-mas*) and Red Campion (*Selene dioica*), as well as sometimes dense masses of Bluebell

(*Hyacinthoides non-scripta*), often flowering profusely in spring as the young Bracken fronds are beginning to emerge. Common Adder's-tongue (*Ophioglossum vulgatum*—see below) is one of the few pteridophytes to be able to survive beneath the summer canopy of the Bracken fronds, whilst Spring Squill (*Scilla verna*) may grow in shallower soils around it in many localities. Amongst other associates of several of the pteridophytes of cliff-ledge and especially cliff-top sites are sub-maritime, disturbed-habitat and grassland species.

In wind-pruned and often rabbit-grazed grassland turf which stretches back from the tops of cliffs, Moonwort (*Botrychium lunaria*) and Common Adder's-tongue (*Ophioglossum vulgatum*) can form diffuse and probably very old, established patches in what is probably natural turf. Their leafy shoots may be of very small size, except where they gain local shelter from prevailing winds behind outcropping boulders, fence-posts, gorse bushes, lighthouses, ancient earthworks or even abandoned cliff-top military fortifications.

Even smaller, however, and also very characteristic of remote Atlantic headland cliff-top grassland are the other two species of native Adder's-tongues: Small Adder's-tongue (*Ophioglossum azoricum*), with shoots which reach a maximum size of around 8 cm but which, in these sites are often nearer 2–3 cm, and Least Adder's-tongue (*Ophioglossum lusitanicum*), which is usually not so large. Indeed, with the leafy parts of the blade usually 1.0–1.5 cm in length and frequently lying flat on the ground, *O. lusitanicum* is easily the smallest native pteridophyte, and is usually overtopped by almost every member of the identically-coloured grass turf community around it. Searching for any of these species in windswept cliff-top turf can be a time-consuming business, and is certainly best done (and indeed can usually only be done) on hands and knees, when other appointments are not too pressing.

Ophioglossum azoricum is a highly Atlantic species in its discontinuous native distribution around Britain and Ireland, from where is spreads south also to the Azores and Canary Islands, and north to Iceland. The majority of its sites are on exposed, grassy headlands and peninsulas, and on exposed aspects of inshore and offshore islands lying along western English, Irish and Scottish coasts, scattered from the Channel Islands, Scillies and Lundy Island in southern Britain, to the North Wales, Cumbrian, Northumberland (Lindisfarne), west Highland (Inverpolly and Tongue) and north Highland (Dunnet Head) coasts, Orkneys, Shetlands, Fair Isle, North Rona and St Kilda, and in Ireland in equally isolated stations from Great Blasket Island and the Dingle Peninsula of Kerry to Clare and Inishea Islands and to peninsulas of the Connemara, Mayo and west Donegal coasts. The reasons for this extraordinarily discontinuous, 'insular–peninsular', highly Atlantic distribution, and the way it has been achieved, are unknown, but might well imply the operation of some dispersal agent other than mere chance. The possibility of the involvement of migrating seabirds of such habitats carrying spores either externally or internally between these isolated localities should be investigated. In this connection it is of interest to note the close similarity in the distribution round the British and Irish coasts of *Ophioglossum azoricum* to that of the nesting sites of at least three seabirds: the Storm Petrel (*Hydrobates pelagicus*), and the ground-nesting, burrow-inhabiting Puffin (*Fratercula arctica*), and the Manx Shearwater (*Puffinus puffinus*).

Ophioglossum lusitanicum is much more local and of distinctly southern distribution. It is known from discontinuous stations around the coastal fringes of Brest, Spain and Portugal, eastwards on mainly coastal–insular sites across the Mediterranean to the Middle East, and south and westwards to the Azores and Canary Islands. In Britain, it seems confined to a small number of cliff-top and rocky coastal downland sites, in short, turfy vegetation on the Scilly Isles (St. Agnes) and the Channel Islands (south and west Guernsey). Rather surprisingly, it has not been found anywhere on the southern or western fringes of Ireland, but such a diminutive plant could easily be overlooked, and, indeed, its presence in the Scilly Island was not discovered until the 1950s. However, in the Scilly Islands, where *O. lusitanicum* and *O. azoricum* both occur, their very different seasons of growth help distinguished them. *O. lusitanicum* is mainly a winter-growing species, beginning its above-ground growth during the last months of the year, becoming most prominent from January to April, and shedding its spores during the latter months. After this, it dies-down particularly rapidly and has often disappeared from above ground by late April or May. *Ophioglossum lusitanicum* thus completes the above-ground part of its life-cycle in the very short, winter-grazed turf, before becoming overtopped by taller, summer vegetation. It grows in patches of moist, mossy, sometimes slightly eroding turf, with unshaded, southerly exposure, which warm rapidly in spring, and where slight seepage of groundwater helps maintain patches of moist, spongy soil which also slope sufficiently to avoid becoming too waterlogged in winter. Its patches of vegetation are usually thus marked by an increase in the moss (especially *Polytrichum*) components of the surrounding, floristically-rich turf, whilst other species occurring nearby may include Buck's-horn and Ribwort Plantain (*Plantago coronopus* and *P. lanceolata*),

The small, prostrate, boat-shaped leaves of Ophioglossum lusitanicum, *like* Isoetes histrix, *grow mostly in the winter and can be difficult to spot in cliff-top grassland. South-west Guernsey, late March*

Autumnal Squill (*Scilla autumnalis*), Lady's Bedstraw (*Galium verum*), Scarlet Pimpernel (*Anagallis arvensis*), Parsley Piert (*Aphanes arvensis*), with scattered Bluebell (*Hyacinthoides non-scripta*) and *Vulpia* grasses, and English Stonecrop (*Sedum anglicum*) marking patches of adjacent shallower soils.

Another winter growing and diminutive pteridophyte, which shares with the last species a rather similar native and overseas distribution in cliff-top and associated Atlantic downland turf, is the Land Quillwort (*Isoetes histrix*). Land Quillwort is a small, inconspicuous, rosette-like, perennial plant, with short, pointed, quill-like leaves. The leaves arise in spreading clusters from small, knobbly, subterranean corms; each plant resembling a miniature pineapple half-submerged in the ground. It is a rare and highly local species, occurring in limited patches in winter-wet, peaty hollows, confined in these islands

Small plants of Isoetes histrix, *which grow very early in the season in shallow, moist depressions in close-cropped cliff-top turf, can be difficult to find. South-west Guernsey, late March*

to the cliff-top downland of the Lizard peninsula of Cornwall and to similar habitats (as well as spreading in one locality into fixed dune pasture) on the Channel Islands of Alderney and Guernsey. Its range spreads southward from Britain along the western coast of France and the west of the Iberian peninsula and eastwards, in mainly coastal and insular habitats, into the Mediterranean.

Land Quillwort is a slightly amphibious pteridophyte, which can be extremely difficult to spot, occurring as it does in small patches amongst a fairly close-sward of vegetation. It generally grows in the more sparsely-vegetated hollows which are flooded or well-irrigated in winter and spring, but which partially or largely dry out and bake in most summers. Like *Ophioglossum lusitanicum*, it is mainly a winter-growing species, which completes the above-ground part of its annual cycle during early spring, appearing above ground about mid-March. Thereafter it usually withers back to its underground corm by mid-May to late June, persisting for longer only in occasional, particularly wet summers. Most of its sites are on southward or westward slopes, where the soil is shallow but silty in winter, warming rapidly in spring sunshine. Its locations seem to differ from those of *Ophioglossum lusitanicum* (near to which it grows in at least one of its Channel Island localities) in being sited in more distinct hollows which are more subject to rainwater collection in winter, but which are less seepage-fed in summer. Its sites consequently are less mossy and generally floristically poorer, but can include a number of other individuals also of rosette-form, such as assorted-aged (and perhaps annually colonising) plants of Buck's-horn Plantain (*Plantago coronopus*), Sand Crocus (*Romulea columnae*), Autumnal Squill (*Scilla autumnalis*), Sand Sedge (*Carex arenaria*), and numerous young turf-inhabiting plants of Sea Thrift (*Armeria maritima*).

The close adaptation to these exacting sites of the turf-inhabiting pteridophytes and their notably discontinuous distributions, suggest that these species have, for the most part, probably had a long association with such windswept cliff-top locations. Certainly, many of the larger colonies of *Botrychium* and all three species of *Ophioglossum*, could only have gradually established their present colonies over considerable periods of time, with probably constant exposure and minimal turf disturbance. There is, however, some evidence that parts of such areas as the Scilly Islands have carried a more wooded vegetation at periods in the Post-glacial past than they do at present, and that at least some of the now open, non-wooded vegetation on these islands is probably of partly anthropogenic origin. It therefore seems probable that both open patches and a low-canopied deciduous woodland in more sheltered hollows, may well have formerly occupied many such cliff-top sites. In addition to the probably ancient distribution of the turf-inhabiting pteridophytes in the open patches, it seems likely that the woodland species of pteridophytes still persisting in inaccessible cliff-ledge sites may also be relics of former more numerous wooded coastal-fringe populations, some of the genetic diversity of which the modern plants in these sites may well still preserve.

Clay Coasts and Dunes of South-east Ireland

The clay coasts and sand dunes of south-east Ireland are pteridologically unique for the widespread occurrence of a horsetail unknown elsewhere within the British Isles, Moore's Horsetail (*Equisetum × moorei*). Moore's Horsetail is the natural hybrid between Dutch Rush (*Equisetum hyemale*) and Ramose Horsetail (*E. ramosissimum*), and although it is present very sporadically elsewhere in continental central and southern Europe where the *E. ramosissimum* parent also grows, its apparently quite natural, extensive and probably very long-established occurrence in Ireland where the *E. ramosissimum* parent is absent, is of particular phytogeographical interest. Within south-east Ireland, *Equisetum × moorei* is confined to Co. Wicklow and Co. Wexford, where it occurs in numerous localities along about 30 miles (ca. 50 km) of coast from Ardmore Point south to Wexford Harbour. Here it almost always grows in the immediate neighbourhood of the sea, on low sandy and clayey banks, seldom penetrating more than a few score metres inland. In some of its sites it is extremely abundant in local patches on many steeply shelving, moist clay banks flanking low headlands immediately overlooking long sandy strands. Locally it also spreads into sandy grassed hinterland as well as into various areas of adjacent, eroded, much-modified dune systems with wet and dry, stable and more mobile areas. Within its particular habitats, it appears to be a plant of often aggressive and vigorous growth as well as of somewhat variable appearance, very closely mimicking, in places, either parent, as well as adopting virtually every intermediate condition. In the more exposed sites, its shoots annually die down to near their bases, but in nearby, sheltered, slumping cliff pockets may persist nearly intact through mild winters and into the following summer. Often surviving shoots of the previous year grow new, strong, ascending branches from some of their upper nodes during their second year.

Cultivation experiments I have carried out show that the stem fragments of this hybrid from these Irish sites have a very considerable ability to strike as new plants when washed up on damp, sandy shores, even after periods of flotation in agitated sea-water of three days or more. Such abilities exceed those of most other horsetails, with the exception of Mackay's Horsetail (*Equisetum* × *trachyodon*), and thus open very considerable potential for local spread of this plant by natural dispersal of vegetative fragments by seaborne longshore drift, along the whole area of coastline in which appropriate habitats occur. This, indeed, is just what the plant appears to have achieved in south-east Ireland.

Even though *E.* × *moorei* is restricted to a single coast of Ireland, the plant nevertheless encounters in its range of sub-maritime habitats a considerable number of other species. Those noted comprise a range of grassland, sea-coast and marsh or flush species, and include Common and Great Horsetail (*Equisetum arvense* and *E. telmateia*) – as well as Wild Carrot (*Daucus carota*), Sea and Buck's-horn Plantain (*Plantago maritima* and *P. coronopus*), Field Penny-cress (*Thalaspi arvensis*), Large Birdsfoot-trefoil (*Lotus ulignosus*), Tufted Vetch (*Vicia cracca*), Meadow Vetchling (*Lathrus pratensis*), Sea Pea (*L. maritimus*), Wild Pansy (*Viola tricolor*), Milkwort (*Polygala vulgaris*), Ribwort Plantain (*Plantago lanceolata*), Restharrow (*Ononis repens*), Self-heal (Prunella vulgaris), Lady's Bedstraw (*Galium verum*), Cat's Ear (*Hypochoeris radicata*), Sheep's-bit (*Jasione montata*), Common centaury (*Centaurium erythraea*), Creeping Cinquefoil (*Potentilla reptans*), Silverweed (*Potentilla anserina*), Yarrow (*Achillea millefolium*), Bracken (*Pteridium aquilinum*), Bramble (*Rubus fruticosus* agg.), Willowherbs (*Epilobium* spp.), Purple Loosetrife (*Lythrum salicaria*), Meadowsweet (*Filipendula ulmaria*), Water-pepper (*Polygonum*

Equisetum × moorei.
Co. Wicklow, July

hydropiper), Fleabane (*Pulicaria dysenterica*), Yellow Flag (*Iris pseudacorus*), Wild Angelica (*Angelica sylvestris*), Cow Parsnip (*Heracleum sphondylium*), Marsh Thistle (*Circium palustre*), Marsh Bedstraw (*Galium palustre*), Marsh Marigold (*Caltha palustris*), Hemp Agrimony (*Eupatorum cannabinum*), Fragrant Orchid (*Gymnadenia conopsea*), Remote Sedge (*Carex remota*), Carnation Grass (*C. flacca*), Hard Rush (*Juncus inflexus*), Oatgrass (*Arrhenatherum elatius*), Yorkshire Fog (*Holcus lanatus*), Cock's-foot (*Dactylis glomerata*), Slender False-brome (*Brachypodium sylvaticum*), Common Bent (*Agrostis tenuis*), and *Festuce* and *Vulsia* grasses.

The particularly suitable environment for the survival of this hybrid on this coastline appears to be a combination of geology, topography and a maritime but south-easterly climate. The coasts of this region are unusual within Ireland in being characterised by their great stretches of sandy strands and gravels backed by low boulder clay cliffs. The boulder clay overlies an old, well eroded platform of mixed hard Cambrian, Ordovician and Silurian rocks, and where these outcrop, clays still form much of the capping to the many low headlands. The yellow-grey clays, of Pleistocene age, derive in large part from the massive glaciation of the central limestone core of Ireland, bringing appropriately basic rocks into close proximity with more acidic ones. The present extensive exposure of these clays to marine erosion creates a rich mosaic of habitats in the numerous, actively eroding seaward faces. Such topographic and geologic conditions are ideal for horsetails in general, and although shoots of *Equisetum × moorei* may occur for some distance back from the cliff tops, its colonies are often at their most vigorous where they continually re-pioneer the eroding seaward clay cliff-faces and shoulders, and may become especially dense and vegetationally dominant where moist lines of seepage emerge along slumping cliff-faces. Shoots, in places, spread also into loose and sometimes damp sand-dune accumulations lying over the clay, and at the foot of the faces, may also enter the sandy upper seashore communities, right down to the winter strand line, emerging amongst such saltwater-tolerant flowering plants as Sea Sandwort (*Honkenya peploides*), Sea Buckthorn (*Hippophae rhamnoides*), Sea Bindweed (*Calystegia soldanella*), and Sea Holly (*Eryngium maritimum*). The area, by day, is also rich in Lizards, Six-spot Burnet Moths in summer, Meadow Brown and Grayling Butterflies, and abundant snails, especially *Cepaea nemoralis*, seemingly indicative of the generally calcareous nature of the terrain.

Climatically, not only is this south-eastern coastal fringe of Ireland one in which the northward-bound marine currents in the western Irish Sea constantly bring considerable winter warmth, but experience in summer also suggests the extreme coastal fringe to be one of unusually high number of hours of summer sunshine. For the shores often appear to be bathed in summer sun when the Wicklow mountains rising only a few miles behind, are wrapped in low cloud and soft, light rain.

Praeger (1934) notes that the whole area of this coast is, indeed, a focus of the strand flora of Ireland, and that a number of flowering-plant species of generally southern affinity also occur within this region, including Sea Stock (*Matthiola sinuata*), Sea and Portland Spurge (*Euphorbia paralias* and *E. portlandica*), Sand-spurrey (*Spergluria rubra*), Golden Samphire (*Inula crithmoides*) and Wild Asparagus (*Asparagus officinalis*). The absence of one parent of *Equisetum × moorei* from the whole of Ireland and Britain, yet the widespread range of this hybrid on this coast, suggests it to be an ancient native plant which is a survivor from a past, wider parental range, from a warmer, Post-glacial (or even earlier?) time. It appears to have survived here because of the unusual combination of geological and climactic conditions, which have probably also restricted the other southern species that occur here.

Limestones of Western Atlantic Coasts

Outcrops of limestone rocks in the oceanic climates of the extreme west of these islands are of considerable pteridological interest. Such sites provide rocky habitats which are moist, lime-yielding, and typically well-drained, and, especially where well-sheltered, are frequently rich in ferns. They also provide sites in which, under the frequent light rainfall, lime-loving ferns often grow in close proximity to more acidic ones, as well as ones in which unusual combinations of southern elements and low-altitude enclaves of more montane ones may meet. Climatic conditions for pteridophyte prothallial, as well as sporophyte, growth also seem especially good and opportunities for unusual hybridisations and survival of resulting offspring often appear excellent.

More major outcrops of limestones of various geological ages occur widely scattered around the western margins of our islands, from Cape Wrath and Wester Ross, southward to Co. Sligo, Clare and Kerry. Others occur near the extreme northwest Welsh coast and locally in south Wales and south Devon. Between these also occur many additional much smaller and more local outcrops in western locations. Habitats in all of these sites differ somewhat from each other, depending partly on location and partly on the more detailed geological make-up and erosional structure of the rock itself.

North-west Highland Limestones of Scotland

In the Scottish north-west Highlands, the limestone outcrops are almost exclusively those of the Durness limestone, largely of Ordovician age. This old, hard limestone forms a highly discontinuous outcrop which runs from Durness, west of Loch Eriboll, on the north-west coast of Highland, in an approximately SSW direction to appear again at Loch Kishorn in Wester Ross, some 90 miles (ca. 145 km) further south.

Between these extreme ends, the limestone is exposed mainly in the Assynt area of west Highland, notably near Inchnadamph, where it forms tall, west-facing inland cliffs with block-boulder scree at their bases. Nearby, streams in small valleys have numerous base flushed slopes along their flanks, in which occurs Variegated Horsetail (*Equisetum variegatum*), spreading locally into a turf rich in Mountain Avens (*Dryas octopetala*), which also includes Lesser Clubmoss (*Selaginella selaginoides*). In similar sites further north in Sutherland, recent exploration by Dr R.E.C. Ferreira has also shown Dutch Rush (*Equisetum hyemale*) and Mackay's Horsetail (*E.* ×

trachyodon) to be present. The cliffs themselves form sites for Maidenhair and Green Spleenwort (*Asplenium trichomanes* subsp. *quadrivalens* and *A. viride*) as well Brittle Bladder-fern (*Cystopteris fragilis*). Hard Shield-fern (*Polystichum aculeatum*) and Holly Fern (*P. lonchitis*) occur amongst the grey-white stones of the screes, often with only the tips of the fronds emerging from amongst the coarse, loose boulders. Alpine Hybrid Shield-fern (*Polystichum* × *illyricum*) is also known here, and in similar habitats on these limestones, Limestone Oak-fern (*Gymnocarpium robertianum*) has also been recently discovered.

Near to Loch Kishorn, the exposures of the Durness limestone occur along the coastal fringes of a much more massively

Polystichum
lonchitis. *Wester Ross, August*

Polystichum
aculeatum *on a steep
limestone valley side,
inaccessible to grazing
animals. Wester Ross,
August*

mountainous landscape of predominantly acidic basalt-quartzites and extensive Lewisian gneiss. The surface run-off from these high and impermeable hinterland rocks forms tumbling, mountain streams which cross the limestone locally to form small, twisting, steep-sided gorges. Within the limestone gorge sites the run-off of peaty surface water down the rocky sides promotes an intimate mosaic of wet, but freely-drained, high acidity niches and of high base-status ones in particularly close proximity.

Thus ferns more widespread in western, acidic sites usually fringe the tops of the gorge sides and occur in the wetter places down its walls, whilst in the nearby fissures and on the ledges of the gorge walls, calcicolous species, including ones more characteristic of alpine cliff-ledges, grow in particular luxuriance nearly at sea-level. Most characteristic of the dripping fringes of the shoulders of the gorge walls are usually numerous plants of Hard Fern (*Blechnum spicant*), Sweet Mountain Fern (*Oreopteris limbosperma*), Lady-fern (*Athyrium filix-femina*), and Broad Buckler-fern (*Dryopteris dilatata*), sometimes with Common and Golden-scaled Male-ferns (*Dryopteris filix-mas* and *D. affinis* subsp. *borreri* or subsp. *affinis*), along with Bilberry (*Vaccinium myrtillus*) and Greater Woodrush (*Luzula sylvatica*). Common and Western Polypody (*Polypodium vulgare* and *P. interjectum*) are sometimes present in drier spots, and there may be scattered plants of Northern Buckler-fern (*Dryopteris expansa*), Hay-scented Buckler-fern (*D. aemula*), and the Filmy-ferns *Hymenophyllum wilsonii* and *H. tunbrigense* forming an intimate mosaic with numerous mosses. Further down the gorge sides, many of these species follow the courses of dripping acidic water, but where fissures and ledges are influenced by lime-rich seepage, rich enclaves of calcicoles are usually present amongst them. Such sites are often marked by the presence of cushions of Saxifrages, including especially Yellow Mountain-saxifrage (*Saxifraga aizoides*) on the gorge walls and Golden Saxifrage (*Chrysosplenium oppositifolium*) where dripping basic water falls. In the larger basic fissures, Hard Shield-fern (*Polystichum aculeatum*) is usually frequent, often forming especially large plants with the fronds of successive years hanging pendulously beneath the rhizomes against the gorge walls. In smaller basic fissures are typically numerous and luxuriant plants of Brittle Bladder-fern (*Cystopteris fragilis*), Common Maidenhair-spleenwort (*Asplenium trichomanes* subsp. *quadrivalens*), scattered Black Spleenwort (*Asplenium adiantum-nigrum*), and luxuriant clumps of Green Spleenwort (*A. viride*), in a site at the lowest altitude at which I have seen them.

In addition to the oceanic climate, the deep shade cast by the steep sides of the gorges is an additional, important factor in the occurrence of alpine species at such low altitude. The frequency of cloud-cover is also high, induced by the close presence of such large mountain masses, whilst the high humidity and abundant wet rock surfaces help ensure that the small heat input of brief periods of sunshine is usually entirely consumed in evaporation, and even on a warm day the area can seem as cool as a shaded mountain slope.

Ben Bulben Limestones of North-west Ireland

In the Ben Bulben area of the Co. Sligo–Co. Leitrim border in north-west Ireland, hard, Carboniferous limestone outcrops form abrupt, flat-topped hills only a few miles inland from the sea. Here, in one site, where a small, lush, grassy, inland limestone valley is almost surrounded by tall limestone cliffs, the phenomenon of alpine and southern elements growing closely together in Atlantic climates is graphically demonstrated by the fern genus *Polystichum*. It is the only site in which I have seen all three native species of *Polystichum* growing together: the mostly alpine Holly Fern (*Polystichum lonchitis*), the mainly northern

Hard Shield-fern (*P. aculeatum*) and the generally southern Soft Shield-fern (*P. setiferum*).

This profusion of *Polystichum* is made even more complex by the ability of these three species to apparently also form all three potential hybrid combinations under these wet, oceanic conditions. Not only do the hybrids, known from other sites between *P. lonchitis* and *P. aculeatum* (Alpine Hybrid Shield-fern, *P.* × *illyricum*) and between *P. aculeatum* and *P. setiferum* (Lowland Hybrid Shield-fern, *P.* × *bicknellii*), occur here, but there occurs too what appear to be several examples of the hybrid between *P. lonchitis* and *P. setiferum* (Atlantic Hybrid Shield-fern, *P.* × *lonchitiforme*), unique in the world, so far as I am aware, to this unusual and spectacularly beautiful western Irish site.

Polypodium Rich Southern Limestones

Epiphytic Polypodium interjectum, *with Ivy, characteristic of woodlands of our western coasts. Isle of Anglesey, March*

A somewhat analogous situation occurs in the genus *Polypodium* in certain limestone areas of Atlantic-fringe climates of probably both Britain and Ireland, where acidic and mixed habitats occur near to such limestone ones, in sites which are especially rich in *Polypodium*. Such sites occur in widely scattered locations especially in west and south Wales, south

Devon and southern and western Ireland, but has been especially studied in *North Wales on the Tournaisian rocks of the Carboniferous Limestone Series of the Isle of Anglesey*, by R.H. Roberts. Here, all three species of *Polypodium* reach particular abundance in the vicinity of the outcropping limestone. Southern Polypody (*Polypodium australe*) occurs mainly directly on the many cliff-faces within the Ash-dominated woodlands growing over the much dissected, low-lying and sheltered limestone topography. Western Polypody (*P. interjectum*) is abundant, sometimes epiphytically or capping the slightly more acidic tops of limestone boulders, its rhizomes spreading widely through rich mossy layers where some humus has accumulated. Common Polypody is somewhat less common, but appears to occur epiphytically and on adjacent lanebank walls, as well as, perhaps, in more acidic pockets on the limestone tops. Throughout the Ash woodlands which occur on the limestone, colonies of *Polypodium*, like those of *Polystichum* above, occur in a variable and dauntingly bewildering array. Excellent opportunities for hybridisation occur between each species in these mild and moist Atlantic conditions and these seem to be fully realised by the members of this genus. All three theoretically possible hybrid combinations in Polypodium do, indeed, occur: Manton's Polypody (*P. × mantoniae = P. interjectum × vulgare*), Shivas' Polypody (*P. × shivasiae = P. australe × interjectum*), and Font-Quer's Polypody (*P. × font-queri = P. australe × vulgare*).

Polypodium × shivasiae *on a limestone cliff in an ash woodland. Isle of Anglesey, March*

Of these, the rare *P.* × *shivasiae* is a particularly spectacular hybrid, which on steep, highly sheltered, cliff-face exposures, can form large, pure stands of massive arching fronds. Another interesting point is that amongst the variable populations of *P. australe* present, some have particularly sawtooth-edged pinnae, and this phenomenon occurs too in some of the local colonies of *P. interjectum*. The occurrence of a similar morphological trait such as this in both the diploid, and in the polyploid species which is known to involve the diploid in its parentage, raises the question of whether some of the colonies of *P. interjectum* might have originated locally, involving adjacent, morphologically unusual, colonies of *P. australe* in their particular parentage. I am indebted to R.H. Roberts for showing me this site, for all of these hybrid taxa, like the parent species, seem quite variable here, and it takes the systematically-applied skill and patience of an expert, like Mr Roberts, to sort and identify every species and hybrid.

The Burren and Aran Limestones of Western Ireland

The Burren area of Co. Clare and the adjacent Aran Islands in Galway Bay consist of terraces of low-altitude Carboniferous limestone strata alternating with beds of calcareous shales extensively exposed to the moist Atlantic climate of western Ireland. In both areas, soils are thin, and the white, rocky terrain of these 'lands of stone' presents extensive habitats of bare karst and deeply-fissured limestone pavement habitats to plant colonisation, under unusually mild conditions.

Amongst the many lime-loving ferns which abound in the area, especially notable here is Maidenhair Fern (*Adiantum capillus-veneris*), and the extensive occurrence of Rusty-back Fern (*Ceterach officinarum*).

Maidenhair Fern indeed occurs naturally through a number of western sites in Britain and Ireland, on or close to the winter-warming influence of the Atlantic, mostly on limestones (and sometimes where limestone tufa is actively forming). It is present on the coasts of Devon, Cornwall and south Glamorgan, in the Channel and Scilly Islands, West Cork, Clare, West and North-east Galway, Sligo and West Donegal, the Isle of Man and the south Cumbrian coast. For a species whose range in Europe is, however, otherwise Mediterranean, and which on a world-scale is essentially warm-temperate to subtropical, its widespread occurrence at high latitude in these islands (reaching to over 55°N on Ireland's north-west coast) speaks much for the extreme winter-mildness of these Atlantic fringe climates.

In the Aran Islands and Atlantic fringes of the Burren lime-stones Maidenhair Fern occurs in numerous, low-altitude pockets and deep crevices of shelly corraline limestone rock, where shade and moisture are present, and which are well-sheltered from every direction. As befits a generally Mediterranean species, the plant makes much of its growth during the very early spring months of the year, with fronds beginning to appear as early as March in most years. In the more exposed sites, plants are small and may have numerous fronds scarcely over a few centimetres in length, but in sites of greater shelter and often moisture, large plants with fronds reaching 10–15 cm or more in length may occur, sometimes penetrating deep into the gloom of large rock fissures, beneath seaward-facing rock overhangs, and hanging pendulously from the roofs of occasional caves, where it shows considerable tolerance to very low levels of illumination.

By contrast, Rusty-back Fern (*Ceterach officinarum*) is always a high-light demanding species, which therefore seldom competes for the same habitats as those occupied by Maidenhair Fern. It too is a southern species of many limestone areas in southern and western Britain and Ireland, which are not necessarily coastal. It is, however, especially extensively

Ceterach officinarum vigorously colonises wall tops in western Ireland. Co. Clare, July

developed both in natural habitats and on the tops of lime-mortared walls within and around low-altitude sites on the Burren limestones and adjacent western Ireland. Other members of its small genus are, like those of *Adiantum*, essentially warm-temperate to subtropical in range, with allied species spreading to Madeira and the Canary Islands, the foot-hills of the Himalayas and to South Africa.

Within western Ireland, and especially in sites near to the Burren, luxuriant plants and sometimes large colonies of *Ceterach officinarum* are frequently in a form which is seldom seen elsewhere. This form has somewhat crenulate margins to the already-lobed frond outline, and was recognised as distinctive by the Irish botanist R.L. Praeger and appropriately named var. *crenatum*. The distinctiveness of this plant from the normal (inland) form of the species has been largely overlooked by most botanists, but the structural differences in frond form, though small, are constant and appear to be genetically determined ones. I have the impression too, that its plants seem to be rather more vigorous and to eventually grow larger and in more massive clumps than does the typical form of this species. Plants of this western form of Rusty-back Fern grow in a variety of limestone sites, from limestone pavement fissures to limestone cliff ledges. In parts of the Burren limestone pavements, it occasionally almost forms a local turf over bare lime-stone surfaces, and may, equally extensively, cap the tops of local, lime-mortared walls.

Hebridean Machair

Machair is a habitat largely confined to the Scottish Western Isles and Orkneys, consisting of the wide, flat, fixed dune pasture of unusually calcareous sand, formed under highly wind-swept conditions, but with a mild climate temperatures.

Such habitats tend to develop wherever topographic conditions have allowed the accumulation of extensive offshore, marine sand along shallowly-shelving shorelines. In many places, accumulations of such sand occur in small sheltered bays, but the machair undoubtedly reaches its greatest development along the Atlantic-facing, western shores of the Outer Hebridean islands, including Lewis, south Harris and Barra, but is especially extensive on the western coasts of North Uist, South Uist and Benbecula, with smaller, more local patches, elsewhere.

In these islands there is a particularly gently sloping western coastal topography and a 10-fathom depth of water is not reached until 3–5 miles (5–7 km) offshore. Here, the extensive

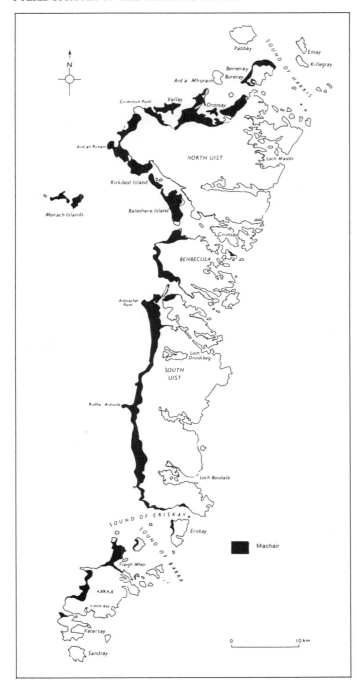

Fig. 14
*Distribution of
machair habitats
(black) in the Uists and
adjacent islands. Outer
Hebrides. (After
Ritchie, 1979)*

Machair grasslands flanked by white shell-sand strands. South Uist, Outer Hebrides. (Cambridge University Collection: copyright reserved)

and almost flat intertidal areas and mild conditions are ideal for the occurrence of large populations of calcareous-shelled, marine, bivalve molluscs, such as the Banded Wedge Shell (*Donax vittatus*) and the Thin Tellin (*Tellina tenuis*), and numerous wading birds which feed upon them. Natural, high, winter mortality rates are supplemented by the feeding of the birds, and piles of broken shells contribute to the availability of a shell supply. Continuous accumulations of dead shells exposed to the elements are pulverised by wave action, resulting in the formation of a highly calcareous shell sand. Steady onshore winds continually transport this fine material on to the exposed island shores, resulting in the accumulation of a fringe of unusually calcareous dunes backed by broad flat calcareous sand plains overlying otherwise acidic terrain.

This distinctive, often wide, gradually accreting, coastal, sand system results in terrestrial sites which have a much higher proportion of their total area fixed as mobile dune stages than other dune systems. It also differs in that the sand is usually at least 20% calcium carbonate, and sometimes as much as 80%, with a declining gradient from the shore inland, as organic matter gradually increases in the soil.

The extremely wind-planed profile of the machair, lying mostly no more than 2–5 m above sea level, ensures also an almost permanently high water table and moisture retention. In practice, several different machair landforms occur, and under the predominantly onshore winds, both depositional and erosional processes operating over a long period of time, are important. Carbon–14 dating suggests that initiation of many machair habitats probably took place in Post-glacial times, certainly before the Iron Age and probably at least 5,700 years ago. The machair development subsequently seems to have been characterised by long periods of stability, interrupted by episodes of more major environmental disturbance. These have variously extended the machair, perhaps both in landward and seaward directions, at many different times, whilst more local areas of erosion by rivers or the sea have probably usually been present.

The climate of the machair is mild, moist and often extremely windy. The summer/winter temperature range in areas such as the Uists is lower than in any other part of the British Isles, except for the Shetland Islands and possibly the Scillies; but the average windspeed is higher than anywhere else in Britain except for even more remotely outlying islands such as St Kilda. Driving sand and salt-spume laden winds from the sea are common, as is fine, driving rain. The total amounts of rain falling are not high by the normal standards of western Scotland—averaging about 50 inches (1,270 mm) or less—but it is frequent, with as many as 240 rain days a year, and potential evapotranspiration deficits are uncommon. Harsh winters are almost unknown. Snow is infrequent, and seldom lies long. Precipitation falls throughout the year, usually in the form of brief but driving light showers, interspersed with frequent short sunny spells—a year-round rapid oscillation of conditions more characteristically associated with April weather elsewhere in Britain. Indeed, most of the cloud which forms as westerly winds rise over the mountain backbones of the islands, does not form over the flat, low-lying machair, with resulting local rainfall and higher sunshine climates over these habitats quite different from those only a mile or two inland.

Botanically, the machair vegetation is not a single plant community, but an intricate mosaic of different green and turfy communities, mostly in a dense vegetational sward. Species present within it vary according to the local base status of the soil, the drainage, and the degree of disturbances by man and by grazing animals. The highest, and hence generally the best drained ground, usually lies along the coastal edge of the machair behind the dunes. Its wettest edge is usually its most

Machair turf with Equisetum × trachyodon *and* Selaginella selaginoides. Equisetum × litorale *is also present where water runs. South Harris, August*

inland one, where the machair abuts on to, and partly dams, the drainage off the surrounding inland rocky or peaty country, known locally as 'blackland'. Here, ponding of water produces frequent machair lochs, whilst in winter, many areas of the low, flat plain partly flood or are at least considerably marshy. Most of the better-drained habitats present are dominated by a *Festuca rubra* grass turf. Grazing pressure (by rabbits throughout the year, and in addition cattle in the winter, in the Uists, and by Red Deer in Rhum), in addition to the extremely windy environment, ensures that the vegetation retains a particularly low wind-profile, becoming taller only in the local shelter of hollows in the lee of occasial rocks. Thus, even in the absence of grazing, this vegetation would be unlikely to become excessively rank. Very many of the habitats are particularly floristically rich, and it is not exceptional for more than sixty species of plants to be present in the turf alone. The resulting botanical interests in such a diversity of habitats are thus considerable and fully warrant considerable conservation action to prevent its disappearance.

The pteridophytes of the machair are best considered under two different communities. The first are the low-growing pteridophytes of the machair turf itself. The second are the slightly taller ones in the wetland habitats of small brackish lochs, streams and man-made ditches on the landward side of the machair turf, where basic and acidic habitats meet.

Machair Turf Communities

The pteridophytes present in the machair turf reflect the general botanical interest in the machair vegetation as a whole. At least six species of lime-loving, low-growing pteridophytes occur widely within the dune turf, with at least two further hybrids in local sites which are subject to natural sand erosion. All are plants which can form small and sometimes minute aerial growth, which appear to be widely and sparsely scattered in the machair turf, but which, through their size, seem widely overlooked. The species to occur in dense turf are Moonwort (*Botrychium lunaria*), Common Adder's-tongue (*Ophioglossum vulgatum*) which, despite its name, is seldom common, Lesser Clubmoss (*Selaginella selaginoides*), Variegated Horsetail (*Equisetum variegatum*), Common Horsetail (*E. arvense*) and Marsh Horsetail (*E. palustre*). In sites where there is some natural erosion, the two hybrids: Mackay's Horsetail (*Equisetum × trachyodon*) and Shore Horsetail (*E. × litorale*) are present in several machair systems. It is additionally possible that the rare Lesser Adder's-tongue (*Ophioglossum azoricum*) might well also occur in machair habitats, in which it would be extremely easy for it to be overlooked.

The low-growing form of all of these species offer little resistance to wind. The presence of *Botrychium* and *Ophioglossum* shows a close link between these machair grasslands and the moist grassy hollows of more widespread calcareous links of fixed dune pasture, as well as with more inland grasslands. Plants of both genera are usually under 4 cm in height,

Selaginella
selaginoides *in
machair turf. South
Harris, July*

with *Botrychium* frequently no more than about 1.5 cm, and to find them at all can involve long searching on hands and knees! Equally difficult to find but probably widespread in machair is Lesser Clubmoss (*Selaginella selaginoides*). Its club-shaped, often slightly pinkish or yellowish-cream cone shoots stand erect, but are usually under 3 cm in height in machair turf, and often smaller. Its vegetative shoots twine closely amongst the bases of surrounding plants and grass, where they are scarcely visible without careful dissection of the turf itself, and these could readily be taken to be some rather lank moss.

For both *Botrychium*, *Ophioglossum* and *Selaginella*, their machair habitats form parts of dense turfy swards of vegetation, with the *Botrychium* and *Selaginella* most often present towards the machair's drier seaward edges and the *Ophioglossum* in moister slight hollows. For both *Botrychium* and *Ophioglossum*, the high density of turf may be advantageous in creating the appropriate root environment for its associated mycorrhizal fungi, which is dependent on other decaying vegetable matter in the soil around. Unusually, here, *Selaginella* succeeds in, and indeed appears to thrive in, a density of plant competition with which it is seldom associated in mountain habitats, and which here at least, it seems well able to tolerate.

Within the machair, Variegated Horsetail (*Equisetum variegatum*), Common Horsetail (*E. arvense*), Marsh Horsetail (*E. palustre*) and Shore Horsetail (*E.* × *litorale*) occur in local patches or as very diffuse communities, with diminutive shoots emerging from dense turf, or, in the case of Common and Shore Horsetail, with often totally prostrate shoot systems.

All of these horsetails form colonies produced by long-continued growth of their slender, creeping rhizomes, usually at depths of between 2–10 cm beneath the surface of the sand. Shoots of all the species can be freely fertile in these habitats, those of *E. variegatum* bearing especially diminutive, rounded, spine-tipped cones scarcely 2–3 mm in length on the tips of their shoots. Locally, all, and especially *E. variegatum*, also succeed in areas where communities are more open, either through recent sand deposition or especially through erosion of the turf sites, in which they were already present in diffuse form, and in such sites probably contribute greatly to stabilisation and recolonisation of the eroded habitats concerned.

Machair sites of *Botrychium*, *Ophioglossum* and *Selaginella*, are usually thought to mark areas where the turf itself has not been ploughed or otherwise disturbed. Some additional evidence of the ancientness of these communities comes additionally from *Equisetum*. For in at least two places in the machair habitats of south Harris and at one in Rhum, plants formerly thought to be *Equisetum variegatum* proved to be

extremely small specimens of Mackay's Horsetail (*E.* × *tra-chyodon*). In each of these localities no nearby colonies of parental *E. vareigatum* have been found, nor is *E. hyemale* (the other parent) known as far as I am aware, from the entire Outer Hebrides. It therefore seems probable, however, that the occurrence of *E.* × *trachyodon* marks areas of past distribution of the parental species and that once formed, the hybrid has been able to long outlast the local persistence of its parents. These pteridophyte colonies and the turf communities around them may therefore be extremely ancient indeed.

A fine colony of Equisetum × trachyodon *on a scoured, western streambank. Isle of Skye, July*

Machair Wetland Communities

Between the dry and wet edges of the machair, are a whole range of communities reflecting changing wetness of the ground, through various communities of wet pasture, marsh and fen. Sometimes the water of the lochs is brackish rather than fresh, whilst its degree of acidity is clearly influenced by the degree to which incoming acidic, peaty, run-off water from moorlands behind is neutralised by the basic properties of the sand. These lochs differ somewhat in their vegetation from one another, presumably reflecting differences in their acidity and eutrophic status. In wet pockets of machair towards the margins of open water, Marsh Horsetail (*Equisetum palustre*) may form extensive stands. In deep, soft, silty muds in shallow-water communities around the edges of the machair lochs, Marsh Horsetail becomes replaced by Water Horsetail (*Equisetum fluviatile*). It can, for amphibious plant, occur in quite deep water, with colonies sometimes extending into water 50–60 cm deep. Most colonies, however, occur in water shallower than this, often also spreading far into adjacent, shoreline, marshy communities. Its colonies are typically extensive but fairly open ones, with numerous low, reed-like unbranched shoots all of similar height and yielding by curving slightly away from the direction of each swirl of wind. Branch whorl development is usually totally suppressed in these brightly lit and windy conditions, reducing their area of resistance to the constant wind buffeting.

Sometimes too the machair lochs are partly drained by streams which cross the machair to the sea. Man has, at probably many different times in the past, attempted to further drain the small machair lochs, with ditches in various states of disrepair adding further diversity to the habitat, as well as providing sites in which new vegetational seral successions can

Dense stand of Equisetum fluviatile *at the edge of a machair loch. Isle of Lewis, late June*

occur. In these sites in the machair, *Equisetum fluviatile* and *E. palustre* both spread, in less abundant form, into fen-like Iris-dominated communities, whilst *E. arvense* can be present on better-drained hummocks or sloping banks nearby. In many of the Yellow Flag (*Iris pseudacorus*) communities, and especially those which occur either along natural streamsides crossing the machair or along man-made ditches, Shore Horsetail (*Equisetum × litorale*) occurs. This plant, the hybrid between *E. arvense* and *E. fluviatile* is particularly frequent in such sites in the machair of west Lewis, south Harris and both North and South Uist. It seems to appear very early in the seral succession, forming anew each time after initial opening of these habitats through erosion or by man. Once formed, it rapidly comes to dominate these communities, especially during their early seral stages erosion-scouring helps keep the habitats open. Where such sites eventually stabilise however this hybrid horsetail gradually succumbs to the increasing competition of other vegetation, surviving eventually only as scattered shoots in communities usually dominated by dense Yellow Flag.

Two other, rarer, horsetails may occasionally occur in these habitats: Ditch Horsetail (*Equisetum × rothmaleri*) and Hebridean Horsetail (*E. × dycei*). The thin shoots of each can look very similar to those of either *E. × litorale* or *E. fluviatile* or *E. palustre* in these habitats, and their presence, where they are perhaps more frequent than in any other site in our islands, is probably often overlooked.

Iris-rich lough margin community with at least three hybrid horsetails: Equisetum × litorale, E. × dycei *and* E. × rothmaleri. *Co. Sligo, July*

Horsetail Flushes, Ditches and Stream Margins

Beyond the machair areas, wetland habitats of these types in our Atlantic fringe climates are, in suitable sites, ones which may be exceptionally rich in populations of horsetails. Such habitats occur mostly at relatively low altitude and often within only a few miles of the sea, with varyingly rich, usually diverse and sometimes spectacular concentrations of horsetail species and hybrids occurring in several of the Scottish western Isles (especially Skye, Rhum, Lewis, Harris, Benbecula and the Uists) and in several parts of western Ireland. In a few of these sites, all eight native species of the genus may grow close together, or there may be a complex mixture of locally-formed hybrids, themselves of variable appearance, occurring profusely in a wide range of habitats with or without their parents, forming a sometimes bewildering array.

The sites which are richest in horsetails are always those where edaphic chemical conditions offer an appropriate combination of lime-rich habitats combined with an adequate supply of available silica in the substrate. It is of interest in relation to the edaphic aspects of their sites that the two evergreen species of horsetail (of subgenus *Hippochaete*) — *Equisetum variegatum* and *E. hyemale* (as well as their hybrid *E.* × *trachyodon*) — seem more often to succeed, in these Atlantic climates, in lime-flushed sites in which the available silica source is a quartzose one, while those of the deciduous-stemmed species (subgenus *Equisetum*) and their hybrids are usually most characteristic of lime-flushed sites in which the silica source is more often one of complex hydrated alumino-silicates in the form of shales and clays. Within such edaphically suitable locations, the concentration of horsetails appears to be a function largely of the unusual climatic conditions of the Atlantic fringe, which seems to be not so much the lack of extremes of temperature, as all of the species are adequately hardy elsewhere. But under conditions of mild winters and cool summers coupled with frequent light rain and almost permanently moist substrates, horsetails which elsewhere are of somewhat different climatic and edaphic persuasions appear to find the habitats almost equally environmentally suitable, and their habitat differences become minimised.

Perhaps the best indicator of sites in our Atlantic fringe most likely to be rich in horsetails is the prolific presence of Great Horsetail (*Equisetum telmateia*), which usually extensively colonises the sites of the most actively seeping lime-rich water, where adequate silica sources are available in the form of heavy clay substrates. In the progressively drier sites around it are likely to be found Wood Horsetail (*E. sylvaticum*), Shade

Horsetail (*E. pratense*) and Common Horsetail (*E. arvense*), and in wetter and more generally deoxygenated ones are typically Marsh Horsetail (*E. palustre*) and Water Horsetail (*E. fluviatile*), the former where the water begins to become more stagnant, the latter where it becomes even more so and may also be deep. Additionally, Dutch Rush (*E. hyemale*) may be present where there is actively running seepage, perhaps in more sandy sites, and Variegated Horsetail in lime-flushed sandy streamside gravels.

Equisetum × litorale in a typical Iris-marsh shoreline community. Kirkudbrightshire, late June

Undoubtedly the most common hybrid throughout our western Atlantic fringe localities in both Britain and especially Ireland is Shore Horsetail (*Equisetum × litorale*), the hybrid between *E. arvense* and *E. fluviatile*. Its most typical habitats in western Scotland are in marshes and flushes of all types, including man-made drainage channels and roadside ditches—often ones in which, like its machair habitat a species-rich Iris and Juncus vegetation is also established. In Ireland *E. × litorale* also occurs widely on the shores of small ponds and of relatively calcareous lochs.

Also widely occurring in very similar habitats and sites in Atlantic climates to those occupied by *E. × litorale*, are Ditch Horsetail (*E. × rothmaleri*), the hybrid between *E. arvense* and *E. palustre*, and Hebridean Horsetail (*E. × dycei*), the hybrid

Roadside ditches and adjacent flushes marsh vegetation rich in Equisetum × rothmaleri. Trotternish, Isle of Skye, June

between *E. fluviatile* and *E. palustre*. Both are known in several scattered sites through the western Isles of Scotland and western Ireland, chiefly in marsh, Iris-flush, lakeshore or ditch habitats, with or without their parents, and each varying greatly in form and abundance. When in dense Iris-flush or marshy ditch vegetation, both are extremely easy to overlook.

Much more local, although remarkably spectacular are the relatively large plants of Bowman's Horsetail (*E. × bowmanii*), the hybrid between *E. telmateia* and *E. sylvaticum*, and Skye Horsetail (*E. × font-queri*), the hybrid between *E. palustre* and *E. telmateia*. Bowman's Horsetail is the most geographically outlying of these, known only from a single climatically mild site in the New Forest of Hampshire, where it occupies damp, disturbed, low roadside banks. Skye Horsetail is probably the most vigorous of all our horsetail hybrids, occurring in its Skye locality throughout an enormous range of habitats from roadside banks and ditches to almost all aspects of adjacent moorlands, through ridges, valley sides, flushes, marshes and streambanks, occupying virtually all habitats which are intermediate between those of its parents. Experience suggests that, despite their size and distinctive appearance, both *E. × bowmanii* and *E. × font-queri* are also easily generally overlooked. *E. × bowmanii* was found, for example, only very recently, thanks to the sharp eyes of a local botanist, R.P. Bowman (Page, 1988). *Equisetum × font-queri* was also unknown in these islands until the mid-1960s (Page, 1972) where it is the dominant plant over about two square miles of one of the best botanised parts of the Isle of Skye.

In extreme western, Atlantic fringe climates, mainly in riverside gravels, Mackay's Horsetail (*E.* × *trachyodon*), the hybrid between *E. hyemale* and *E. variegatum*, may also be present, and like Moore's Horsetail in south-eastern Ireland, seems to have a very high potential for vegetative fragmentation and establishment of new streamside colonies through establishment of natural stem cuttings. Lastly Milde' Horsetail (*E.* × *mildeanum*), the hybrid between *E. pratense* and *E. sylvaticum*, is known from central Scotland (Page, 1988), but is also very probably present in wet flushes in parts of Skye as well.

The distinctive fat cones of Equisetum × font-queri. *Trotternish, Isle of Skye, late June*

Luxuriant stands of Equisetum × font- queri *flank the base- flushed banks of a trickling burn. Trotternish, Isle of Skye, late July*

Water Margin *Osmunda* Habitats

Royal Fern (*Osmunda regalis*) is a slow-growing, markedly calcifuge fern, which occurs locally along the margins of both standing and flowing water. It is more abundant in sites with mild, wet, western climates near to the Atlantic fringe of our islands than in any other region. It thrives in predominantly wet, peaty conditions, especially where there is some movement of water in the soil. It is mainly confined to within about 100 ft (ca. 30 m) of sea level, although scattered individuals may occur much higher than this. Near to western coasts, plants seem highly tolerant of salt-laden air. Under conditions of mild climate and high rainfall, it thrives in a variety of water margin sites, especially where there is both some shelter and good protection from grazing. It is present locally around the stony, peat-fringed margins of many western Highland Scottish moorland lochs at low altitude, and more occasionally along the small streams feeding to or from them through a myriad of sheltered streamlets and rills incised often deeply into the surrounding peat. Such sites are usually the least accessible to grazing animals, and for this reason *Osmunda* is often also amongst the vegetation of small isolated islands within low-altitude moorland lochs. In western Ireland it is especially frequent in districts such as south-west Kerry, where extensive peat accumulations occur near to western shores. Here, it spreads extensively around the margins of valley bogs, where there is considerable seepage of peaty water, and frequent plants also colonise many lake shore margins,

Lake margin community of massive, old clumps of Osmunda regalis. *Co. Kerry, July*

Fern-rich western habitats, with many small Spleenworts on the bridge mortar and luxuriant Osmunda regalis, *fringing an Atlantic stream. Co. Kerry, July*

streambanks and the shoulders of many roadside ditches. In south-west England, it occurs as occasional, but sometimes locally extensive, stands, in several sheltered valleys along fast-flowing streamcourse margins of some of the larger rivers, such as the Dart, draining from the acidic, peaty uplands of the larger, granitic moorland areas.

In its western Irish and south-west English sites in particular, plants may reach impressive size, with fronds growing to around head height, or more. Such plants typically have also massive rhizome clumps, sometimes a metre or more in diameter, although others are known, historically, which are reported to have been over two metres across, eventually forming hollow centres within big, circular clumps of fronds. Such large clumps are probably very ancient indeed, and this impressive plant would certainly seem to rank amongst the longest lived of our native ferns.

Western, Low-lying, Wet, Acid, Woodlands

Acidic woodlands which are soft, wet and boggy underfoot, have probably long been characteristic of very many, rather poorly-drained, low-lying, valley bottom sites within the original wildwood of Britain and Ireland. Typically dominated by a low, thin, Birch–Alder tree canopy, with a dense ground layer beneath composed mainly of soft cushions of sodden bog-mosses and emergent rushes and ferns, their forest floors have permanently high, scarcely flowing, water tables, which are usually strongly acidic and low in available bases. Fragments of such woodland are widely scattered over Britain and Ireland, especially in regions of high rainfall. Many typically occur where the course of slow-flowing streams is obstructed by the growth of peat-bogs spreads across broad, flat, lowland valleys, developed over fans of glacial gravels or former stream alluvium. Others occur along low-lying lake margins or from the typical 'lagg' vegetation associated with the margins of raised bogs.

Low-lying woodland of this general type is, of course, highly susceptible to drainage, and such woodlands have probably greatly diminished almost throughout these islands since the Middle Ages. Their rate of loss, however, seems to have increased during the last century or so, suffering particularly from the implementation of widespread drainage activities, for their conversion to forest plantations or to agriculture. Some of the pteridologically most interesting still survive, however, especially in the high-rainfall Atlantic fringes of the British Isles.

Woodlands of these types are characteristically dominated by Birch (*Betula pubescens*) and Alder (*Alnus glutinosa*), the latter usually marking the wettest areas. Various Sallows (*Salix* spp.) and sometimes Alder Buckthorn (*Frangula alnus*) may be present, and shrubby masses of Bog Myrtle (*Myrica gale*) some-times mark the edges of narrow, clear-water, slow-flowing stream channels. Numerous species of *Sphagnum* are usually present, forming a hummocky mosiac, including *Sphagnum recurvum*, *S. palustre*, *S. subnitens* and *S. squarrosus*, usually with scattered dense hummocks of *Polytrichum commune*. Other mosses occasionally present include *Dicranum majus*, *Mnium hornum* and *Thuidium tamariscinum*, whilst clumps of rushes, usually Soft Rush (*Juncus effusus*) are frequent. Because of their

Dryopteris carthusiana *in fen carr vegetation.* Kirkudbrightshire, June

Enclaves of wet woodland occasionally still also occur away from the extremes of the Atlantic fringe, mostly on low-lying land around lake-margins. West Gloucestershire, late May

location, the damp interiors of such woodlands are usually also sheltered ones, and a high, permanent humidity exists. Such habitats seem largely avoided by grazing animals, preferring drier, firmer ground, and under these conditions the interiors of such woodlands are usually particularly rich in ferns.

Confined to better drained sites, which are principally around the boles of trees and amongst dense, loose moss growths on fallen, rotting trunks, are usually numerous and often large, old plants of Broad Buckler-fern (*Dryopteris dilatata*), often accompanied by more scattered plants of Hard Fern (*Blechnum spicant*). In somewhat wetter ground, but still usually within slightly better-drained hummocks, often those of larger *Sphangum* or *Polytrichum*, are occasional plants of Lady Fern (*Athyrium filix-femina*), and, especially in more northern localities of England and Scotland, usually much more frequent specimens of Northern Buckler-fern (*Dryopteris expansa*). Most abundant of all, however, are usually specimens of Narrow Buckler-fern (*Dryopteris carthusiana*),

*Dryopteris ×
ambrosiae.
Westmorland, July*

confined chiefly to the damper hollows of the hummocky topography, and usually distinguishable from the other species of *Dryopteris*, by their rather pale-coloured, narrow, much more upright fronds, with their shiny, very pale brown scales giving their crown buds, half-buried amongst the *Sphagnum* carpet, a distinctly glassy appearance when exposed.

It is not, however, merely the species of *Dryopteris*, and their often unusual abundance, that add pteridological interest and diversity to these sites, for the three species of Buckler-ferns are able to (and often do) hybridise with each other in one, two or three combinations, with different frequencies, different ecologies and different degrees of vigour, and, indeed, what often appear to be substantially more than three crosses sometimes seem to be present!

The ability of such dense communities of closely inter-related fern species to closely co-exist in such numbers seems to arise from the exploitation and constant recolonisation by each of the edaphically distinct spots within the hummocky mosaic of the forest floor. The same seems true generally for at least two of the resultant hybrids. Preliminary observations on sites in western Scotland suggest that in the close competition arising, the hybrids generally appear to occupy those niches which are intermediate edaphically between those of the parents. As the sequence of parental preference for differing moisture conditions seems to generally run *D. dilatata, D.*

expansa, D. carthusiana in order of increasing wetness, the hybrids of *D. dilatata* × *D. expansa* (*D.* × *ambroseae*) and *D. expansa* × *D. carthusiana* (*D.* × *sarvelae*) might well be expected not to essentially interfere with the ecology of those of any of the species. In practice, neither of these two crosses seems to be an excessively vigorous hybrid, and such an ecology seems, indeed, to be generally the case, with the hybrids co-existing and perhaps long-persisting generally alongside or near to their original parents and geographically within the over-lapping portions of the range of all of them, particularly in the wetter climates of the west of Scotland. The third hybrid, however, which theoretically could and does form, that of *D. dilatata* × *D. carthusiana* (*D.* × *deweveri*), is theoretically likely to be close in its ecological preference to the species of the intermediate sites, *D. expansa*. Where the two are present, some close ecological overlap and perhaps displacement might well be expected. In practice, *D.* × *deweveri* seems to be a fairly vigorous hybrid, and such competition with *D. expansa* might well be the case, were this hybrid to form in the same habitats. Perhaps it is partly in consequence of this that *D. expansa* has an unusually narrowly geographic range in wet, lowland habitats in Britain and Ireland, exclusively in the high-rainfall, northern oceanic fringe of these islands, from the English Lake District northward around western Scotland and perhaps through western Ireland, whilst *D.* × *deweveri* occurs most extensively in many wet, lowland habitats elsewhere in England and Wales, where *D. expansa* is absent.

Two other species of ferns are much rarer in these woodland sites, and are very largely confined to marginal habitats, where the ground rises higher above the water table or to the vicinity of soil pockets amongst outcropping boulders. These are the Common and Golden-scaled Male-ferns (*Dryopteris filix-mas* and *D. affinis* subsp. *affinis*). Of further pteridological interest is that in areas where these species occur in adjacent habitats, the possibility of yet further hybridisation exists, and indeed the rather similar-looking hybrids *D. carthusiana* × *D. filix-mas* (*D.* × *brathaica*) and *D. affinis* subsp. *affinis* × *D. expansa* (*D.* × *remota*) are known. The former has been described from damp woodland in the vicinity of Lake Windermere in the English Lake District, and the latter from the shore of Loch Lomond and in at least two localities in western Ireland. *Dryopteris* × *remota* is of particular interest in that it inherits in part the apogamous life-cycle of its *D. affinis* subsp. *affinis* parent, and is therefore itself potentially able to reproduce further by spores, once initially formed.

In addition to the hybrids outlined above, the possibility of other hybrids arising with other combinations of parents in or around these rather under-explored and very fern-rich habitats cannot be ruled out. For example, in many areas of western Scotland, such habitats occur near to ones in which Hay-scented Buckler-ferns (*Dryopteris aemula*) can occur with some abundance, and plants of intermediate appearance between it and some of the other Buckler-ferns (especially, perhaps, *D. expansa*), but of as yet unproven identity, appear to occasionally occur.

Western Oak and Oak–Birch Woodlands and Ravines

Western Oak and Oak-Birch woodlands, on the Atlantic periphery of these islands, are often the habitats of uniquely 'western' assemblages of ferns and fern allies, some of which are typical and largely confined to this habitat and which can grow in considerable luxuriance. Such woodlands, typically dominated by Sessile (Durmast) Oak (*Quercus petraea*), often with a small admixture of other broadleaves, including patches of Birch (*Betula pubescens*), enclose especially fern-rich habitats either where they occur over steep, rocky, usually north-facing slopes, or where they clad narrow stream ravines.

In both of these habitats, ground conditions of enhanced local moisture, shade, shelter and humidity usually prevail, whilst the sites are also ones to which larger grazing mammals have a very restricted access. In such sites, ferns may consequently grow in luxurious profusion, not only in terms of species diversity, but also in terms of numbers of individuals and the undamaged health of each.

By contrast, flatter oak woodland sites, especially when they occur on deeper soils, may also have once contained many of the same fern species (which can be shown to return in grazing exclusion experiments). But almost wherever their understorey layer is accessible to grazing animals, the pteridophyte diversity is normally exterminated, to be replaced by widespread Bracken (*Pteridium aquilinum*).

Oakwood Slopes

Shaded, north-facing, oakwood, rocky-boulder, steep slopes rising from southern seaward, shorelines of sea lochs, are a feature of the landscape of the fjord-like indented coastline of many parts of the extreme western Highlands of Scotland, on the mainland from Kintyre to Wester Ross and on some of the more sheltered inner western Scottish islands, notably on

Arran and Jura. Many mark the cliffed shorelines between raised beaches.

Their boulder-strewn, steep terrain, often with slippery rock faces and crevasse-strewn boulders hidden entirely by thick moss blankets, provide their own natural deterrent to grazing through the sheer insubstantiality of their footholds to wary browsers. Clumps of terrestrial woodland ferns are also abundant, but where the moss blankets are at their most luxuriant, the ferns are usually restricted to luxuriant cappings to the tops of each of the boulders and to occasional epiphytic growth on fallen wood.

Such fern communities are typically composed entirely of shade-tolerant Buckler-ferns, often with intimate admixtures of Broad Buckler-fern (*Dryopteris dilatata*), Northern Buckler-fern (*D. expansa*) and Hay-scented Buckler-fern (*D. aemula*), of which the latter is especially typical and very often by far the most abundant and luxuriant. It seldom occurs in such communities far inland of extreme western coasts, in habitats more or less directly influenced by the winter-ameliorating warmth of the Atlantic Gulf Stream. Most of its habitats consequently occur within about 100 ft (ca. 30 m) of sea-level, only occasionally ascending higher, such as in Ireland, where scattered plants reach exceptional heights of 1,430 ft (440 m) in Co. Down and 2,100 ft (640 m) in Co. Kerry.

Each season, the fronds of *Dryopteris aemula* unroll only slowly, with an initial flush followed usually by several further fronds unfurling in a steady succession throughout the summer season. Most fronds mature by autumn, and stand overwinter until about May of the following year. One of the main factors confining the plant to highly oceanic areas is probably the requirement for permanently moist and summer-cool conditions combined with adequate winter-warmth and the long duration of the growing season required for the slow-growing wintergreen fronds to fully harden. Along these moist, cool Atlantic habitats of the western fringe of our islands, it finds its exacting growing conditions to be met in a similar manner to its similarly luxuriant growth in the even more oceanic climate of its headquarters in the Azores archipelago. Indeed, I suspect that it may very well be that *Dryopteris aemula* is a direct Atlantic-coast survivor from the long extinct preglacial Tertiary evergreen forest flora, which was spread much more widely over southern Europe during the Miocene.

Oakwood Stream Ravines

Stream ravines in western oak woodlands are necessarily

Western streamside woodland rich in Athyrium *and* Hymenophyllum *Dartmoor, South Devon, August*

Hymenophyllum wilsonii *covering wet boulder surfaces. Merionethshire, September*

mainly a feature of Atlantic sites where rapid run-off of substantial torrents of water result from an immediate hinterland of considerable relief. Western oak woodland habitats such as these are thus scattered intermittently from the higher areas of Devon, Cornwall and the south-west of Ireland to the western Highlands of Scotland. Such higher relief usually owes its origins to its geological constitution of older, harder, sedimentary or metamorphic rocks. In many cases, these hard rocks are of extensively acidic types, such as the granites of Dartmoor and

Boulders thick with carpets of Hymenophyllum wilsonii *flank the spray-zone of a waterfall in a western woodland. Merionethshire, September*

the granites and gneisses of the north-west Scottish Highlands, and in these areas, predominantly or exclusively acid-loving species may exist over large areas of terrain and thus throughout such ravines. In other regions, such as in several parts of West Argyll, where metamorphic rocks largely composed of highly-foliated mica schists occur very extensively, numerous, thin, basic layers are regularly exposed along such ravine sides. In many other areas, including south-west and north-east Ireland, North Wales and the English Lake District, rocks of a wide mixture of origins and types are exposed in such valleys and glens, and the resulting pteridophyte flora is especially diverse.

The high, adjacent, upland topography helps ensure that these regions are ones where the valley sides have often been enlarged and deepened by considerable erosive forces of rushing torrents, often creating many abrupt valley sides, with rock-strewn watercourses, numerous plunging waterfalls, and often with many small side stream valleys hurling their watercourses directly into larger ones. Undercut rock faces may flank the steep outsides of bends, small stream-scoured shallow gravel fans frequently flank their inner curves, and fallen, semi-rotten trunks of trees may straddle streams where winter storms have lodged them. In the cool, turbulent air above the plunging torrents, shelter, shade and a cool humidity are high, and are probably all important factors not just for the levels which they achieve, but also for their constancy within these ravine environments. From all the wet rock faces, local dissolution rates of available bases are likely to be especially enhanced, resulting in the close and frequent juxtaposition of acid and base-loving plant species. The erosive action of surface run-off may be pteridologically important, available for fern colonisation, but also for re-exhuming and re-distributing any existing accumulations of old but still viable pteridophyte spore-reserves that may be stored within the ground.

These aspects of the environment of such wooded, steep ravines are reflected closely in the vegetational dominance which pteridophytes usually achieve, as well as in the size and sheer luxuriance of most individuals present.

Such ravines are flanked above by woodland communities which are themselves already inherently pteridophyte-rich, but which, so often, carry little but dense stands of Bracken (*Pteridium aquilinum*), the result of constant intensive grazing by larger herbivores, especially sheep. This community is maintained so long as the grazing pressure continues, and is typical of so many such communities, especially in west Wales and western Scotland. Such Bracken communities then persist if the canopy is thinned or removed, especially in the absence of tree regeneration caused by the same grazing regimes. In one such area of the Killarney oakwoods of Co. Kerry, for example, extensive stands of Bracken dominate the floor beneath large, old trees, with little sign of other fern species or of much tree

Dryopteris aemula is almost always found on steep slopes in western woodlands. Dorset, July

regeneration. In an adjacent, now well-established, fenced grazing exclusion experiment, abundant tree regeneration is accompanied not only by abundant upgrowth of herbs, but most notably by reduction in vigour and thinning of the canopy of Bracken. In the moister and more shaded conditions this results in the re-establishment of many of the former forest understorey fern species, including especially Hard Fern (*Blechnum spicant*), Lady Fern (*Athyrium filix-femina*), Male-fern (*Dryopteris filix-mas*), Hay-scented Buckler-fern (*D. aemula*), Broad Buckler-fern (*D. dilatata*) and possibly sporelings of Northern Buckler-fern (*D. expansa*). Elsewhere, in the grazed parts of such woodlands, most of these ferns, plus others, become luxuriant only in the relatively inaccessible ravines.

Along the upper edges of ravines, dense fringes of Greater Woodrush (*Luzula sylvatica*) and clumps of Bilberry (*Vaccinium myrtillus*) frequently mark the lines of the steeper shoulders, where there is abundant surface run-off and lateral movement of acidic surface water. Along such fringes, marking the beginning of the habitats inaccessible to grazing animals, Broad Buckler-fern (*Dryopteris dilatata*) frequently predominates, with Hard Fern (*Blechnum spicant*), Lady-fern (*Athyrium filix-femina*) and Sweet Mountain Fern (*Oreopteris limbosperma*) also often present where dripping water flows, the fronds of the latter often standing with pale yellow and sometimes totally white blades, persisting well into November. In addition to the lemon fragrance of its fronds, *Oreopteris* is easily recognised in early spring when its fronds are expanding, by the silver-white colour of its scales, and by the peculiar habit of its pinnae expanding outwards sideways, before the still-curled crozier has yet fully exposed them. In western sites at low altitude, plants of Hay-scented Buckler-fern (*Dryopteris aemula*) may sometimes also colonise the tops and fringes of ravines, often with *Blechnum spicant*, and there may also be small plants of Northern Buckler-fern (*D. expansa*), and these two species of the genus *Dryopteris* often predominate in the rockiest situations.

Below the valley crests, the main aspects of the valley slopes are usually composed of numerous hummocky ledges separated by steeper, more regular slopes and sheer rock faces. The whole habitat is strongly influenced by the varying degrees of stability and by the surface (frequently acidic) run-off or by locally emerging (sometimes basic) water seepage.

Drier, outcropping rocky bluffs, may interrupt the pattern and the spatial distribution of pteridophytes species, and on various rocky knolls, Common Male Fern (*D. filix-mas*) and various subspecies of Golden-scaled Male-fern may occur, especially *Dryopteris affinis* subsp. *borreri* and *D. affinis* subsp. *affinis*. Frequently, spreading masses of Common Polypody (*Polypodium vulgare*) and Western Polypody (*P. interjectum*) cap the tops of scattered, drier, outcropping boulders and spread in mossy layers on to the bases of the trunks of rough-barked trees. Here, all species of *Polypodium*, occasionally accompanied by scattered specimens of Broad Buckler-fern (*Dryopteris dilatata*) in moister niches where humus collects, clad the upper aspects of leaning trunks of oaks, overhanging cool, tumbling watercourses far below.

On steeper parts of the banks, where ledges and knolls are usually damper and irrigated by dripping or emergent acidic water, plants of Lady-fern (*Athyrium filix-femina*) and Hard Fern (*Blechnum spicant*) may co-dominate, or *Blechnum*, accompanied by *Luzula*, may be confined to the ledge margins. On other acidic ledges, Lady-fern (*Athyrium filix-femina*), Broad Buckler-fern (*Dryopteris dilatata*) or Hay-scented Buckler-fern (*D. aemula*) may largely or entirely replace *Blechnum*, or there may be a mixture of some or all of these species, often with more scattered specimens of Northern Buckler-fern (*D. expansa*) and Sweet Mountain Fern (*Oreop-*

teris limbosperma). Where cushions of moss are frequent, filmy ferns may also begin to appear.

Plants of Hard Fern (*Blechnum spicant*) may continue to dominate on most of the steeper slopes, where these are moist and acidic. By contrast, where base-rich rocks form a component of the geology are exposed below the valley crests, Hart's Tongue (*Phyllitis scolopendrium*) and Soft Shield-fern (*Polystichum setiferum*) may be present as scattered plants. Usually restricted to only the steepest of slopes and, like *Blechnum*, often in a hanging position, Hard Shield-fern (*Polystichum aculeatum*) frequently marks locations where some of the most base-rich moisture seepage emerges, with previous year's fronds slowly turning brown but not always decaying, so that in such hanging specimens, they sometimes accumulate annually for many years, suspended beneath the living plant in eventually dense, chaffy masses. In these sites in northern districts, Maidenhair Spleenwort (*Asplenium trichomanes* subsp. *quadrivalens*), and Green Spleenwort (*A. viride*) often grow. In the most shaded and humid sites, Brittle Bladder-fern (*Cystopteris fragilis*), sometimes forms luxuriant curtains. These ferns are usually confined to sites where there are direct

Filmy-fern rich streambank habitats of Trichomanes speciosum. *Co. Kerry, July*

mineral exposures of base-rich rock, and the latter to sites where this is well shaded and permanently moist.

Along shaded soil banks, usually deep within ravines, scattered plants of Common Male-fern and Sweet Mountain Fern usually occur. Woodland Oak-fern (*Gymnocarpium dryopteris*) and Beech Fern (*Phegopteris connectilis*) sometimes form large colonies on deep, moist, well-drained soil slopes of fine, downwash alluvium to ravine bases and above larger outcropping shoulders, while Wood Horsetail (*Equisetum sylvaticum*) may grow on steep, well-irrigated, banks. Common Male-fern (*Dryopteris filix-mas*) and Golden-scaled Male-fern (*D. affinis* subsp. *borreri*) may be frequent along lower banks retained by larger, fixed boulders, as may fine specimens of Woodland Lady-fern (*Athyrium filix-femina*), or, in appropriately more basic soils, Soft Shield-fern (*Polystichum setiferum*), Hart's Tongue (*Phyllitis scolopendrium*) and Robust Golden-scaled Male-fern (*D. affinis* subsp. *robusta*). Lady-fern frequently occurs in more stable boulder-pockets along the water margins, sometimes in sites which become briefly inundated during winter months, where it is usually the most abundant waterside fern. Royal Fern (*Osmunda regalis*) may occur in wet, acidic, peaty pockets near to running water, where it may occasionally reach nearly 2 m in height.

In the bases of ravines, outcropping boulders may be abundant, and fallen, semi-rotten trunks of trees may straddle

The largest of our native filmy ferns. Trichomanes speciosum. *Cornwall, June*

streams where winter storms have lodged them. Undercut rock faces occur frequently, especially on the outer aspects of bends. Along tumbling river courses, scattered and often large and old plants of Hay-scented and Broad Buckler-fern often persist in local acidic pockets on the tops of mossy boulders, and on the tops of semi-rotten fallen logs, Wilson's and Tunbridge Filmy Ferns (*Hymenophyllum wilsonii* and *H. tunbrigense*) may occur in abundance on the sides of boulders, especially in cool, moist, shaded sites in the vicinity of waterfalls, and, less commonly also grow epiphytically on the bases of nearby trees. In almost all such habitats, these filmy ferns grow typically embedded within spongy cushions of luxuriant mosses. In rare and widely scattered, sheltered, moist and deeply shaded ravines, stands of the extremely beautiful and delicate Killarney Fern (*Trichomanes speciosum*) may cling to the sides of steep, rocky gorges, spreading by long, dark, scale-clad rhizomes along rocky fissures, always close to moving water. In one native site, its firmly rigid yet thin and pellucidly delicate fronds may exceed 14 inches (over 35 cm) in length.

As in more inland ravines, it seems likely that the occurrence of large colonies of many of these pteridophytes, but especially of Woodland Oak-fern, Beech Fern, Wood Horsetail, and all of the filmy ferns, along with many of their associated species, probably indicate sites with a long history of little disturbance, and often of especially ancient woodland.

One cannot help but be impressed by the sheer luxuriance and verdure here of our native ferns, and the ecological dominance which they can retain under such optimal conditions for growth. In their undisturbed state, the absence of grazing through the steepness of ravine sides, and under the mild and equable climate of the Atlantic fringe of our islands, the fern communities of these habitats are, without doubt, some of the most diverse and pteridologically fascinating within probably the whole of western Europe. The population dynamics of the communities and the habitats as a whole, however, of micro-successions and species replacements with time, on both larger and smaller scales, seems, in all probability, to be an extremely complex one, upon the detailed ecological aspects of which, studies have, as yet, scarcely begun.

Sat squarely upon a smooth-washed stone, one cannot but help reflect on the grandeur of such habitats, with the immense erosive forces of fast-moving water, reverberating between cliff-faces, hung with the delicate tracery of fern fronds waving slightly in the passing, cool air. We admire a situation – a geology, a landscape, and a natural history—which has probably changed but little in many a million year.

Bibliography

For further details on the taxonomic aspects of the native Pteridophyta the reader should refer to Page, 1982.

Adam, P., Birks, H. J. B. & Huntley, B. (1977). Plant communities of the Island of Arran, Scotland. *New Phytol.* 79: 689–712.

Allen, D. E. (1969). *The Victorian Fern Craze.* Hutchinson, London.

Allen, D. E. (1978). *The Naturalist in Britain. A Social History.* Penguin Books, London.

Allen, D. E. (1987). Changing attitudes to nature conservation: the botanical perspective. *Biol. J. Linn. Soc.* 32: 203–212.

Anderson, F. W. & Dunham, K. C. (1966). *The Geology of Northern Skye.* Memoirs of the Geological Surv. Great Britain.

Anderson, M. C. (1964). Studies of the woodland light climate. II. Seasonal variation in the light climate. *J. Ecol.* 52: 643–663.

Anderson, R., Bridges, P. W., Leeder, M. R. & Sellwood, B. W. (1979). *A Dynamic Stratigraphy of the British Isles.* Allen & Unwin, London.

Angus, I. S. (1979). The macrofauna of intertidal sands in the Outer Hebrides. *Proc. Roy. Soc. Edinb.* 77: 155–171.

Antonovics, J., Bradshaw, A. D. & Turner, R. G. (1971). Heavy metal tolerance in plants. *Adv. Ecol. Res.* 7. 1–85.

Applebaum, S. (1972). *Roman Britain.* In Finberg, H. P. R. (ed.) *Agrarian History of England and Wales. I. AD 43–1042.* Cambridge University Press.

Arber, M. A. (1940). The coastal landscape of south-east Devon. *Proc. Geol. Assoc.* 51: 257–271.

Arkell, W. J. (1933). *The Jurassic System in Great Britain.* University Press, Oxford.

Arnwell, D. S. (1960). Newborough Warren, Anglesey. III. Changes in the vegetation in parts of the dune system after loss of rabbits by myxomatosis. *J. Ecol.* 48: 355–395.

Bailey, B. (1982). *The Industrial Heritage of Britain.* Ebury Press, London.

Balchin, W. G. V. (1983). *The Cornish Landscape.* Hodder & Stoughton, London.

Balme, D. E. (1953). Edaphic and vegetational zoning on the Carboniferous limestone in the Derbyshire Dales. *J. Ecol.* 41: 331–344.

Barber, A. J., Beach A., Park R. G., Tarney, J. & Stewart, A. D. (1978). The Lewisian and Torridonian Rocks of North-West Scotland. Geologists Association Guide No 21, London.

Bazeley, M. L. (1921). The extent of the English forest in the thirteenth century. *Trans. Roy. Hist. Soc., 4th Ser.* 7: 140–172.

Bell, B. R. & Harris, J. W. (1986). An Excursion Guide to the Geology of the Isle of Skye. Geological Society of Glasgow.

Bell, P. R. (1985). Introduction: The essential role of the Pteridophyta in the study of land plants. *Proc. Roy. Soc. Edinb.* 86B: 1–4.

Benedict, R. C. (1941). The Gold Rush: a fern ally. *Am. Fern. Journ.* 31: 127–130.

Berry, R. J. (1979). The Outer Hebrides: where genes and geography meet. *Proc. Roy. Soc. Edinb.* 77B: 21–43.

Berry, R. J. & Johnston, J. L. (1980). *The Natural History of Shetland.* Collins New Naturalist, London.

Bick, D. (1980). *The Old Industries of Dean.* Pound House, Newent.

Bick, D. (1982). *The Old Copper Mines of Snowdonia.* Pound House, Newent.

Bilham, E. G. (1934). The sea-breeze as a climatic factor. *J. State Med., London* 42: 40.

Bilham, E. G. (1938). *The Climate of the British Isles.* Macmillan, London.

Birks, H. H. (1975). Studies in the vegetational history of Scotland. IV Pine stumps in Scottish blanket seats. *Phil. Trans. Roy. Soc. Lond.* B270: 181–226.

Birks, H. J. B. (1973). *Past and Present Vegetation of the Island of Skye.* Cambridge University Press.

Birks, H. J. B. (1976). The distribution of European pteridophytes: a numerical analysis. *New Phytol.* 77: 257–287.

Birks, H. J. B. & Birks, H. H. (1974). Studies on the bryophyte flora and vegetation of the Isle of Skye. I. Flora. *J. Bryol.* 8: 19–64, 197–254.

Birks, H. J. B. & Birks, H. H. (1980). *Quaternary Palaeoecology.* Edward Arnold, London.

Birks, H. J. B., Deacon J. & Peglar, S. (1975). Pollen maps for the British Isles 5,000 years ago. *Proc. Roy. Soc. Lond. ser. B* 189: 87–105.

Birse, E. C. (1982). Plant communities on serpentine in Scotland. *Vegetatio* 49(3): 141–162.

Blunden, J. (1975). *The Mineral Resources of Britain. A Study in Exploitation and Planning.* Hutchinson, London.

Bolton, J. (1785–1789). *Filices Britannicae. An history of the British proper ferns, etc., with plain and* accurate descriptions and new figures of all the species and varieties. Vol 1. John Binns, Leeds. Vol. 2. J. Brooke, Huddersfield.

Boorman, L. A. (1977). Sand-dunes. pp. 161–197 in Barnes, R. S. K. (ed.) The Coastline. John Wiley & Sons, London and New York.

Boorman, L. A. & Fuller, R. M. (1981). The changing status of reedswamp in the Norfolk Broads. J. Appl. Ecol. 18: 241–269.

Boswall, J. T. & Brown, N. E. (1886). Sowerby's English Botany. 3rd edn. Vol. 12. George Bell, London.

Box, J. D. & Cossons, U. (1988). Three species of clubmoss (Lycopodiaceae) at a lowland station in Shropshire. Watsonia 17: 69–71.

Boycott, A. E. (1934). The habitats of land Mollusca in Britain. J. Ecol. 22: 1–38.

Boyd, J. M. (ed.) (1979). The natural environment of the Outer Hebrides. Proc. Roy. Soc. Edinb. 77B.

Braithwaite, M. E. (1976). A Railway Flora of Teviotdale. Buccleuch, Hawick.

Brander, M. (1980). The Making of the Highlands. Constable, London.

Brian, M. V. (1977). Ants. Collins New Naturalist, London.

Brian, A. D., Price, P. S., Redwood, B. C. & Wheeler, E. (1987) The flora of the marl-pits (ponds) in one Cheshire parish. Watsonia 16: 417–426.

Brooks, R. R. (1987). Serpentine and its Vegetation. A multi-disciplinary approach. Croom Helm, London.

Brown, G. M. (1969). The Tertiary Ingneous Geology of the Isle of Skye. Geologists Association Guide No 13, Colchester.

Brunker, J. P. (1950). Flora of Count Wicklow. Dundalgan Press, Dundalk.

Bunce, R. G. H. & Jeffers, J. N. R. (eds) (1977). Native Pinewoods of Scotland. Institute of Terrestrial Ecology, Cambridge.

Burnett, J. H. (ed.) (1964). The Vegetation of Scotland. Oliver & Boyd, Edinburgh.

Burton, A. (1981). The Canal Builders. David & Charles, Newton Abbot.

Busby, A. R. (1976). Ferns in canal navigations in Birmingham. Fern Gaz. 11: 269.

Cadell, H. M. (1982). Geological changes wrought by Man within the Forth Basin. Trans. Edinburgh Geol. Soc. 6: 275–286.

Caird, J. B. & Moisley, H. A. (1964). The Outer Hebrides. pp. 374–390 in Steers, J. A. (ed.) Field Studies in the British Isles. Nelson, London.

Callaghan, T. V. (1980). Age-related patterns of nutrient allocation in Lycopodium annotinum from Swedish Lapland. Oikos 35: 373–386.

Cameron, L. B. & Stephenson, D. (1985). British Regional Ecology. The Midland Valley of Scotland (3rd edn). HMSO, London.

Cameron, J. (1883). Gaelic Names of Plants (Scottish and Irish). W. Blackwood, Edinburgh.

Campbell, M. S. (1985). The Flora of Uig (Lewis). T. Buncle & Co, Arbroath.

Carlquist, S. (1974). Island Biology. Columbia University Press, New York and London.

Chandler, T. J. & Gregory, S. (1976). The Climate of the British Isles. Longmans, London.

Charlesworth, J. K. (1930). Some geological observations on the origin of the Irish fauna and flora. Proc. Roy. Irish Acad. 39B: 358–390.

Charlesworth, J. K. (1963). The Historical Geology of Ireland. Oliver & Boyd, Edinburgh.

Clapham, A. R., Tutin, T. G. & Warburg, E. G. (1962). Flora of the British Isles. Cambridge University Press.

Clark, W. A. (1956). Plant distribution in the Western Isles. Proc. Linn. Soc. Lond. 167: 96–103.

Cole, G. A. J. & Hallissy, T. (1924). Handbook of the Geology of Ireland. Thomas Murby, London.

Condry, W. (1974). Woodlands. David & Charles, Newton Abbot.

Cousens, M. I., Lacey, O. G. & Kelly, E. M. (1985). Life-history studies of ferns in a consideration of perspective. Proc. Roy. Soc. Edinb. 86B: 321–380.

Coombe, D. E. (1957). The special composition of shade light in woodlands. J. Ecol. 45: 823–830.

Coombe, D. E. & Frost, L. C. (1956a). The heaths of the Cornish serpentine. J. Ecol. 44: 226–256.

Coombe, D. E. & Frost, L. C. (1956b). The nature and origin of the soils over the Cornish serpentine. J. Ecol. 44: 605–615.

Cooper-Driver, G. (1985). Anti-predation strategies in pteridophytes—a biochemical approach. Proc. Roy. Soc. Edinb. 86B. 397–402.

Coppins, B. J. (1976). Distribution patterns shown by epiphytic lichens in the British Isles. pp. 249–278 in Brown, D. H., Hawksworth, D. L. & Bailey, R. H. (eds) Lichenology: Progress and Problems. Academic Press, London.

Courtney, M. A. (1887). Cornish folk-lore. Folk Lore J. 5: 215.

Craig, G. Y. (1965). The Geology of Scotland. Oliver & Boyd, Edinburgh.

Crampton, C. B. (1911). The Vegetation of Caithness Considered in Relation to Geology. Committee for the Survey and Study of British Vegetation, Edinburgh.

Crocker, R. C. & Major, J. (1955). Soil development in relation to vegetation and surface age at Glacier Bay, Alaska. J. Ecol. 43: 427–488.

Currie, A. (1979). The vegetation of the Outer Hebrides. *Proc. Roy. Soc. Edinb.* 77B: 719–765.

Darby, H. C. (1951). The clearing of the English woodlands. *Geography* 36: 71–83.

Darling, F. F. & Boyd, J. M. (1964). *The Highlands and Islands.* Collins New Naturalist, London.

Darlington, A. (1981). *Ecology of Walls.* Heinemann, London.

Davey, F. H. (1909). *Flora of Cornwall.* Chegwidden, Penshy.

Davies, A. (1964). The south-west peninsula of England. pp. 14–25 in Steers, J. A. (ed.) *Field Studies in the British Isles.* Nelson, London.

Davies-Shiel, M. (1972). A little-known Late Mediaeval Industry, part I. The making of potash for soap in Lakeland. *Trans. Cumb. & Westmor. Antiqu. & Archaeol. Soc.* 72: 83–111.

Deevey, E. S. (1949). Biogeography of the Pleistocene. Pt 1. Europe and North America. *Bull. Geol. Soc. America* 60: 1315–1416.

Department of Physical Planning (1976). *Biological Survey of the Union Canal.* Lothian Regional Council, Edinburgh.

Derrick, L. N., Jermy, A. C. & Paul, A. C. (1987). Checklist of European Pteridophytes. *Summerfeldtia* 6: 1–94.

Dewey, W. (1925). The mineral zones of Cornwall. *Proc. Geol. Assoc.* 36: 107–135.

Dick, D. E. (1978). The Old Metal Mines of Mid-Wales. Pound House, Newent.

Dickinson, C. H., Pearson, M. C. & Webb, D. A. (1978). Some microhabitats of the Burren, their micro-environments and vegetation. *Proc. Roy. Irish Acad.* 63B: 221–302.

Dickinson, G. (1968). The Vegetation of Grogarry Machair, South Uist. Nature Conservancy Council, unpublished report.

Dickinson, G. (1977). The submarine fringe. pp. 271–288 in Barnes, R. S. K. (ed.) *The Coastline.* John Wiley & Sons, London and NY.

Dickson, J. (1973). *Bryophytes of the Pleistocene. The British Record and its Chronological and Ecological Implications.* Cambridge University Press.

Dimbleby, G. W. (1962). The development of British heathlands and their soils. *Oxford Forestry Memoirs* 23: 1–121.

Dimbleby, G. W. (1978). *Plants and Archaeology (2nd edn).* John Baker, London.

Dimbleby, G. W. (1984). Anthropogenic changes from Neolithic through Medieval times. *New Phytol.* 98: 57–72.

Directorate of Fisheries Research (1981). *Atlas of the Seas around the British Isles.* Ministry of Agriculture, Fisheries and Food, London.

Dony, J. G. (1955). Notes on the Bedfordshire railway flora. *Beds. Nat.* 9: 2–16.

Down, W. L., Farrand, W. R. & Ewing, M. (1962). Pleistocene ice volumes and sea-level lowering. *J. Geol.* 70: 206–214.

Druery, C. T. (undated). *British Ferns and their Varieties.* Routledge, London.

Dunham, K. C. (1931). Mineral deposits of the North Pennines. *Proc. Geol. Ass.* XLII (3): 274–281.

Du Rietz, G. E. (1935). Glacial survival of plants. *Proc. R. Soc. Lond. Ser. B.* 118(808).

Durno, S. E. & McVean, D. N. (1959). Forest history of the Beinn Eighe nature reserve. *New Phytol.* 58: 228–236.

Dyer, A. F. (ed.) (1979). *The Experimental Biology of Ferns.* Academic Press, London.

Dyer, A. F. & Page, C. N. (eds) (1985). *Biology of Pteridophytes.* Royal Society, Edinburgh.

Edmonds, E. A., Mckown, M. C. & Williams, M. (1975). *British Regional Geology: South-West England (4th edn).* HMSO, London.

Edwards, D. (1986). Robert Kidston, the most professional palaeobotanist. *Forth Naturalist and Historian* 8: 65–93.

Edwards, W. & Trotter, F. M. (1954). *British Regional Geology: The Pennines and Adjacent Areas (3rd edn).* HMSO, London.

Eggling, W. J. (1965). Checklist of the plants of Rhum, Inner Hebrides. *Trans. Bot. Soc. Edinb.* 40: 20–59.

Ellett, D. J. & Baxter, G. C. (1965). Surface temperatures in the southern North Sea, January–March, 1963. *Ann. Biol. Copenhagen* 20: 28–39.

Elton, C. S. (1966). *The Pattern of Animal Communities.* Chapman & Hall, London.

Emeleus, C. H. & Forster, R. M. (1979)., *Field Guide to the Tertiary Igneous Rocks of Rhum, Inner Hebrides.* Nature Conservancy Council.

Evans, J. G. (1979). *The Environment of Early Man in the British Isles.* Paul Elek, London.

Eyers, A. M. (1980). *Scottish Place Names.* Sphere Books, London.

Feachem, R. (1977). *Guide to Prehistoric Scotland (2nd edn).* Batsford, London.

Fenton, E. W. (1937). The influence of sheep on the vegetation of hill-grazings in Scotland. *J. Ecol.* 25: 428–430.

Ferreira, R. E. C. (1959). Scottish mountain vegetation relative to geology. *Trans. Bot. Soc. Edin.* 37: 229–250.

Finberg, H. P. R. (1972). *The Gloucestershire Landscape.* Hodder & Stoughton, London.

Finberg, H. P. R. (ed.) (1972). The Agrarian History of England and Wales. I. Cambridge University Press.

Fisher, R. A. & Taylor, G. L. (1940). Scandinavian influence on Scottish ethnology. *Nature, Lond.* 145: 590.

Fitter, A. S. R. (1945). London's Natural History. Collins New Naturalist, London.

Fletcher, H. R. & Brown, W. H. (1970). The Royal Botanic Garden, Edinburgh 1670–1970. HMSO, Edinburgh.

Fowler, P. J. (1983). *The Farming of Prehistoric Britain.* Cambridge University Press.

Fraser-Darling, F. (1947). *Natural History in the Highlands and Islands.* Collins New Naturalist, London.

Fraser-Darling, F. (1955). *West Highland Survey.* Clarendon Press, Oxford.

Freethy, R. (1981). *The Making of the British Countryside.* David & Charles, Newton Abbot.

Freethy, R. (1983). *The Naturalists Guide to the British Coastline.* David & Charles, Newton Abbot.

Geiger, R. (1959). *The Climate Near the Ground.* Harvard University Press.

Geikie, A. (1897). *The Ancient Volcanos of Great Britain.* Macmillan, London.

Gemmel, R. P. (1977). *Colonisation of Industrial Wasteland.* Arnold, London.

George, T. N. (1961). Economic minerals in Scotland. pp. 28–51 in Elgood, L. A. (ed.) *Natural Resources in Scotland.* Scottish Council (Development and Industry).

Gilbert, O. L. (1968). Bryophytes as indicators of air pollution in the Tyne Valley. *New Phytol.* 67: 15.

Gilbertson, D. D. (1973). The construction of hedgebanks around Filham Moor, Ivybridge. *J. Devon Trust for Nature Conservation* 5(1): 41–44.

Gimmingham, C. H. (1972). *Ecology of Heathlands.* Chapman & Hall, London.

Godwin, H. (1944). The age and origin of the 'Breckland' heaths of East Anglia. *Nature, Lond.* 154: 6–7.

Godwin, H. (1944a). Neolithic forest clearance. *Nature, Lond.* 153: 511–512.

Godwin, H. (1949b). The spreading of the British Flora considered in relation to conditions of the Late-glacial period. *J. Ecol.* 37: 140–147.

Godwin, H. (1975). *The History of the British Flora.* Cambridge University Press.

Godwin, H. (1978). *Fenland: its Ancient Past and Uncertain Future.* Cambridge University Press.

Goldberg, E. D. (ed.) (1973). *North Sea Science.* NATO North Sea Science Conference, Aviemore.

Goldsmith, F. B. (1975). The sea-cliff vegetation of Shetland. *J. Biogeogr.* 2: 297–308.

Goldsmith, F. B. (1977). Rocky cliffs. pp. 237–251 in

Barnes, R. S. K. (ed.) *The Coastline.* John Wiley & Sons, London and New York.

Goodier, R. (1971). Aerial photography and the ecologist. pp. 1–5 in Goodier, R. (ed.) *The Application of Aerial Photography to the Work of the Nature Conservancy.* Nature Conservancy. Edinburgh.

Grant, J. (1845). A few remarks on the large hedges and small enclosures of Devonshire and adjoining counties. *J. Royal Agric. Soc.* 5: 420–429.

Gray, J. M. (1974). Late glacial and Postglacial shorelines in western Scotland. *Boreas* 3, 129–138.

Gray, J. M. & Lowe, J. J. (1977). *Studies in the Scottish Late-glacial Environment.* Pergamon Press, Oxford.

Green, F. H. W. (1964). A map of annual average potential water deficit in the British Isles. *J. Appl. Ecol.* 1: 151–158.

Green, F. H. W. & Harding, R. J. (1979). The effects of altitude on soil temperature. *Met. Mag.* 208: 81–91.

Green, G. W. & Welch, F. B. A. (1965). *Geology of the Country around Wells and Cheddar.* HMSO, London.

Greenwood, E. F. & Gemmell, R. P. (1978). Derelict industrial land as a habitat for rare plants in S. Lancs (V.C. 59) and W. Lancs (V.C. 60). *Watsonia* 12: 33–40.

Gregory, M. A. (1954). Temperature maps of the British Isles. *Publ. Inst. Brit. Geographers* 20: 59–73.

Greig, D. C., Wright, J. E., Hains, B. A. & Mitchell, G. H. (1968). *Geology of the Country around Church Stretton, Craven Arms, Wenlock Edge and Brown Clee.* Memoirs of the Geological Survey of Great Britain. HMSO, London.

Grigg, D. B. (1967). The changing agricultural geography of England: a commentary on the sources available for the reconstruction of the agricultural geography of England 1750–1850. *Inst. of British Geographers Publ. No. 41.*

Grim, R. E. (1969). *Clay Mineralogy, (2nd edn).* McGraw-Hill, New York.

Grime, J. P. (1974). Vegetation classification in relation to strategies. *Nature, Lond.* 250: 26–31.

Grime, J. P. (1977). Evidence for the existence of three primary strategies in plants and its relevance to ecological and evolutionary theory. *Amer. Natur.* 111: 1169–1194.

Grime, J. P. (1984). The ecology of species, families and communities of the contemporary British flora. *New Phytol.* 98: 15–33.

Grime, J. P. (1984). Factors limiting the contribution of pteridophytes to a local flora. In A. F. Dyer & C. N. Page (eds) *Biology of*

Pteridophytes. Edinburgh: Royal Society of Edinburgh.

Guppy, E. M. & Sabine, P. A. (1956). *Chemical analysis of igneous rocks, metamorphic rocks and minerals*. Mem. Geol. Surv. Great Britain. HMSO, London.

Hadfield, C. (1966). *The Canals of the West Midlands*. David & Charles, Newton Abbot.

Haldane, A. R. B. (1952). *The Drove Roads of Scotland*. Edinburgh University Press.

Halen, F. H. A. (1978). *Man and the Landscape in Ireland*. Academic Press, London.

Hall, A. R. (1983). Evidence of dye plants from Viking age York and Medieval Beverley. pp. 25 in Dalrymple, G. *Dyes in Historical and Archaeological Textiles*. Nat. Mus. Antiquities, Scotland.

Hall, A. R., Tomlinson, P. R., Hall, R. A., Taylor, G. W. & Walton, P. (1984). Dye plants from Viking York. *Antiquity* 55: 58–60.

Hall, L. G. (1957). The ecology of disused pit heaps in England. *J. Ecol.* 45: 685–720.

Hall, N. (1983). The mysterious magic of ferns. *Countryside N.S.* 25: 176–180.

Handley, J. E. (1953). *Scottish Farming in the 18th Century*. Faber, London.

Harding, D. W. (1974). *The Iron Age in Lowland Britain*. Routledge & Keegan Paul, London.

Hardy, E. (1977). *The Naturalist in Lakeland*. David & Charles, Newton Abbot.

Harley, J. C. & Lewis, D. H. (1984). *The Flora and Vegetation of Britain. Origins and Changes—the Facts and their Interpretation*. Academic Press, London.

Harper, J. L. (1977). *Population Biology of Plants*. Academic Press, London.

Havins, P. J. N. (1976). *The Forests of England*. Robert Hale, London.

Hepburn, I. (1943). A study of the vegetation of sea-cliffs in North Cornwall. *J. Ecol.* 31: 30–39.

Herity, M. & Eogan, G. (1977). *Ireland in Pre-History*. Routledge & Keegan Paul, London.

Heslop-Harrison, J. W. et al. (1936). The natural history of Raasay and the adjacent islands of South Rona, Scalpay, Fladday and Longay. *Proc. Univ. Durham Phil. Soc.* 10: 246–351.

Heslop-Harrison, J. (1953). The North American and Lusitanian elements in the flora of the British Isles. pp. 105–123 in Linsley, J. E. (ed.). *The Changing Flora of Britain*. BSBI.

Heslop-Harrison, J. (1960). A note on the temperature and vapour pressure deficit under drought conditions in some microhabitats of the Burren limestone, Co. Clare. *Proc. Roy. Irish Acad.* 61B: 109–114.

Heyworth, A. (1978). Submerged forests around the British Isles. *British Archaeological Reports International Series* 51: 279–288.

Hibbert, F. A. (1978). The vegetational history of the Somerset Levels. pp. 90–95 in Limbrey, S. & Evans, J. G. *The Effect of Man in the Landscape: The Lowland Zone. CBA Research Report No 21*. Council of British Archaeology, London.

Hickin, N. E. (1971). *The Natural History of an English Forest*. Hutchinson, London.

Hill, David (1981). *An Atlas of Anglo-Saxon England*. Blackwell, Oxford.

Hill, H. W. (1973). Currents and water masses. pp. 17–42 in Goldberg, E. D. (ed.) *North Sea Science*. NATO North Sea Conference, Aviemore.

Hinde, T. (1985). *Forests of Britain*. Victor Gollancz, London.

Hoeg, O. A. (1984). Country people in Norway and their knowledge of plants. pp. 111–119 in Vickery, R. (ed.) *Plant-Line Slides*. The Folklore Society, London.

Hohn, R. (1973). On the climatology of the North Sea. pp. 183–236 in Goldberg, E. D. (ed.) *North Sea Science*. NATO North Sea Conference, Aviemore.

Holdgate, M. W. (1955). The Vegetation of some springs and wet flushes in Tarn Moor, near Orton, Westmorland. *J. Ecol.* 43: 80–89.

Hollam, D. (1980). Somerset Ferns. *Somerset Arch. & Nat. Hist.* 123: 119–124.

Holland, P. G. (1972). The pattern of species density of old stone walls in western Ireland. *J. Ecol.* 60: 799–805.

Holland, S. C. (1986). *Supplement to the Flora of Gloucestershire*. Grenfell Publications, Bristol.

Hollingworth, S. E. (1951). The influence of glaciation on the topography of the Lake District. *Journ. Inst. Water Engineers* 5: 485–496.

Hooke, D. (1981). Anglo-Saxon landscapes of the West Midlands: the evidence. *Br. Arch. Reports* 95: 300–307.

Hooper, M. D. (1970). The botanical importance of our hedgerows. pp. 58–62 in *The Flora of a Changing Britain. BSBI Conf. Report. No 11*.

Hoppe, G. (1963). Some comments on the 'ice-free refugia' of northern Scandinavia. In A. Love & D. Love (ed.) *North Atlantic Biota and their History*. Pergamon Press, New York.

Hoskins, W. G. (1970). *The Making of the English Landscape*. Hodder & Stoughton, London. New ed. Penguin, London.

Howarth, F. G. (1980). The zoogeography of specialised cave animals: a bioclimatic model. *Evolution* 34: 394–406.

Hulten, E. (1958). The Amphi-Atlantic plants and their phytogeographical connections. *K. Vet. Akad. Handl.* IV: 7.

Hume, J. R. (1976–77). *The Industrial Archaeology of Scotland.* 2 vols. Batsford, London.

Hunter, J. R. S. (1884). The Silurian districts of Leadhills and Wanlockhead, and their early and recent mining history. *Trans. Geol. Soc. Glasgow* 7: 373–392.

Hunter, R. F. (1962). Hill sheep and their pasture: a study of sheep-grazing in south-east Scotland. *J. Ecol.* 50: 651–680.

Innes, J. L. (1983). Landuse changes in the Scottish Highlands during the 18th century: The role of pasture degeneration. *Scottish Geogr. Mag.* 99(3): 141–149.

Institute of Geological Sciences (1980). *The Geology of Northern Skye.* HMSO, London.

Irish National Committee for Geography (1979). *Atlas of Ireland.* Royal Irish Academy, Dublin.

Iversen, J. (1956). Forest clearance: the stone-age. *Sci. Amer.* 194: 36–41.

Iversen, J. (1964). Retrogressive vegetational succession in the post-glacial. *J. Ecol.* (Suppl.) 52: 59–70.

Ivimey-Cook, R. B. (1984). *Atlas of the Devon Flora.* Devonshire Association, Exeter.

Ivimey-Cook, R. B. & Proctor, M. C. F. (1966). The plant communities of the Burren, Co. Clare. *Proc. Roy. Irish Acad.* B64: 212–307.

Jacobi, R. M. (1978). Population and landscape in Mesolithic lowland Britain, pp. 75–85 in S. Limbrey & J. G. Evans (ed.) *The effects of man on the landscape: the lowland zone.* CBA Research Report 21.

Jalas, J. & Suominen, J. (1979). *Atlas Florae Europaeae. Pteridophyta.* Committee for Mapping of the Flora of Europe, Helsinki.

Jee, N. (1972). *Guernsey's Natural History (2nd edn).* Guernsey Press, St Peter Port.

Jermy, A. C., Arnold, H. R., Farrell, C. & Perring, F. H. (eds) (1978). *Atlas of Ferns of the British Isles.* Botanical Society of the British Isles and British Pteridological Society, London.

Jermy, A. C. & Crabbe, J. (1978). *The Island of Mull. A Survey of its Flora and Environment.* British Museum (Natural History). London.

Jessen, K. (1949). Studies in Late Quaternary deposits and Flora-history of Ireland. *Proc. R. Ir. Acad.* 52B: 85–290.

Jessen, K., Andersen, S. T. & Farrington, A. (1959). The interglacial deposit near Gort, Co. Galway, Ireland. *Proc. Roy. Irish Acad.* 36o: 1–77.

Johnson, C. G. & Smith, L. P. (eds) (1965). *The Biological Significance of Climatic Changes in Britain.* Academic Press, London.

Johnston, J. B. (1970). *Place-names of Scotland.* S. R. Publishers, Wakefield, Yorkshire.

Johnstone, G. S. (1966). *British Regional Geology: the Grampian Highlands (3rd edn).* HMSO, London.

Jones, D. K. C. (1980). *The Shaping of Southern England.* Academic Press, London.

Jones, M. & Dimbleby, G. W. (eds) (1981). *The Environment of Man: the Iron Age to the Anglo-Saxon Period.* British Archaeological Reports (British Series) vol. 87, Oxford.

Keble Martin W. & Fraser, G. T. (1939). *Flora of Devon.* Devonshire Association, Exeter.

Kellaway, G. A., Redding, J. H., Shepard-Thorn, E. R. & Destombes, I.-P. (1975). The Quaternary History of the English Channel. *Proc. Trans. Roy. Soc. Lond.* A279: 189–218.

Kelly, D. L. (1981). The native forest vegetation of Killarney, south-west Ireland: an ecological account. *J. Ecol.* 69: 437–472.

Kent, D. A. (1961). The flora of Middlesex walls. *Lond. Nat.* 40: 29–43.

Kidson, C. (1964). The coasts of south and south-west England. pp. 36–42 in Steers, J. A. (ed.) *Field Studies in the British Isles.* Nelson, London.

Kidson, C. & Tooley, M. J. (eds) (1972). *The Quaternary History of the Irish Sea.* Seel House Press, Liverpool.

Kidston, R. & Lang, W. H. (1917–1921). On Old Red Sandstone plants showing structures from the Rhynie Chart Bed, Aberdeenshire. *Trans. Roy. Soc. Edinb.* 51–52.

Kirkby, M. J. (ed.) (1978). *Hillslope Hydrology.* Wiley, London and New York.

Kohlmaier, G. & Sartory, S. (1981). *Houses of Glass.* MIT Press, London.

Lamb, H. H. (1964). The early medieval warm epoch and its sequel. *Palaeogeogr. Palaeoclimatol. Palaeocol.* 1: 13–37.

Lamb, H. H. (1977). *Climate, Past, Present and Future.* Methuen, London.

Lamb, H. H. (1985). Climate and landscape in the British Isles. pp. 148–167 in Woodell, S. R. J. (ed.) *The English Landscape. Past, Present and Future.* Oxford University Press.

Lamb, H. H. & Woodruffe, A. (1970). Atmospheric circulation during the last Ice Age. *Quatern. Research* 1: 29–58.

Large, D. C. & Robinson, G. W. S. (1964). The Channel Islands. pp. 1–13 in Steers, J. A. (ed.) *Field Studies in the British Isles.* Nelson, London.

Lawson, J. A. & J. D. (1976). *Geology Explained around Glasgow and South-West Scotland, including Arran.* David & Charles, Newton Abbot.

Leach, W. (1930). The vegetation of some non-calcareous British screes. *J. Ecol.* 18: 321–332.

Leitch, D. (1942). The Upper Carboniferous rocks of Arran. *Trans. Geol. Soc. Glasgow* 20: 142–154.

Le Suer, F. (1984). *Flora of Jersey*. Societe Jeriaise, Jersey.

Lewis, C. A. (ed.) (1970). *The Glaciations of Wales and Adjoining Regions*. Longmans, London.

Lindsay, John (1794). Account of the germination and raising of ferns from the seed. *Trans. Linn. Soc. Lond.* 2: 93–100.

Linton, D. L. (1959). Morphological contrasts of eastern and western Scotland. pp. 16–45 in Miller, R. & Watson, J. W. (eds) *Geographical Essays in honour of Alan G. Ogilvie*. Nelson, Edinburgh.

Linton, W. J. (1965). *The Ferns of the English Lake Country (2nd edn)*. Garrett, Windermere.

Longsley, J. E. (1971). *The Flora of the Isles of Scilly*. David & Charles, Newton Abbot.

Lotn, H. (1962). *Anglo-Saxon England and the Norman Conquest*. Longman, London.

Lotschert, W. (1982). The heavy-metal content of some Irish plants. *J. Life Sci. R. Dubl. Soc.* 3: 261–266.

Lovis, J. D. (1977). Evolutionary patterns and processes in ferns. *Adv. Bot. Res.* 4: 229–415.

Lowe, E. J. (1865). Our Native Ferns. George Bell, London.

Macan, T. T. (1970). *Biological Studies of the English Lakes*. Longmans, London.

MacArthur, R. H. & Wilson, E. O. (1963). An equilibrium theory of insular biogeography. *Evolution* 17: 373–387.

MacArthur, R. H. & Wilson, E. O. (1967). *The Theory of Island Biogeography*. Princeton University Press.

McClintock, D. (1975). *The Wild Flowers of Guernsey*. Collins, London.

McCracken, E. (1971). *The Irish Woods since Tudor Times*. David & Charles, Newton Abbot.

McCullagh, P. (1978). *Modern Concepts in Geomorphology*. Oxford University Press.

MacDonald, J. G. & Herriot, A. (1983). *Geology of Arran (3rd edn)*. Geological Society of Glasgow. Glasgow.

McKay, M. M. (1980). *The Rev. Dr John Walker's Report on the Hebrides of 1764 and 1771*. John Donald Publishers, Edinburgh.

McLean, W. N. (1940). Windermere basin: rainfall, run-off and storage. *Q. J. R. Met. Soc.* 66: 337–362.

McNally, K. (1978). *The Islands of Ireland*. Batsford, London.

McVean, D. N. (1958). Snow cover and vegetation in the Scottish Highlands. *Weather* 13: 197–200.

McVean, D. N. & Ratcliffe, S. A. (1962). *Plant Communities of the Scottish Highlands. Nature Conservancy Monographs, No 1*. HMSO, London.

MacVicar, S. (1901). On the comparative state of the flora of the West Highlands during the 18th century and at the present time. *Proc. Bot. Soc. Edinb.* 22: 17–30.

McWhirr, A. (1981). *Roman Gloucestershire*. Sutton, Gloucester.

Muirburn Working Party (1977). *A Guide to Good Muirburn Practice*. HMSO, Edinburgh.

Maitland, P. S. (1976). Fish in the large freshwater lochs of Scotland. *J. Scott. Wildl.* 12: 13–17.

Malloch, A. J. C. (1971). Vegetation of the maritime clifftops of the Lizard and Land's End Peninsulas, West Cornwall. *New Phytol.* 70: 1155–1197.

Manley, G. (1935). Some notes on the climate of NE England. *Q. J. Roy. Met. Soc.* 61: 405–410.

Manley, G. (1939). On the occurrence of snow-cover in Great Britain. *Q. J. Met. Soc.* 65: 2–27.

Manley, G. (1952). *Climate and the British Scene*. Collins New Naturalist, London.

Manley, G. (1959). The late-glacial climate of north-west England. *Lpool. Manchr, Geol. I.* 2: 188–213.

Manley, G. (1979). The climatic environment of the Outer Hebrides. *Proc. Roy. Soc. Edinb.* 77B 47–59.

Manton, I. (1950). *Problems of Cytology and Evolution in the Pteridophyta*. Cambridge University Press.

Margetts, L. J. & David, R. W. (1981). *A Review of the Cornish Flora. 1980*. Institute of Cornish Studies, Redruth.

Marquand, E. D. (1901). *Flora of Guernsey and the Lesser Channel Islands*. Dulau & Co., London.

Matthews, J. R. (1937). Geographical relationships of the British flora. *J. Ecol.* 25: 2–90.

Matthews, J. R. (1955). *Origin and Distribution of the British Flora*. Hutchinson, London.

Matthews, L. H. (1982). *Mammals in the British Isles*. Collins New Naturalist, London.

Messenger, K. G. (1968). A railway flora of Rutland. *Proc. Bot. Soc. Bri. Isl.* 7: 325–344.

Miller, J. (1964). The geography of the Scottish Highlands. pp. 360–373 in Steers, J. A. (ed.) *Field Studies in the British Isles*. Nelson, London.

Millman, R. N. (1975). *The Making of the Scottish Landscape*. Batsford, London.

Millward, R. & Robinson, A. (1980). *Upland Britain*. David & Charles, Newton Abbot.

Mitchell, G. F. (1976). Post-Boreal pollen diagnoses from Irish raised bogs. *Proc. Royal Irish Acad.* 57B: 183–251.

Mitchell, F. (1976). *The Irish Landscape*. Collins.

Mitchell, G. F. (1972). The Pleistocene history of the Irish Sea. *Sci. Proc. Roy. Dublin Soc.* A4: 181–199.

Mitchell, G. F. (1977). Periglacial Ireland. *Phil. Trans. R. Soc.* 280: 199–209.

Mitchell, G. F. (1981). The Littletonian Warm Stage—post 10,000 BP. pp. 259–271 in Holland, C. H. (ed.) *A Geology of Ireland.* Scottish Academic Press, Edinburgh.

Mitchell, J. (1972). *A report on the past and present status of* Woodsia ilvensis *in the Moffat Hills.* Nature Conservancy Council.

Moore, T. (1862). *A Popular History of British Ferns and the Allied Plants.* Routledge, Warne, London.

Moore, T. (1863). *British Ferns and their Allies.* Routledge, Warne, London.

Morgan, S. W. (1936). Domesday woodland in South-West England. *Antiquity* 10: 306–324.

Morton, A. G. (1981). *History of Botanical Science.* Academic Press, London.

Murray, C. W. & Birks, H. J. B. (1980). *The Botanist on Skye. A Guide to the Flowering Plants and Ferns.* BSBI, Cambridge.

Nairn, R. & O'Sullivan, A. (1978). *Irish Hedges.* Folens, Dublin.

Neale, J. & Flenley, J. (eds) (1981). *The Quaternary in Britain.* Pergamon Press, Oxford.

Nef, J. U. (1932). *The Rise of the British Coal Industry.* Routledge and Heyn Paul, London.

Newman, E. (1844). *A History of British Ferns and Allied Plants.* van Voorst, London.

Newman, E. (1854). *A History of British Ferns.* van Voorst, London.

Nicol, E. A. T. (1936). The brackish-water lochs of North Uist. *Proc. Roy. Soc. Edinb.* 56: 169–195.

O'Dell, A. C. (1939). A Geographical examination of the development of Scottish Railways. *Scot. Geogr. Mag.* 55: 129–148.

Ollier, C. D. (1969). *Weathering.* Oliver and Boyd, Edinburgh.

O' Malley, D. J. S. (1979). *Asplenium cuneifolium* Viv. new to West Mayo. *Irish Nat. J.* 19: 315.

O'Sullivan, P. E. (1977). Vegetation history of the native pinewoods. pp. 60–69 in Bunce, R. G. H. & Jeffers, J. N. R. (eds) *Native Pinewoods of Scotland.* Institute of Terrestrial Ecology, Cambridge.

Page, C. N. (1976). The taxonomy and phytogeography of bracken—a review. *Bot. J. Linn. Soc.* 73: 1–34.

Page, C. N. (1979). The diversity of ferns—an ecological perspective. pp. 10–56 in Dyer, D. F. (ed.) *The Experimental Biology of Ferns.* Academic Press, London.

Page, C. N. (1979b). Experimental aspects of fern-ecology. pp. 551–589 in Dyer, A. F. (ed.) *The*

Experimental Biology of Ferns. Academic Press, London.

Page, C. N. (1982). *The Ferns of Britain and Ireland.* Cambridge University Press.

Page, C. N. & Barker, M. A. (1985). Ecology and geography of hybridisation in British and Irish horsetails. *Proc. Roy. Soc. Edinb.* 86B: 265–272.

Palmer, J. & Neilson, R. A. (1962). The origin of granite tors on Dartmoor, Devonshire. *Proc. Yorks. Geol. Soc.* 33: 315–340.

Parry, M. C. & Slater, T. R. (eds) (1980). *The Making of the Scottish Countryside.* Croom Helm, London.

Payne, R. & Craig, R. E. (1966). Temperature and salinity in Scottish Waters 1964. *Annls. Biol. Copenh.* 21: 26–28.

Pears, N. V. (1968–1970). Post-glacial tree lines in the Cairngorm mountains, Scotland. *Trans. Bot. Soc. Edinb.* 40: 363–394, 1968; 40: 536–544, 1970.

Pearsall, W. H. (1917). The aquatic and marsh vegetation of Esthwaite Water. *J. Ecol.* 5: 180–202.

Pearsall, W. H. (1950). *Mountains and Moorlands.* Collins New Naturalist, London.

Peck, S. B. (1976). The effect of cave entrances on the distribution of cave inhabiting terrestrial arthropods. *Int. J. Speliol.* 8: 309–321.

Pennington, W. (1974). *The History of British Vegetation* (2nd edn). English Universities Press, London.

Perring, F. (ed.) (1974). *The Flora of a Changing Britain.* Botanical Society of the British Isles, London.

Peterken, G. F. (1974). A method for assessing woodland flora for conservation using indicator species. *Biological Conservation* 6(4): 239–285.

Peterken, G. F. (1977). Habitat conservation priorities in British and European woodlands. *Biological Conservation* 11: 223–236.

Peterken, G. F. (1981). Woodland Conservation and Management. Chapman & Hall, London.

Peterken, G. F. (1986). The status of native woods in the Scottish uplands. pp. 14–19 in Jenkins, D. (ed.) *Trees and Wildlife in the Scottish Uplands.* Institute of Terrestrial Ecology, Natural Environment Research Council, Huntingdon.

Petersen, R. L. (1985). Towards an appreciation of fern edaphic niche requirements. *Proc. Roy. Soc. Edinb.* 86B: 93–103.

Pigott, C. D. (1956). The vegetation of Upper Teesdale in the North Pennines. *J. Ecol.* 44: 545–586.

Pigott, C. D. (1983). Regeneration of oak-birch woodland following exclusion of sheep. *J. Ecol.* 71: 629–649.

Pigott, C. D. & Walters, S. M. (1954). On the interpretation of the discontinuous distributions shown by certain British species of open habitats. *J. Ecol.* 42: 96–116.

Plomer, W. (ed.) (1944). Kilvert's Diary 1870–1879. Jonathan Cape, London.

Poel, L. W. (1961). Soil aeration as a limiting factor in the growth of *Pteridium aquilinum. J. Ecol.* 49: 107–111.

Pollard, E., Hooper, M. D., Moore, N. W. (1974). *Hedges*. Collins New Naturalist, London.

Poore, M. E. D. (1956). The ecology of Woodwalton Fen. *J. Ecol.* 44: 455–492.

Poore, M. E. D. & Robertson, V. C. (1949). The Vegetation of St Kilda in 1948. *J. Ecol.* 37: 87–99.

Porter, J. (1980). *The Making of the Central Pennines*. Moorland Publishing, Ashbourne.

Powell, A. T. & Chamberlain, Y. M. (1956). Plant life in Rockall. pp. 171–176 in Fischer, J. (ed.). *Rockall*. Geoffrey Bles, London.

Praeger, R. L. (1901). *Irish Topographical Botany*. Hodges, Figgis, Dublin.

Praeger, R. L. (1934). *The Botanist in Ireland*. Deans Hodges Figgis & Co., Dublin.

Praeger, R. L. (1950). *Natural History of Ireland*. Collins, London.

Price, R. J. (1973). *Glacial and Fluvioglacial Landforms*. Oliver & Boyd, Edinburgh.

Price, R. J. (1983). *Scotland's Environment during the last 30,000 years*. Scottish Academic Press, Edinburgh.

Proctor, J. (1971). The plant ecology of serpentine, II. Plant responses to serpentine soils. *J. Ecol.* 59: 397–410, 877–842.

Proctor, J. & Woodell, S. R. J. (1975). The ecology of serpentine soils. *Adv. Ecol. Res.* 9: 255–366.

Proctor, M. C. F., Spooner, G. M. & Spooner, M. F. (1980). Changes in Wistman's Wood, Dartmoor: photographic and other evidence. *Trans. Devon Assoc. Adv. Sci.* 112: 43–79.

Rackham, O. (1975). *Hayley Wood. Its History and Ecology*. Cambridgeshire and Isle of Ely Naturalist's Trust, Cambridge.

Rackham, O. (1976). *Trees and Woodlands in the British Landscape*. Dent, London.

Rackham, O. (1980). *Ancient Woodland – its History, Vegetation and Use in England*. Edward Arnold, London.

Rackham, O. (1986). *The History of the Countryside*. Dent, London.

Raistrick, A. & Jennings, B. (1965). *A History of Lead Mining in the Pennines*. Longmans, London.

Randall, R. E. (1976). Machair zonation of the Monach Isles NNR. *Trans. Bot. Soc. Edinb.* 42: 441–462.

Ratcliffe, D. A. (1960). The mountain flora of Lakeland. *Proc. Bot. Soc. Br. Isl.* 4: 1–25.

Ratcliffe, D. A. (1968). An ecological account of the Atlantic Bryophytes in the British Isles. *New Phytol.* 67: 365–439.

Ratcliffe, D. A. (ed.) (1977a). *A Nature Conservation Review*. Cambridge University Press.

Ratcliffe, D. A. (1977b). *Highland Flora*. Highlands and Islands Development Board.

Ratcliffe, D. A. (1981). The vegetation. pp. 42–76 in Nethersole-Thompson, D. & Watson, A. *The Cairngorms*. Melven Press, Perth.

Ratcliffe, D. A. (1984). Post-medieval and recent changes in British vegetation: the culmination of human influence. *New Phytol.* 98: 73–100.

Raven, J. & Walters, M. (1956). *Mountain Flowers*. Collins New Naturalist, London.

Read, H. H. (1960). *Rutley's Elements of Mineralogy*. Murby, London.

Reaney, P. H. (1960). *The Origin of English Place Names*. Routledge & Keegan Paul, London.

Reid, I. (1973). The influence of slope orientation upon the soil moisture regime and its hydro-geomorphological significance. *J. Hydrol.* 19: 309–321.

Reney-Smith, J. (1973). *The old railway. Some recollections*. Mimeographed publication: Wirral Country Park.

Richey, J. E. (1961). *Scotland: The Tertiary Volcanic Districts*. HMSO, London.

Rickard, M. H. (1972). The distribution of *Woodsia ilvensis* and *W. alpina* in Britain. *British Fern Gazette* 10: 269–280.

Riddelsdell, H. J., Hedley, G. W. & Price, W. R. (1948). *Flora of Gloucestershire*. Cotswold Naturalists Field Club, Cheltenham.

Ritchie, W. (1967). The machair of South Uist. *Scott. Geogr. Mag.* 83: 161–173.

Ritchie, W. (1976). The meaning and definition of machair. *Trans. Bot. Soc. Edinb.* 42: 431–440.

Ritchie, W. (1979). Machair development and chronology in the Uists and adjacent islands. *Proc. Roy. Soc. Edinb.* 77B 107–122.

Roberts, R. H. & Page, C. N. (1979). A second British record for *Equisetum × font-queri*, and its addition to the English flora. *Fern Gaz.* 12: 61–62.

Robertson, R. H. S. & Whitehead, T. H. (1954). *Serpentine and Olivine-rock in Scotland*. Rep. Miner. Resear. Fund, Edinburgh.

Robinson, G. W. S. (1977). *Guernsey*. David & Charles, Newton Abbot.

Rohan, P. K. (1975). *The Climate of Ireland*. Stationery Office, Dublin.

Rowley, T. (1978). *Villages in the Landscape*. Dent, London.

Rums, F. E. (1961). Seasonal variation in sea surface temperatures in coastal waters of the British Isles. *Sci. Pap. 6, Met Office Mo 685*.

Rymer, L. (1976). The history and ethnobotany of bracken. *Bot. J. Linn. Soc.* 73: 151–176.

St Joseph, J. K. S. (ed.) (1966). *The Uses of Air Photography.* John Baker Publisher, London.

Salisbury, E. J. (1939). Ecological aspects of meteorology. *Q. J. Roy. Met. Soc.* 65: 337–357.

Salisbury, E. J. & Tansley, A. G. (1921). The durmast oakwoods (*Quercus sessiliflorae*) of the Silurian and Malvernian strata near Malvern. *J. Ecol.* 9: 19–38.

Salter, P. J. & Williams, J. B. (1965). The influence of texture on the moisture characteristics of soils. II. Available water capacity and moisture release characteristics. *J. Soil Sci.* 26: 310–317.

Sargent, C. (1984). *Britain's Railway Vegetation.* Institute of Terrestrial Ecology, Cambridge.

Scannell, M. J. P. (1974). *Asplenium cuneifolium* Viv. in West Galway, Ireland. *Ir. Nat. J.* 19: 245.

Scannell, M. J. P. & Synnott, D. M. (1987). *Census Catalogue of the Flora of Ireland* (2nd edn). Stationery Office, Dublin.

Schumer, B. (1984). The evolution of Wychwood to 1400: pioneers, frontiers and forest. *University of Leicester Occasional Paper No 6.*

Scully, R. W. (1916). *Flora of Co Kerry.* Folens, Dublin.

Segal, S. (1969). *Ecological notes on Wall Vegetation.* Junk, The Hague.

Seward, A. C. (1941). *Plant Life Through the Ages.* Cambridge University Press, Cambridge.

Seward, M. R. D. (1976). Bracken at Vindolanda, in *The Vindolanda Environment.* Barcombe Publications, Hartwhistle, Northumberland.

Shakespeare, W. (1960). *A Midsummer Nights Dream.* Fisher, London.

Shand, S. J. (1952). Rocks for Chemists. Murby, London.

Sheail, J. (1971). *Rabbits and their History.* David & Charles, Newton Abbot.

Sheail, J. (1979). *British Rail land – biological survey. Interim report. The history of railway formations. CST Report No 276.* Nature Conservancy Council, Banbury.

Sheail, J. (1982). Wild plants and the perception of land-use change in Britain: an historical perspective. *Biological Conservation* 24: 129–146.

Shimwell, D. W. (1973). Recent and fossil records for club-mosses in the Derbyshire Limestones. *Watsonia* 9: 271–272.

Shotton, F. W. (ed.) (1977). *British Quaternary Studies.* Oxford University Press.

Silvertown, J. W. (1982). *Introduction to Plant Population Ecology.* Longmans, London.

Silvertown, J. W. (1982). Measuring plant distribution in limestone pavement. *Field Studies* 5: 651–662.

Simmons, I. G. (1964). Pollen diagrams from Dartmoor. *New Phytol.* 65: 165–180.

Sinclair, J. (1936). The natural history of Barra, Outer Hebrides. *Proc. Roy. Phys. Soc. Edinb.* 22: 241–296.

Sissons, J. B. (1963). Scottish raised shoreline heights with particular reference to the Forth Valley, *Geogr. Ann.* 45: 180–185.

Sissons, J. B. (1967). The Loch Lomond readvance in southern Skye and some palaeoclimatic implications. *Scott. J. Geol.* 18: 23–36.

Sissons, J. B. (1974). The quaternary in Scotland: a review. *Scott. J. Geol.* 10: 311–357.

Sissons, J. B. (1981). British shore platforms and ice-sheets. *Nature, Lond.* 291: 473–475.

Sissons, J. B. & Grant, A. J. W. (1972). The last glaciers in the Lochnagar area. *Scott. J. Geol.* 8: 85–89.

Skinner, B. L. (1969). *The Lime Industry of the Lothians.* University of Edinburgh, Department of Adult Education and Extra-Mural Studies.

Smith, D. I. & Drew, D. P. (eds) (1975). *Limestone Caves in the Mendip Hills.* David & Charles, Newton Abbot.

Smith, I. & Lyle, A. (1979). *Distribution of Freshwaters in Great Britain.* Institute of Terrestrial Ecology, Edinburgh.

Smith, R. A. H. & Bradshaw, R. D. (1972). Stabilisation of toxic mine wastes by the use of tolerant plant populations. *Trans. Inst. Min. Metall.* 81A: 230–237.

Sowerby, J. E. (1859). *The Ferns of Great Britain.* Bohn, London.

Sparks, B. W. & West, R. G. (1972). *The Ice Age in Britain.* Methuen, London.

Spence, D. H. N. (1959). Studies in the vegetation of Shetland. II. Reasons for the restriction of the exclusive pioneers to serpentine debris. *J. Ecol.* 47: 641–649.

Spence, D. H. N. (1960). Studies in the vegetation of Shetland. III. Scrub in Shetland and on South Uist, Outer Hebrides. *J. Ecol.* 48: 73–95.

Spence, D. H. N. (1964). The macrophytic vegetation of lochs, swamps and associated ferns. pp. 306–425 in Burnett, J. H. (ed.) *The Vegetation of Scotland.* Oliver & Boyd, Edinburgh.

Spence, D. H. N. (1967). Factors controlling the distribution of freshwater macrophytes with particular reference to the lochs of Scotland. *J. Ecol.* 55: 147–170.

Spence, D. H. N., Allen, E. D. & Fraser, J. (1979). Macrophyte vegetation of fresh and brackish waters in and near the Loch Druidibeg National Nature Reserve, South Uist. *Proc. R. Soc. Edinb.* 77B: 307–328.

Sporne, K. R. (1975). *The Morphology of Pteridophytes (4th edn).* Hutchinson, London.

Stace, C. A. (ed.) (1975). *Hybridisation and the Flora of the British Isles.* Academic Press, London.

Stacey, W. F. (1915). Distribution of relative humidity in England and Wales. *Quart. J. R. Met. Soc., London* 41: 45.

Stamp, D. (1948). *The Land of Britain, its Use and Misuse.* London.

Stamp, L. D. (1955). *Britain's Structure and Scenery (4th edn).* Collins New Naturalist, London.

Steers, J. A. (1962). *The Sea Coast.* Collins New Naturalist, London.

Steers, J. A. (ed.) (1964). *Field Studies in the British Isles.* Nelson, London.

Steers, J. A. (1967). *The Coastline of England and Wales.* Cambridge University Press.

Steven, H. M. & Carlisle, A. (1959). *The Native Pinewoods of Scotland.* Oliver & Boyd, Edinburgh.

Stewart, S. A. & Corry, T. H. (1938). *A Flora of the North-East of Ireland.* Quota Press, Belfast.

Synge, J. M. (1921). *The Aran Islands.* London.

Syson, L. (1980). *The Watermills of Britain.* David & Charles, Newton Abbot.

Tansley, A. G. (1949). *Britain's Green Mantle.* Allen & Unwin, London.

Tansley, A. G. (1949). *The British Islands and their Vegetation (2 vols).* Cambridge University Press.

Taylor, B. J., Burgess, I. C., Land, D. H., Mills, D. A. C., Smith, D. B. & Warren, P. T. (1971). *British Regional Geology: Northern England (4th edn).* HMSO, London.

Taylor, C. (1975). *Fields in the English Landscape.* Dent, London.

Taylor, C. (1979). *Roads and Tracks of Britain.* Dent, London.

Taylor, J. A. (1976). Upland climates. pp. 264–287 in Chandler, T. J. & Gregory, S. (eds) *The Climates of the British Isles.* Longmans, London.

Temple, A. K. (1956). The Leadhills-Wanlockhead lead and zinc deposits. *Trans. Roy. Soc. Edinb.* 63: 86–113.

Thiselton-Dyer, T. F. (1888). *The Folk-Lore of Plants.* Chatto & Windus, London.

Tittensor, R. M. (1970). History of Loch Lomond oakwoods. *Scott. For.* 24: 100–118.

Tittensor, R. M. & Steele, R. C. (1971). Plant communities of the Loch Lomond oakwoods. *J. Ecol.* 59: 561–582.

Thomas, A. S. (1963). Changes in vegetation since the advent of myxomatosis. *J. Ecol.* 48: 287–356, 51: 151–186.

Thomas, D. S.-J. (1981). *A Regional History of the Railways of Great Britain. Vol. 1. The West Country (5th edn).* David & Charles, Newton Abbot.

Thompson, F. M. L. (1985). Towns, industry, and the Victorian landscape. pp. 168–187 in Woodell, S. R. J. *The English Landscape. Past, Present and Future.* Oxford University Press.

Trueman, A. E. (1971). *Geology and Scenery in England and Wales.* Penguin Books, London.

Tubbs, C. R. (1986). *The New Forest.* Collins New Naturalist, London.

Turner, J. (1965). A contribution to the history of forest clearance. *Proc. Roy. Soc. B.* 161: 343–354.

Turner, J. S. & Watt, A. S. (1939). The Oakwoods (*Quercetum sessiliflorae*) of Killarney, Ireland. *J. Ecol.* 27: 202–233.

Turner, D. (1982). *Railways in the British Isles. Landscape, land use and society.* A. & C. Black, London.

Turrill, W. B. (1948). *British Plant Life.* Collins New Naturalist, London.

Vasari, Y. & Vasari, A. (1968). Late- and post-glacial macrophytic vegetation in the lochs of southern Scotland. *Acta Bot. Fenn* 50: 1–120.

Vevers, H. G. (1936). The land vegetation of Ailsa Craig. *J. Ecol.* 24: 424.

Wager, L. R. (1953). The extent of glaciation in the island of St Kilda. *Geol. Mag.* 90: 177–181.

Walker, M. J. C. (1975). Late glacial and early post-glacial environmental history of the Central Grampian Highlands, Scotland. *J. Biogeogr.* 2: 265–284.

Walker, T. G. (1979). The cytogenetics of ferns. pp. 87–132 in Dyer, A. F. (ed.) *The Experimental Biology of Ferns.* Academic Press, London.

Wallwork, K. L. (1974). *Derelict Land.* David & Charles, Newton Abbot.

Walters, S. M. (1978). British Endemics. pp. 263–273 in Street, H. E. (ed.) *Essays in Plant Taxonomy.* Academic Press, London.

Walton, J. (1959). Palaeobotany in Great Britain. pp. 230–242 in Turrill, W. B. *Vistas in Botany, Vol. 2.*

Walton, K. (1959). Ancient elements in the coastline of north-east Scotland. pp. 93–109 in Miller, R. & Watson, J. W. (eds) *Geographical Essays in Memory of Alan G. Ogilvie.* Nelson, Edinburgh.

Ward, N. B. (1942). *On the Growth of Plants in Closely Glazed Cases.* London.

Washburn, A. L. (1973). *Periglacial Processes and Environments.* Edward Arnold, London.

Watling, R. & Seaward, M. R. D. (1981). James Bolton: mycological pioneer. *Archiv. Nat. Hist.* 10: 89–110.

Watson, J. A. S. (1932). The size and development of the sheep industry in the Highlands and North of Scotland. *Trans. Highland Agric. & Statistical Soc. 5 ser.* XLIV: 1–25.

Watt, A. S. (1947). Pattern and process in the plant community. *J. Ecol.* 35: 1–22.

Watt, A. S. (1976). The ecological status of Bracken. *Bot. J. Linn. Soc.* 77: 217–239.

Watts, W. A. (1963). Late-glacial pollen-zones in western Ireland. *Ir. Geog.* 4: 367–376.

Webb, D. A. (1980). The Biological Vice-counties of Ireland. *Proc. R. Ir. Acad.* 80B: 179–196.

Webb, D. A. (1983). The flora of Ireland in its European context. *J. Life Sci. Roy. Dublin Soc.* 4: 143–160.

Webb, D. A. & Scannell, M. J. P. (1983). *Flora of Connemara and the Burren.* Cambridge University Press.

Webb, N. (1986). *Heathlands.* Collins New Naturalist, London.

West, R. G. (1963). Problems of the British Quarternary. *Proc. Geol. Assoc.* 74: 147–186.

West, R. G. (1968). *Pleistocene Geology and Biology.* Longmans, London.

Wheeler, B. D. (1984). British Fens: A Review. pp. 237–281 in Moore, P. D. (ed.) *European Mires.* Academic Press, London.

White, D. J. B. (1961). Some observations on the vegetation of Blakeney Point, Norfolk, following the disappearance of the rabbits in 1954. *J. Ecol.* 49: 113–118.

White, J. (ed.) (1982). *Studies on Irish Vegetation.* Royal Dublin Society.

Whiteside, E. P. (1953). Some relationships between the classifications of rocks by geologists and the classification of soil by soil scientists. *Soil Sci. Soc. Amer. Proc.* 17: 138–143.

Whitcock, R. (1980). *The Shaping of the Countryside.* David & Charles, Newton Abbot.

Whitton, J. B. (1974). *Geology and Scenery in Ireland.* Penguin Books, London.

Wilkins, D. A. (1984). The Flandrian woods of Lewis (Scotland). *J. Ecol.* 72: 251–258.

Willmot, A. J. (1985). Population dynamics of *Dryopteris* in Britain. *Proc. Roy. Soc. Edinb.* 86B: 307–313.

Wilmanns, O. & Brun-Hool, J. (1982). Plant Communities of Human Settlements in Ireland. 1. Vegetation of Walls. pp. 79–90 in White, J. (ed.) *Studies in Irish Vegetation.* Royal Dublin Society.

Wood, E. S. (1979). *Field Guide to Archaeology.* Collins, London.

Woodell, S. A. J. (ed.) (1985). *The English Landscape. Past, Present and Future.* Oxford University Press.

Woodhead, T. W. (1906). Ecology of woodland plants in the neighbourhood of Huddersfield. *J. Linn. Soc. Bot.* 37: 333–406.

Wright, G. N. (1977). *The Yorkshire Dales.* David & Charles, Newton Abbot.

Wright, H. E. Jr (1961). Late Pleistocene climate of Europe: a review. *Bull. Geol. Soc. Amer.* 72: 933–982.

Appendix 1

Checklist of the British Ferns and Allies (Pteridophyta)

The nomenclature follows that of Page (1982), with subsequent additions, including hybrids and infra-specific taxa recognised in this text.

Lycopodiaceae
Interrupted Clubmoss	*Lycopodium annotinum* L.
Stag's-horn Clubmoss	*L. clavatum* L.
Marsh Clubmoss	*Lycopodiella inundata* (L.) Holub
Fir Clubmoss	*Huperzia selago* (L.) Bernh.
Alpine Clubmoss	*Diphasiastrum alpinum* (L.) Holub
Hybrid Alpine Clubmoss	*D.* × *issleri* (Rouy) Holub (*D. alpinum* × *complanatum*)

Selaginellaceae
Lesser Clubmoss	*Selaginella selaginoides* (L.) Link

Isoetaceae
Quillwort	*Isoetes lacustris* L.
Spring Quillwort	*I. echinospora* Durieu
Land Quillwort	*I. histrix* Bory

Equisetaceae
Dutch Rush	*Equisetum hyemale* L.
Moore's Horsetail	*E.* × *moorei* Newm. (*E. hyemale* × *ramosissimum*)
Mackay's Horsetail	*E.* × *trachyodon* A. Braun (*E. hyemale* × *variegatum*)
Variegated Horsetail	*E. variegatum* Schleich. ex Weber & Mohr
Praeger's Horsetail	*E. variegatum* var. *majus* Syme
Newman's Horsetail	*E. variegatum* var. *wilsonii* Newm.
Water Horsetail	*E. fluviatile* L.
Hebridean Horsetail	*E.* × *dycei* C. N. Page (*E. fluviatile* × *palustre*)
Field Horsetail	*E. arvense* L.
Shore Horsetail	*E.* × *litorale* Kuhlew. ex Rupr. (*E. arvense* × *fluviatile*)
Ditch Horsetail	*E.* × *rothmaleri* C. N. Page (*E. arvense* × *palustre*)
Shade Horsetail	*E. pratense* Ehrh.
Wood Horsetail	*E. sylvaticum* L.
Milde's Horsetail	*E.* × *mildeanum* Rothm. (*E. pratense* × *sylvaticum*)
Marsh Horsetail	*E. palustre* L.
Skye Horsetail	*E.* × *font-queri* Rothm.
Great Horsetail	*E. telmateia* Ehrh.
Bowman's Horsetail	*E.* × *bowmanii* C. N. Page (*E. telmateia* × *sylvaticum*)

Ophioglossaceae
Moonwort	*Botrychium lunaria* (L.) Swartz
Adder's-tongue	*Ophioglossum vulgatum* L.

Small Adder's-tongue   *O. azoricum* C. Presl
Least Adder's-tongue   *O. lusitanicum* L.

Osmundaceae
Royal Fern   *Osmunda regalis* L.

Adiantaceae
Parsley Fern   *Cryptogramma crispa* (L.) Hook.
Jersey Fern   *Anogramma leptophylla* (L.) Link
Maidenhair Fern   *Adiantum capillus-veneris* L.

Hymenophyllaceae
Tunbridge Filmy-fern   *Hymenophyllum tunbrigense* (L.) Sm.
Wilson's Filmy-fern   *H. wilsonii* Hook.
Killarney Fern   *Trichomanes speciosum* Willd.

Polypodiaceae
Common Polypody   *Polypodium vulgare* L.
Western Polypody   *P. interjectum* Shivas
Manton's Polypody   *P.* × *mantoniae* Rothm. (*P. interjectum* × *vulgare*)
Southern Polypody   *P. australe* Fee
Font-Quer's Polypody   *P.* × *font-queri* Rothm. (*P. australe* × *vulgare*)
Shivas' Polypody   *P.* × *shivasiae* Rothm. (*P. australe* × *interjectum*)

Hypolepidaceae
Common Bracken   *Pteridium aquilinum* (L.) Kuhn var. *aquilinum*
Northern Bracken   *P. aquilinum* subsp. *latiusculum**
White-scaled Bracken   *P. aquilinum**

Thelypteridaceae
Marsh Fern   *Thelypteris palustris* Schott
Beech Fern   *Phegopteris connectilis* (Michx.) Watt
Sweet Mountain Fern   *Oreopteris limbosperma* (All.) Holub

Aspleniaceae
Hart's Tongue Fern   *Phyllitis scolopendrium* (L.) Newm.
Confluent Maidenhair   × *Asplenophyllitis confluens* (T. Moore ex Lowe) Alston
  Spleenwort   (*Asplenium trichomanes* subsp. *quadrivalens* × *Phyllitis scolopendrium*)
Guernsey Fern   × *A. microdon* Alston (*Asplenium billotii* × *Phyllitis scolopendrium*)
Jackson's Fern   × *A. jacksonii* Alston (*Asplenium adiantum-nigrum* × *Phyllitis scolopendrium*)
Black Spleenwort   *Asplenium adiantum-nigrum* L.
Caernarvonshire Spleenwort   *A.* × *contrei* Calle, Lovis & Reichstein (*A. adiantum-nigrum* × *septentrionale*)
Acute-leaved Spleenwort   *A. onopteris* L.

Hybrid Black Spleenwort | *A.* × *ticinense* D. E. Meyer (*A. adiantum-nigrum* × *A. onopteris*)

Lanceolate Spleenwort | *A. billotii* F. W. Schultz

Guernsey Spleenwort | *A.* × *sarniense* Sleep (*A. adiantum-nigrum* × *A. billotii*)

Sea Spleenwort | *A. marinum* L.

Delicate Maidenhair Spleenwort | *A. trichomanes* L. subsp. *trichomanes*

Hybrid Maidenhair Spleenwort | *A.* × *lusaticum* D. E. Meyer

Common Maidenhair Spleenwort | *A. trichomanes* L. subsp. *quadrivalens* D. E. Meyer emend. Lovis

Green Spleenwort | *A. viride* Huds.

Wall Rue | *A. ruta-muraria* L.

Lady Clermont's Spleenwort | *A.* × *clermontiae* Syme (*A. ruta-muraria* × *A. trichomanes* subsp. *quadrivalens*)

Murbeck's Spleenwort | *A.* × *murbeckii* Dorfl. (*A. ruta-muraria* × *A. septentrionale*)

Forked Spleenwort | *A. septentrionale* (L.) Hoffm.

Alternate-leaved Spleenwort | *A.* × *alternifolium* Wulf.

Rusty-back Fern | *Ceterach officinarum* DC.

Athyriaceae

Woodland Lady-fern | *Athyrium filix-femina* (L.) Roth

Alpine Lady-fern | *A. distentifolium* Tausch ex Opiz

Flexile Lady-fern | *A. flexile* (Newm.) Druce

Woodland Oak-fern | *Gymnocarpium dryopteris* (L.) Newm.

Limestone Oak-fern | *G. robertianum* (Hoffm.) Newm.

Brittle Bladder-fern | *Cystopteris fragilis* (L.) Bernh.

Dickie's Fern | *C. dickieana* Sim

Mountain Bladder-fern | *C. montana* (Lam.) Desv.

Oblong Woodsia | *Woodsia ilvensis* (L.) R. Br.

Alpine Woodsia | *W. alpina* (Bolton) S. F. Gray

Aspidiaceae

Holly Fern | *Polystichum lonchitis* (L.) Roth

Atlantic Hybrid Shield-fern | *P.* × *lonchitiforme* (Halacsy) Becherer (*P. lonchitis* × *setiferum*)

Hard Shield-fern | *P. aculeatum* (L.) Roth

Lowland Hybrid Shield-fern | *P.* × *bicknellii* (Christ) Hahne (*P. aculeatum* × *setiferum*)

Alpine Hybrid Shield-fern | *P.* × *illyricum* (Burbas) Hahne (*P. aculeatum* × *lonchitis*)

Soft Shield-fern | *P. setiferum* (Forsk.) Woynar

Mountain Male-fern | *Dryopteris oreades* Fomin

Common Male-fern | *D. filix-mas* (L.) Schott

Manton's Male-fern | *D.* × *mantoniae* Fr.-Jk. & Corley (*D. filix-mas* × *oreades*)

Hybrid Male-fern | *D.* × *tavelii* Rothm. (*D. filix-mas* × *D. affinis* agg.)

Yellow Golden-scaled Male-fern | *D. affinis* (Lowe) Fr.-Jk. subsp. *affinis*

Narrow Golden-scaled Male-fern | *D. affinis* subsp. *stilluppensis* (Sabransky) Fr.-Jk.

Common Golden-scaled Male-fern	*D. affinis* subsp. *borreri* (Newm.) Fr.-Jk.
Robust Golden-scaled Male-fern	*D. affinis* subsp. *robusta* Oberholz. & von Tavel ex Fr.-Jk.
Distant-leaved Buckler-fern	*D.* × *remota* (A. Br.) Druce (*D. affinis* subsp. *affinis* × *D. expansa*)
Hay-scented Buckler-fern	*D. aemula* (Ait.) Kuntze
Mull Fern	*D.* × *pseudoabbreviata* Jermy (*D. aemula* × *oreades*)
Rigid Buckler-fern	*D. submontana* (Fr.-Jk. & Jermy) Fr.-Jk.
Crested Buckler-fern	*D. cristata* (L.) A. Gray
Narrow Buckler-fern	*D. carthusiana* (Vill.) H. P. Fuchs
Brathay Fern	*D.* × *brathaica* Fr.-Jk. & Reichstein (*D. carthusiana* × *filix-mas*)
Hybrid Fen Buckler-fern	*D.* × *uliginosa* (Newm.) Kuntze ex Druce (*D. carthusiana* × *cristata*)
Broad Buckler-fern	*D. dilatata* (Hoffm.) A. Gray
Hybrid Narrow Buckler-fern	*D.* × *deweveri* (Jansen) Jansen & Wachter (*D. carthusiana* × *dilatata*)
Gibby's Buckler-fern	*D.* × *ambrosiae* Fr.-Jk. & Jermy (*D. dilatata* × *expansa*)
Northern Buckler-fern	*D. expansa* (C. Presl) Fr.-Jk. & Jermy
Kintyre Buckler-fern	*D.* × *sarvelae* Fr.-Jk. & Jermy (*D. carthusiana* × *expansa*)

Blechnaceae
Hard Fern	*Blechnum spicant* (L.) Roth

Marsileaceae
Pillwort	*Pilularia globulifera* L.

*Taxon under description or revision.

Appendix 2

Overwintering Strategies of the British Pteridophytes

	Winter-Green Aerial Parts Remaining mostly green and standing in most habitats in normal winters	Winter-Deciduous Aerial Parts Mostly or completely dying down seasonally (in winter, unless otherwise stated)
Lycopods	All *Lycopodium, Lycopodiella, Huperzia* and *Diphasiastrum* spp.	*Selaginella selaginoides*
Quillworts	*Isoetes lacustris I. echinospora*	*Isoetes histrix***
Horsetails	*Equisetum hyemale E. × trachyodon E. variegatum*	All other *Equisetum* spp. and hybrids
Moonworts and Adder's-tongues		*Botrychium lunaria Ophioglossum vulgatum O. azoricum O. lusitanicum***
Royal Fern		*Osmunda regalis*
Pteridoid Ferns		*Cryptogamma crispa Anogramma leptophylla*** *Adiantum capillus-veneris**
Filmy Ferns	*Hymenophyllum tunbrigense H. wilsonii Trichomanes speciosum*	
Polypodies	All *Polypodium* spp. and hybrids	
Bracken		*Pteridium aquilinum*
Thelypteroid Ferns		*Thelypteris palustris Phegopteris connectilis Oreopteris limbosperma*

	Winter-Green Aerial Parts Remaining mostly green and standing in most habitats in normal winters	Winter-Deciduous Aerial Parts Mostly or completely dying down seasonally (in winter, unless otherwise stated)
Asplenioid Ferns	All *Phyllitis, Ceterach, Asplenium* spp. and hybrids	
Lady Ferns		All *Athyrium*
Oak Ferns		All *Gymnocarpium*
Bladder Ferns and Woodsias		All *Cystopteris* and *Woodsia*
Shield Ferns	All *Polystichum* spp. and hybrids	
Male Ferns and Buckler Ferns	*D. aemula* *D.* × *pseudoabbreviata?*	*D. filix-mas** *D.* × *tavelii** All other *Dryopteris* spp. and hybrids
Hard Fern	*Blechnum spicant*	
Pillwort		*Pilularia globulifera**

*   Variable, persisting in mild winters in sheltered localities
** Dying down in summer, resuming growth in winter

Appendix 3

Pteridophyte Hybrids in the British Isles

Frequency of involvement of native pteridophyte species in hybrid formation known to 31 December 1987.

Involvement in one hybrid	Involvement in two hybrids	Involvement in three hybrids	Involvement in four hybrids
Equisetum pratense	Equisetum telmateia	Equisetum palustre	Asplenium adiantum-nigrum
Asplenium onopteris	E. sylvaticum	Phyllitis scolopendrium	Dryopteris carthusiana
Cystopteris fragilis 4n	E. fluviatile	Asplenium septentrionale	
C. fragilis 6n	E. arvense	A. trichomanes subsp. quadrivalens	
Dryopteris aemula	E. hyemale	Dryopteris filix-mas	
D. cristata	Polypodium vulgare	D. affinis agg.	
	P. interjectum	D. expansa	
	P. australe		
	Asplenium billotii		
	A. ruta-muraria		
	A. trichomanes subsp. trichomanes		
	Polystichum lonchitis		
	P. aculeatum		
	P. setiferum		
	Dryopteris oreades		
	D. dilatata		

Taxonomic distribution of potential parent taxa and numbers of known wild hybrids amongst the British and Irish native pteridophyte genera in which hybrids are known, to 31 December 1987. In the case of *Equisetum* and *Diphasiastrum*, the presence of the two presumed former species *E. ramosissimum* and *D. complanatum* are included in parenthesis, to account for the parentage of the total hybrids given.

Genus	Number of native potential parent taxa	Number of known wild hybrids in Britain and Ireland
Dryopteris	11	9
Asplenium	9	7
Equisetum	8(+1 in past?)	9
Polypodium	3	3
Polystichum	3	3
Cystopteris	4	1?
Phyllitis	1	3 (crossing with Asplenium)
Diphasiastrum	1(+1 in past?)	1

Native pteridophyte hybrids in Britain and Ireland with predominantly non-western geographic ranges

Species	Distribution
× *Asplenophyllitis confluens*	Kerry, Westmorland, north-east Yorkshire
Dryopteris × *deweveri*	Widely scattered over Britain and Ireland?
D. × *tavelii*	Widely scattered over Britain and Ireland?
D. × *uliginosa*	Now confined to Norfolk, formerly elsewhere
Diphasiastrum × *issleri*	Southern England and Midlands, perhaps elsewhere
Equisetum × *bowmanii*	Hampshire (New Forest)
E. × *mildeanum*	Central Scotland, perhaps also Skye

Native pteridophyte hybrids in Britain and Ireland with predominantly western geographic ranges and likely factors contributing to this.

	Western range in large part resulting from particular suitability of Atlantic edaphic and climatic conditions	Western range in part resulting from descent of one montane parent to low altitudes under western climates	Western range in part resulting from predominantly western/south-western geographic range of at least one parent
Polypodium × *shivasiae*	+		+
P. × *font-queri*	+		+
Asplenium × *sarniense*	+		+
A. × *ticinense*	+		+
A. × *contrei*	+		+
× *Asplenophyllitis jacksonii*	+		+
× *A. microdon*	+		+
Dryopteris × *pseudoabbreviata*	+	+	+
D. × *mantoniae*	+	+	
D. × *ambroseae*	+	+	
D. × *sarvelae*	+	+	
D. × *remota*	+	+	
Polystichum × *illyricum*	+	+	
P. × *lonchitiforme*	+	+	
Polypodium × *mantoniae*	+		
Asplenium × *murbeckii*	+		
A. × *alternifolium*	+		
A. × *clermontiae*	+		
A. × *lusaticum*	+		
Polystichum × *bicknellii*	+		
Dryopteris × *brathaica*	+		
Equisetum × *trachyodon*	+		
E. × *dycei*	+		
E. × *litorale*	+		
E. × *rothmaleri*	+		
E. × *font-queri*	+		
E. × *moorei*	(+)		

Index

The main discussions of the habitats of each species are indicated in bold.